The Grand Tour

THE GRAND TOUR

NEWCASTLE UNITED'S ADVENTURES IN EUROPE

PAUL JOANNOU

Foreword by Bob Moncur

NEWCASTLE UNITED

An official publication

MAINSTREAM
PUBLISHING

EDINBURGH AND LONDON

First published in Great Britain in 2006 by
MAINSTREAM PUBLISHING COMPANY (EDINBURGH) LTD
7 Albany Street
Edinburgh EH1 3UG

ISBN 1 84596 022 X

A catalogue record for this book
is available from the British Library

Typeset in Caflish, Meta and New Baskerville

Printed and bound in Germany by
Appl Druck, Wemding

AUTHOR'S NOTES & ACKNOWLEDGEMENTS

As a teenaged Newcastle United fanatic, I was captivated, like many, by the team's entry into European football in 1968. I was not quite old enough to travel on those early pioneering trips to Rotterdam, Lisbon or behind the Iron Curtain to Budapest and had to be content, like most football fans on Tyneside, to squeeze into a packed St. James' Park along with 50,000 others to see how the Continentals played the game we all love. Those terrific European nights are still vivid some 30-odd years later.

Feyenoord, Real Zaragoza, Sporting Lisbon as well as Újpesti Dózsa, Porto, Anderlecht and the mighty Internazionale – Inter Milan to us back then – were the great unknowns to the somewhat insular British at the time – and certainly so in the far north-east corner of England.

It was bewitching, the romantic side of football. With so few foreign players in our game at that time, seeing at first hand the stars of Europe on Tyneside made you starry-eyed. They were so different to the players of the home nations we saw week in, week out in regulation action in the First Division. Feyenoord's Ove Kindvall, Újpesti's Ferenc Bene, Anderlecht's Paul van Himst and Jan Mulder – that supreme No. 9 – those famous names of Inter and Italy, and later the Dutch maestro Johnny Rep.

Several years afterwards, as the Black 'n' Whites returned to the European trail in 1994, much had changed: in society and in football. Now a good few years older, well travelled and part of an open European Union, following the Magpies around the Continent was much easier. As one of the Toon Army on tour, I was able to witness the lively way that the distinctive black and white flag of our club and our region was proudly flown across Europe – in a way only Geordies can do. To Rome and Athens; to Barcelona and Milan. What could be better than watching your football club at the highest level and, as a bonus, exploring the many fascinating sights of Europe, as well as experiencing the fabulous Continental way of life?

Now we are all Europeans: part of a big family. And as the lucrative Champions League has clearly shown, European football is an essential, if not the most important, ingredient of the modern game. Newcastle United will strive to continue to be part of that exciting picture. *The Grand Tour* captures Newcastle United's adventures across Europe and also covers the Magpie's first 100 games in Continental action.

Notes

Generally, the Continental spelling and nomenclature of the club, city and stadium in question is used and not the sometimes different UK styling. For example, Rome's venue is noted as Stadio Olimpico rather than the Olympic Stadium, while the Milan giants are given as Internazionale rather than the British – and totally wrong – Inter Milan. Champions League opponents Dynamo Kyiv are given the spelling used by UEFA and the Ukrainian club, instead of the Anglo version, Kiev. There are some exceptions commonly used in football: Munich is given its English version, rather than München, and Feyenoord is used instead of the Dutch Feijenoord.

Care has been taken to attempt to identify the correct spelling of club titles and the names of places, players and officials. Annoyingly, the details of player substitutions made during the early

European matches were not well recorded, unlike now, and some gaps result. When noted, players' appearances and goal totals are for senior competitive fixtures and include substitute outings. They do not include friendlies. *The Grand Tour* covers United's 102 European matches up to May 2005 with a brief postscript for season 2005–06.

Acknowledgements

Newcastle United club directors have assisted in the production of this book, most notably Ken Slater, Russell Cushing and Trevor Garwood, as well as staff members Hazel Greener, Steve Spark, Tony Toward, Serena Taylor and especially Mark Hannen, who helped enormously. So too has Publications Editor Paul Tully, who assisted appreciably with his professional advice and knowledge of over 40 years watching the Magpies. Club photographer Ian Horrocks is especially acknowledged for his pictures of United in European action, both at home and abroad, used extensively in this book.

Players past and present have contributed, too: Alan Shearer, Shay Given, Peter Beardsley, Mick Martin, Tommy Craig and Bob Moncur – the man who lifted United's European trophy back in 1969 and who also compiled the foreword. Bryan Robson, who scored so many great goals in those early years of Newcastle's European adventures, was also a great help.

Journalists who have followed the fortunes of the Magpies, since those opening rounds back in 1968, are acknowledged for their enduring reports, notably John Gibson, Tony Hardisty, Doug Weatherall, Ivor Broadis and Bob Cass from the pioneering days, as well as more recently Alan Oliver and the many other local journalists on the north-east beat, past and present, especially from the morning daily, *The Journal*. John Gibson is also due further acknowledgement for his record of United's Fairs Cup quest in his early series of books, *The Newcastle United Story*, which were an invaluable source in the writing of *The Grand Tour*. Bob Moncur and Bryan Robson also produced autobiographies during that era, *United We Stand* and *The Sporting Worlds of Bryan 'Pop' Robson*, both important sources in my research. So too were the club's official publications: *Black and White*, *Scene@StJames* and the various editions of the match-day programme.

The excellent football logo website *www.hqfl.dk* has been an essential point of reference and of use in reproducing club badges. Population figures are taken from *www.citypopulation.de*. The Rough Guide's *European Football – A Fans' Handbook*, *The Guinness Record of World Soccer* and Dorling Kindersley's *Football Yearbook – The Complete Guide to the World Game* have all been a central point of reference. United supporters Alan Candlish and Bill Swann have both assisted me, filling gaps and answering niggling queries. Several other people have assisted in various ways:

Bo Karlsson (Sweden), Fabrizio Pugi (Italy), Mike Hammond, John Edminson, Mick Worrell, Robert Marcz (Hungary), Jurgen Witlox (Holland), Jerome Demeraux (France), Pat Pierpoint, Mike Bolam, Stephane Renauld (France), Mick & Mark at The Back Page, Dave Hewson and the staff at Typestyles as well as Athletic Club Bilbao, Chris Brown, Christos Sotiropoulos (Greece), Antoni Mysona (Denmark), Tomas Rademacher (Czech Rep.) and George Xenides (Greece). All are thanked.

The majority of photographs used in the text are from Newcastle United's official library, but additional illustrations are courtesy of *Newcastle Chronicle & Journal*. Postcard and memorabilia reproductions are mainly from the author's historical archive.

Appreciation to Mainstream Publishing for producing this fine official record of United's European fixtures, particularly to director Bill Campbell and designer Becky Pickard.

Finally, a big thank you to the Toon Army on tour . . . for their exuberant support and often humorous dedication to United's cause.

Paul Joannou, Club Historian, May 2006.

CONTENTS

INTRODUCTION

THE GRAND TOUR

An extended tour through the major cities of Europe . . .
One undertaken by a rich or aristocratic Englishman.
Collins English Dictionary

By the time European football had taken hold during the '60s, Newcastle United had already been regular and experienced travellers to the Continent. But the matches were purely friendlies, exhibition contests or local tournaments. Indeed, as early as the summer of 1904, the Magpies had packed their bags and set off for European destinations. Travel, of course, was not as easy as jumping on a plane, as it is now. At the end of the 1903–04 season, it was by sea, not air, that United headed to Denmark and played a four-game mini-tour in Copenhagen.

From that point onwards, Newcastle continued to visit the Continent on frequent end-of-season tours. On their travels, United faced some of Europe's greatest clubs: Barcelona, Ajax, Internazionale and Real Madrid. And the Spanish giants from the capital were also a rare pre-war visitor to St. James' Park in 1925. At the time, they were not so mighty and not so famous: they were promptly thrashed 6–1. But the Europeans were quick to learn, and by the time UEFA had been formed, the Continentals had in many ways overtaken their teachers in ability and modern thinking about the game.

It was in June 1954 that the Union of European Football Associations was formed – then under the title of the European Football Association – now known to everyone as UEFA. A little over 30 countries were represented by the association, with the aim of introducing structured European-wide competitions for both club and national teams. Despite early resistance to the new form of competition, during the latter seasons of the '50s the European Cup, Cup Winners Cup and Inter Cities Fairs Cup – then initially sitting outside UEFA's umbrella of control – all flourished. Most clubs quickly wanted to be a part of the new kind of football.

The success of UEFA and its tournaments has now seen them develop to the point that the Champions League and UEFA Cup are regarded as, perhaps, even more important than domestic competition. Now, with over 50 member countries across the Continent, the football map of Europe stretches far and wide: in the east to Russia's Ural Mountains; in the north to the Arctic Circle; and in the south to the entire Mediterranean region and the fringe of Africa. With the introduction of Israel, it even covers the Middle East too.

Europe has a richly diverse history and culture, fascinating cities, spectacular architecture and many differing ways of life; a passion for football spreads across all. In many ways, the beautiful game has brought Europeans closer, and Europe is now without doubt the centre of world football. It has the most clubs, most fans, most players and most money, and the world's best players play in the world's best leagues: the Premiership, *Serie A*, *La Liga* and *Bundesliga*.

When Newcastle United entered the action in 1968 it was a step into the unknown. By the end of that first season, manager Joe Harvey said, 'European football is just great. It brings us a completely fresh competition against teams who are normally beyond our reach.' He added, 'This kind of football is going to boom in the future.'

European football has always been something of an adventure for Newcastle United and the Toon Army, just as it was for the young aristocrats who had, in years gone by, embarked on the original 'Grand Tour'. Then, well-to-do and fashionable gentlemen headed for Paris and the Alps, then to Venice, Florence and Rome, returning through Switzerland, Germany and the Low Countries. One description of those young noblemen on their Grand Tours noted that 'many had a riotous time'. The Toon Army of a much later era may not have been so wealthy or so learned, and hardly treated their travels around the Continent as a finishing school, but they were to have boisterous and friendly encounters just the same.

United's European adventures soon became hugely significant as television money flooded into the game, and European football became big, big business. Indeed, qualification for the Champions League was considered in some quarters an even bigger achievement than winning the FA Cup.

Newcastle United have led the way in the north east of England as far as European football is concerned. The Black 'n' Whites have now played over 100 games – one of only a handful of clubs in the country to do so.

There are several stops Newcastle United have yet to make on their Grand Tour. To Paris, to Amsterdam and to Madrid – and the marvellous Bernabéu – as well as to more far away centres of football excellence like Moscow and Istanbul. The adventure continues. Here's to the next 100 games in Europe.

Newcastle's Champions League visit to Turin and the Stadio Delle Alpi to face Juventus was a memorable journey for the Toon Army.

FOREWORD

by Bob Moncur

European football was a bit of a great unknown when Newcastle United started out in Continental action back in 1968. We knew very little about the clubs and players at that time, unlike now. It was all a bit of an adventure to begin with – a nice break from league and cup competition at home. We all wanted to know where we were off to next: 'Lisbon again – great!' But it soon became serious stuff.

Newcastle United's supporters took to European football in those early years. They packed into St. James' Park. It was incredible, really, how they backed us. We had three fabulous seasons, and winning the Inter Cities Fairs Cup at the first time of asking was truly remarkable. It remains the highlight of my career – and the wonderful Geordies will never let me forget it!

Now, over 30 years later, European football has developed into a huge business and is immensely important to major clubs like Newcastle United. Apart from the financial benefits and prestige, top players will only join clubs with a European pedigree. If your club is not a regular in either the Champions League or UEFA Cup, they will go elsewhere. Newcastle have now played over 100 games in European football and can be recognised as a European power. Like everyone associated with the Black 'n' Whites, I've been on the edge of my seat watching some of the action of recent years. Nothing would please me more than to see a United skipper again lift a European trophy.

Bob Moncur

COMPETITIONS & TROPHIES

EUROPEAN CUP (1955–56 to 1991–92) / CHAMPIONS LEAGUE (1992–93 to date)

Proposed in 1955 by the editor of French sports paper *L'Equipe*, the European Cup was originally contested by each country's leading clubs, then solely the national champions. It has developed into a glittering and prestigious tournament for the biggest and most successful sides in Europe – almost in the form of a super-league. First contested in 1955–56, the *Coupe des Clubs Champions Européens* is the premier prize of all club football and has a formidable trophy to go with it. The rebranded UEFA Champions League was introduced for the 1992–93 season and has steadily expanded into a money-spinning showpiece.

Most victories: Real Madrid (9), AC Milan (6), Liverpool (5)

INTER CITIES FAIRS CUP/EUROPEAN FAIRS CUP (1955–56 to 1970–71)

Starting life in the same year as the European Cup under the banner of the 'International Industries Fairs Inter-Cities Cup', the name of the competition was later shortened to the Inter Cities Fairs Cup. Proposed as early as 1950 by FIFA's vice-president Ernst Thommen to create a competition between select teams from Europe's top industrial cities, it was also backed by the powerful Sir Stanley Rous, who sat on the Fairs Cup committee. The first competition took almost three years to complete – from 1955 to 1958 – but was thereafter competed for on a yearly basis, although it did not officially come under the umbrella of UEFA control for some time. It was renamed the European Fairs Cup in 1969 with qualification criteria similar to its successor the UEFA Cup but with a bizarre one-club-one-city rule.

Most victories: FC Barcelona (3)

UEFA CUP (1971–72 to date)

In 1971, UEFA took over the administration of the Fairs Cup, renamed the competition the UEFA Cup and introduced a new trophy. Entry was given to the highest league clubs not qualifying for either the European Cup or Cup Winners Cup – and without the unfair and controversial one-club-one-city rule. For many years to come, the final was played on a home and away basis, only changing in 1998 to a more traditional one-off final at a neutral venue. From the 1999–2000 season, domestic cup winners also qualified for entry.

Most victories: Internazionale (3), Juventus (3), Liverpool (3)

EUROPEAN CUP WINNERS CUP (1960–61 to 1998–99)

The success of the European Cup, as well as the restrictions on entry to the Fairs Cup, saw pressure mount to introduce a further European competition as the '50s came to a close. In 1960, the European Cup Winners Cup was unveiled at a meeting in Vienna. It was open only to the winners of individual national knockout competitions – such as the FA Cup or *Copa del Rey* – or to the losing finalist, if the winner was already destined to compete in the European Cup. Fiorentina won the first tournament in season 1960–61, and it developed into an important competition for 39 years until the expanded Champions League and UEFA Cup contributed to its demise in 1999.

Most victories: FC Barcelona (4)

SUPER CUP (1972–73 to date)

The Super Cup was brought into play during 1972 and was originally contested by the winners of the European Cup and Cup Winners Cup. It is now held between the victors of the Champions League and UEFA Cup. The competition has now developed to culminate in a grand final held in Monaco at the Stade Louis II and is broadcast around Europe. The winners earn the right to compete in the European/South American Cup, with the champions of Europe playing the champions of South America in what is in essence a world play-off.

Most victories: AC Milan (4)

INTERTOTO CUP (1994–95 to date)

The Intertoto Cup was introduced by UEFA during 1994 to provide one of two routes for additional places in the UEFA Cup – the other being by way of the Fair Play League. At first there were two extra places available via the competition, then three, with teams competing in so-called Intertoto Cup finals. There is no actual trophy, and the competition runs in three parallel strands, resulting in a trio of finals during late summer. Several big-guns of Europe have qualified via the Intertoto Cup, including Valencia and the mighty Juventus. Bordeaux did likewise in 1995 and went all the way to the UEFA Cup final.

Footnote: Trophy wins up to cs 2005.

1

A EUROPEAN ADVENTURE

1968–69

United and Real Zaragoza line up and wave to the
St. James' Park crowd before the Fairs Cup tie on
Tyneside in 1969.

hen Newcastle United entered competitive action on the Continent 38 years ago – back in 1968 – the scene was very different to the new, modern Europe with its cosmopolitan lifestyle that is accessible to us all today. In 1968, the Iron Curtain still hung a fearful veil across Central Europe, with communism at its draconian height and some 20 years from its extraordinary collapse. The European Union (EU), as we know it today, was then in its infancy. Popularly known as the Common Market – although officially it was called the European Economic Community (EEC) – it was formed when the Treaty of Rome was signed in 1957 by only a handful of

founding members and developed further by the Brussels Treaty of 1965. The United Kingdom did not become a member until 1973 and then a somewhat hesitant one. Air travel for the masses was some way off, with holidays abroad on the Costa del Sol just starting to become a sunny and welcome alternative to the much maligned British seaside.

Football on the Continent had developed substantially since the formation of UEFA as the governing body of the European game in 1954. By the late '60s, all member countries took European soccer seriously, unlike the formative years when, most notably, British associations and certain clubs remained sceptical about any innovative idea of regular competition with the top sides across the English Channel.

Back in 1954, UEFA had 35 founding members, and the new association spurred on development of the European club competitions, replacing such tournaments as the Latin Cup and Mittel Europa Cup, which began inter-nation club competition as far back as 1927. The European Cup, and later Cup Winners Cup, Inter Cities Fairs Cup and UEFA Cup, as well as the Super Cup and qualifying fledgling the Intertoto Cup, all gradually came to the fore. Yet, in the '60s the European Cup, Cup Winners Cup and the Fairs Cup, as it was then, were still light years away from the glitzy television spectacular and money-spinning tournaments of the present day: the Champions League and, to a lesser extent, the UEFA Cup.

Newcastle United were the first club from the north east of England to enter Europe and still are, in 2006, the only local side with any UEFA pedigree. Neighbours Sunderland, by comparison, have played only four games, back in 1973–74, and Middlesbrough only made their European debut as late as the 2004–05 season.

The Black 'n' Whites laid the foundations for European qualification in the 1967–68 season. Manager Joe Harvey had transformed a struggling side, largely thanks to the strike combination of Wyn Davies and Albert Bennett, as well as a strong defensive formation with Bob Moncur at its heart. Moncur was a player who had emerged as a top-rated defender and would go on to skipper Scotland. However, an end of season slump, in which United fell from fifth place in the table to tenth, looked like ruining any thoughts for the club of European competition for the first time in its history. Luckily, Newcastle received a slice of fortune, and qualification came through the back door.

Manchester United's triumph in the European Cup helped. It gave England two places in the top competition, and together with the proposed enlargement of the tournament it meant that four clubs could now be provisionally nominated for the Fairs Cup,

although that number was still to be sanctioned by the governing Fairs Cup committee. Newcastle looked like they would scrape in – the fourth team to make it along with Leeds United, Liverpool and Chelsea – with the help of the controversial one-club-one-city rule. That much maligned piece of football legislation meant sides above United in the league – Everton, Tottenham and Arsenal – could not be admitted: to many people it was an injustice, and it created much debate.

John Gibson of the *Evening Chronicle*, who followed United's early European ventures closely, recorded, 'The Fairs Cup entries had to be increased from 48 to 64 for Newcastle to make it.' And that enlargement was by no means a certainty. Gibson commented at the time, 'FIFA president Sir Stanley Rous, who is also chairman of the Fairs Cup committee, had blandly announced he was against increasing the entries because it would lower the standard of the competition.' At the deciding meeting of the Fairs Cup committee the odds would be stacked against the Magpies.

No one knew United's fate until the actual draw for the new season's competition was made. Gibson was there in Copenhagen. He said, 'It was absolute agony, and the tension was even worse as the minutes slipped away.' But at last an announcement was made. Gibson recorded that he was elated when the words 'Group 13, Newcastle United versus Feyenoord, Rotterdam' were voiced as the draw continued.

Newcastle were in and Tyneside was jubilant.

Favourites for the 1968–69 trophy were holders Leeds United, at the time boasting a formidable yet infamous side built by Don Revie. The Elland Road club were joined by such experienced European campaigners as Athletic Club Bilbao, Fiorentina, Valencia, Napoli, Juventus, Locomotive Leipzig and United's opening opponents, Feyenoord.

That season, Joe Harvey's United developed into a resolute side, but one with an attack that could be very effective, scoring some wonderful goals. The focal point of the team was centre-forward Wyn Davies, who along with Irishman Willie McFaul between the posts, a central defence dominated by Moncur – alongside either Ollie Burton or John McNamee – and midfield workhorses in Tommy Gibb and Benny Arentoft, made up a first-class spine to the team. Frank Clark and David Craig were reliable full-backs while on the flanks of midfield, Jim Scott and Jackie Sinclair grew in confidence as the season unfolded. And as a partner for Davies, Bryan 'Pop' Robson was sensational, hitting 30 goals in the year. The side may have lacked creative skills, but as Frank Clark said, 'We were a solid unit and very hard to get past.'

The season, however, did not start well. St. James' Park was rocked by the news that defensive kingpin and skipper Bob Moncur would be out for the opening weeks of the programme with a cartilage injury picked up in a friendly with Hibernian. Then more bad news. Albert Bennett broke down in the first match of the season and 21-year-old Geoff Allen, who had impressed many, suffered a bad knee injury – one that wrecked his career. But in stepped Pop Robson up front to forge a potent pairing

with Davies, expensive signing Jackie Sinclair started to look the part, while the emergence of youngsters Alan Foggon and Keith Dyson was also a bonus. And Moncur recovered in double-quick time to lead United in inspirational fashion.

From that history-making first match against Feyenoord in September 1968 to their memorable victory in Budapest in June 1969, Newcastle had utterly confounded everybody in football, in and out of the North East. Almost all the pundits said that the Magpies had no chance from the off. Clark noted, 'Our incredible cup run was all the more enjoyable for being totally unexpected.' United's full-back – and later European Cup victor with Nottingham Forest – added in his biography *Kicking With Both Feet* that the players had 'a sense of adventure' and noted that United had been 'written off at the start by the press as a bunch of provincial no-hopers. By any sensible criteria, we should never have been in the competition.'

Backed by a Tyneside public that took to the new form of football that the Inter Cities Fairs Cup brought – with near sell-out gates on a regular basis – reaching the final made people

Bryan Robson drills the ball home against Setúbal during a lull in the snowstorm. The United striker scored twice in the quarter-final tie.

at home and abroad take notice. And United's victory was no fluke. They toppled some of the finest sides in Europe: Feyenoord, Sporting Clube, Real Zaragoza and Glasgow Rangers. Only Setúbal were an unknown quantity before Newcastle played them. In the final they met Újpesti Dózsa, who had knocked out Leeds United in style and were rated one of the finest sides on the Continent at the time. Newcastle marched on and on with Geordie spirit and resolute footballing application.

Newcastle United's trek behind the Iron Curtain for their first European final was the biggest event in the North East since the glory days of the '50s. Media reporting back then was very different to the slick and high-tech programming we are used to these days. Television coverage appeared to be something

of an afterthought: amateurish block titles, black and white pictures (and grainy at that), odd camera shots and Alan Weaks as a commentator – and it wasn't live with only highlights being broadcast late in the evening. But at least the BBC covered the match, and thousands of Geordies, who waited impatiently to experience their team's night of glory, were thankful for that.

Only a handful of Newcastle supporters made the trip to Hungary. Travelling abroad for the masses was in its infancy, and a journey behind the Cold War divide was almost unheard of. But soon thousands of the Toon Army were to begin a Grand Tour of Europe as they followed the Black 'n' Whites on the highways and byways across the Continent.

Jim Scott (left) and John McNamee (right) with the Fairs Cup trophy during the homecoming at St. James' Park in 1969.

MATCHES 1 – 12

Jim Scott fires United into the lead during the Fairs Cup semi-final with Rangers at Gallowgate.

1968–69

Holland, Rotterdam	v. Feyenoord	4–0, 0–2 Agg 4–2	Inter Cities Fairs Cup, R1
Portugal, Lisbon	v. Sporting Clube	1–1, 1–0 Agg 2–1	Inter Cities Fairs Cup, R2
Spain, Zaragoza	v. Real Zaragoza	2–3, 2–1 Agg 4–4	Inter Cities Fairs Cup, R3
Portugal, Lisbon	v. Vitória Setúbal	5–1, 1–3 Agg 6–4	Inter Cities Fairs Cup, QF
Scotland, Glasgow	v. Glasgow Rangers	0–0, 2–0 Agg 2–0	Inter Cities Fairs Cup, SF
Hungary, Budapest	v. Újpesti Dózsa	3–0, 3–2 Agg 6–2	Inter Cities Fairs Cup, Final

Euro Facts & Figures

Qualifying Seasons

14 seasons: 1968–69, 1969–70, 1970–71, 1977–78, 1994–95, 1996–97, 1997–98, 1998–99, 1999–2000, 2001–02, 2002–03, 2003–04, 2004–05, 2005–06

Milestones

First game: v. Feyenoord (h) Sept 1968 (ICFC) won 4–0

50th game: v. FK Partizan (a) Oct 1998 (ECWC) lost 0–1

100th game: v. Olympiacos CFP (h) March 2005 (UEFAC) won 4–0

Away Goals

Won on away goals:

4–4 v. Real Zaragoza (ICFC) 1968–69

1–1 v. Southampton (ICFC) 1969–70

Lost on away goals:

3–3 v. RSC Anderlecht (EFC) 1969–70

3–3 v. Athletic Bilbao (UEFAC) 1994–95

2–2 v. FK Partizan (ECWC) 1998–99

4–4 v. Troyes-Aube (ITC) 2001–02

Match 1

1968–69

Inter Cities Fairs Cup, Round 1: Newcastle United v. Feyenoord (Holland)
FIRST LEG Wednesday, 11 September 1968, St. James' Park

Feyenoord

UNITED McFaul, Craig, McNamee, Burton, Clark, Gibb, Elliott, Scott, Robson (B), Davies, Allen. Subs not used: Marshall, Iley, Sinclair.
Manager: Joe Harvey

FEYENOORD Graafland, van den Heide, Israel, Laseroms, Veldhoen, Boskamp, Jansen, van Hanegem (Geels), Wery, Kindvall, Moulijn. Subs not used: Treytel, Romeijn.
Manager: Goos Brox

REFEREE H. Carlsson (Sweden)

RESULT Won 4–0 (3–0)

AGGREGATE 4–0

ATTENDANCE 46,348

SCORERS United: Scott (7), Robson (35), Gibb (44), Davies (70)

MATCH HIGHLIGHTS

A Wednesday evening in mid-September marked a historic moment in the story of Newcastle United, and the newcomers to Continental football gave their experienced opposition from Holland a hiding in the very first competitive European fixture on Tyneside. Without injured skipper Bob Moncur, Joe Harvey's side tore the Dutchmen apart in a magnificent performance, providing the fans with a feast of attacking football. Local lad Geoff Allen, playing on the left-wing, was a constant menace all evening, while Feyenoord's defenders could not cope at all with the aerial menace of Wyn Davies at centre-forward. Newcastle grabbed four goals, but it could easily have been six or seven. The opening strike arrived early, inside the first ten minutes, after Allen scorched past van den Heide, and the winger's cross was turned in by Jim Scott from close range following Bryan Robson's knock-down into space. Then Davies tried a 25-yard shot that cannoned off the woodwork, only for Robson to dive forward and head it home. A minute from half-time, United were cruising when a Tommy Gibb effort glanced into the net off defender Israel, following a fine run down the wing by Scott. Big Wyn Davies deservedly got onto the score sheet in the second period when he soared to meet a Scott free-kick, striking the ball perfectly into the corner of the net. United also hit the post and bar through Allen and Clark, while defender Laseroms almost scored an own-goal with another effort that fired against the woodwork.

MAN OF THE MATCH

Geoff Allen – a sizzling display.

| MATCH RATING | ● | ● | ● | ● | ● | Pulsating opening. |

STAR COMMENT

Geoff Allen: 'There had been a fair bit of rain, and the pitch was a bit greasy on top, so I knew the conditions were going to suit me.'

EYEWITNESS

Tony Hardisty (*Sunday Express*): 'A truly sensational start to a memorable first European campaign which instantly captured the imagination of the fans whose support was inspirational.'

OPPONENT FILE

One of the two giants of Dutch football – along with Ajax – Feyenoord were experienced European campaigners. The Dutch league pacesetters at the time, Feyenoord developed into one of Europe's finest sides of that era, winning the title and toppling Celtic in the European Cup final two years later in 1970. They also lifted the UEFA Cup in 1974. Like Newcastle, the Dutch club possessed a great support with an average crowd of over 49,000 in 1968, although latterly the club has been in the shadow of both Ajax and PSV in terms of success.

STAR VISITOR

Ove Kindvall – Feyenoord's centre-forward was recognised as one of the best strikers in Europe at the time. Born in Sweden, he arrived in Rotterdam from Norrköping in 1966 as an up-and-coming youngster who quickly developed as an exciting player in Feyenoord's emerging side at the time. He became a regular international for his country and a constant danger to the opposition. Tall and elegant on the ball, Kindvall was top scorer in Holland, and Tyneside was mightily impressed with their first view of a Continental striker.

DID YOU KNOW

Wyn Davies had not scored for 21 games, but in European action the Welsh centre-forward was to break his duck and prove a relentless threat.

Match 2

1968–69

Inter Cities Fairs Cup, Round 1: Feyenoord (Holland) v. Newcastle United
SECOND LEG Tuesday, 17 September 1968, De Kuip Stadion (Rotterdam)

Feyenoord

UNITED McFaul, Craig, Clark (Iley), Gibb, McNamee, Burton, Scott, Robson, Davies, Elliott, Allen. Subs not used: Marshall, Sinclair.
Manager: Joe Harvey

FEYENOORD Graafland, Romeijn, Israel, Laseroms (van den Heide), Veldhoen, Boskamp, Jansen, Wery, Kindvall, van Hanegem, Moulijn. Subs not used: unknown.
Manager: Goos Brox

REFEREE H. Fritz (West Germany)

RESULT Lost 0–2 (0–1)

AGGREGATE Won 4–2

ATTENDANCE 45,000

SCORERS Feyenoord: Kindvall (27), van den Heide (54)

MATCH HIGHLIGHTS

United learnt their first lesson of European football in the return leg at the noisy, cauldron-like De Kuip stadium. Newcastle's defence – again without the influence of Moncur – were second best for most of the contest. United did not play as a unit, largely panicked in defence and continually gave up possession as Feyenoord attacked the Magpies from the off. But they managed to survive despite a Dutch onslaught, and the same mistake was not repeated for the rest of the campaign. In a physical, tough contest, the Dutch showed they were a fine side and took the lead almost on the half-hour as Kindvall blasted home Israel's chipped free-kick with a low shot that took a deflection. With goalkeeper Willie McFaul kept busy making a string of fine stops, the Black 'n' Whites held firm from conceding a second until the 54th minute when the sustained pressure eventually told. Van den Heide knocked the ball into the net from a narrow angle, following his penetrating run into the box. The Dutch pressed more and more and penned United back inside their penalty area. There were plenty of last-ditch tackles and blocks to prevent Feyenoord from scoring a third, resulting in a tense finale to the game.

MAN OF THE MATCH

John McNamee – tenacious, no-nonsense defence.

| MATCH RATING | • | • | | | | | Just watchable. |

STAR COMMENT

Jim Scott: 'They piled on the pressure, and our lads at the back had to perform heroics to keep them down to two.'

EYEWITNESS

Doug Weatherall (*Daily Mail*): 'I spent most of the 90 minutes in the Feyenoord stadium worrying. Worrying whether United could hold out against fantastic Feyenoord pressure.'

TOUR STOP – ROTTERDAM

Europe's largest port, situated where the mighty Rhine meets the North Sea, Rotterdam was devastated by German bombing in the Second World War and, as a consequence, is largely a city of modern architecture, with commercial might and a no-nonsense, hard-working people. With the 600-ft Euromast Tower and many avant-garde buildings, Rotterdam also gave United's fans a taste of Continental life at its most liberal. (pop. 600,000.)

STADIA FILE – DE KUIP

On the left bank of the Maas River, close to the heart of Rotterdam and at the time just fresh from a £4 million refurbishment, the De Kuip – or Stadion Feijenoord – was then years ahead of anything in Britain. With a capacity on two tiers of 62,000, it was first opened in 1937 next to the vast Varkenoord shipyards. When United first played there, it was an open bowl with one main covered stand, yet it still produced an intimidating atmosphere. The complex had lavish facilities compared to most stadiums of the time, including a hotel, restaurant and plush bars. Much changed recently, it is now one of Europe's finest stadiums.

DID YOU KNOW

United had a following of around 2,000 supporters on their first voyage abroad for European football. A two-day trip cost £19 10s 0d while a standing ticket was priced at 6s 6d.

The pre-match pennant presented by the Dutch captain.

Tour Stop

Rotterdam – Holland

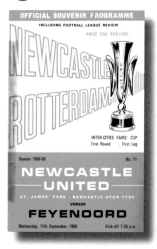

Feyenoord 1968–69

1 Postcard from Rotterdam

Gateway to Europe, a major port and commercial centre of the Netherlands.

2 Postcard from... De Kuip Stadion

Feyenoord's arena as it looked back in 1968, then an ultra-modern venue compared to the traditional British stadiums of the time.

3 Match action

United's debut in Europe ended in a marvellous 4–0 victory. Bryan Robson goes close at St. James' Park, this effort called up for offside.

4 Programme cover

United's match-day programme from the club's opening game in Europe.

Lisbon – Portugal

Sporting Clube 1968–69

Lisbon was an attractive destination. Pictured is the statue of Joao I in the Praca da Figueira, one of the capital's many grand squares. In the background is the hilltop fortress of Castelo de Sào Jorge.

Sporting Clube's original arena, the stadium was largely an open bowl, and on a stormy, rain-lashed evening, it was not a pleasant place to be.

In the return leg at St. James' Park, Pop Robson's cracking volley sealed the tie for the Magpies – a goal ranked as one of the very best in all United's Euro matches.

The Portuguese programme from the first-leg contest in Lisbon.

Match 3

1968–69

Inter Cities Fairs Cup, Round 2: Sporting Clube de Portugal v. Newcastle United
FIRST LEG Wednesday, 30 October 1968, Estádio José Alvalade (Lisbon)

Sporting Clube

UNITED McFaul, Craig, Clark, Gibb, Winstanley, Burton, Scott, Robson, Davies, Moncur, Foggon (Dyson). Subs not used: Clarke, Elliott.
Manager: Joe Harvey

SPORTING Damas, Celestino, Hilario, José Carlos, Armando, Goncalves (Marinho), Pedras, José Morais, Lourenco, Chico, Ernesto. Subs not used: Carvalho.
Manager: Fernando Caiado

REFEREE J. Wetter

RESULT Drew 1–1 (1–0)

AGGREGATE 1–1

ATTENDANCE 9,000

SCORERS United: Scott (32); Sporting: José Morais (89)

MATCH HIGHLIGHTS

Not many judges gave United much hope against one of Europe's top clubs, but, in an electric rainstorm, United came very close to pulling off a memorable victory in Portugal. Newcastle led courtesy of a Jim Scott close-range strike until ten seconds from the final whistle. At the death, Sporting claimed a precious equalising goal when José Morais hit a speculative long-range shot that struck the bar, then Willie McFaul's arm and rebounded into the net. With Bob Moncur back to fitness to marshal the defence, United gave a gritty and determined performance, keeping Sporting at bay and stunning the home crowd by taking the lead. Robson set up the opening, chasing an irretrievable-looking ball from a Clark free-kick. He won possession near the touchline and whipped in a terrific cross for Jim Scott to convert a side-foot shot from six yards out. It was a textbook European performance: avoiding defeat and recording an away goal. United perhaps came of age in Lisbon on that wet evening in October.

MAN OF THE MATCH

Bob Moncur – magnificent on his return.

MATCH RATING	•	•	•		

Average fare.

STAR COMMENT

Bryan Robson: 'Although they played a lot of good football, they rarely looked like getting through our back-line.'

EYEWITNESS

John Gibson (*Evening Chronicle*): 'Sporting only managed to snatch a 1–1 draw with a lucky goal ten seconds from time.'

TOUR STOP – LISBON

The city is one of Europe's finest capitals situated majestically on the Tagus estuary, and a football hotbed. Built on a series of hills, the small band of Toon supporters wandered through the fascinating old quarter of Alfama, visited the Castelo de São Jorge and rode the century-old trams as any tourist would do in this enchanting city. Lisbon is also a busy international port, as well as the industrial and commercial centre of Portugal. (pop. 565,000.)

STADIA FILE – ESTÁDIO JOSÉ ALVALADE

A massive concrete bowl close to Benfica's Estádio da Luz in the north of the capital, the José Alvalade stadium became Sporting's home in 1956 and, when United arrived there, had a capacity of 49,000. With only one covered cantilevered stand, the stadium was open to the elements and offered little protection from the storm that engulfed the arena the night of Newcastle's visit. The stadium was much developed afterwards with an imaginative seating design of green and white stripes. It was newly built for the 2004 European Championships.

DID YOU KNOW

Due to the torrential rain, Sporting changed kit at half-time from their green-and-white hooped shirts to tops with green-and-white halves.

Jim Scott netted the opening goal.

Match 4

1968–69

Inter Cities Fairs Cup, Round 2: Newcastle United v. Sporting Clube de Portugal
SECOND LEG Wednesday, 20 November 1968, St. James' Park

Sporting Clube

UNITED McFaul, Craig, Clark, Gibb, Burton, Moncur, Scott, Robson, Davies, Elliott, Dyson (Bennett). Subs not used: Clarke, Winstanley.
Manager: Joe Harvey

SPORTING Damas, Celestino, Hilario, José Carlos, Armando, José Morais, Pedras, Chico, Lourenco (Sitoi), Ernesto, Joao Carlos. Subs not used: Carvalho, Joao Morais.
Manager: Abraham Sorin

REFEREE G. Schulenburg (West Germany)

RESULT Won 1–0 (1–0)
AGGREGATE Won 2–1

ATTENDANCE 53,747

SCORERS United: Robson (10)

MATCH HIGHLIGHTS

United, playing in an unusual all-white kit on home soil, came out on top in a close contest with Sporting Clube. It was a spectacular goal from Bryan Robson, early in the game, that won the tie for United. A Tommy Gibb free-kick on the edge of the box was headed across goal by Wyn Davies for Robson, who had run around the back of the wall, to jump and volley the ball into the roof of the net from 14 yards out. It was a superbly worked goal, previously practised on the training ground over and over again. Although the visitors kept possession of the ball for sustained periods, they rarely threatened McFaul's goal, and it was Sporting's highly rated goalkeeper Vitor Damas who was the busier: he saved shot after shot as the match progressed. With a packed St. James' Park crowd roaring the Magpies forward, United kept a grip on the contest, and Davies and Scott twice went agonisingly close to registering another goal, while David Craig and Robson missed chances as well. Damas, though, was in brilliant form. At the other end of the field, United keeper McFaul had a quiet night as Sporting's pretty possession football all came to nothing in the box. Newcastle's deserved victory over another of Europe's most distinguished clubs raised eyebrows across the Continent.

MAN OF THE MATCH

Bryan Robson – influential performance.

MATCH RATING ● ● ● ☐ ☐   Accomplished display.

STAR COMMENT

Bryan Robson: 'The goal gave us a solid advantage to build on and with our strong defence we were always likely to hold on to it.'

EYEWITNESS

Tony Hardisty (*Sunday Express*): 'Bryan Robson's winning volley was technique and timing at its very best – magnificent, magical.'

OPPONENT FILE

An institution in Portugal, at the time United faced Sporting they were in the shadow of a great Benfica line-up, but they were still good enough to lift the title in 1970 and were runners-up in both 1968 and 1971 as well as European Cup Winners Cup victors in 1964. The 'Lions of Portugal' are recognised as the most loyally and vociferously supported team in the country, although they have recently been eclipsed by Porto's success.

STAR VISITOR

José Morais – One of Sporting's star forwards, Morais was a well-built, chunky striker who appeared for Portugal in the 1966 World Cup. It was his goal that defeated MTK in Sporting's European Cup Winners Cup triumph in 1964. A favourite of the Lisbon crowd, Morais returned from injury to face United and was noted for his power shooting. He was also especially dangerous from dead-ball positions.

DID YOU KNOW

The match attendance of almost 54,000 produced record receipts of £20,000. United's European debut season continually broke records at the turnstile with an average gate of 55,392 for the six home matches.

Match 5

1968–69

Inter Cities Fairs Cup, Round 3: Real Zaragoza (Spain) v. Newcastle United
FIRST LEG Wednesday, 1 January 1969, Estádio de la Romareda (Zaragoza)

Real Zaragoza

UNITED McFaul, Craig, Clark, Gibb, Burton, Moncur, Dyson, Robson, Davies, Scott, Foggon. Subs not used: Clarke, McNamee, Sinclair.
Manager: Joe Harvey

ZARAGOZA Neives, Borras, Irusquieta, Planas II, Santamaria, Santos (Violeta), Moya (Planas I), Gonzales, Bustillo, Marcelino, Martin. Subs not used: Diaz.
Manager: Cesar Rodrigues

REFEREE A. Ott (West Germany)

RESULT Lost 2–3 (2–2)

AGGREGATE 2–3

ATTENDANCE 22,000

SCORERS United: Robson (6), Davies (31); Zaragoza: Santos (5), Bustillo (20), Planas II (57)

MATCH HIGHLIGHTS

Newcastle spent New Year in sunny Spain and, in front of a fiesta crowd, performed well against a very good Real Zaragoza side, going down by only the odd goal in five, claiming two important away strikes. After an electrifying opening to the tie, the home side held a 2–1 advantage approaching the half-hour mark. Santos had rocketed home a rebound from the edge of the box after a drive had been blocked to open the scoring. Newcastle then levelled thanks to a goal from Bryan Robson, who rounded the keeper following a Tommy Gibb break. With 20 minutes gone, Bustillo's fine header from a free-kick went past Willie McFaul to restore Real's lead, but the two sides went in level at the break thanks to a brilliant Wyn Davies stooped header from another Gibb inspired attack, this time from a free-kick. With Newcastle's tactics working a treat – having decided to play a counter-attacking style – the match flowed from end to end. The Spanish outfit grabbed a winner almost on the hour, in a thriller of a match, as Martin ended a scintillating run down the right flank with a quick pass to Planas, who cracked a thunderbolt past United's keeper. Many reckoned Real Zaragoza would end United's pretence of European grandeur – the critics, though, were to be confounded yet again.

MAN OF THE MATCH

Wyn Davies – caused problems.

| MATCH RATING | ● ● ● ● ▢ | Captivating Hogmanay. |

STAR COMMENT

Bob Moncur: 'Zaragoza probably went closer than anyone to stopping us winning the cup.'

EYEWITNESS

John Gibson (*Evening Chronicle*): 'United, brave as always, were matching a great attacking side kick for kick.'

TOUR STOP – ZARAGOZA

A historic Roman city in northern Spain, situated on the River Ebro and backed by the Pyrenees, Zaragoza is rich in history and is marked by splendid, broad avenues. The city is also the capital of the Aragon region. Its main landmark is the Moorish palace of Aljafería as well as the cathedrals of La Seo and El Pilar. An important commercial hub, Zaragoza is at the heart of Spain's northern agricultural region. (pop. 626,000.)

STADIA FILE – LA ROMAREDA

Like many stadiums on the Continent at the time, La Romareda was an open bowl with one covered main stand. Built in 1957, Zaragoza's home underwent much modernisation after the Magpies' visit, to such an extent that it is now one of the finest in Spain, and is completely covered with a capacity of almost 50,000, complete with striking blue and white seating. It is set in an open piazza off one of Zaragoza's main thoroughfares and is surrounded by high-rise offices, apartments and urban greenery as well as the Hotel Romareda.

DID YOU KNOW

United supporters could spend New Year in Spain with a package trip to watch the Magpies at a cost of £33, which included flights, transport, match tickets, a sightseeing trip and overnight stay.

Bryan Robson became a key player.

Match 6

1968–69

Inter Cities Fairs Cup, Round 3: Newcastle United v. Real Zaragoza (Spain)
SECOND LEG Wednesday, 15 January 1969, St. James' Park

Real Zaragoza

UNITED McFaul, Craig (Guthrie), Clark, Gibb, Burton, Moncur, Dyson, Robson, Davies, Scott, Foggon. Subs not used: Clarke, McNamee.
Manager: Joe Harvey

ZARAGOZA Neives (Alarcia), Rico, Irusquieta, Borras, Santamaria, Gonzales, Martin, Violeta, Bustillo, Santos, Fontenla (Tejedor). Subs not used: Diaz.
Manager: Cesar Rodrigues

REFEREE M. Barde (France)

RESULT Won 2–1 (2–1)

AGGREGATE Drew 4–4, won on away goals

ATTENDANCE 56,055

SCORERS United: Robson (2), Gibb (29); Zaragoza: Martin (43)

MATCH HIGHLIGHTS

Zaragoza arrived without five of their stars for the return leg on a frosty Tyneside and after only two minutes were rocked when Pop Robson crashed home a 30-yard shot into the top corner after going past two defenders. But the stylish Spaniards looked the part, were cunning and dangerous, and pressed United hard. The Magpies needed a second goal, and after a mistake by keeper Neives, who fumbled a Robson cross, Tommy Gibb dived to head the ball into the net. The Spanish goalkeeper was soon to leave the field injured, having dived at the feet of Alan Foggon, and it was only substitute goalie Alarcia that stopped the Magpies from increasing their lead with a remarkable performance of heroics between the posts. In between United's attacks, Zaragoza pulled a goal back to keep the tie on a knife-edge: just before half-time, Martin had found the net after fine link-up play between Bustillo and Santos. With Zaragoza now only needing another goal to win the tie, the second period was tense, and chances came at both ends, but United hung on to their lead to go through on away goals.

MAN OF THE MATCH

Tommy Gibb – outstanding in midfield.

| MATCH RATING | ● | ● | ● | | |

Nail-biting finale.

STAR COMMENT

Keith Dyson: 'Zaragoza were a very good side and gave us one of the toughest games of the Fairs Cup run.'

EYEWITNESS

John Gibson (*Evening Chronicle*): 'Zaragoza never looked like getting a second, but Alarcia was inspired after the interval to leave United relying on the away goals rule.'

OPPONENT FILE

Another of Europe's finest club sides, Zaragoza were one of the Continent's elite, playing their 50th European fixture. They were winners of the Cup Winners Cup in 1964 and finalists in 1966. They were consistent performers in the Spanish league, although they have only ever once been close to winning the championship (as runners-up in 1975). At the time, they were just behind the might of Barca and Real Madrid; however, Zaragoza were four times finalists and twice winners of the Copa del Rey during the era that Newcastle met them. They were noted as being a side that were suspect in defence but brilliant in attack.

STAR VISITOR

Bustillo – A tough yet cultured little player who caused United all sorts of problems in both games. Highly rated in Spain, he had just completed a headline-grabbing £50,000 transfer to Barcelona, but was then loaned back to Zaragoza so he could complete his National Service. Strong and dangerous, he was powerful in the air and skilled on the deck.

DID YOU KNOW

Zaragoza failed to turn up for the second half with United's players, as well as the officials, left waiting for fully five minutes on the pitch. One of the French linesmen was sent to call the Spaniards out, yet they still didn't appear. In the end, the referee had to go to the dressing-room to lay down the law!

Tour Stop

Zaragoza – Spain

Real Zaragoza 1968–69

Situated on the River Ebro, the city of Zaragoza is rich in history. The impressive Basilica and Plaza del Pilar are pictured to the right of the river.

Zaragoza's home captured after United's visit, following redevelopment in 1982 for the World Cup.

Another spectacular goal from Bryan Robson: a 30-yard screamer past the diving Neives. United won the closely fought tie on away goals.

Match poster advertising the New Year's Day clash in Spain.

Setúbal – Portugal

Vitória Setúbal 1968–69

1

A Postcard from Lisbon

With the away leg switched to Lisbon, United quickly returned to the Portuguese capital some 25 miles up the coast from Setúbal. There were plenty of sights to see, including Ponte 25 de Abril (top left) and the Torre de Belém (top middle).

2

A Postcard from Estádio José Alvalade

With modern rail and road links, Sporting's arena was in total contrast to the pre-war English stadiums Newcastle were accustomed to in domestic action.

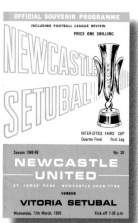

4

OFFICIAL SOUVENIR PROGRAMME
INCLUDING FOOTBALL LEAGUE REVIEW
PRICE ONE SHILLING

NEWCASTLE SETUBAL

INTER-CITIES FAIRS' CUP
Quarter Final   First Leg

Season 1968-69   No. 38

NEWCASTLE UNITED
ST. JAMES' PARK · NEWCASTLE UPON TYNE

VERSUS

VITORIA SETUBAL
Wednesday, 12th March, 1969   Kick-off 7-30 p.m.

Match Action

Just before the Setúbal players took to the St. James' Park pitch, a snowstorm engulfed the arena. Skipper Bob Moncur exchanges formalities with the Setúbal captain and match officials before the kick-off.

Memorabilia

United's distinctively designed match programme from the opening years of European action.

3

Match 7

1968–69

Inter Cities Fairs Cup, Quarter-Final: Newcastle United v. Vitória Setúbal (Portugal)
FIRST LEG Wednesday, 12 March 1969, St. James' Park

Vitória Setúbal

UNITED McFaul, Craggs, Clark, Gibb, Burton, Moncur, Robson, Horsfield (Sinclair), Davies, Scott, Foggon. Subs not used: McNamee, Clarke.
Manager: Joe Harvey

SETÚBAL Vital, Herculano, Carrico, Batista, Cardoso, Alfredo, José Maria, Wagner, Figueiredo, Arcanjo (Petita), Joao (Tome). Subs not used: Torres.
Manager: Fernando Vaz

REFEREE C. Liedberg (Sweden)

RESULT Won 5–1 (2–0)

AGGREGATE 5–1

ATTENDANCE 57,662

SCORERS United: Foggon (23), Robson (36), Davies (65), Robson (75), Gibb (88); Setúbal: José Maria (82)

MATCH HIGHLIGHTS

United crushed Portuguese side Vitória Setúbal in a snowstorm on Tyneside and counted their blessings that the north-east weather had given them a distinct advantage over their opponents. Many of Setúbal's players had never seen snow before, took time to adjust to the conditions and, in the end, never came to terms with the weather. A display full of assurance and skill in difficult conditions saw danger-men Wyn Davies and Bryan Robson cause havoc. United adopted the right tactics on a slippery pitch, with Setúbal completely baffled by the wintry conditions they were far from accustomed to. Newcastle took the lead in the 23rd minute when Davies won the ball in midfield and skipped past two defenders. He fed John Craggs, whose cross was met full on by Alan Foggon, his header flashing past Vital. Thirteen minutes later, it was 2–0 when another Craggs cross was capitalised on, and Robson belted the ball home after chaos in the box. Just after the hour, Davies had the ball in the net again in a hotly disputed goal. Robson's hooked pass put him through, and as the visitors called for offside, United's No. 9 swivelled to slide the ball home. Robson then claimed his second with an opportunist's strike, before Setúbal gained a consolation for their efforts – José Maria rifling the ball past Willie McFaul. But Newcastle wrapped up a great night by striking their fifth, in the final minutes, as Tommy Gibb struck a beauty from 20 yards that skimmed off the snow.

MAN OF THE MATCH

Bryan Robson – a danger all night.

MATCH RATING • • • •   Bizarre evening.

STAR COMMENT

Antonio Petita: 'Newcastle were brilliant – so strong – but then we aren't snowmen. We are footballers.'

EYEWITNESS

Tony Hardisty (*Sunday Express*): 'Another outstanding team performance, but the attendance of almost 58,000 – in a snowstorm! – was what made this night so special.'

OPPONENT FILE

Although founder members of Portugal's national league, Setúbal were largely an unknown club outside their own country. At the time, they possessed a young, attack-minded side and sat in fourth place in the Portuguese table. With a largely home-grown eleven that had impressed many, and having scored seventeen goals in the three rounds so far, Setúbal were an obvious danger. They had recently regained their top status in Portugal by winning promotion and for a short but sweet period challenged Benfica and Sporting, reaching the Portuguese cup final on four occasions around that time. The minnows of Setúbal, though, could only attract gates of around 10,000 and were never to sustain their development.

STAR VISITOR

José Maria – In season 1968–69 such was José Maria's reputation that he challenged the great Eusébio as Portugal's finest player. An established international for Portugal, and younger brother of skipper Conceição, he patrolled midfield and often arrived late into the box to pose a goal-scoring threat. Much courted by Portugal's giants, he scored two goals that saw Setúbal knock out Italian league leaders Fiorentina in an earlier round of the competition.

DID YOU KNOW

Due to a colour clash with Setúbal's green-and-white stripes, United appeared in an all-blue change strip at St. James' Park.

Match 8

1968–69

Inter Cities Fairs Cup, Quarter-Final: Vitória Setúbal (Portugal) v. Newcastle United
SECOND LEG Wednesday, 26 March 1969, Estádio José Alvalade (Lisbon)

Vitória Setúbal

UNITED McFaul, Craggs, Clark, Gibb, Burton (McNamee), Moncur, Sinclair, Robson, Davies, Scott, Foggon. Subs not used: Elliott, Hope.
Manager: Joe Harvey

SETÚBAL Vital, Conceição, Carrico, Batista, Cardoso (Petita), Alfredo, José Maria, Arcanjo, Figueiredo, Wagner, Joao. Subs not used: Torres.
Manager: Fernando Vaz

REFEREE O. Huber (Switzerland)

RESULT Lost 1–3 (1–1)

AGGREGATE Won 6–4

ATTENDANCE 34,000

SCORERS United: Davies (42); Setúbal: Arcanjo (26), Petita (60), Figueiredo (65)

MATCH HIGHLIGHTS

The return game with Setúbal, switched to Lisbon's José Alvalade arena, saw a remarkable carnival atmosphere, as seemingly the whole population of the small town of Setúbal descended on the capital. The Portuguese side were determined to have a go and attempt to claw back the five goals United had scored on Tyneside. As a consequence, the Magpies found themselves on the rack. Setúbal were both skilful and aggressive, in what was at times a testy match. They went ahead midway through the opening period when Arcanjo scored with a fine header at the far post, but Davies equalised, running in to nod home at an opportune moment, just before the break. The Welshman's peach of a goal made Setúbal's task really difficult, if not impossible. Newcastle were rocked, however, by a second-half onslaught by the Portuguese side with two quick goals – one a Petita free-kick and the other a Figueiredo header – and their physical, indeed at times savage, approach to the match made for an uncomfortable ending. Newcastle, though, courageously kept their heads and progressed into the semi-finals, those goals on a snow-filled night at St. James' Park proving the cushion they needed.

MAN OF THE MATCH

Bob Moncur – cool and masterful.

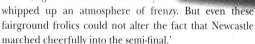

MATCH RATING ● ● ●   Torrid stuff.

STAR COMMENT

Alan Foggon: 'There was all sorts going on. We held out pretty well, and they knew they were beaten, even before the final whistle.'

EYEWITNESS

Arnold Howe (*Daily Express*): 'Bands, clowns, girls and drummer boys whipped up an atmosphere of frenzy. But even these fairground frolics could not alter the fact that Newcastle marched cheerfully into the semi-final.'

TOUR STOP – LISBON/SETÚBAL

Newcastle supporters did not get to explore the small, picturesque fishing town of Setúbal sandwiched between the Arrabida Mountain and the Atlantic, due to the match being switched to nearby Lisbon. Only 25 miles south from the capital, Setúbal is an old and interesting destination and now a popular tourist stop, with the Castelo de São Filipe occupying a breathtaking position overlooking the sea and town. (pop. 97,000.)

STADIA FILE – ESTÁDIO JOSÉ ALVALADE

Setúbal's Estádio do Bonfim was undergoing refurbishment at the time of the tie and temporarily without floodlights, so the match had to be switched to the home of Sporting Lisbon, a venue United had already visited only three and a half months before. The José Alvalade complex was then totally uncovered and far from the state-of-the-art stadium it is today.

DID YOU KNOW

The festival atmosphere at the José Alvalade arena was contributed to by a constant din of drums and trumpets, and there was also the bizarre sight of a motorcycle that raced round and round the perimeter track during the match waving a huge Setúbal flag.

Match 9

1968–69

Inter Cities Fairs Cup, Semi-Final: Glasgow Rangers (Scotland) v. Newcastle United
FIRST LEG Wednesday, 14 May 1969, Ibrox Park (Glasgow)

Glasgow Rangers

UNITED McFaul, Craggs, Clark, Gibb, McNamee, Moncur, Scott (Sinclair), Robson, Davies, Arentoft, Foggon. Subs not used: Burton, Hope.
Manager: Joe Harvey

RANGERS Neef, Johansen, Provan, Greig, Jackson, Smith (D), Henderson, Penman, Stein, Jardine, Persson. Subs not used: Martin.
Manager: David White

REFEREE J. Adair (Northern Ireland)

RESULT Drew 0–0 (0–0)

AGGREGATE 0–0

ATTENDANCE 75,580

SCORERS None

MATCH HIGHLIGHTS

It was an Anglo–Scots contest that made the blood tingle, a Battle of Britain encounter that had everyone in the North talking. In a hard but sporting match, Rangers could have built a crucial lead at Ibrox, as they missed several chances to find the net. Newcastle defended resolutely, and at times with good fortune, while the Glasgow club also missed a first-half penalty, after Persson was felled in the 34th minute. Willie McFaul brought the Danish forward down, when attempting to punch the ball clear as Persson ran onto a Smith pass. But United's Ulster-born keeper made amends by brilliantly diving across goal and pushing Andy Penman's low spot-kick round the post. It was the key moment of the tie, and the Newcastle contingent behind McFaul's goal were jubilant. McFaul, in fact, had an inspired day, pulling off several other worthy saves, too, while Bob Moncur and John McNamee were solid in the centre of United's defence in a terrific all-round team performance. With confidence high after that penalty stop, United held firm, were resolute at the back and caught Rangers on the break. With a slice of luck, they could have pinched victory. Robson lobbed a shot over the bar, then United's striker almost capitalised on a slip by Jardine, only for a last-ditch tackle by Kai Johansen to save a certain goal. The unlucky Robson almost sneaked it at the death with a 25-yard attempt. United, though, were well pleased with a goalless draw.

MAN OF THE MATCH

Willie McFaul – for his penalty save.

| MATCH RATING | ● | ● | | | |

Dogged display.

STAR COMMENT

Joe Harvey: 'It was a heart-stirring performance. I was proud of every one of them.'

EYEWITNESS

Arnold Howe (*Daily Express*): 'Newcastle owe their position to their magnificent defence at Ibrox. Courage, camaraderie and team spirit came through against Rangers.'

TOUR STOP – GLASGOW

Unlike United's previous ports of call, Glasgow was a familiar stop to many of the Geordies who made the trip to Clydeside. At the time of United's semi-final visit, Scotland's largest city was a still an industrial giant but one starting to decline, reliant, in the main part, on the country's ageing core industries: shipbuilding, manufacturing and coal mining. Then in much need of renovation, Glasgow is now a thriving and regenerated metropolis. (pop. 630,000.)

STADIA FILE – IBROX PARK

In 1969, Rangers' famous home was a much different stadium to the inspiring twenty-first-century venue that it is now. Then a vast bowl, and only two years before the 1971 tragedy left sixty-six fans killed on the Ibrox steps, the ground featured the historic Leitch grandstand and vast terraces with oval ends. Opened as far back as 1877, Ibrox began to be completely remodelled at the start of 1978 and with later upgrading, apart from sections of the Leitch Main Stand, is now unrecognisable today compared to when United visited.

DID YOU KNOW

The crowd of over 75,000 was a Fairs Cup record and the largest attendance Newcastle United had played in front of at that time, other than in cup finals. Around 12,000 Geordies made the trip to Glasgow.

Goalkeeper Willie McFaul.

Match 10

1968–69

Inter Cities Fairs Cup, Semi-Final: Newcastle United v. Glasgow Rangers (Scotland)
SECOND LEG Wednesday, 21 May 1969, St. James' Park

Glasgow Rangers

UNITED McFaul, Craig, Clark, Gibb, Burton, Moncur, Scott, Robson, Davies, Arentoft, Sinclair. Subs not used: Foggon, Craggs, Hope.
Manager: Joe Harvey

RANGERS Neef, Johansen, Mathieson, Greig, McKinnon (Provan), Smith (D), Henderson, Penman, Stein, Johnston, Persson. Subs not used: Martin.
Manager: David White

REFEREE W. Gow (Wales)

RESULT Won 2–0 (0–0)

AGGREGATE Won 2–0

ATTENDANCE 59,303

SCORERS United: Scott (52), Sinclair (77)

MATCH HIGHLIGHTS

On an emotion-and-tension-filled early summer night, Newcastle progressed to their first European final, in their first year of entry. But it was a bitter, bruising encounter against the men from Glasgow, and the game saw a disturbing pitch invasion by the hordes that had travelled to support the famous Ibrox club. In a game littered with stoppages, Newcastle took hold of the match with two second-half goals, one from Jackie Sinclair and the other by Jim Scott. The first effort was a great shot by Scott, eight minutes after half-time, following a perfect Gibb through ball. The former Hibs man left Mathieson in his wake and struck a fierce drive across the keeper. Thirteen minutes from time, United sealed victory when Sinclair fired in a volley following a Davies knock-down in the box from a long Ollie Burton free-kick. Ironically, both players were Scots by birth. Play was stopped three times due to crowd trouble, including a seventeen-minute period when the players were led from the field as Rangers fans invaded the pitch in a futile attempt to call a halt to the match when United were in an unassailable position. Play resumed with police lining the Gallowgate End, shoulder to shoulder. However, those alarming moments of soccer hooliganism couldn't overshadow United's remarkable achievement of reaching a European final at the first attempt.

MAN OF THE MATCH

Bob Moncur – inspirational throughout.

MATCH RATING ● ● ● ●   Grim but stirring.

STAR COMMENT

Bob Moncur: 'The second leg was never going to be an easy game, and while Gers didn't really create a lot, they weren't easy to break down either.'

EYEWITNESS

Ivor Broadis (*The Journal*): 'It was hard, relentless stuff with man-to-man marking limiting space and nobody prepared to yield an inch of it.'

OPPONENT FILE

At the time United met the mighty Rangers, the Ibrox men were noted as having appeared in more European ties than any other British club. In 1967 they reached the Cup Winners Cup final and lifted the trophy in 1972, but in domestic action Rangers were second best to the dominant Celtic side of the time and had just been beaten by their Old Firm rivals in the Scottish Cup final. Nevertheless, Rangers' side was full of famous names and international stars.

STAR VISITOR

Colin Stein – The subject of the first six-figure transfer between Scottish clubs when he moved from Hibs to Rangers for £100,000, Colin Stein was noted as a 'brilliant centre-forward and restless forager'. A member of the Scotland squad, Stein was a fiery character having already been sent off on three occasions in all games during the 1968–69 season. In the match against United he had just returned from a five-week suspension. He later moved to England with Coventry City. Stein scored almost 100 goals for the Gers.

DID YOU KNOW

Alex Ferguson – later more famously Manchester United's boss – was in the Rangers party for the semi-final. A striker, he found himself axed by boss Dave White for the latter stages of the European run.

Tour Stop

Glasgow – Scotland

①

IBROX PARK, GLASGOW · Home of Rangers F.C.

5127

②

Postcard from Glasgow

United had a 12,000 following of Geordies for the semi-final on Clydeside. No aircraft were needed, just a long and tedious drive in pre-motorway Scotland.

Postcard from Ibrox Park

Unrecognisable now, apart from the listed Archibald Leitch main stand, Ibrox was packed with a record Fairs Cup crowd of over 75,000. Shortly after United's visit, 66 Rangers supporters were killed on the steep exit steps of the stadium.

④

In the event of the game to which this ticket admits being postponed for any reason, the ticket will be available on the postponed date. On no account will money be refunded.

21

INTER CITIES' FAIRS CUP—SEMI-FINAL FIRST LEG

RANGERS v. NEWCASTLE UNITED

IBROX STADIUM, GLASGOW
WEDNESDAY, 14th MAY, 1969
KICK-OFF 7.30 p.m.

Section F

Row E

Seat No. 24

Manager

THIS PORTION TO BE RETAINED BY HOLDER

Match Action

Jackie Sinclair sweetly volleys the ball past keeper Neef in the deciding second leg at Gallowgate.

Memorabilia

Match-day ticket for the contest at Ibrox: a 30-shilling prime main-stand seat.

③

Budapest – Hungary

Újpesti Dózsa 1968–69

1. Postcard from Budapest

The Hungarian capital was an attractive destination for United's first European final – even if in 1969 it was deep behind the Iron Curtain. Pictured is the Royal Palace situated on Buda hill overlooking the majestic Danube.

2. Postcard from Megyeri úti Stadion

Small, compact and surrounded by trees, this is a venue etched into the history of Newcastle United.

3. March

Jim Scott, running onto a return pass and flicking the ball over keeper Szentimihalyi, scores the crucial third goal in the first leg on Tyneside.

4.

The Fairs Cup final programme for the match in Budapest, a game that was played well into June.

Match 11

1968–69

Inter Cities Fairs Cup, Final: Newcastle United v. Újpesti Dózsa (Hungary)
FIRST LEG Thursday, 29 May 1969, St. James' Park

Újpesti Dózsa

UNITED McFaul, Craig, Clark, Gibb, Burton, Moncur, Scott, Robson, Davies, Arentoft, Sinclair (Foggon). Subs not used: Craggs, McNamee, Hope.
Manager: Joe Harvey

ÚJPESTI Szentimihalyi, Kaposzta, Bankuti, Dunai (E), Solymosi, Nosko, Fazekas, Gorocs, Bene, Dunai (A), Zambo. Subs not used: Borbely, Szini, Nyiro, Nagy.
Manager: Lajos Baroti

REFEREE J. Hannet (Belgium)

RESULT Won 3–0 (0–0)

AGGREGATE 3–0

ATTENDANCE 59,234

SCORERS United: Moncur (63), (71), Scott (84)

MATCH HIGHLIGHTS

On a warm summer evening United played their biggest game for 14 years. A tense first half brought stalemate that saw Újpesti stars Gorocs and Bene shine and give Newcastle supporters plenty to worry about. Newcastle needed something special to break the Hungarians down: in stepped Bob Moncur to give a skipper's performance. Once United grabbed the opening goal just after the hour mark, the tide turned the Geordies' way. The breakthrough came when Wyn Davies brought down a long ball from a Tommy Gibb free-kick and drilled in a low shot, which saw unlikely scorer Bob Moncur whip home a rebound off the keeper low into the net. Minutes later, United's captain again stepped forward from the back, exchanged a one-two and drilled another low shot into the net from the edge of the box. Then Jim Scott gave Newcastle a comfortable lead, racing into the box to clip the ball over the advancing keeper, following yet another delightful one-two move with Ben Arentoft. Újpesti had the ball in the net right on the final whistle when Solymosi fired home a free-kick. The referee, though, had blown for time just before the ball flew past Willie McFaul. The 3–0 advantage came at a cost, though, with star centre-forward Wyn Davies sustaining a nasty facial injury: a fractured cheekbone courtesy of his teammate Moncur. But, courageously, Davies made sure he was able to play in the deciding leg in Budapest.

MAN OF THE MATCH

Bob Moncur – a captain's role.

MATCH RATING	●	●	●	●	

Terrific exhibition.

STAR COMMENT

Joe Harvey: 'I think we have got one hand on the cup now. I hoped for two [goals] at the most – but three – it's fantastic.'

EYEWITNESS

Denis Lowe (*Daily Telegraph*): 'Newcastle's performance must rank as one of the most worthy by any British club in European competition.'

OPPONENT FILE

Újpesti had just finished the 1968–69 season as runners-up in Hungary and were recognised as a free-scoring side, spearheaded by the dangerous combination of Bene and Antal Dunai. They had taken care of Leeds United – Football League champions to be – in the run-up to the final and were regarded as one of the top teams on the Continent. Regular champions in Hungary, alongside their great rivals Ferencváros, they held ascendancy in the years after facing the Magpies, lifting seven titles in a row. Backed by the communist Ministry of the Interior, the club was later reformed and known as Újpesti TE following the downfall of the communist regime.

STAR VISITOR

Ferenc Bene – A great favourite of the Hungarian public and an automatic choice for his country at a time when they were a force in Europe. Bene was a tricky, skilled and astute centre-forward respected throughout Europe. A player who roamed across the forward line, Bene had joined Újpesti from the age of sixteen, lifted an Olympic gold medal in Tokyo and appeared for the Hungarians during the 1966 World Cup two years later. Not tall but well built, Bene went on to become a Hungarian legend spoken of in the same breath as the great Ferenc Puskás.

DID YOU KNOW

Bob Moncur had never before scored a senior goal for United, in over six years since making his debut, but United's skipper made it a Euro final hat-trick with another strike in the second leg in Hungary. All three goals were from his left foot, too – not bad for a right-footed player!

Match 12

1968–69
Inter Cities Fairs Cup, Final: Újpesti Dózsa (Hungary) v. Newcastle United
SECOND LEG Wednesday, 11 June 1969, Megyeri úti Stadion (Budapest)

Újpesti Dózsa

UNITED McFaul, Craig, Clark, Gibb, Burton, Moncur, Scott (Foggon), Robson, Davies, Arentoft, Sinclair. Subs not used: McNamee, Hope.
Manager: Joe Harvey

ÚJPESTI Szentmihalyi, Kaposzta, Solymosi, Bankuti, Dunai (E), Nosko, Fazekas, Gorocs, Bene, Dunai (A), Zambo. Subs not used: unknown.
Manager: Lajos Baroti

REFEREE J. Heymann (Switzerland)

RESULT Won 3–2 (0–2)

AGGREGATE Won 6–2

ATTENDANCE 34,000

SCORERS United: Moncur (48), Arentoft (52), Foggon (68); Újpesti: Bene (30), Gorocs (42)

MATCH HIGHLIGHTS

A remarkable evening in Budapest began with Newcastle on the rack as the Magyars battled back into the tie with a brilliant opening half. They rocked United with flair and imagination, and two goals found the back of United's net. It could have been three but for a marvellous flying save from Willie McFaul, who was at his best that night. The Magyars first arrived as Bene collected the ball out wide, surged inside and crashed a terrific shot screaming into the net. Then Újpesti's other star player, Gorocs, had the crowd roaring as he raced into the box and left United's defence for dead to send the ball past McFaul from close in. The 3–0 advantage now looked vulnerable, but Joe Harvey's interval team-talk did the trick as the Magpies shocked the confident Hungarians with a three-goal burst that ensured that the trophy ended up on the plane back to Tyneside with the team. Bob Moncur, with another captain's performance, set the Black 'n' Whites on their way with a hooked volley from 18 yards following a Sinclair cross, immediately after the interval. It was a goal that stunned the home players and partisan crowd. Within four minutes, the game was level at 2–2 as Arentoft picked up a rebound after a Scott effort had been blocked, the Dane hammering the ball home from fifteen yards. With Newcastle in total control, substitute Alan Foggon ran onto a great Davies flick to sprint clear and crash the ball against the bar before following up to convert the rebound. It made the score on the night 3–2,

clinching an amazing fight-back from two goals down. As a result, Newcastle United were European champions.

MAN OF THE MATCH

Bob Moncur – once more a hero.

| MATCH RATING | ● ● ● ● ● | Scintillating comeback.

STAR COMMENT

Joe Harvey: 'I have not seen any cup final or played in one that matched this game for excitement and fighting courage.'

EYEWITNESS

Joe Cummings (*Daily Mirror*): 'Newcastle came out for the second session full of fight. They caught Újpesti cold and blasted in two goals in a fabulous four-minute spell.'

TOUR STOP – BUDAPEST

The capital of Hungary was formed as late as 1873 following the unification of three separate towns: Buda – the historic centre – Obuda and Pest. Situated on the Danube, the city boasts magnificent architecture, including the famous Parliament building modelled on Westminster, the old walled town on Buda hill, the Royal Palace and St Stephen's Basilica. The city is a football hotspot with six senior clubs, and after the fall of communism at the end of the '80s, Budapest became a popular and lively tourist destination. (pop. 1,760,000.)

STADIA FILE – MEGYERI ÚTI STADION

Situated in the north of Pest with a capacity of 34,000, the stadium was a completely open bowl with modest facilities and prominent V-shaped floodlights, and was attached to an adjacent sports complex, when the Magpies visited. Opened in 1923, the stadium was refurbished in 1972, shortly after United's triumphant visit, with the addition of a continuous roof.

DID YOU KNOW

Newcastle United celebrated two birthdays on that 11 June evening in Budapest – Joe Harvey was 50 years old and centre-half John McNamee turned 28. Only around 200 fans made the trip behind the Iron Curtain for that victorious night. Another 200,000 or so listened to and watched the BBC back home.

Glory against

Against the Magyars of Hungary, the Black 'n' Whites performed in a manner that impressed many. Taking a heartening 3–0 advantage to Budapest, after a victory in front of a near 60,000 crowd on Tyneside, was a tremendous start. But Newcastle had to dig deep in the Hungarian capital as Újpesti showed exactly why they were rated so highly. United were two goals adrift by the interval. Yet boss Joe Harvey remained confident. He said at the time, 'I wasn't worried at half-time when we were two down. I knew if they had scored one it would be tricky, but all we needed was one ourselves, and then they would be up against the wall.'

The players weren't as confident as their boss, though. Bryan Robson recalled, 'They started with a high tempo, and we were taken aback by the pace of the game. We struggled and nothing really constructive was said at half-time to change it.' However, the experienced Harvey, winner of two FA Cup finals with United, knew his football. Newcastle stormed into the second half and hit the Hungarians cold. They scored not once but twice in the space of the opening seven minutes. Harvey was right in his prediction that Újpesti would have little stomach to fight back. They collapsed as Joe had predicted. Robson added, 'We capitalised after that. Újpesti ran out of gas. It was a real surprise.' Newcastle went on to score a third goal and turn the match into a marvellous 3–2 victory, winning the trophy by a wide margin of 6–2 on aggregate.

Top: Moncur hits the net to score a goal for United in the first leg at St. James' Park.
Second top: The skipper then receives rapturous congratulations from his teammates.
Second bottom: Postcard from Budapest.
Right: Programme from the game on Tyneside.
Far right: Captain Bob Moncur holds aloft the Inter Cities Fairs Cup after being presented with the trophy by Sir Stanley Rous (right) following the victory in Budapest.

OFFICIAL SOUVENIR PROGRAMME

PRICE
1/-

INTER CITIES
FAIRS' CUP

FINAL TIE
First Leg

Season 1968-69   No. 1

NEWCASTLE UNITED
ST. JAMES' PARK · NEWCASTLE UPON TYNE
versus
UJPEST DOZSA
THURSDAY, 29th MAY, 1969   KICK-OFF 7.30 p.m.

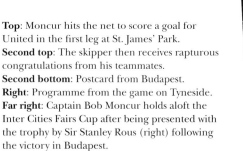

the Magyars

Left: United's party arrive back at St. James' Park on an open-top bus; Moncur leads the celebrations.
Below: The ball is in the back of the Hungarians' net. Alan Foggon (No. 11) turns away to take the acclaim.
Bottom: Skipper Bob Moncur holds the trophy with Willie McFaul as the players parade around the Gallowgate arena.

'He would be worth millions if he was playing now, because born leaders like him are...

Terry McDermott

Bob Moncur

It is often said every successful team needs both an inspirational skipper and a commanding central defender at the heart of its team. In the 1968–69 season, as Newcastle United embarked on their first European voyage, the Black 'n' Whites possessed both – all rolled into one in the shape of Bob Moncur. A tough and uncompromising centre-half who read the game well, Moncur marshalled Newcastle's rearguard like few before or since and can perhaps be recognised as the club's finest-ever defender. As a captain, he was a chip off the block of his manager Joe Harvey: a sergeant-major type who yelled his way through matches getting the very best from his players.

During United's European triumph Moncur was in inspired form, producing performances second to none. His fantastic leadership of the team culminated in a truly remarkable show in the final against Újpesti Dózsa when he netted a much celebrated, trophy-winning hat-trick over the two legs.

Originally from Perth, Moncur was a Scottish schoolboy international before heading for Tyneside as a teenager in October 1960. The young Scot took to Newcastle from the start, and he was to spend the vast majority of his playing career with the Magpies: in all, he spent thirteen and a half years at St. James' Park. More a budding attacking inside-forward when he arrived, he was soon lifting silverware in the shape of the FA Youth Cup, in which Moncur scored the winning goal against Wolves in 1962. He then began a lengthy period of trying to establish himself in United's first team.

A move into a more defensive role suited Moncur, and once he became a no-nonsense central defender during the mid-'60s his career flourished. He was tough – with legs like tree trunks – good in the air and as resolute as any. Teammate Bryan Robson said of his colleague, 'Apart from being a good defender he was a really good leader with a strong personality.' More than anyone it was Moncur who fostered United's marvellous togetherness. Robson added, 'Moncs bonded the team spirit. He organised nights out and brought us all closer together.'

Moncur missed the opening contest with Feyenoord, out injured with cartilage trouble, but he returned to give a series of formidable displays as United continued their progress to the final. The Scot was especially prominent in the Geordies' away legs when his resolute defending and organising ability were in prime demand. In the 1–1 draw with Sporting Lisbon Bob noted, 'We had to keep our heads, something we learnt early into the cup run.' He rallied the troops when the going got tough and kept his cool in torrid encounters with Zaragoza in Spain and back in Portugal against Setúbal. Moncur recalled, 'Zaragoza were a brilliant

Bob Moncur

attacking team and probably went closer than anyone to stopping us winning the cup.'

Then against the might of Glasgow Rangers the rugged defender frustrated the masses at Ibrox by guarding the United box as if on a life-or-death mission. Bob said, 'As a Scot it was a great occasion to lead out the Magpies at Ibrox. We played a perfect away game and kept the likes of Henderson and Stein quiet, survived a harsh penalty and ultimately hushed the Scots fans who had been baying for our blood from the start.'

He went on to say, 'In the return at St. James' Park it was quite a match, not a brilliant one, but a tense and dour battle. Rangers didn't create much, but they were difficult to break down. But we got two fantastic goals and had to encounter that remarkable pitch invasion.'

The stage was set for a hero's performance in the final with Újpesti Dózsa, and Bob Moncur proved to be that hero by striking an unlikely three goals over the two legs. It was the perfect captain's performance – something straight out of the *Roy of the Rovers* comic-strip. Amazingly, Moncur had never before scored a first-class goal in his near decade of wearing the black and white shirt. The Scot's only taste of hitting the net was in that FA Youth Cup final some seven years before.

United's captain noted, 'I was not known for venturing over the halfway line too often. Indeed, Joe didn't want me to. That was not my job. But we needed a breakthrough. So, up I went from my normal back-line position. Gibbo hit a free-kick to the back of the box, as he so often did, for big Wyn Davies. He chested the ball down and as the tall Újpesti keeper came out hammered the ball against him. The rebound flew towards me and I just connected first time, sweet as you like.' Bob couldn't believe it: 'My first senior goal and in a European final.'

But it didn't end there. Bob continued, 'I

BOB MONCUR: FACT FILE

Position: Centre-half

Born: Perth, January 1945

Joined United from: Schools football, October 1960

Left for: Sunderland, June 1974, £30,000

Other major clubs: Carlisle United

Full international: Scotland (16 caps, 1968 to 1972)

United career, senior games: 361 app., 10 goals

United Euro record: 22 app., 4 goals

Did you know: Bob unleashed upon the football world the very special talent of Peter Beardsley when in charge of Carlisle United.

moved forward again from the half-way line and with Újpesti defenders backing off, played a one-two with Ben Arentoft. Suddenly, the ball stood up perfectly, and I just let fly. The ball hardly lifted as it flashed across the box and into the far corner of the net. It may have bounced a few times, but I wasn't bothered. It was another goal.'

United took a 3–0 lead to Hungary, and Moncur was at the centre of the action again. He said, 'The crucial goal just after the break was to bring me that amazing hat-trick and complete the triumph I could never have even dreamt about. My goal in Budapest rates as the most important. We were two goals down and looked dead and buried as the Hungarians murdered us. At half-time, I was utterly convinced we had lost it. But as Joe famously said to us in the dressing-room, all we needed was a goal and they would die. He was absolutely right.

'I got one within a minute or so of the restart. A corner saw the keeper punch out under

Bob Moncur

pressure. Sinclair returned it into the box, and the ball dropped just right. I swung at it and connected almost spot-on. The ball rocketed high into the net off the keeper's hands. I'd got three goals and all with my left foot. And that's pretty remarkable, too, as I am right-footed!'

Newcastle United had won the Inter Cities Fairs Cup. Moncur, as could be expected, was elated. He recalled, 'It was a fabulous occasion. I received the trophy from FIFA President Sir Stanley Rous but cannot remember much else. Everything was a bit of a haze, with all the celebration and emotion. We had been dubbed back-door entrants into Europe, and that hurt a bit. For a team not good enough we did pretty well.'

Bob considered that the side in 1969 was the best he played in, noting, 'We were solid, organised and professional. Nobody felt bigger than anyone else. There were no inflated egos. We all gelled together.

'There weren't any great stars, but it was a great team. We were just a couple of players short of having a really brilliant side. Apart from buying Jimmy Smith from Aberdeen, we didn't strengthen when we should have done.

'Willie McFaul had a fabulous season. We had the class of David Craig; the experience of Frank Clark. Tommy Gibb and Benny Arentoft used to get through a load of work on the pitch. Pop Robson and Wyn Davies combined well with Pop snapping up the chances from big Wyn's knock-downs. Pop was the best striker never to play for England.'

Moncur's emergence as a top defender – upon which much of United's success was based – saw the Scot blossom at international level, too. First capped by his country in May 1968 against the Netherlands, he was taken to heart by his nation's fanatical supporters after a rugged display in an England v. Scotland clash in 1970 at Hampden Park. He spectacularly cleared

off the line to save the game for his country, then was led off the field with concussion to a standing ovation from the massive crowd of 134,000, following his spirited performance. He was handed the captaincy of Scotland in that year and was by then highly rated by many in the game, including the great Sir Matt Busby, who once said, 'He is a splendid captain and leader of men.' Terry McDermott remembered Moncs as a 'special player'. Newcastle colleagues during the '70s, McDermott said, 'He would be worth millions if he was playing now, because born leaders like him are a rarity.'

Moncur led the Magpies into more European action during 1969–70 and 1970–71 and took part in the infamous battle with Internazionale at St. James' Park. It was a match Moncur will never forget. It even prompted him to ask for police protection in the tunnel at the end of the game to stop any brawling as they came off! And Captain Bob got on the score sheet again – opening United's account with a header in that extraordinary match.

United's skipper remembered, 'I've never seen anything like it before or since. There was no interest in the ball at all from Inter.' Two minutes before the flashpoint of the dismissal of the visitors' goalkeeper Vieri occurred, Moncur had given United a deserved lead with a well-taken header from a corner. He sent the ball flying past the Italian international keeper – who was in his country's squad for the 1970 Mexico World Cup – and high into the roof of the net. It was Vieri's last act – or almost. He then went on to thump the referee and, not surprisingly, was ordered to the dressing-room. Bob noted, 'My outstanding memory is of two policemen coming onto the pitch at the Gallowgate End to lead the keeper off. They led him along the front of the paddock to the tunnel.'

The year before, when United were the trophy holders, Moncur had almost guided the

Bob Moncur

One of United's finest captains, Bob Moncur was an inspiration and a top-class defender.

Bob Moncur

Magpies to another semi-final, just failing by a matter of 120 seconds in a dramatic quarter-final with Anderlecht. Earlier in that campaign, Moncur had been the linchpin as Newcastle defeated Porto. He was an inspiration in Portugal as United battled out a goalless draw, in spite of the fact that he was decidedly unwell with a stomach bug. Then, with United needing a convincing victory over the Belgians after going down 0–2 in Brussels, it was Moncur who led from the front in the fight-back, continually waving his colleagues forward to claw back the deficit and grab what looked like a winner only for a dramatic late Anderlecht strike to stun the Tyneside faithful. Bob remembered, 'All the lads just dropped: it was dreadful.' He added, 'If we hadn't lost that late goal against Anderlecht, I am still convinced we would have won the Fairs Cup two years running.'

Moncur remained at Gallowgate until the summer of 1974, leading the Black 'n' Whites to Wembley in the FA Cup final before heading for Wearside to conclude his playing career with United's great rivals, Sunderland. Following a stint in management with Carlisle United, Hearts, Plymouth Argyle and Hartlepool United, Moncur settled back on Tyneside, his adopted home since he was a teenager. A keen golfer and expert yachtsman, Bob is now involved in celebrity golf events and organises sailing tours at home and abroad, once completing the notable Fastnet Race as well as the Whitbread Round the World Yacht Race in 1993.

A popular local radio presenter, too, he also appears on television as a knowledgeable pundit and is a regular corporate host at St. James' Park on match days. Bob is also chairman of Heroes, the club's ex-players' association, and remains a hugely popular figure on Tyneside. He is the last United skipper to hold aloft a major trophy, but that's an unwanted tag Bob would love to lose. He simply longs to see the Magpies win another one.

The encounter with Glasgow Rangers was a highlight for Moncur. The match included a pitch invasion at St. James' Park, the Gallowgate End terrace eventually having to be lined by police officers to control the Scottish fans.

2

OPULENT BRUSSELS TO COMMUNIST PÉCS

1969–70, 1970–71

Bob Moncur rises to bullet a header past the Internazionale goalkeeper at St. James' Park in the epic 1970 tie.

In the aftermath of Newcastle United's magnificent triumph in Budapest, the soccer-mad public of Tyneside wanted more of the same. The experience of European football had been a rousing and highly enjoyable one. The fact that the Magpies had started as no-hopers but had gone on to topple some of the cream of Europe and lift a major trophy – the club's first for 14 years – was much heralded across the country. Geordies overflowed with pride. Players, officials and supporters all wanted a repeat performance, although Bryan Robson recalled there wasn't any real optimism about retaining the trophy. He said, 'It was such a surprise and a fantastic achievement to win the cup with the group of players we had. There was a great team spirit, and we were looking forward to defending the trophy, but we never thought we would win it again.' Nevertheless, club chairman Lord Westwood noted at the time, 'Right now, there is more potential at Newcastle United than at any time in the club's history.'

Tyneside took to the new form of European football like few other places in the country. Attendances for that opening campaign approached 56,000, a remarkable average. While the mass of United's boisterous support stayed very much on north-east soil, at this stage, a handful – by comparison with what was to follow – did start their Grand Tour around Europe. They were the Toon Army's advance troops: pioneers in what was later to become a huge and popular season-by-season exodus to the many appealing destinations that the Continent had to offer.

For the next two European campaigns, Newcastle United and their fans certainly experienced the vast disparity of a Continent split at the time by the East–West divide. They headed for opulent Brussels, centre of the rapidly emerging EEC, as well as to fashionable Milan, but then saw the other extreme, travelling deep behind the Iron Curtain to communist Hungary and the town of Pécs. The contrast was acute.

Newcastle's triumphant Fairs Cup-winning side was bolstered with new blood for the start of the 1969–70 season with the record purchase of the elegant Scottish playmaker Jimmy Smith from Aberdeen. Costing £100,000 – United's first six-figure signing – manager Joe Harvey spent just about all his hard-earned European windfall. Smith was not an instant hit, taking time to settle, but the fans adored his silky, smooth and tantalising skills that contrasted well with the other players in United's tough and industrious line-up. In addition, the further development of two eager youngsters from the junior ranks in Alan Foggon – who had scored that marvellous goal in the Fairs Cup final in Budapest – and Keith Dyson was heartening for the future.

Although to some the Geordies had qualified for European football again by the back door – finishing ninth and seventh in the table in the 1968–69 and 1969–70 seasons respectively – once more being helped by the one-club-one-city rule, as well as a controversial ban on Derby County due to irregularities, Newcastle United did not make up the rules. Skipper Bob Moncur noted that the back-door jibes simply 'spurred us on'. And in the following two seasons they performed with much credit, holding their own against much more experienced European sides. For the Magpies' first game in the defence

of the Fairs Cup trophy, the whole of Tyneside wanted a glamour tie: a match against one of the Continent's magical names. Instead, they faced a short trip across the Cheviots to face Dundee United. It was a big disappointment but it at least gave the Black 'n' Whites a good chance to progress in the now renamed European Fairs Cup – soon to be rebranded the UEFA Cup.

The men from Tannadice were no match for the trophy holders and, like many teams in those days, simply had no answer to the aerial menace of Wyn Davies. Newcastle cruised through to the second round and faced an attractive tie against FC Porto. It proved to be a tight, close encounter decided by a single and vital goal from Jim Scott. United's supporters had to wait again for a mouth-watering European clash as the Magpies were paired with fellow First Division outfit Southampton. A stereotypical English confrontation resulted, settled by a late Pop Robson effort at The Dell. Newcastle then at last received a glamour tie in the quarter-final against Belgian aristocrats RSC Anderlecht, at the time one of the finest and most respected sides in Europe.

A classic match with the grandiose Belgian side representing Brussels resulted; it was a tie high in drama and mixed emotions as United went from being joyous heir apparents to the semi-finals to gallant losers in a matter of seconds. At the very end of the enthralling contest they suffered a cruel knockout punch, conceding a late goal and losing on away goals when the club looked like heading towards another final. It was hard to take.

By the time the next campaign started, in the 1970–71 season, Tyneside's Black 'n' White Army dreamed for another tie like the epic with Anderlecht. They did not have to wait long as they received probably the biggest draw possible in the opening round, facing the might of Internazionale, recently twice back-to-back European Champions. The team from Milan bristled with famous names, several of whom had played in Italy's 1970 World Cup campaign in Mexico that summer. It was a classic tournament and had every football supporter stuck to their armchair as the *Azzuri* faced Brazil in one of the game's greatest-ever matches.

What a confrontation was in store. United, as usual, were given absolutely no chance against the superstars of Inter. Yet Joe Harvey's gutsy and spirited team completely outplayed their illustrious opponents over both legs in an Anglo–Italian encounter that had everything. It was one that was to live in every Newcastle player and supporter's memory long after the final whistle. Pop Robson remembered, 'It was a big test, but we put on a fantastic performance over the two legs.'

United brought a magnificent 1–1 draw back to Tyneside from the San Siro – although they could have recorded a sensational victory but for a late equaliser – and then roared into the lead against Inter at a packed St. James' Park. The contest then erupted as referee Joseph Minnoy was floored boxing-style by the bizarre actions of the Italian keeper, deteriorating into Latin assault as Inter failed to cope with a Magpie onslaught and Wyn Davies in particular. Another goal – by Davies, who else – rocked United's eminent visitors and was enough to take the Magpies into the next round.

Moving from chic and lively Milan to the historic but communist town of Pécs, deep inside the Iron Curtain, Newcastle were shown Europe as it was during the '60s and '70s: a continent divided culturally, politically and economically. When the Hungarians arrived on Tyneside they could have been, in many ways, aliens landing

Manager Joe Harvey: a grand servant to Newcastle United as player, coach and manager.

on a different planet. The East—West partition was at its height; tanks and missiles lined up along the length of the European divide. It was to take many years before they were removed and the Continent was reunited as friends rather than enemies.

United's most potent weapon, Welsh centre-forward Wyn Davies, was yet again the key player. He destroyed the Hungarians with his flame-haired assault at St. James' Park, only for the Magpies to fall on a bumpy, below-standard pitch in Pécs, losing in a humiliating penalty shoot-out. 'A penalty fiasco,' Robson remembered. United's talented striker also noted that the 'facilities, travel arrangements and surface were awful and decisions didn't go our way either'. He added, 'Everything went wrong.' It was an eventful adventure in Europe once again.

Penalty agony in Pécs; János Máté strikes the ball one way as Willie McFaul goes the other.

MATCHES 13 – 24

United's trophy-winning squad in 1969, pictured as they are about to defend the cup.

1969–70

Scotland, Dundee	v. Dundee United	2–1, 1–0, Agg 3–1	European Fairs Cup, R1
Portugal, Porto	v. FC Porto	0–0, 1–0, Agg 1–0	European Fairs Cup, R2
England, Southampton	v. Southampton	0–0, 1–1, Agg 1–1	European Fairs Cup, R3
Belgium, Brussels	v. RSC Anderlecht	0–2, 3–1, Agg 3–3	European Fairs Cup, QF

1970–71

Italy, Milan	v. Internazionale	1–1, 2–0, Agg 3–1	European Fairs Cup, R1
Hungary, Pécs	v. Pécsi Dózsa	2–0, 0–2, Agg 2–2	European Fairs Cup, R2

Euro Facts & Figures

Penalty Shoot-outs
Lost v. Pécsi Dózsa (EFC) 1970–71
Lost v. FK Partizan (UCL) 2002–03

Largest Victories
5–0 v. R. Antwerp (UEFAC) 1994–95 (h)
5–0 v. NAC Breda (UEFAC) 2003–04 (h)

Heaviest Defeats
0–3 v. AS Monaco (UEFAC) 1996–97 (a)
1–4 v. Internazionale (UCL) 2002–03 (h)
1–4 v. Sporting Clube (UEFAC) 2004–05 (a)

Match 13

1969–70

European Fairs Cup, Round 1: Dundee United FC (Scotland) v. Newcastle United
FIRST LEG Monday, 15 September 1969, Tannadice Park (Dundee)

Dundee United

UNITED McFaul, Craggs, Clark, Gibb, Burton, Moncur, Robson, Dyson, Davies, Arentoft, Smith (J). Subs not used: Elliott, Hope, Sinclair.
Manager: Joe Harvey

DUNDEE UNITED MacKay, Rolland, Cameron (J), Gillespie, Smith, Markland, Wilson, Reid, Cameron (K), Scott, Mitchell. Subs not used: Riley, Briggs.
Manager: Jerry Kerr

REFEREE P. Coates (Ireland)

RESULT Won 2–1 (0–0)

AGGREGATE 2–1

ATTENDANCE 21,000

SCORERS United: Davies (56), (59); Dundee United: Scott (77)

MATCH HIGHLIGHTS

Newcastle United were more than a match for an ordinary Dundee United side on their short trip across the border. The Magpies quickly took control of the game in midfield, with Tommy Gibb and Benny Arentoft the engine-room of the team, and always posed a threat with Wyn Davies and Bryan Robson in attack. In the end, they should have won by a far bigger margin. Big Welshman Davies netted with two marvellous second-half goals in the space of three minutes – after twice striking the woodwork in the opening period. Dundee United centre-backs Gillespie and Smith had no answer to the flame-haired Welshman and Davies was a menace each time the ball was delivered in the air. He first struck the bar from an Ollie Burton free-kick, then from another dead-ball opportunity he out-jumped the defence to rattle the woodwork once more. But Davies was to have his glory, and he met a perfect Craggs delivery with a well-timed run to power a header into the net. Almost from the restart the No. 9 was back looking for a second. Robson collected a Gibb throw and his centre was met by the Welshman who pinpointed his header past MacKay and into the top corner of the net. Dundee United offered little until the latter stages of the game when United relaxed and allowed the Scots to pull a goal back. Following a free-kick, Ian Mitchell headed on a cross for Jocky Scott to squeeze home the ball from close range. It kept the tie alive, much to the annoyance of the Newcastle support that had travelled north for the game.

MAN OF THE MATCH

Wyn Davies – unstoppable on the night.

| MATCH RATING | ● | ● | ● | | |

Reliable victory.

STAR COMMENT

Wyn Davies: 'I was completely surprised at the easy time I was given. Usually I am roughed up or cleverly impeded. But I was given the freedom of the park.'

EYEWITNESS

Ivor Broadis (*The Journal*): 'Newcastle won the midfield battle, and from midway in the opening half you could never see them being beaten.'

TOUR STOP – DUNDEE

On the north shore of the famous River Tay, Dundee is a significant port, bridging point and university city. Noted for confectionery and publishing – the *Beano*, *Dandy* and all that – it is the administrative centre of the Tayside region sporting two football clubs side by side on Tannadice Street. Captain Scott's *Discovery* is now docked in the revamped waterfront area. (pop. 155,000.)

STADIA FILE – TANNADICE PARK

A goal-kick from Dens Park, home to city rivals Dundee, Tannadice has much changed since United visited the stadium in 1969. Then a traditional ground of old with outdated and oddly designed stands as well as the terraced 'Kops' behind each goalmouth. There was only one sign of improvement in the shape of an early-style cantilevered stand, which gave the stadium a 28,000 capacity. The '80s saw the arena much developed and the capacity much reduced as a consequence.

DID YOU KNOW

Local Newcastle newspaper *The Journal* at the time gave merit marks for performances – 1 out of 10 was dreadful while 10 out of 10 was magnificent. Wyn Davies was awarded a rare maximum score for his astonishing display.

Tommy Gibb, midfield dynamo for United.

Dundee United

UNITED McFaul, Craig, Clark, Gibb, McNamee, Moncur, Robson, Dyson, Davies, Smith, Foggon (Arentoft). Subs not used: Burton, Hope.
Manager: Joe Harvey

DUNDEE UNITED MacKay, Rolland, Cameron (J), Gillespie, Smith, Markland, Hogg, Reid, Gordon, Scott, Mitchell. Subs not used: Riley, Stuart, Cameron (K).
Manager: Jerry Kerr

REFEREE L. Callaghan (Wales)

RESULT Won 1–0 (0–0)

AGGREGATE Won 3–1

ATTENDANCE 37,470

SCORERS United: Dyson (85)

MATCH HIGHLIGHTS

Dundee United had learnt their lesson in the first leg and marked Wyn Davies tightly all evening on Tyneside. The Scots' defence gave United's centre-forward hardly a sniff all night, and United found it tough going for much of the contest. But with two away goals, United had a distinct advantage and another goal, late into the game, ended the visitors' European hopes, even though the Scots had tussled gamely with the Magpies in the deciding leg of the tie. The Tayside club gave a below par Newcastle United some anxious moments as they showed they were going to be no pushovers. They were the better side for spells, and the impressive Alex Reid hit the woodwork for the visitors before Jim Smith set up Newcastle's winner. The former Aberdeen playmaker, who had joined the Magpies to give Joe Harvey's resilient side a touch of sparkle, took hold of the ball and stroked a delightful pass to Keith Dyson on the edge of the box. The young Newcastle striker bustled his way past two defenders before finding the net from close to the penalty spot with a low right-foot shot. The Dundee United goalkeeper, Don MacKay, could only watch it power into the net. It was enough to take United into the second round and was another step in their defence of the trophy.

MAN OF THE MATCH

Jimmy Smith – spread a web of class.

MATCH RATING ● ● ☐ ☐ ☐ Mediocre skirmish.

STAR COMMENT

Bryan Robson: 'It was a bit of a damp squib. We were used to some great trips away and the tie was a let down.'

EYEWITNESS

Tony Boullemier (*The Journal*): 'Only Smith, the back four, and McFaul could feel satisfied with their displays.'

OPPONENT FILE

Dundee United were lying in fifth spot in the Scottish league and only two points behind the Old Firm when they faced United. The Tayside club had rarely hit the high spots north of the border, their golden period under Jim McClean during the '80s, when they reached the final of the UEFA Cup, being some ten years off. In 1966–67 they had qualified for Europe for the first time and shocked both Barcelona and Juventus in the process, while the 1969–70 campaign was – like Newcastle United's – only their second in Europe. The foundations for the emergence of the club from Tannadice Park were just being laid.

STAR VISITOR

Ian Mitchell – A prolific goalscorer north of the border, Mitchell was a rising star and part of the Scotland Under-23 side when he faced the Black 'n' Whites. From Falkirk, he raided from the flank and eventually scored over 100 goals for Dundee United. Newcastle United paid £50,000 for his talent in July 1970, but Mitchell failed to recapture his potent scoring touch south of the border and soon returned to Tannadice.

DID YOU KNOW

Another Dundee United player, Alex Reid, also impressed boss Joe Harvey and soon he joined the Gallowgate staff as well, heading south to join the Magpies in October 1971.

Dundee – Scotland

Tay Road Bridge, Dundee. Angus.

AT 1714

Dundee United 1969–70

The famous Tay Road Bridge with Dundee in the background. The city is noted for its cakes, marmalade and the DC Thompson publishing empire as well as two celebrated football clubs.

A much later bird's-eye view of Dundee United's stadium after extensive redevelopment. When Newcastle visited Tannadice, the arena was quite different. Dens Park is just off picture, bottom centre.

Centre-forward Wyn Davies climbs to meet a cross to head United into the lead.

Dundee United's programme from the first leg on Tayside.

Porto – Portugal

FC Porto
1969–70

A typical postcard view of the prosperous city of Porto showing the old town, the River Douro and Ponte De Luís I bridge.

An extensive open bowl set on the outskirts of the city. Latterly, Porto have moved to the magnificent Estádio do Dragão.

Bryan Robson (right) causes problems for the Porto defence at a snow-covered St. James' Park.

United's programme for the clash with Porto.

Match 15

1969–70

European Fairs Cup, Round 2: FC Porto (Portugal) v. Newcastle United
FIRST LEG Wednesday, 18 November 1969, Estádio das Antas (Porto)

Porto

UNITED McFaul, Craig, Clark, Gibb, Burton, Moncur, Robson, Dyson, Davies, Arentoft, Guthrie (Scott). Subs not used: Cowan, Craggs, Hope.
Manager: Joe Harvey

PORTO Rui, Gualter, Valdemar, Nunes, Sucena, Rolando, Salim, Pavao, Seninho, Pinto, Nobrega. Subs not used: Anibal.
Manager: Elek Schwartz

REFEREE R. Marendaz (Switzerland)

RESULT Drew 0–0 (0–0)

AGGREGATE 0–0

ATTENDANCE 25,000

SCORERS None

MATCH HIGHLIGHTS

Newcastle gave a brave defensive display, holding a highly talented Porto side, and were praised for their solid performance, with Wyn Davies and Bob Moncur playing on despite illness and injury. United's centre-forward nursed a shoulder ailment while the Geordie's skipper fell ill just before the game. On a warm evening in northern Portugal, the Magpies found themselves under tremendous pressure for long periods of the match. The skilled Porto side pushed the ball around in silky fashion, but Bob Moncur and Ollie Burton at the centre of the Black 'n' Whites' rearguard were a solid pair and held firm when the home side reached the danger area. Moncur in particular deserved praise, having a tremendously positive influence on his side. And with the tactical addition of full-back Ron Guthrie operating in midfield to stifle the Porto forward play, the Magpies were difficult to break down. Newcastle could have sneaked a victory when two good chances fell to Bryan Robson and Guthrie. United's European L-plates had now been despatched to the rubbish bin as the Black 'n' Whites looked assured and convincing away from their Tyneside stronghold.

MAN OF THE MATCH

Bob Moncur – courageous skipper.

| MATCH RATING | ● | ● | | | | Competent show. |

STAR COMMENT

Joe Harvey: 'We contained Porto with a magnificent job of professional football.'

EYEWITNESS

Ivor Broadis (*The Journal*): 'Harvey's plan to spoil and contain was eminently successful.'

TOUR STOP – PORTO

The centre of northern Portugal, Porto is in many ways a quaint city, famous over the centuries for its connection with the wine and port trade. On the Douro river, it is the second largest city in the country and boasts the landmark Dona Maria Pia (designed by Gustave Eiffel) and Ponte De Luís I bridges. A thriving historic centre, it has old, narrow streets around the hillside Barredo quarter leading to a busy and lively riverside area. (pop. 263,000.)

STADIA FILE – ESTÁDIO DAS ANTAS

Porto's almost circular-shaped concrete bowl was opened in 1952 and featured one large cantilevered stand and vast single-tier open terraces. With a capacity of 50,000 the stadium is situated in the north east of Porto, in the affluent setting of the Antas district. In both 1976 and 1986 it was much refurbished and extended with both the upper and lower decks featuring prominent blue seating in the colours of Porto. Remodelled again for the Euro 2004 Championships with a capacity of 52,000, the new Estádio do Dragão is a first-class venue.

DID YOU KNOW

United fielded a substitute's bench without a goalkeeper when reserve custodian John Hope was injured in the lead-up to the game with an ankle knock and failed to take his place.

Ollie Burton, solid in defence.

Match 16

1969–70
European Fairs Cup, Round 2: Newcastle United v. FC Porto (Portugal)
SECOND LEG Wednesday, 26 November 1969, St. James' Park

Porto

UNITED McFaul, Craig, Clark, Gibb, Burton, Moncur, Scott, Robson, Davies, Arentoft, Foggon. Subs not used: Guthrie, Hope, Sinclair, Smith.
Manager: Joe Harvey

PORTO Rui (Salim), Gualter, Valdemar, Nunes, Sucena, Rolando (Jaoa), Salim, Albano (Acacio), Pavao, Pinto, Nobrega. Subs not used: Anibal.
Manager: Elek Schwartz

REFEREE W. Riedel (East Germany)

RESULT Won 1–0 (1–0)

AGGREGATE Won 1–0

ATTENDANCE 44,833

SCORERS United: Scott (22)

MATCH HIGHLIGHTS

Newcastle needed a victory against the stars of northern Portugal. A score draw would send the visitors through, but United received an advantage from the heavens when, just like the last time Portuguese visitors arrived at Gallowgate, a flurry of snow covered the St. James' Park surface. United were at the Porto defence from the off in hunt of a crucial first early strike. Davies went close, then a superb goal by Scotland international Jim Scott settled the close tie. Wyn Davies held the ball on the edge of the box and then the hardworking Dane Benny Arentoft danced round two defenders before setting up Scott, who drove the ball low into the net on twenty-two minutes. With the blanket of snow, conditions hindered the visitors from Portugal, but with Newcastle wasting a string of opportunities, Porto always had the opportunity to sneak an away goal and clinch the tie. They kept possession well and tested the Magpies on occasion, which meant the match produced a tense finish. Yet the Magpies were always the more dangerous and potent going forward. Rui denied Pop Robson, and the Newcastle striker also had a shot that was booted from the line – most observers believing that the effort was over the line – while Jim Scott nearly grabbed a second goal when a shot hit Salim as the ball was entering the net. Newcastle played in an all-red strip to avoid a clash with Porto's broad blue-and-white striped shirts.

MAN OF THE MATCH
Jim Scott – tricky in the snow.

| MATCH RATING | ● | ● | | | | Watchable and edgy. |

STAR COMMENT
Frank Clark: 'I was surprised at their performance in the snow. They never allowed us defenders to dwell on the ball like other Continental sides have.'

EYEWITNESS
John Gibson (*Evening Chronicle*): 'Flowing football was out, and it became a matter of strength and persistence – hardly the sort of 90-minutes to stir the blood.'

OPPONENT FILE
Porto were at the time lagging behind in Portugal's title race, but were a side full of experience with a European pedigree that went back to 1956–57. However, it was not until after the Portuguese club had played the Magpies that they were triumphant in Europe. 'The Dragons' endured some lean times in the '60s but made up for it in the following decades and are now recognised as one of the best clubs in European football, having lifted two European Cups and the UEFA Cup.

STAR VISITOR
José Rolando – The 25-year-old midfielder was Porto's skipper and an international for his country having been in the squad for the World Cup in England during 1966. The tall, blond playmaker had developed through the ranks at Porto and was noted as being a danger at setting up opportunities and also for getting into the box himself.

DID YOU KNOW
Porto were forced to play out the final minutes of the match with only ten men after goalkeeper Rui was badly injured and Porto had used their permitted two substitutes, meaning reserve keeper Anibal was unable to get onto the pitch.

Match 17

1969–70

European Fairs Cup, Round 3: Newcastle United v. Southampton FC (England)
FIRST LEG Wednesday, 17 December 1969, St. James' Park

Southampton

UNITED McFaul, Craig, Clark, Gibb, Burton, Moncur, Robson, Dyson, Davies (W), Arentoft, Scott (Foggon). Subs not used: Craggs, Hope.
Manager: Joe Harvey

SOUTHAMPTON Martin, Kirkup, Byrne, Fisher, McGrath (Stokes), Gabriel, Paine, Channon, Davies (R), Walker, Jenkins. Subs not used: unknown.
Manager: Ted Bates

REFEREE R. Davidson (Scotland)

RESULT Drew 0–0 (0–0)

AGGREGATE 0–0

ATTENDANCE 38,163

SCORERS None

MATCH HIGHLIGHTS

With potential opponents such as Barcelona, Inter and Ajax in the draw, hopes of an attractive tie were dashed when United were drawn with Southampton. On a cold and snowy evening, a tough, all-English encounter developed with the Saints back-line battling against a wave of United attacks. Despite losing ex-Magpie defender John McGrath to injury early in the game, the Saints were always determined in defence and fought a splendid rearguard action. Gabriel was a tower of strength following his switch into the back four once McGrath, who had been pulled apart by Wyn Davies, had left the action. The Scot stepped into the breach and almost played United's danger-man out of the game. Newcastle ended the night frustrated after putting Southampton under heavy pressure. Goalkeeper Eric Martin was the other Saints hero, stopping everything that came his way in style with a string of fine saves notably from Keith Dyson and Jim Scott. Wyn Davies and Pop Robson also had chances, but it was one of those evenings that was never going to see a United goal. At the other end of the field, the visitors, while being on the rack for most of the match, did create opportunities, too, and Ron Davies was only inches away from clinching a well-earned victory on Tyneside. The advantage in the tie had swung towards the Saints.

MAN OF THE MATCH

Bryan Robson – unlucky not to score.

| MATCH RATING | • | | | | | Dour battle. |

STAR COMMENT

John McGrath: 'Jimmy Gabriel filled in for me and did a great job to help us get the 0–0 draw.'

EYEWITNESS

Charlie Summerbell (*Daily Mirror*): 'Nothing went right for the Geordie side. Despite heavy pressure chances galore were wasted.'

OPPONENT FILE

At the time Southampton were struggling in the First Division table, fourth from the bottom, but this was far from being a true indication of their ability. The Saints had only gained Division One status for the first time in 1966, and their rise into European football had been meteoric, reaching the Fairs Cup through the back door like Newcastle. However, Southampton consolidated and maintained their top-flight standing for many years, until they were relegated at the end of the 2004–05 season.

STAR VISITOR

Ron Davies – Described by the media as 'world class', the Welsh international centre-forward was highly rated by many and often a partner of his Newcastle namesake in the Welsh side. Davies joined the staff at The Dell in 1966 for a £55,000 fee after spells with Chester, Luton Town and Norwich. He went on to score over 153 goals for the Saints, becoming a celebrated goal poacher during his playing days. He was often linked with a move to Gallowgate.

DID YOU KNOW

Southampton became the first visiting club to avoid defeat in European action at St. James' Park. It was the first time in nine European ties United had failed to record a victory.

Match 18

1969–70

European Fairs Cup, Round 3: Southampton FC (England) v. Newcastle United
SECOND LEG Wednesday, 14 January 1970, The Dell (Southampton)

Southampton

UNITED McFaul, Craig, Clark, Gibb, McNamee, Moncur, Robson, Smith, Davies (W), Young (Guthrie), Ford. Subs not used: Dyson, Hope.
Manager: Joe Harvey

SOUTHAMPTON Martin, Kirkup, Byrne, Fisher, Gabriel, Walker, Jenkins, Channon, Davies (R), Paine, Sydenham (Stokes). Subs not used: Springett, Jones, McGrath, Saul.
Manager: Ted Bates

REFEREE W. Gow (Wales)

RESULT Drew 1–1 (0–1)

AGGREGATE Drew 1–1, won on away goals

ATTENDANCE 25,182

SCORERS United: Robson (84); Southampton: Channon (28)

MATCH HIGHLIGHTS

The odds were in Southampton's favour in the second leg and when Mick Channon put the Saints ahead, as he latched onto a Terry Paine free-kick to head the opening goal, Newcastle's season in European football looked to be coming to an end. The Magpies' goal had further narrow escapes as a Ron Davies effort hit the bar, Frank Clark cleared a shot off the line and John Sydenham missed a golden chance near the end. United rode their luck, but Joe Harvey's side always possessed resilience, and the Black 'n' Whites battled their way back into the tie, following almost constant one-way traffic by the Saints, orchestrated by England veteran Paine in midfield. In a storming finish, and only six minutes from the final whistle, Jim Smith chipped a delightful ball into the middle, and Davies nodded it down into a ruck of legs and boots in the six-yard box. Pop Robson pounced on the loose ball and fired home the equaliser through a crowd of players to send Newcastle into the quarter-final on the away goals rule. It was a cruel knockout punch for the Saints, who deserved better. There was still time for Southampton to clinch victory, but that Sydenham miss proved costly, although credit had to go to United's centre-half John McNamee, who cleared his line when a goal – and a Saints victory – looked certain. The clearance was as important as Robson's equaliser.

MAN OF THE MATCH

Jimmy Smith – starting to impress.

| MATCH RATING | ● | ● | | | |

Notable robbery.

STAR COMMENT

Joe Harvey: 'Pop Robson has a tremendous flair for producing the vital goal. It came at the right time, and I felt we deserved it.'

EYEWITNESS

Charlie Summerbell (*Daily Mirror*): 'The odds were heavily in Southampton's favour. Even today Southampton are probably still wondering how they missed out.'

TOUR STOP – SOUTHAMPTON

The centre of Hampshire at the head of the Solent, Southampton is the principal passenger port for the UK and the home of the great liners, being ideally situated on the English Channel. The city is rich in history, going back to Roman times, with many fine landmarks of distinction from the medieval era, including the notable city walls, Bargate and the Tudor House. (pop. 217,000.)

STADIA FILE – THE DELL

The quaint, ramshackle arena of The Dell, with its tight pitch, is now long gone, put under the bulldozer like many English football stadiums, but for a century it was both loved and loathed by many. The Saints moved there in 1898, and over the years, a mix of traditional and not so traditional stands were packed into a confined space next to residential semis and terraces. With a capacity of 30,000, it was one of the most unusual grounds in the country and totally outdated by the time European football arrived in Southampton.

DID YOU KNOW

Newcastle also faced Southampton in the FA Cup in between those two Fairs Cup games. The Saints won 3–0 at The Dell, and of course the two clubs also met in Division One action. They faced each other three times in eleven days in three different competitions.

Jimmy Smith, signed for £100,000, a record at that time.

Tour Stop

Southampton – England

Southampton 1969–70

At one time a strategic port, it is a city with an intriguing past and plenty to see. Pilgrim Stone (left) and Bargate (top right), the thirteenth-century entrance to the city, are pictured.

For years one of the most curious and under-developed stadiums in top-flight soccer, it was home to the Saints from 1898 to 2001.

Saints keeper Eric Martin saves at the feet of Keith Dyson at St. James' Park.

Southampton's programme for the Fairs Cup clash, including a cover picture of the same month's FA Cup meeting with the Magpies.

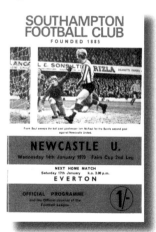

Brussels – Belgium

RSC Anderlecht 1969–70

The capital of Europe, perhaps, Brussels has many sights including the magnificent Grand Place.

Anderlecht's headquarters, at the time one of the finest stadiums in Europe.

Tempers become frayed at St. James' Park. Wyn Davies (left) is manhandled after a clash with the Belgian goalkeeper.

Programme from the meeting in Brussels.

Anderlecht

UNITED McFaul, Craggs, Guthrie, Gibb, McNamee (Burton), Moncur, Robson, Dyson, Davies, Smith (Elliott) Foggon. Subs not used: Ford, Hope, Young.
Manager: Joe Harvey

ANDERLECHT Trappeniers, Heylens, Velkeneers, Kialunda, Maertens, Nordahl, Desanghere, Devrindt, Mulder, van Himst, Puis. Subs not used: Vandenbossche, Peeters, Deraeve, Cornelis, van Binst.
Manager: Pierre Sinibaldi

REFEREE M. Schiller (Austria)

RESULT Lost 0–2 (0–1)

AGGREGATE 0–2

ATTENDANCE 30,000

SCORERS Anderlecht: Desanghere (30), Puis (62)

MATCH HIGHLIGHTS

The Magpies fielded a patched-up side due to injury and, significantly, a makeshift defence with David Craig and Frank Clark missing and Bob Moncur far from fit. They showed little of the defensive authority of previous European ties and were battered by a cultured and potent Belgian side. Pressurised unmercifully for most of the game, they were fortunate to return to Tyneside only two goals adrift. With Devrindt and centre-forward Mulder especially wreaking havoc, Willie McFaul saved Newcastle from a mauling that would have made the second leg elementary. Anderlecht's opener came after a right-wing run by Mulder, who cut the ball back for Desanghere to strike the ball hard and true past McFaul. Newcastle held the Belgians at bay for long periods, but on the hour the home side broke through again, after Tommy Gibb gave away a free-kick on the edge of the box. From 25 yards, Puis hit a fierce angled drive into the top corner of the net past the diving McFaul. United's travelling one-thousand-strong support were far from confident for the return leg.

MAN OF THE MATCH

Willie McFaul – a series of fine stops.

STAR COMMENT

Tommy Gibb: 'We had a bad game and got the runaround. It could have been more, but two goals down gave us a decent chance.'

EYEWITNESS

Bob Cass (*Sunday Sun*): 'United, patched-up and injury torn, showed little of the cool control that marked earlier matches on the Continent.'

TOUR STOP – BRUSSELS

Capital of Belgium, seat of the European Union and one of the finest cities in Europe, Brussels is a popular tourist destination. The city boasts many fine buildings and landmarks such as the Grand Place – the splendid main square – the Atomium, the Manneken Pis statue and the vast EU headquarters. A diverse commercial and industrial centre, Brussels has also a lively nightlife like any Euro capital. It also houses the headquarters of NATO. (pop. 983,000.)

STADIA FILE – PARC ASTRID

Also known as the Stade Constant Vanden Stock or Stade Emile Versé with a capacity of 36,000, Anderlecht moved to the site in 1918 and by 1935 the stadium had been developed into one of the finest around. Situated alongside parkland, the four stands in place when United played there have since been totally remodelled, and the Parc Astrid is now a modern venue to match most on the Continent. For bigger games Anderlecht often switch matches to the Heysel Stadium in the capital.

DID YOU KNOW

In May 1951, United played Anderlecht in Brussels a month after their triumph at Wembley in the FA Cup and won emphatically 6–0.

David Craig, a polished performer at full-back.

Anderlecht

UNITED McFaul, Craig, Clark (Young), Gibb, Burton, Moncur, Robson, Dyson, Davies, Guthrie, Foggon. Subs not used: Cowan, Elliott, Ford, Hope.
Manager: Joe Harvey

ANDERLECHT Trappeniers, Heylens, Maertens, Nordahl, Velkeneers, Kialunda, Desanghere, Devrindt, Mulder, van Himst, Puis. Subs not used: unknown.
Manager: Pierre Sinibaldi

REFEREE H. Fritz (West Germany)

RESULT Won 3–1 (2–0)

AGGREGATE Drew 3–3, lost on away goals

ATTENDANCE 59,309

SCORERS United: Robson (4), (20), Dyson (85); Anderlecht: Nordahl (88)

MATCH HIGHLIGHTS

Two goals down from the first leg, Newcastle fought back superbly with a tremendous display, only to be stunned by a late Anderlecht goal. Few who were there will forget the action-packed and drama-filled night at St. James' Park. On a blustery evening, Newcastle went all out from the kick-off to pull back the deficit and received an early boost through a Bryan Robson goal inside the first five minutes. Wyn Davies leapt for a Frank Clark free-kick, the ball swirled in the wind and Robson's looped back-header went towards goal – Foggon making sure it hit the net on the line. Anderlecht lost their composure and Newcastle's pressure paid off: they grabbed two more goals that looked like securing another semi-final place. For the first, Robson took a pass from Tommy Gibb, advanced to the edge of the box from the right and unleashed a screamer that rammed into the net from 30 yards. That effort levelled the tie, then Newcastle appeared to grab the all-important third goal with only five minutes left. A Moncur free-kick was lofted into a crowded box, and Keith Dyson stole in behind Davies to bang the ball into the net from six yards. United were through – or so everyone thought. With seconds remaining, however, van Himst moved forward with menace. His ball saw an Ollie Burton clearance rebound to Nordahl, and the Swede picked up the loose ball to fire a sweet shot high across Willie McFaul to win the tie with a crucial away goal.

MAN OF THE MATCH

Bryan Robson – a menace to the Belgians.

MATCH RATING ● ● ● ● ● Glorious exit.

STAR COMMENT

Joe Harvey: 'I just couldn't believe it. One minute we were in the semi-final – the next we were out of the cup. I was proud of the lads. We have proved ourselves over 20 matches, and the Continent knows the name of Newcastle United.'

EYEWITNESS

Bob Cass (*Sunday Sun*): 'Nobody expected the sickening blow that fate had reserved until the dying seconds.'

OPPONENT FILE

The Royal Sporting Club of Anderlecht are the aristocrats of Belgian football, highly experienced in Europe's competitions and a big draw. Before facing the Magpies, they had lifted the Belgian title five seasons in a row – from 1964 to 1968 – although disappointingly came third in the season prior to heading for Tyneside. Afterwards, Anderlecht reached seven European finals and lifted both the European Cup Winners Cup and UEFA Cup, while the Mauves have latterly been matched by Club Brugge as Belgium's top club.

STAR VISITOR

Paul van Himst – Captain of Anderlecht and of Belgium, the talented midfielder had played over 50 internationals for his country and was recognised as one of the best players in the world at the time. Twenty-seven years of age, van Himst would become Belgium's most capped player with eighty-two appearances. He oozed silky ability and had the touch of a master. Developed by Anderlecht as a teenager, he was only 17 years of age when he was first capped by Belgium. He was noted as being a fast-raiding and quick-footed linkman, able to create openings for others, although he could also operate as a striker, too.

DID YOU KNOW

Anderlecht went on to reach the final but fell narrowly to another English club, Arsenal. On nine occasions between 1967 and 1977 English sides reached the final of the Fairs Cup.

Match 21

1970–71

European Fairs Cup, Round 1: Internazionale Milano (Italy) v. Newcastle United
FIRST LEG Wednesday, 23 September 1970, Stadio di San Siro (Milan)

Internazionale

UNITED McFaul, Craig, Clark, Gibb, Burton, Moncur, Robson, Dyson, Davies, Arentoft, Young. Subs not used: Elliott, Ford, Guthrie, Hindson, Hope.
Manager: Joe Harvey

INTER Vieri, Burgnich, Facchetti, Fabbian, Giubertoni, Cella, Pellizzaro, Mazzola, Achilli, Frustalupi, Corso. Subs not used: unknown.
Manager: Heriberto Herrera

REFEREE H. Seibert (West Germany)

RESULT Drew 1–1 (1–0)

AGGREGATE 1–1

ATTENDANCE 14,460

SCORERS United: Davies (42); Inter: Cella (84)

MATCH HIGHLIGHTS

Not many in Milan turned up to see the visit of the relative unknowns from England in the giant San Siro. The Italian public – and many in the Inter camp – took it for granted that the Milan giants would cruise into the next round. They failed to give Newcastle United due respect and paid the penalty. Newcastle turned on a tremendous defensive show to hold the mighty Internazionale and almost snatched a remarkable victory. After a shaky start, United settled well, soaking up the Inter pressure during the first period of the match. Wyn Davies put the Geordies in front when he sprinted to the near post just before half-time to convert a Bryan Robson free-kick with a superb stooped header low past Vieri from 12 yards out. Inter struggled to crack the unfancied Black 'n' Whites, with Bob Moncur and Ollie Burton holding firm at the heart of United's determined back-line. Their studied build-up play suited the Magpies, who massed in front of the Inter superstars – Mazzola and Corso in particular. And the Italian giants only managed to break down United's defensive wall six minutes from time when Cella moved forward to take a pass from Mazzola and fired past the unsighted Willie McFaul from the edge of the penalty box. Newcastle would have settled for the result before the start of play and boarded the plane home with a well-earned draw and an away goal.

MAN OF THE MATCH

Wyn Davies – a threat in the air.

| MATCH RATING | • | • | • | | | Accomplished show. |

STAR COMMENT

Wyn Davies: 'It was a cracking result, and we were effectively ahead because of the away goal.'

EYEWITNESS

Bob Cass (*Sunday Sun*): 'Newcastle were going to get murdered, but raised their game and gave a great performance against one of Europe's finest teams.'

TOUR STOP – MILAN

Italy's second city in Lombardy, on the edge of the Alps and Italian Lakes, Milan is the chief financial, industrial and commercial centre of the country. It is a city with a wealth of impressive sights from La Scala and the Castello Sforzesco to the Piazza del Duomo and its gigantic cathedral. One of the world's great football cities, Milan oozes style and provides visitors with plenty of nightlife and entertainment of every kind. (pop. 1,250,000.)

STADIA FILE – SAN SIRO

Situated on the outskirts of Milan, and also known from 1979 as the Stadio Giuseppe Meazza after a famous Milan player, United's first visit to the San Siro lacked passion and atmosphere in an almost empty arena. At the time an open, double-tiered towering bowl, it was first used by AC Milan in 1926 with Inter moving in as joint tenants during 1947. The stage for many top games at club and international level, the capacity in 1970 was 82,000, but the stadium was much altered for the 1990 World Cup.

DID YOU KNOW

Newcastle first played the Italian giants back in May 1929 when they were known as Ambrosiana Milan. The match, played in the Milan Arena, was won by United by a single goal but not until a controversial and heated contest had taken place.

Souvenir plaque gifted by Inter to United.

Match 22

1970–71
European Fairs Cup, Round 1: Newcastle United v. Internazionale Milano (Italy)
SECOND LEG Wednesday, 30 September 1970, St. James' Park

Internazionale

UNITED McFaul, Craig, Clark, Gibb, Burton, Moncur, Robson, Dyson, Davies, Arentoft, Young. Subs not used: Hope, Guthrie, Ford, Hindson, Smith.
Manager: Joe Harvey

INTER Vieri, Righetti, Facchetti, Bellugi, Giubertoni, Cella, Jair, Fabbian, Boninsegna, Archilli (Bordon), Corso. Subs not used: Mazzola, Burgnich.
Manager: Heriberto Herrera

REFEREE J. Minnoy (Belgium)

RESULT Won 2–0 (1–0)

AGGREGATE Won 3–1

SENT OFF Vieri (31)

ATTENDANCE 56,495

SCORERS United: Moncur (29), Davies (70)

MATCH HIGHLIGHTS

The near-capacity St. James' Park crowd witnessed high drama against the Milan giants, as the temperamental Inter superstars completely lost their heads against Newcastle's solid, uncompromising team. And included in a quite remarkable match was the sending-off of goalkeeper Lido Vieri after the Italian international had floored the referee! By then United had already gone in front through a great Moncur opener. Bryan Robson's corner saw Vieri go for the ball, but United's skipper got there first to power a header down into the turf and up into the net. Minutes later, all hell broke loose in a bad-tempered match. Davies feigned a challenge on the keeper, Vieri reacted and elbowed United's centre-forward: the referee awarded an indirect free-kick inside the box. Inter snapped, surrounded the referee Joseph Minnoy, and Vieri then proceeded to land a lovely right-hook on the poor Belgian official that put him on his knees! Not surprisingly, Vieri was ordered off, leading to the fiery Italians swarming around the referee again, only to be calmed down by two burly local policemen. After that, Inter resorted to every tactic, except football, to stop the Black 'n' Whites. United's powerful attack, led by the magnificent Wyn Davies, gave the Italians all sorts of trouble with experienced defenders Facchetti and Guibertoni again unable to cope with United's aerial menace. Davies deservedly doubled the Tynesiders' lead in the second half, diving forward, despite a body check, to nod home the rebound after Keith Dyson had crashed the ball against the bar from a Tommy Gibb cross.

MAN OF THE MATCH

Wyn Davies – battled away with great spirit.

| MATCH RATING | • | • | • | • | | Unforgettable night. |

STAR COMMENT

Bob Moncur: 'I've never seen anything like it before or since. It was the most violent game of football I have ever played in and the most violent game I ever saw.'

EYEWITNESS

John Gibson (*Evening Chronicle*): 'Inter's record was so impressive as to be blinding. The Tyneside public were expecting great things from the thoroughbreds of the soccer world. Such expectancy was to be shattered in no uncertain terms.'

OPPONENT FILE

Internazionale became a modern giant under the guidance of coach Helenio Herrera in the '60s, and were crowned Italian champions at the end of the season United faced them. They were the most celebrated club United had played up until that point, having recently twice won the European Cup in 1964 and 1965 as well as being finalists in 1967. They boasted several stars that had graced the television screen from the recent World Cup in Mexico. Inter went on to appear in the 1972 European Cup final, too. They are now regarded as Italy's third club behind Juventus and rivals AC Milan.

STAR VISITOR

Giacinto Facchetti – Captain of club and country and having just skippered the Azzuri to the World Cup final, the tall and elegant Facchetti was a world-famous name. At full-back or centre-half he could handle the best forwards in the business but found United's Welsh Flier, Wyn Davies, an immense handful. Capped 94 times for his country, he later became Inter President and returned to Gallowgate in 2003 as the two sides met again, this time in Champions League action.

DID YOU KNOW

Newcastle, unusually, played in an all-red strip against Internazionale, the home side changing colours due to a clash with the Milan club's famous blue-and-black stripes, known as the *Nerazzurri*.

Tour Stop

Milan – Italy

Internazionale 1970–71

One of Europe's finest cities and a football crazy one at that. Teatro alla Scala (top left) and the Duomo cathedral on the grand Piazza del Duomo (bottom) are both pictured.

United's first visit to the mighty San Siro saw the stadium less than a quarter full and somewhat different to the majestic upgraded arena of over 30 years later.

The flash point of the return leg: keeper Vieri is sent off by referee Joseph Minnoy, who needs the assistance of a Geordie PC.

United's programme for the glamour tie with Inter; note the dual pricing of 1 shilling and '5 New pence'.

Pécs – Hungary

**Pécsi Dózsa
1970–71**

A historic town, Pécs has been occupied by the Celts, Romans, Mongols and Turks and is full of treasures that testify to these many different periods in its history.

A modest arena, comparable to a non-league stadium in the UK. It is pictured here after the club recently moved to a new stadium in Pécs.

United's No. 9 Wyn Davies was a handful at Gallowgate, seen here netting the first goal.

Top: Match ticket from the St. James' Park contest.
Bottom right: Match-day programme from the fixture in Hungary, probably the rarest of all modern Newcastle programmes.

63

Match 23

1970−71
European Fairs Cup, Round 2: Newcastle United v. Pécsi Dózsa (Hungary)
FIRST LEG Wednesday, 21 October 1970, St. James' Park

Pécsi Dózsa

UNITED McFaul, Craig, Clark, Gibb, Young, Moncur, Robson, Dyson, Davies, Smith, Ford. Subs not used: Arentoft, Burleigh, Craggs, Hindson, McNamee.
Manager: Joe Harvey

PÉCSI Rapp, Hernadi, Maurer, Kincses, Kocsis, Konrad, Berczesi, Daka, Máté, Ronai (Tuske), Toth. Subs not used: Kingis, Kol, Dol.
Manager: Mihaly Czibulka

REFEREE H. Weyland (West Germany)

RESULT Won 2−0 (1−0)

AGGREGATE 2−0

ATTENDANCE 50,550

SCORERS United: Davies (43), (59)

MATCH HIGHLIGHTS

Wyn Davies was Newcastle's danger-man again at St. James' Park as an astonishing crowd of over 50,000 came to see the unknowns from Hungary. The Welsh international striker gave a display of awesome power and sent two majestic headers into the Hungarian net to cap a fine second-half showing. This followed a disappointing opening display by the Magpies, as they failed to click into top gear against the men from behind the Iron Curtain, only making the breakthrough minutes before the interval. Jimmy Smith clipped a hanging ball into the box, and up soared Davies high above the Pécsi defence to nod the ball powerfully into the back of the net. Newcastle, in fact, should have sealed their passage into the next round by taking more chances: their missed opportunities were to prove costly. Bob Moncur struck the woodwork as the Hungarians had no answer to balls flighted into the box. Davies grabbed a second just before the hour mark, again jumping to meet another high ball from a David Ford corner, heading past the Pécsi keeper Rapp. Davies should have had more goals and nearly registered a hat-trick, rattling the crossbar and having another goal cancelled for offside, a decision that was highly debatable. The German referee also turned down two clear penalty appeals as Newcastle penned the visitors into their own half for most of the second period. Pécsi defender Laszlo Maurer even conceded after the game that one of his fouls on Tommy Gibb should have resulted in a spot-kick.

MAN OF THE MATCH

Wyn Davies – majestic performance.

MATCH RATING	●	●	●		

Good, but not enough.

STAR COMMENT

Joe Harvey: 'The worst penalty decision I have ever seen.'

EYEWITNESS

Ivor Broadis (*The Journal*): 'Once United took a grip on things after the interval, the Hungarians were struggling to keep pace.'

OPPONENT FILE

Totally unheard of outside their own country, Pécsi Dózsa were only part timers and had been in existence for only 20 years. They finished the Hungarian league to qualify for the Fairs Cup in their highest ever position – sixth – and surprised many with their ability. The club was totally reformed in 1973 and retitled as Pécsi Munkás when five local clubs merged: Dózsa, Bányász, Ércbányász, Helyipari and Építők. Later a new name of Pécsi Mecsek was adopted.

STAR VISITOR

János Máté – A clever striker with good footwork and a penetrating turn of pace. Twenty-two years of age, Máté developed into a fine Hungarian forward and was at the time a rising star in his homeland. He joined Pécsi in 1968 from Bonyhadi Vasas and was on the fringe of the national side. He proved a difficult opponent for United in the second leg. Later joining Ferencváros, Máté appeared on seven occasions for Hungary.

DID YOU KNOW

Pécsi skipper János Dunai is the brother of Antal Dunai who faced United in the Inter Cities Fairs Cup final for Újpesti Dózsa.

Match 24

1970–71

European Fairs Cup, Round 2: Pécsi Dózsa (Hungary) v. Newcastle United
SECOND LEG Wednesday, 4 November 1970, Pécsi Vasutas Sport Kör (Pécs)

Pécsi Dózsa

UNITED McFaul, Craig, Clark, Gibb, McNamee, Moncur, Robson, Dyson (Hindson), Davies, Young, Ford (Mitchell). Subs not used: Arentoft, Craggs, Hope.
Manager: Joe Harvey

PÉCSI Rapp, Hernadi, Maurer, Konrad, Kincses, Kocsis, Daka, Toth, Berczesi (Dunai), Máté, Ronai (Koller). Subs: Tuske (on).
Manager: Mihaly Czibulka

REFEREE R. Marendaz (Switzerland)

RESULT Lost 0–2 (0–1) after extra time
AGGREGATE Drew 2–2, lost 2–5 on penalties

ATTENDANCE 25,000

SCORERS Pécsi: Máté (18), (81) (pen)
Penalty shoot-out, Lost 2–5 – Pécsi: Konrad, Daka, Tuske, Dunai, Kincses (all scored).
United: Robson (missed), Mitchell (missed), Gibb (missed), Clark (scored), McFaul (scored).

MATCH HIGHLIGHTS

The return leg in Pécs resulted in one of Newcastle's worst displays in European competition. On a sunny day and against an average team, United fell apart on a bumpy, below-standard pitch that favoured the home side. Nevertheless, United defended badly, allowed the Hungarians to take the lead through a scrappy goal then conceded a crucial spot-kick near the final whistle that took the game into extra time and on to a penalty shoot-out. Pécsi made a game of it by attacking United from the start and sensed the professionals from England were having a bad afternoon. A Konrad free-kick caused panic in United's box, and the ball fell for Máté to shoot home off Bob Moncur's legs, with Willie McFaul already committed to diving the other way. That goal opened up the tie. Pécsi smelt victory and a shock, although United held out uncomfortably until nine minutes from time when Maurer was pulled down in the box by John McNamee. Máté coolly slotted home the spot-kick to the joy of their small but vociferous following. Newcastle might have won it when a header by Wyn Davies almost found glory, but, instead, his effort was kicked off the line. Extra time came and went without United imposing themselves on the Hungarians, and the tie ended in disaster for the Black 'n' Whites with an embarrassing penalty shoot-out. Pécsi were clinical: five penalties, five

goals. United, on the other hand, were woeful – their first three kicks failed to find the net – and were eliminated.

MAN OF THE MATCH

Tommy Gibb – impressive work rate.

MATCH RATING | ● | | | | | Hideous ending.

STAR COMMENT

Bryan Robson: 'We conceded two, and they controlled the game. We just didn't get going at all and blew our 2–0 home victory.'

EYEWITNESS

Ivor Broadis (*The Journal*): 'It was like facing an obscure non-league side in a cup-tie at home in midsummer.'

TOUR STOP – PÉCS

An industrial but attractive historic old town in the south-west of Hungary near the Yugoslav border, at the time Pécs was deep behind the Iron Curtain under an oppressive communist regime. With one of Europe's oldest universities – founded in 1367 – Pécs is a town of rich history and architecture, with a strong Roman and Turk influence. However, Széchenyi tér, the city's main square, was just about devoid of any early Toon Army travellers: only around 50 media and fans made the trip due to difficulties getting into Eastern Europe at the time. (pop. 163,000.)

STADIA FILE – VASUTAS SPORT KÖR

Back in 1970, the local Pécs stadium, linked to the regional state railway company Vasutas, was anything but a venue Newcastle United were used to. With a capacity of 26,000 it wasn't up to usual standards and wouldn't pass any modern UEFA regulations. Without a directors' box or press enclosure and with no floodlights, the match had to kick off at 1.30 pm, and the surface was hard and rutted. Surrounded by poplar trees, the open terraces, including a grass bank at one end, ran round to a small main stand. The stadium was then of non-league standard and is now used only for local football with the Pécsi Mecsek club playing at a compact and modern arena in the town.

DID YOU KNOW

Newcastle had to complete their spot-kicks after the result was secure, the referee insisting the teams conclude the formalities of taking five kicks each. Pécsi had already scored, and United missed, their first three kicks, and so Frank Clark and goalkeeper Willie McFaul completed the statistics by netting both penalties. It was United's first penalty shoot-out in any competition.

'Without Wyn Davies United would never have won the Inter Cities Fairs Cup.'

Lord Westwood

Wyn Davies

Wyn Davies may not have been a prolific goalscorer in the true tradition of Newcastle United's No. 9 heroes, and he received almost as much criticism as praise, yet the big Welshman had a huge cult following in the North East. On many occasions he had thousands of the Geordie crowd singing over and over again, 'You've not seen nothing like the Mighty Wyn'. He was the undisputed king of St. James' Park for almost five years, and he more than any other player wrote Newcastle United's name on the football map of Europe. Chairman Lord Westwood said at the time of United's shock opening triumph, 'Without Wyn Davies, United would never have won the Inter Cities Fairs Cup.'

United's record £80,000 purchase from Bolton Wanderers, in October 1966, proved to be a secret weapon as the Magpies entered European action as virtual unknowns in 1968.

Yet those unheard of figures in black-and-white stripes, with the tall and physical presence of Davies as a spearhead, gave some of the best in Europe quite a headache.

Davies was the one player in United's ranks the Continentals, including the likes of accomplished defenders Santamaria, Hilario and Facchetti, had no answer to. His towering leaps for the ball and never-say-die spirit up front ruffled their composure. They weren't used to the long- and high-ball game. They liked to keep the ball on the grass, most European teams preferring to play possession football, and Newcastle's different tactical style had them rattled. In the Magpies' opening season, he scored goals and created them – usually for his fellow strike partner Bryan Pop Robson, who flourished alongside the Welsh centre-forward. Robson noted, 'Wyn always upset opponents with his presence. He could hang in the air, and the ball in the box caused them a problem. He always made lots of space and openings. Yet he wasn't just an aerial threat. He drifted to the wings and could cross a good ball too.'

Against Feyenoord's experienced international centre-half Cor Veldhoen, in United's first-ever European match, the Welshman started as he was to continue, harassing the opposition for the full 90 minutes. Wyn struck a 25-yarder against the bar for Robson to convert, then grabbed United's fourth goal, getting on the end of a Jim Scott cross to the far post.

Sporting Lisbon's Hilário da Conceição was, like Veldhoen, a polished international stopper with over 30 caps to his name, appearing in the 1966 World Cup. The mainstay of the Sporting back-line, he had no answer to the threat of Davies either. Wyn's exquisite head down for Robson's expertly finished goal, early in the deciding leg, is one of the enduring moments of the Fairs Cup era. Pop reckoned it was his

Wyn Davies

best and noted 'it was important and a lovely volley to score'.

Against Real Zaragoza, Wyn's away strike in the 3–2 defeat proved to be crucial and what a brave one it was too. It characterised the Welshman's wholehearted attitude. Diving in amongst the defenders' boots to get his head to the ball, the United No. 9 powered the ball into the net, while centre-half Santamaria could only stand by and watch. Joe Cummings, writing in *The Sun*, noted, 'The big, muscular Spaniard, very much a local hero, had pranced and preened at the start with a cocky self-assurance. After 90 minutes of Davies' attention he looked sick and bedraggled.' In the second leg the Spaniards put Gonzalez on Davies to help regular centre-back Santamaria. It made little difference as Wyn had a 'tenacious battle' with his twin markers and, as it was reported, 'tormented the pair of them'.

Then in the quarter-final with Setúbal, he was again prominent, scoring in both legs. United recorded what was to be a winning 5–1 first leg advantage. He slammed home the Magpies' third goal, a strike that saw Setúbal lose their cool, claiming Davies was offside. In a torrid second leg in Lisbon, Wyn settled United's nerves by grabbing a crucial away goal, rising above Cardoso to head home Clark's cross.

A great scrap took place with Scottish centre-halves Ron McKinnon and Colin Jackson against Rangers and it was Davies – playing with a broken nose – who created the goal that clinched the tie for the Magpies, leaping to meet a long Ollie Burton free-kick to nod the ball down into the path of Jackie Sinclair, who volleyed home. *The Journal*'s report noted that as Burton's ball glided forward, 'Davies hoisted himself to meet it. A brief flick towards the Rangers goal and Sinclair, reading the situation admirably, was in like a hungry barracuda to blast the ball home.'

That was typical of the tactics of Davies and

WYN DAVIES: FACT FILE

Position: Centre-forward

Born: Caernarfon, March 1942

Joined United from: Bolton Wanderers, October 1966, £80,000

Left for: Manchester City, August 1971, £52,500

Other major clubs: Wrexham, Manchester United, Blackpool, Crystal Palace, Stockport County, Crewe Alexandra

Full international: Wales (34 caps, 1964 to 1974)

United career, senior games: 216 app., 53 goals

United Euro record: 24 app., 10 goals

Did you know: Wyn Davies missed out on winning a league championship medal in 1972 when Manchester City fell short by one point in a close title race with Derby County.

Newcastle. A long punt up field or looping cross would search out the flame-haired head of the No. 9, who usually drew the attention of two defenders. A leap towards the heavens and a knock-down into space creating a goal opportunity: the strategy worked a treat, over and over again.

In the final against Újpesti Dózsa, regular Hungarian international defender Ern Solymosi had his work cut out, too. Davies was in the thick of the action for the all-important opening strike at St. James' Park, chesting the ball down in the box before firing a shot towards goal that Moncur capitalised on. Then in Budapest, Davies sealed United's triumphant victory with a flick on for Alan Foggon to surge past the Magyars' defence and score the third goal.

Wyn played through the pain barrier during that magnificent display in Hungary, having

Wyn Davies

fractured a cheekbone in a clash with his own skipper Bob Moncur in the first leg on Tyneside. At St. James' Park, with Newcastle pushing for goals in the second half, both Davies and Moncur went for a Robson corner. Moncur got there first, but in the process clashed with Davies, the captain's head whacking into Wyn's cheekbone. It wasn't a worry to Davies, he just kept on playing in his typical brave style, but after the match, club director and surgeon Fenton Braithwaite noted that Davies would need an operation and would miss the return leg of the final in Budapest. Wyn was adamant: 'No, I'm not having that.' The operation could wait: Davies would play through the pain barrier in Hungary. However, he did have to cut short the celebrations on his return to Tyneside with the trophy. He went straight to see Braithwaite and had the operation the next day.

Davies was used to pain and injuries. Although he wasn't powerfully built, he was lean and fit, and the Welshman was as strong and courageous as they come. Colleague Bob Moncur said, 'Wyn was one of the bravest guys I ever saw on a football pitch. He wasn't the heftiest of blokes – he was tall and quite thin – but he could take a hammering.' Davies possessed the heart of a lion and as one *Evening Chronicle* comment recorded, 'took more punishment in Newcastle United's Fairs Cup cause than probably any other player and still came back for more'.

Journalist John Gibson recalled that the 'Welshman terrorised Continental defences', while Davies himself once noted, 'My job was to take the knocks and come back for more. I accepted it, and we had a lot of success because Continental defenders weren't used to the way I played.' Manager Joe Harvey was more than satisfied at his centre-forward's attitude and commitment, although acknowledged that Davies 'gets more stick than any player I know'.

It was much the same story in the 1969–70 campaign. Against Dundee United *The Journal*'s reporter Ivor Broadis, an ex-United and England star, described Davies as having a 'prodigious leap and cobra-like strike', after he had scored two cracking headers in the space of three minutes and sent two more against the woodwork. And Broadis also noted that, 'Dundee dithered every time he rose inside the box'.

Against Anderlecht, as United stormed forward to claw back a two-goal shortfall, he caused sufficient confusion in the Belgian side's defence to allow Robson the chance to score the Magpies' opener. And he did the same for Dyson to grab what looked like the United winner, until Nordahl's late, late strike.

The following season, Davies had perhaps his finest 90 minutes for the Toon – in fact, his finest two matches – in a double header with Internazionale. Against some of the world's toughest defenders of the time, including Giacinto Facchetti – captain of Italy – Mario Giubertoni and Tarcisio Burgnich, Wyn caused the Latin temperament of the Internazionale side to boil over and explode. In the San Siro, Davies was a handful, nodding the opening goal just before half-time. He frightened the stars of Inter to death. Bob Moncur said for Inter it was simply 'a question of stopping Wyn by any means possible'. It was reported that the Nerazzurri defence changed their tactics against Davies for the second leg, with Facchetti, arguably the world's finest defender at the time, given the role of man-marking Wyn.

They changed other tactics too. The Milan players now resorted to punching, kicking and any other foul means they could muster to halt the big leader. He roughed up and aggravated the Italians, and the great Facchetti in particular, by first creating the space for Moncur to score the opener then for his part in a flare-up with

Wyn Davies

Wyn Davies in characteristic action; he was an aerial menace to the Sporting Clube defence in 1968.

Wyn Davies

Lido Vieri, the Inter goalkeeper, which saw the international sent off. One report noted that after Davies and Vieri tussled for the ball just inside the six-yard box, the keeper was penalised and United were awarded an indirect free-kick in a dangerous position. The visitors' custodian then lost his head, and the unfortunate referee was 'pushed and punched to the ground'. It was extraordinary. After the game the Belgian referee Joseph Minnoy said, 'It was the first time I have ever been punched by a player.'

Davies soon created more grief for the visitors by scoring himself, diving forward to head into the net after Keith Dyson had struck the bar. Moncur remarked, 'Inter were so afraid of him that they tried everything to get him, but Wyn rode it all, took all the fouls and knocks, and kept going.'

Following that memorable, drama-packed evening on Tyneside, Davies was also the match-winner against the Hungarian side Pécsi Dózsa. In the first leg at Gallowgate, he was supreme. He sent three glorious headers into the net, although one was ruled out due to a marginal offside call. Centre-half László Maurer, like many before him, simply had no answer to the Davies menace. But his efforts were wasted in the return leg, United going out on penalties instead of capitalising on the lead Wyn had secured against the Eastern Bloc minnows.

Ten goals in twenty-four European appearances was a tremendous personal record for Wyn, and represented a far better return than his domestic league and cup goal ratio. It remained a club record for a lengthy period, until Alan Shearer broke it more than 30 years later.

Soon after that European exit in the town of Pécs, manager Joe Harvey changed the focus of his side. The United boss decided to discard the high-ball game and give the Magpies a makeover. Although Davies was far from being only a high-ball striker, also possessing a decent touch with the ball at his feet, Harvey was to transform Newcastle into a more flamboyant side with the introduction of new blood, and the big Welshman was a casualty. As Malcolm Macdonald arrived, big Wyn quickly departed, joining Manchester City in August 1971.

Immensely popular – Newcastle United's first hero of the modern game – Davies continued on a much-travelled career. His five years on Tyneside, though, remained the highlight of his days in football. As he said, they were 'the best years of my life'. Moving around in his concluding seasons, Davies saw service with the other half of Manchester's football set, at Old Trafford, and also with Crystal Palace, Blackpool, Stockport and Crewe. He even spent a few months in South Africa. Wyn also played on in non-league football with Bangor City in his native North Wales for a while.

Davies later settled in Bolton, and to this day, a generation of Geordies, who witnessed his dedicated endeavours for the Toon, hold him in great esteem – a true No. 9 hero of United folklore.

Wyn Davies (centre, dark shirt) against FC Porto.

3

DUTCH MASTER CLASS

1977–78

Tension in Dublin: goalkeeper Mick Mahoney (back, middle) receives treatment after being hit by a missile during United's UEFA Cup meeting with Bohemians.

By the time Newcastle United entered Europe for their second spell in the 1977–78 season, six years had passed since their opening adventure, and Tyneside eagerly awaited a return to the excitement of Continental action. With new manager Gordon Lee – the ex-Blackburn boss – in the Gallowgate hot seat, having replaced old warhorse Joe Harvey, United had progressed into a side able to compete with the likes of Liverpool and Nottingham Forest, league champions that year.

Lee was, in many ways, a completely different character to Harvey. He was one of a new breed of manager: a tracksuit boss who forged a work ethic and stood in front of a tactic board, a rarity in the '50s management-style of his predecessor. But it was a football philosophy that lacked flair and superstars. Indeed, Lee controversially sold No. 9 hero, and supporters' favourite, Malcolm Macdonald to Arsenal for a record fee.

The new manager, though, had taken the Magpies within a whisker of a trophy in his first season in charge, reaching the Football League Cup final in 1975–76, only to lose narrowly to Manchester City. And United also challenged strongly in the First Division table, at one point reaching third place. Yet Gordon Lee departed just as things were beginning to knit together. He dropped a bombshell, sensationally quitting Tyneside to join Everton midway through the 1976–77 season.

Into the breach stepped his assistant Richard Dinnis, an almost unknown in the football world. Without any real pedigree in the game, Dinnis did not inspire the club's directorate but held much respect in the dressing-room. And an unsavoury feud resulted, as one part of the club wanted to appoint a new high-profile boss – in the shape of Lawrie McMenemy, Graham Taylor or Brian Clough – while the playing staff wanted their coach installed as manager. Revolt and a near coup followed, played out, as is Newcastle's way, unsatisfactorily in the media. The result was an away victory for the players, Dinnis eventually being appointed boss.

Once the mutiny had died down, the one-time schoolteacher incredibly led United to their highest position in the table for 26 years. He continued the good work of the previous manager by developing the foundations laid by Gordon Lee, and many judges still do not know quite how he did it. The players backed him all the way, though, and Dinnis guided the Black 'n' Whites to fifth place in the table and to UEFA Cup qualification – this time with no need for any back doors. Newcastle United returned to Europe on merit and very much through the front door.

By now, European competition had fully taken hold in the game of football. UEFA possessed huge influence and the revamped Fairs Cup – now called the UEFA Cup with a glittering new trophy – was one of three prestigious competitions every club in Europe wanted to compete for. Taking part in action on the Continent was becoming the goal for all major clubs. Unlike the formative years, now no one thought twice about taking part.

English clubs were in the middle of dominating much of European competition at the time. Liverpool lifted the European Cup on four occasions, Nottingham Forest succeeded twice, then Aston Villa followed with another

victory in 1982. In the UEFA Cup, English sides dominated, too. Following on from the Fairs Cup victories of Leeds United in 1968 and Newcastle in '69, Arsenal, Leeds again, Tottenham (twice), Liverpool (twice) and Ipswich Town all lifted the trophy. Newcastle's re-emergence on the European scene, and as a past winner, was recognised as a welcome boost to the competition.

United's line-up possessed many very good players but few of top international quality and no superstars. Mick Mahoney had developed into a formidable last line of defence, a great shot stopper, while the defence was anchored around two highly rated players in Alan Kennedy and Irving Nattrass. They were assisted by the experience of David Craig – sole survivor of the Fairs Cup glory days – as well as John Bird and home-grown youngsters Aidan McCaffery, Ray Blackhall and Peter Kelly.

Midfield hinged around the considerable talents of Scot Tommy Craig and Irishman Tommy Cassidy, both internationals and both with influential ball skills – the left foot in Craig's case and the right in Cassidy's. They were supported by Stuart Barrowclough and the underrated talent of skipper Geoff Nulty. Up front, the waning career of one-time Busby Babe Alan Gowling had been given a lifeline, and he grasped the opportunity, scoring 30 goals in 1975–76. Tall and gangly, he linked well with the tricky Micky Burns and the emerging talent of Paul Cannell, a local youngster.

During the summer of 1977, preparation for a return to European football was anything but productive. The manager's relationship with the boardroom was still far from satisfactory, while there were many player issues to resolve too. The squabbling continued throughout the summer break and into the new season. With feuding still simmering in the corridors of St. James' Park, the 1977–78 campaign opened in a catastrophic manner. In First Division action, Newcastle rapidly slid to rock bottom of the table, following a disastrous sequence of results that saw the Magpies without a victory in ten successive league games. On top of that, they were also eliminated from the League Cup by Millwall.

Amongst all this domestic misery, the Black 'n' Whites returned to European football. UEFA's draw threw up an uninspiring but interesting tie with Irish part-timer side Bohemians, at a time when the Anglo–Irish relationship was far from good: the shameful terrorist atrocities were then at their most abhorrent. Despite a hostile reception in Dublin, Newcastle comfortably manoeuvred their way through that tie and faced a much more attractive fixture – and venue to explore – facing Bastia from the Mediterranean island of Corsica in the next round.

The French club had built a gifted side, with several accomplished players like Claude Papi and Felix Lacuestra. Bastia also fielded one extra-special star in Dutchman Johnny Rep, one of the world's top players at the time and part of the entertaining Netherlands side, alongside the likes of Cruyff, Krol and Neeskens.

Despite the quality of the opposition, and United's dire league form, the Geordies played very well in the Armand Cesari stadium. While they went down to the odd goal in three, United very nearly came back home with a draw, Bastia only scrambling a winner in the dying minutes, and Newcastle had scored an away goal, so often vital in European competition. It had been a performance totally out of character, and many people thought that perhaps the Magpies had turned the corner. Unfortunately, that was only a hope and far from the reality.

At Gallowgate, Newcastle's European dream was shattered by a display of superstar magic by Rep and his colleagues, particularly the talented Papi. The Black 'n' Whites were given a lesson in football as the ball pinged around the St. James' Park turf from blue shirt to blue shirt. Almost at will, Bastia stepped up

United's under-fire manager Richard Dinnis, who guided the Magpies into the UEFA Cup for the first time.

to net three times, twice through Rep. United tumbled out of the UEFA Cup – and worse was to follow. Their league results did not improve. United were relegated at the end of the season, and the Magpies started what was to become a calamitous era in the club's eventful and colourful history.

It was to be a long, long wait until European football returned to St. James' Park – all of 17 years. Not until a dramatic revolution on Tyneside had transformed Newcastle United and Kevin Keegan's 'Entertainers' had arrived on the scene did European football come back to St. James' Park.

The Bastia defence holds firm as Paul Cannell challenges the French keeper watched by Micky Burns (No. 10).

MATCHES 25 – 28

Alan Gowling rises to head United's goal against Bastia at St. James' Park.

1977–78

Ireland, Dublin	v. Bohemians FC	0–0, 4–0, Agg 4–0	UEFA Cup, R1
France, Bastia	v. SEC Bastia	1–2, 1–3, Agg 2–5	UEFA Cup, R2

Euro Facts & Figures

Aggregate Margins
Largest winning:
10–2 v. Royal Antwerp (UEFAC) 1994–95
7–1 v. RCD Mallorca (UEFAC) 2003–04
7–1 v. Hapoel Bnei Sakhnin (UEFAC)
2004–05
7–1 v. Olympiacos CFP (UEFAC)
2004–05
Heaviest losing:
0–4 v. AS Monaco (UEFAC) 1996–97

Most Fixtures
14 games: Champions League,
2002–03
14 games: Champions League qualifier
& UEFA Cup, 2003–04
12 games: Inter Cities Fairs Cup,
1968–69
12 games: UEFA Cup, 2004–05

Undefeated Runs
Home & Away:
11 games, 2003–04 & 2004–05*
Home:
13 games, 1968–69 to 1977–78,
13 games 2003–04 to 2005–06
Away:
8 games, 2002–03 to 2003–04
*In 2003–04 and 2004–05 United
played 24 matches, won 18 and only
lost 2.

Match 25

1977–78
UEFA Cup, Round 1: Bohemian FC (Republic of Ireland) v. Newcastle United
FIRST LEG Wednesday, 14 September 1977, Dalymount Park (Dublin)

Bohemians

UNITED Mahoney, Craig (D), Kennedy, Cassidy, Nattrass, Bird, Barrowclough, Cannell, Burns, Callachan, Craig (T). Subs not used: Hardwick, McLean, Blackhall, Oates, McCaffery.
Manager: Richard Dinnis

BOHEMIANS Smyth, Gregg, O'Brien, Kelly, McCormack, O'Connor (P), Byrne (P), Shelly, O'Connor (T), Byrne (E), Ryan. Subs not used: Davis, Brady, Malone, Dixon, Salmon.
Manager: Billy Young

REFEREE G. Owens (Wales)

RESULT Drew 0–0 (0–0)
AGGREGATE 0–0

ATTENDANCE 25,000

SCORERS None

MATCH HIGHLIGHTS

United's return to European action after a break of seven years was an opportune distraction from a poor domestic start to the season but was marred by scenes of violence typical of the '70s. Newcastle's visit to Dublin saw United keeper Mick Mahoney knocked semi-conscious by flying debris just after half-time, and the players were led from the field for 14 minutes as police brought the home crowd under control. Waving tricolour flags and shouting anti-English chants, for a period the atmosphere was unsavoury. The small band of Newcastle supporters in Dublin were innocent and looked on as the Garda intervened. Despite the violence, Newcastle produced the football and largely dominated what was an uninspiring contest, although the Irish part timers gave a spirited display and made it difficult for the Tynesiders. Newcastle created opportunities but couldn't force a goal, lacking punch in the box. Micky Burns and Tommy Craig both went close, while Irving Nattrass had a goal-bound effort cleared off the line. Goalkeeper Mick Mahoney, meanwhile, had to save twice and stop Bohemians from recording a Euro shock. Yet, despite a disappointing performance, United were clear favourites to progress in the UEFA Cup, in what was the Geordies' first taste of the modern competition.

MAN OF THE MATCH

David Craig – his experience proved invaluable.

MATCH RATING ● ☐ ☐ ☐ ☐   Lacklustre on the pitch.

STAR COMMENT

Richard Dinnis: 'Bohemians kept their heads and played football the whole game. They are well organised and they are fit.'

EYEWITNESS

John Donoghue (*The Journal*): 'United have surely clinched their second-round place. In surroundings quite mad they showed they could keep their cool.'

TOUR STOP – DUBLIN

Capital of the Republic, situated on Dublin Bay and the River Liffey, Dublin is now a vibrant commercial and cultural centre as well as popular tourist destination, but back in the '70s it possessed an unpleasant undertone for anyone English. With fine Georgian architecture and many landmarks, such as Christ Church and St. Patrick's cathedrals, strolling the Temple Bar and Grafton Street districts, as well as the giant Guinness brewery, was still a pleasing break for United's small travelling support. (pop. 495,000.)

STADIA FILE – DALYMOUNT PARK

Situated in the Phibsborough area of the capital near Mountjoy Prison, in 1977 Dalymount Park was – and still is – an ill-equipped stadium for top-level football. With a capacity at the time of 45,000, and one main stand of traditional design, facilities were at a minimum. Terraces were the order of the day, yet, despite its shortcomings, the stadium creates its own unique atmosphere, a throwback to football in the '50s and '60s. A landmark church spire is situated just behind the main stand.

DID YOU KNOW

One journalist counted a mere 11 Garda officers to cope with the angry exchanges between fans at the so-called Tram Shed end of the stadium where stones and missiles hailed down on the innocent.

Mick Mahoney, a popular goalkeeper.

Match 26

1977–78

UEFA Cup, Round 1: Newcastle United v. Bohemian FC (Republic of Ireland)
SECOND LEG Wednesday, 28 September 1977, St. James' Park

Bohemians

UNITED Mahoney, Craig (D), Kennedy, McLean, McCaffery, Nattrass, Barrowclough, Callachan, Burns, Gowling, Craig (T). Subs not used: Cannell, Gorry, Hardwick, Mitchell, Oates. Manager: Richard Dinnis

BOHEMIANS Smyth, Gregg, O'Brien, Kelly, Burke, O'Connor (P), Byrne (P), McCormack, Byrne (E), O'Connor (T), Ryan. Subs not used: Dixon, Brady, Shelly, Davis. Manager: Billy Young

REFEREE G. Haraldsson (Iceland)

RESULT Won 4–0 (1–0)
AGGREGATE Won 4–0

ATTENDANCE 19,046

SCORERS United: Gowling (27), Craig (T) (65), Gowling (67), Craig (T) (68)

MATCH HIGHLIGHTS

The Magpies were never in any trouble in the return leg against Irish club, Bohemians. As soon as Alan Gowling put United in front, the Black 'n' Whites cruised into the next round of the UEFA Cup. Gowling and Scotland international Tommy Craig were outstanding and both found the net on two occasions, a flurry of goals coming in the final quarter of the match. Playing in a change kit of green and yellow, United were soon in control. With almost 30 minutes of the game played, they took the lead, with a goal that was finely constructed and smoothly executed. Nattrass started the move, before Ralph Callachan squeezed a pass through to Barrowclough. A run up the line saw the winger's cross cut back to Gowling on the edge of the six-yard box, and the United striker swivelled to fire past Smyth and into the net. In the second period, the Magpies wrapped up the tie. Their second came when a Barrowclough corner saw Gowling head the ball down into the danger zone and skipper Tommy Craig rammed the ball past the Bohemians' keeper. Then, two minutes later, David McLean created an opening, teeing up the ball for Gowling to strike superbly past Smyth. The Irish heads were down as Craig finished off the rout with a magnificent low, angled drive that whizzed past the over-worked goalkeeper.

MAN OF THE MATCH

Tommy Craig – a general in midfield.

MATCH RATING ● ● ● ☐ ☐   One-way traffic.

STAR COMMENT

Tommy Craig: 'We were one up at the interval, and three quick goals in the second half put the tie to bed.'

EYEWITNESS

Tony Hardisty (*Sunday Express*): 'Tommy Craig's wondrous left foot was – predictably – much too good for the Irish part timers. As always, a class act.'

OPPONENT FILE

Traditionally, football has never had a strong support in Ireland, before or after the country's division in 1921. Yet individual stars have always been developed in the Republic and Bohemians, one of several Dublin clubs, have produced many of them. Only part timers earning around £15 per week then, they were still experienced European campaigners and well organised but could never meet the overall ability of United's talented but underperforming side. However, Bohemians did lift the Irish title in the season United met them.

STAR VISITOR

Gerry Ryan – A flying, archetypal winger of the old school from Dublin, he was described as the hottest property in Ireland at the time. At the age of 22, he had pace and an unpredictable genius, characteristic of many a winger. Ryan impressed several watching English scouts and soon moved across the Irish Sea joining Derby County and later Brighton. He appeared in over 200 senior games in England and won 16 caps for the Republic.

DID YOU KNOW

Bohemians' forward Gerry Ryan and full-back Fran O'Brien both impressed boss Richard Dinnis, and United agreed a fee of £50,000 for the pair. But Newcastle were controversially pipped at the post in securing the deal by Derby County and their boss Tommy Docherty.

Tour Stop

Dublin – Ireland

1

Bohemian FC 1977–78

2

The capital of the Emerald Isle, Dublin is impressively situated between the mountains and the sea. Now a friendly and lively city, back in 1977 it was not quite so.

4

Bohemians' stadium, featuring a main stand more accustomed to pre-war football. First erected as far back as 1928, it was the home of Irish international football for over 40 years.

Tommy Craig lashes the ball on the volley to score United's second goal in the comfortable 4–0 victory at Gallowgate.

Match-day programme from United's visit to Dublin.

UEFA CUP

BOHEMIANS v NEWCASTLE UNITED

SEPT 14 1977

15p

3

Bastia – Corsica

SEC Bastia
1977–78

The picturesque waterfront: Bastia is typically Mediterranean with a pleasant mix of French charm and Italian flair.

Bastia's small and compact arena on the edge of the city, adjoining market gardens and featuring a somewhat out-of-place giant double-deck main stand.

The two sides walk into the Cesari de Furiani stadium to a characteristic European welcome of flags, banners and flares. Skipper Geoff Nulty leads the Magpies followed by keeper Steve Hardwick. Tommy Craig, arms raised, salutes the United travelling support.

Newcastle's souvenir programme featuring the symbolic Bastia flag and motif.

BASTIA-Furiani   Stade Armand Cesari

Match 27

1977-78
UEFA Cup, Round 2: SEC Bastia (France) v. Newcastle United
FIRST LEG Wednesday, 19 October 1977, Stade Armand Cesari de Furiani (Bastia)

Bastia

UNITED Hardwick, Kelly, Nattrass, Cassidy, McCaffery, Nulty, Barrowclough, Cannell, Burns, Gowling, Craig (T). Subs not used: Carr, Blackhall, McLean, Bird, Smith.
Manager: Richard Dinnis

BASTIA Weller, Burkhardt, Cazes, Orlanducci, Guesdon, Devignes (Franceschetti) (Larios), Rep, Lacuesta, Felix, Papi, De Zerbi. Subs not used: unknown.
Manager: Pierre Cahuzac

REFEREE E. Linemayr (Austria)

RESULT Lost 1–2 (1–0)

AGGREGATE 1–2

ATTENDANCE 8,500

SCORERS United: Cannell (7); Bastia: Papi (50), (89)

MATCH HIGHLIGHTS

Newcastle United were seconds away from earning a creditable draw on the island of Corsica when the influential Claude Papi drilled home the second of his two goals for Bastia in the dying moments of the match. The Magpies had silenced the noisy home crowd as they took the lead inside the opening ten minutes. Paul Cannell fired past Mark Weller, converting a Stuart Barrowclough pull-back from six yards. The goal was the result of a wonderfully engineered move involving Irving Nattrass and Alan Gowling, before a penetrating run behind the French defence from Barrowclough created the opening. Newcastle took the first-half honours in a competitive match, but Bastia recovered to test United after the break with Steve Hardwick making a series of fine saves. The balding-headed Papi equalised, Hardwick pushing out a Felix shot, only for the French midfielder to scramble home the rebound. Then, at the death, United lost possession, and Papi skipped past two defenders in a brilliant run before striking the ball hard and true towards goal. Hardwick got a hand to it but couldn't stop it entering the net to give Bastia the victory.

MAN OF THE MATCH

Steve Hardwick – busy second half.

| MATCH RATING | ● | ● | ● | | | Spirited action.

STAR COMMENT

Geoff Nulty: 'At 1–1 we got too excited. We got a throw-in, and someone rushed across to take it quickly instead of eating up some time. We lost the ball and it was in the back of our net.'

EYEWITNESS

John Donoghue (*The Journal*): 'A competent all-round team performance, they showed that despite their league troubles they have some fine players.'

TOUR STOP – BASTIA

The centre of a beautiful region of northern Corsica that is steeped in history, Bastia is the island's major commercial centre. It is a thriving port protecting the Tuscan strait and a town full of charm with Italian origins and flair. The delightful old quarter of Terra Vecchia and Terra Nova at the foot of the Citadel provides an enchanting atmosphere, while the harbour area comes alive in the evening in a typically picturesque Mediterranean setting. (pop. 38,000.)

STADIA FILE – ARMAND CESARI DE FURIANA

A small, compact stadium, the Armand Cesari stadium produces a great atmosphere when full. With a capacity of 15,000, at the time it was more reminiscent of an English Third or Fourth Division ground with four modest floodlighting pylons. Since United's visit in 1977, the stadium has been developed into a smart arena, limited in size but complete with modern facilities and a giant double-decked main stand.

DID YOU KNOW

Bastia's club badge features a historic symbol of Corsica called *Tête de Maure*. It depicts the head of a warrior wearing a head scarf, marking the fight against Genoese occupation. The Corsican emblem was emblazoned prominently on the club shirt.

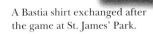

A Bastia shirt exchanged after the game at St. James' Park.

Match 28

1977–78
UEFA Cup, Round 2: Newcastle United v. SEC Bastia (France)
SECOND LEG Wednesday, 2 November 1977, St. James' Park

Bastia

UNITED Hardwick, Blackhall, Nattrass, Cassidy, McCaffery, Nulty (Bird), Barrowclough, Cannell (Hudson), Burns, Gowling, Craig (T). Subs not used: Walker, Smith, Carr.
Manager: Richard Dinnis

BASTIA Weller, Marchioni, Cazes, Knayer, Guesdon, Orlanducci, Rep, Lacuesta, Felix, Papi, De Zerbi (Larios). Subs not used: Assu, Murati, Mattei.
Manager: Pierre Cahuzac

REFEREE S. Thime (Norway)

RESULT Lost 1–3 (1–2)

AGGREGATE Lost 2–5

ATTENDANCE 34,560

SCORERS United: Gowling (35); Bastia: De Zerbi (3), Rep (9), (63)

MATCH HIGHLIGHTS

Newcastle's Euro dream was killed off by Dutch ace Johnny Rep as an impressive and talented Bastia side outplayed the Geordies. Rep – a star of the 1974 and '78 World Cups – struck two superb goals to silence the Gallowgate crowd as the Dutchman stamped his authority on the game. United's only period of ascendancy was for the 15 minutes before half-time when Alan Gowling headed the Tynesiders momentarily back into the match following a Tommy Craig free-kick. For a brief period before the half-time interval, United got going and gave the French visitors a contest, but for the remaining 75 minutes, the French side – and eventual finalists – gave Newcastle a footballing lesson. Bastia killed the game off inside the opening minutes of the match with two goals that stunned United. For the first, De Zerbi converted a move that cut through United's defence after Lacuesta's solo run had made the opening. Within nine minutes of the contest beginning, Bastia were 2–0 ahead, Rep scoring his first of the night. A one-two with Papi saw the Dutch striker hit the ball into the net off the body of Hardwick. In the second period, Rep produced a piece of magic with a stunning goal struck from 25 yards after Larios squared the ball into his path. From that point onwards, the French visitors knocked the ball around with ease and authority. Newcastle had no answer and went out of their first UEFA Cup campaign. Bastia walked off to warm applause, Tyneside's football supporters acknowledging a fine side.

MAN OF THE MATCH

Alan Gowling – battled away up front.

| MATCH RATING | • | • | • | | |

Dazzling visitors.

STAR COMMENT

Geoff Nulty: 'A lot of people had written Bastia off, but they won deservedly.'

EYEWITNESS

John Donoghue (*The Journal*): 'Newcastle's European dream died a death, killed off by the blinding class of Dutchman Johnny Rep.'

OPPONENT FILE

The Sporting Etoile Club de Bastia are proud flag-bearers of the island of Corsica with a small but vociferous following. The side that faced United was one of the club's finest, gaining third position in the French league to qualify for the UEFA Cup. They lifted the French Cup in 1981, and although few people outside France knew much about them, their side was full of top-quality players.

STAR VISITOR

Johnny Rep – A free-roaming striker who earned a huge reputation as one of Holland's top players alongside the likes of Johann Cruyff. Signed by Bastia at the start of the 1977–78 season he had shot to prominence as a 20 year old with Ajax when he netted the winner in the Dutch club's third successive European Cup triumph. Rep appeared in the 1974 and 1978 World Cup finals and moved to France after a spell with Valencia.

DID YOU KNOW

Bastia went on to reach the final of the UEFA Cup after knocking out United. They faced PSV Eindhoven but lost 3–0 on aggregate.

'His left peg was as sweet as you could get. He was a very positive and creative p...

Malcolm Macdonald

Tommy Craig

Now a respected coach of over 20 years and an important aide to United's management behind the scenes at St. James' Park, Tommy Craig was once Britain's first £100,000 teenager when he joined Sheffield Wednesday from Aberdeen. That was back in 1969, when Craig showed his talent as a prospering midfielder with a highly educated left foot, able to open up defences or strike the ball with precision and venom.

The Glaswegian's transfer to England as an 18 year old was a big move for a youngster at the time, and joining a Hillsborough outfit on the slide from the top flight – eventually into the old Third Division – it took a while for Craig to flourish. Indeed, it could be said that the Scot's career stagnated with Sheffield Wednesday for nearly five years.

Although Tommy played over 230 games for the Owls and was a popular player at Hillsborough, it wasn't until he moved back to the First Division with Newcastle United in December 1974 that his career was resurrected and he started playing football at a grade his undoubted skills were suited to. He wanted desperately to appear at the highest level, and Tommy remembers that 'within 20 minutes the transfer was signed, sealed and delivered'. He added, 'I was doing cartwheels at coming to Newcastle.'

Manager Joe Harvey felt that Craig's cultured ability on the left of midfield made him a natural replacement for the injured Terry Hibbitt. A fee of £110,000 was agreed with Wednesday and Craig headed to Tyneside. Short and stocky, the Scot prompted and probed in midfield with good vision and was able to strike a ball that could win a match. Teammate Malcolm Macdonald rated Craig highly. Supermac wrote:

> His left peg was as sweet as you could get. He was a very positive and creative player. What's more, he was a rarity in that he played with his head up which meant he could see everything that was happening around him.

With Gordon Lee soon arriving as boss, Craig had to impress a new manager and the sturdily built Scot did that with ease, Lee preferring Craig to the popular Hibbitt, who was despatched to Birmingham City. It was a credit to Tommy's ability that Newcastle's fans also took to him, as Hibbitt had been an extremely popular player at St. James' Park: Craig could easily have felt a supporter backlash. That never happened, the Scot quickly becoming an automatic choice in Lee's midfield and United's general as the team climbed the table to challenge for trophies in the 1975–76 and 1976–77 seasons.

Tommy Craig

Although not blessed with searing pace, Craig worked hard, tackled back, could hit telling balls – long or short – and was always a danger 20 or 25 yards from goal. He reached the full Scotland set-up, making his debut against Switzerland in April 1976. Tom also skippered the Black 'n' Whites at Wembley in their League Cup final defeat by Manchester City in that same year. The Scot came so close to hoisting a trophy aloft for the Magpies at the top of the famous Wembley steps. Leading United in the absence of the injured Geoff Nulty, Tommy took part in a terrific final, and even though the Black 'n' Whites had to cope with an influenza bug that had spread through the team, United only narrowly went down 1–2.

When Newcastle qualified for the UEFA Cup at the end of the 1976–77 season, Tommy was one of United's most influential players, and their return to European action was a boost for the Magpies. Craig said, 'It was a very significant achievement, especially as we had been as low as 15th the previous year. After a slow start to the season, we had moved up to as high as third before Christmas, and I remember it was our penultimate match, a 3–2 home victory over Aston Villa, that clinched our UEFA Cup spot. After a good season, qualifying for Europe was really the icing on the cake.'

United finished ahead of Manchester United in the league, after recovering from three successive defeats in the space of eight days. The narrow victory over Villa was much needed, and as one report noted, 'Newcastle kept their nerve well enough to hold on to the lead they built up by taking their chances brilliantly.' Along with Tommy Cassidy and Micky Burns, Craig was the architect of the success. Manager Richard Dinnis, who had taken over from Lee, was everyone's hero on that afternoon at St. James' Park. He was carried shoulder-high off the pitch. Yet the cheers were to turn to jeers in

TOMMY CRAIG: FACT FILE

Position: Midfield

Born: Glasgow, November 1950

Joined United from: Sheffield Wednesday, December 1974, £110,000

Left for: Aston Villa, January 1978, £270,000

Other major clubs: Aberdeen, Swansea City, Carlisle United, Hibernian

Full international: Scotland (1 cap, 1976)

United career, senior games: 157 app., 29 goals

United Euro record: 4 app., 2 goals

Did you know: Tommy Craig appeared in the same schoolboy international side as Kenny Dalglish and played at every level for Scotland.

less than four months.

Newcastle started the new season poorly and as United's former midfielder admitted, the reason was mystifying: 'It's very hard to pinpoint. It was more or less the same group of players. We were a good outfit the season before, but the trick of becoming a good team year after year is what distinguishes the good sides from the great sides. The expectations from the previous campaign were very high as far as the league was concerned, but we simply didn't live up to the previous season's form.'

As a consequence, the Magpies' European return was something of a respite to their domestic anguish as they tumbled into relegation danger. Tommy recalled, 'Playing in Europe took the pressure off what was a very worrying time for the team. It was a new experience for us, but, at the same time, we were all very aware that we needed to do something about our league form.'

Tommy Craig

A first-round tie with Dublin club Bohemians gave Newcastle an easy opening passage. Craig said, 'It was a good draw, a side from Division One in England should always prove too strong for an Irish League team and that's how it turned out. That said, they gave us a good game at their place: tough and physical. In terms of Europe, though, drawing away and keeping a clean sheet was a pretty good result, knowing we had the second leg to come at St. James' Park.'

And he remembered the crowd trouble that made all the headlines in that 0–0 draw. 'I recall there was some disturbance behind the goal,' he said, 'and our keeper Mick Mahoney was felled by a brick. It was a little frightening, so the referee was absolutely right to take the teams off the pitch to allow things to cool down. That did the trick, and we came back out to finish the match off without any further undue trouble.'

The Geordies did what was needed in the return clash. Craig said, 'The home leg turned out to be a stroll. We were able to play our football at St. James' Park, and having experienced their style of play from the first leg, we were able to play our own game. The playing surface was much better, too, which helped us as well.' Craig found the net twice in the 4–0 victory, so it was a decent evening for the Newcastle midfield general. 'There was a good build-up to both of them, and I simply slotted them away. We scored three times in four minutes, and I remember I got the second and fourth goals. Scoring twice in a match was unusual for me but twice in four minutes was unheard of!'

It was a different story against much stronger opponents SEC Bastia. Craig said, 'Bastia were a step up. Although not that well known at the time, we knew from scouting reports that they were a decent team. For the first leg, we encountered a very hostile atmosphere and there were plenty of fireworks in evidence – all in all it was very intimidating. But that said, we played extremely well on the night and were very unfortunate not to bring a 1–1 draw back to Tyneside. Paul Cannell put us ahead early on, and after Papi equalised shortly after half-time, we were devastated when the same player popped up two minutes from time to score the winner.'

Tommy faced the Dutch World Cup star Johnny Rep in the midfield battleground and, initially, United's Scotsman wasn't too taken with him. He remembered, 'Unfortunately, after the first game I gave an ill-advised and rash view on Johnny Rep, saying I hadn't been that impressed with him. It was an honest view based on what I had seen in Bastia, but nevertheless it was, looking back, not the right thing to have said.

'At Gallowgate he was different class. The team paid for my comments, which for me personally was very disappointing. Rep ran the show and his two goals, one of which was truly world class, gave Bastia a thoroughly deserved victory. On the final whistle, I shook hands with him and congratulated him on a terrific display. I had learned a valuable lesson!'

Bastia though were not a one-man team and Craig also remembered well another of the stars he faced: 'Papi stood out. He was a little guy but you could see he was a really talented player. He had a real bounce to his game, making terrific darting runs, and, what's more, he played with a smile on his face, which I always think is a great attribute in a footballer.'

Following the Magpies' brief flirtation with European football, it was back to domestic issues for Craig and a relegation dogfight. United had slipped alarmingly, in the space of a few short months, as the club reeled from internal warring between directors, manager and players. Craig recalled, 'Newcastle was a club in turmoil . . . in disarray.' And as he confirmed, 'A lot of things were said that would probably have been better

Tommy Craig

A consoling pat on the back for Tommy Craig from Bastia's Claude Papi following United's exit at St. James' Park.

Tommy Craig

left unsaid.' Craig never really wanted to leave St. James' Park in the wake of the infamous player revolt that rocked the club. He noted, though, 'When I left, it had to happen.'

Richard Dinnis – the subject of the storm – had been sacked after the Bastia exit, and the players did not like it. Following on from a summer of discontent, it was reported in the press that the United players had 'rattled the foundations of soccer by declaring publicly that they have no confidence in the club's directors' and had issued the threat of 'mass transfer requests'; United's dressing-room was a hornets' nest. The senior professionals in the camp, described as 'Geoff Nulty, Alan Gowling, Micky Burns and Tommy Craig', were all determined to leave.

Tommy headed to Aston Villa in a big £270,000 move in January 1978, just two and a half months after the game with Bastia. However, his transfer never worked out. He said, 'After three months at Villa, I knew I had done the wrong thing.' Manager Ron Saunders played the long-ball game and as Craig confessed, 'that sort of football was totally against my style and beliefs'.

After concluding his playing career with Hibernian, the Scot entered coaching at Easter Road and started on a long road that ended back at St. James' Park. Most prominently with Aberdeen and Celtic, and, at one time, in charge of the Scotland Under-21 side, Craig always relished working with kids and developing youngsters.

He rejoined the Magpies in 1998 and worked under a series of managerial regimes led by Kenny Dalglish, Ruud Gullit, Sir Bobby Robson and, latterly, Graeme Souness. He has guided a number of kids into Premiership and European action, most notably Aaron Hughes and recently Steven Taylor.

Craig acknowledges the importance of the European scene on the game nowadays. He said, 'European football has changed in the last 25 to 30 years, from when I played to what it is now. I'm not really an advocate of the numerous group matches we have to face. I much preferred the cut and thrust of two-leg knockout games right through the competition, but money and media demands dictate so much these days.'

Craig and Johnny Rep (No. 7) in action in the first leg of the meeting with Bastia on Tyneside.

4

THE ENTERTAINERS HIT EUROPE

1994–95, 1996–97

Alan Shearer strikes the ball perfectly and into the Ferencváros net during the UEFA Cup contest in Hungary's capital Budapest.

The remarkable Kevin Keegan-led resurgence of Newcastle United into one of football's super-clubs started in 1993 when he steered the Magpies to promotion to the recently introduced Premiership. After a dismal period of mediocrity, near financial ruin and a tumultuous takeover battle for control of the club, lifting the Football League Championship that year in glittering, stylish fashion made people sit up and take notice. Newcastle United were back and determined to become a force in the game once more.

At the time, football was changing rapidly, television companies backing the national sport with millions of pounds. From a position of financial uncertainty, suddenly football was awash with money, and the Premiership was rapidly transformed into a super-league to rival La Liga and Serie A. And United consolidated their place as a Premiership force in double-quick time. Their next objective was to re-establish the Magpies on the European footballing map. The ambition of Sir John Hall, the new chairman, was to see the Black 'n' Whites 'amongst the top ten in Europe'.

As Keegan's flamboyant side took to the Premiership stage in the 1993–94 season, their brand of attacking football soon caught the eye and the imagination of both the media and punters alike. In an era when television and the new Sky Sports channel catapulted football onto another level, broadcasting it to a worldwide audience, the Magpies were branded affectionately as 'The Entertainers'. Players such as Andy Cole, Peter Beardsley, Rob Lee, Barry Venison and John Beresford started to make an impact, and Keegan spent millions as the club refinanced itself and became one of the nouveaux riches. Superstars arrived on Tyneside one after the other: Tino Asprilla, Les Ferdinand, David Ginola and Alan Shearer, who joined his home club in a world record £15 million deal.

Finishing their opening season in the Premier League in a creditable third place, Newcastle qualified for the UEFA Cup; they were back in European action. It marked what was to become a regular occurrence, as the team embarked on expeditions into UEFA's competitions year after year, the Magpies only failing to qualify for Europe in two seasons during the next decade.

Kevin Keegan described United's foray into the modern European football scene as an 'adventure'. He added, 'Nobody knows where it might take us and how long it might last.' After an absence of fully 17 years, everyone was excited: players, officials and supporters alike. The new breed of loyal United fans known as the Toon Army were eager to join in the fun. They were not content to stay at home; they wanted to be on a plane to witness the marvels of Europe. Alan Oliver wrote in the *Evening Chronicle*, 'There was an enormous feeling of anticipation.' United's Grand Tour really took off as the Black 'n' Whites started their UEFA Cup campaign in the 1994–95 season. Newcastle's name was in the hat alongside those of such stately clubs as Juventus and Real Madrid. When it came to the draw, though, an easy hop across the Channel to face experienced European side Royal Antwerp suited everybody, and the Toon Army made the most of it, turning out in force.

As United were set to take on the Belgians, the Magpies were top of the Premier League and playing scintillating football. With a midfield core of Lee, Scott Sellars and Ruel Fox, and a potent attack of Andy Cole backed up by the magical genius of Peter Beardsley, few could stop the Geordie machine. They were soon installed as favourites for the competition, especially after a resounding 10–2 aggregate victory over the Belgians. Rob Lee recalled, 'There was something special about being back in Europe, and that hardly any team won 5–0 away in Europe made it particularly special.' Manager Keegan noted, 'We really announced our arrival on the European map.' And all this was achieved with limited European pedigree in the side. Keegan, of course, had lots of experience from his playing days with Liverpool and Hamburg, and so too did his assistant Terry McDermott, three times winner of the European Cup with the Reds.

The team's lack of experience on the pitch was probably the cause of their exit in the second round. Facing a good Spanish side in Athletic Club Bilbao, the Magpies roared to a 3–0 advantage in the first leg at St. James' Park. Nothing it seemed could stop the Keegan bandwagon, but they allowed the Basque club back into the game when they should have firmly brought down the shutters in defence. Two late goals gave Bilbao the edge, and they eventually went through on away goals.

Everyone was disappointed. Supporters had travelled in huge numbers to both Antwerp and Bilbao and created a friendly if boisterous party atmosphere in both cities. They enjoyed the Continental way of life: the bistros, pavement cafés, bars and liberal attitude. The Toon Army was eager to join the jet set again, and so were the players and manager. Kevin Keegan said at the time, 'Seeing the way the rival fans enjoyed each other's company – in both countries – reminded you of what a wonderful game it is.' He added, 'Our supporters loved our UEFA Cup games, and I know they want more of the same.'

However, at the end of 1994–95 season, United disappointingly missed out on European action on the last day of the league programme by a whisker. But they were back for season 1996–97 for another crack at the UEFA Cup, and they now had Alan Shearer in the famous No. 9 shirt. Kevin Keegan was confident of a good run. He said, 'When we set out on our European travels, I called the UEFA Cup an adventure. This time round, it is much more serious business. We have a realistic chance of winning.' On their bid for trophy success that season, United visited France twice, travelled to Scandinavia and experienced the hostile environment of the old Eastern Bloc for the first time in the modern era, when they journeyed to Budapest, scene of their 1969 triumph.

An easy passage against Swedish club Halmstads in the first round was followed by a much tougher encounter with Hungary's champions Ferencváros in the second, the result of which was two marvellous games of football. In Budapest, a battle royal took place that ended in a five-goal thriller, while in the return leg at Gallowgate, United turned in a top-drawer performance: a 4–0 victory secured with exhilarating football. Next, the Black 'n' Whites faced French club Metz and were inspired by the enigmatic Tino Asprilla. Everything at St. James' Park looked rosy: the team was challenging in the Premiership, having just hit ten goals past Tottenham and Leeds United, were still in with a great shout in the UEFA Cup and were progressing in the FA Cup. But, in January 1997, boss Kevin Keegan sensationally resigned. It was a colossal bolt from the heavens.

Kenny Dalglish, another high-profile manager, was swiftly appointed. Dalglish inherited Keegan's flamboyant squad and the rest of the UEFA Cup campaign, which now had the Magpies paired with Monaco in the last eight of the competition. The team from the small principality were a side bristling with notable names, including Barthez, Petit and Legwinski, as well as a youngster who was to go on to make quite an impression on the English game, Thierry Henry. It looked to be a mouth-watering tie.

United's Belgian international Philippe Albert volleys the ball towards goal against Ferencváros at St. James' Park.

Newcastle and Dalglish, though, were rocked by injuries and had to face the runaway French league leaders – and ultimate champions – without Shearer, Ferdinand or Tino Asprilla, all injured, although the Colombian player returned for the second leg. It was no contest as Jean Tigana's classy side won at a canter.

All that was left was for Dalglish to ensure that the Magpies qualified again for European football the following season. He certainly did that and earned a bonus, too. On the last day of the season, United thrashed Nottingham Forest 5–0 and squeezed into the runners-up spot in the table for the second consecutive year, in the process earning the club a place in the new Champions League. Formed in 1992, the revamped European Cup had its critics, but was to go on to transform the game. A new money-spinning world of Champions League football awaited Newcastle United.

Tino Asprilla clips the ball over Metz goalkeeper Biancarelli in the UEFA Cup tie on Tyneside.

MATCHES 29 – 40

United's pre-match line-up against Halmstads in Sweden.

1994–95

| Belgium, Antwerp | v. Royal Antwerp | 5–0, 5–2, Agg 10–2 | UEFA Cup, R1 |
| Spain, Bilbao | v. Athletic Bilbao | 3–2, 0–1, Agg 3–3 | UEFA Cup, R2 |

1996–97

Sweden, Halmstad	v. Halmstads BK	4–0, 1–2, Agg 5–2	UEFA Cup, R1
Hungary, Budapest	v. Ferencváros TC	2–3, 4–0, Agg 6–3	UEFA Cup, R2
France, Metz	v. FC Metz	1–1, 2–0, Agg 3–1	UEFA Cup, R3
France, Monaco	v. AS Monaco	0–1, 0–3, Agg 0–4	UEFA Cup, QF

Euro Facts & Figures

Consecutive Victories
Home & Away:
5 wins, 1968–69 to 1969–70
5 wins, 2004–05 (twice)
Home:
8 wins, 1968–9 to 1969–70
Away:
5 wins, 2004–05

Fortress St. James
Eight home defeats in 53 played
1–3 v. SEC Bastia (UEFAC) 1977–78
0–1 v. AS Monaco (UEFAC) 1996–97
0–2 v. PSV (UCL) 1997–98
0–1 v. Feyenoord (UCL) 2002–03
1–4 v. Internazionale (UCL) 2002–03
0–2 v. FC Barcelona (UCL) 2002–03
0–1 v. FK Partizan (UCL) 2003–04
1–2 v. RC Deportivo La Coruña (ITC)
2005–06

Most Appearances
Shay Given, 54, 1997 to date
Alan Shearer, 49, 1996 to 2006
Aaron Hughes, 44, 1997 to 2005

1994–95

UEFA Cup, Round 1: Royal Antwerp (Belgium) v. Newcastle United
FIRST LEG Tuesday, 13 September 1994, Bosuil Stadion (Antwerp)

Royal Antwerp

UNITED Srníček, Hottiger, Peacock, Albert, Beresford, Fox, Lee, Venison, Sellars, Beardsley (Watson), Cole (Jeffery).
Subs not used: Hooper, Elliott, Howey.
Manager: Kevin Keegan

ANTWERP Svilar, Kulcsar, Emmerechts, Broeckaert, Smidts, Godfroid, Porte, Zohar (Monterio), Kiekens, Vangompel, Severeyns. Subs not used: van Der Straeten, van Rethy, Moukrim, Aloisi.
Manager: Urbain Haesaert

REFEREE R. Wojcik (Poland)

RESULT Won 5–0 (3–0)

AGGREGATE 5–0

ATTENDANCE 19,700

SCORERS United: Lee (1), (9), Sellars (39), Lee (50), Watson (78)

MATCH HIGHLIGHTS

United's first European fixture for almost 20 years resulted in a truly brilliant display by Kevin Keegan's Entertainers, at a time when they were in top Premiership form. Rob Lee netted a hat-trick of headers, including an opening goal within 50 seconds of the start. Newcastle not only defeated Antwerp with ease but at times toyed with their opponents in a scintillating performance of passing football that left the Belgians totally bemused. United had attacking intentions from the kick-off, and a John Beresford cross picked out a Rob Lee run, his flying header whizzing into the back of the net. Within eight minutes, the Geordies were 2–0 in front when Lee got his second. He fed Fox, who broke down the wing and delivered a telling cross into the box that was challenged for by both Cole and Lee, running for the return. And it was the United midfielder who got there first to score with another header. Then, before half-time, Scott Sellars got on the score sheet after Fox's high centre was miscued by a defender, and Cole was able to set up the chance. Lee went on to complete an amazing hat-trick just after the interval. Full-back Marc Hottiger crossed well, and the future England player guided the ball into the bottom corner of the net. United were in total control when Steve Watson scored the goal of the night with a run that saw him go past three defenders then the goalkeeper before finally rolling the ball home in style. It wasn't all one-way traffic,

though, and Pavel Srníček had to produce a string of good stops to halt the Royal Antwerp strikers.

MAN OF THE MATCH
Rob Lee – brilliant from box to box.

MATCH RATING	● ● ● ● ●	Sparkling return.

STAR COMMENT
Philippe Albert: 'To crush them 5–0 was really something. It's a very rare thing in European football to score so many as that away from home.'

EYEWITNESS
William Johnson (*Daily Telegraph*): 'The remarkable Newcastle United success story moved into a glorious new chapter as Kevin Keegan's team celebrated the ending of a 17-year European exile by tearing apart a bemused Royal Antwerp.'

TOUR STOP – ANTWERP
The travelling Toon Army, some 4,000 strong, enjoyed their first European visit in modern times in the attractive and lively city of Antwerp. The main port of Belgium on the River Scheldt, although heavily bombed during the Second World War, retains a historic charm with a restored old town around the Grote Markt. It bristles with narrow streets, history and museums as well as cafés, bars and clubs. It is also the centre of the international diamond trade. (pop. 455,000.)

STADIA FILE – BOSUIL STADION
Once having a capacity of 60,000, on United's visit the Bosuil arena was undergoing much-needed repairs. A neglected, crumbling stadium left over from the '50s and '60s, the capacity was latterly reduced to 20,000 for safety reasons. Originally opened in 1923, and much altered thereafter, the oval-shaped ground in the style of the old Ibrox eventually underwent modernisation, featuring among its new structures a two-tiered eyesore behind one of the goals.

DID YOU KNOW
Peter Beardsley returned to the United side against Antwerp following a fractured cheekbone injury. It was to be the Newcastle maestro's first game in European competition, having missed out on UEFA action with Liverpool due to the Heysel tragedy in the same country.

Match 30

1994–95
UEFA Cup, Round 1: Newcastle United v. Royal Antwerp (Belgium)
SECOND LEG Tuesday, 27 September 1994, St. James' Park

Royal Antwerp

UNITED Srníček, Hottiger, Peacock, Howey, Beresford, Albert, Beardsley (Clark), Lee (Watson), Sellars, Fox, Cole. Subs not used: Guppy, Holland, Hooper.
Manager: Kevin Keegan

ANTWERP van Der Straeten, Godfroid, Taeymaens, Smidts, Emmerechts (Moukram), Kulcsar, Zohar, Porte, Kiekens, Vangompel (Rubenilson), Severeyns. Subs not used: unknown.
Manager: Urbain Haesaert

REFEREE R. Pedersen (Norway)

RESULT Won 5–2 (4–0)
AGGREGATE Won 10–2

ATTENDANCE 31,383

SCORERS United: Lee (10), Cole (26), Beardsley (35) (pen), Cole (39), (88); Antwerp: Kiekens (79), Severeyns (80)

MATCH HIGHLIGHTS

Against a Belgian side that could not cope with the array of attacking quality in Newcastle's line-up, the Magpies again dominated the game and ran up a 10–2 record aggregate victory. It was Rob Lee who once more gave United an opening boost. The Antwerp keeper van Der Straeten flapped at a ball from a corner, and as it dropped loose, Lee hooked the ball back over his head into the net from just inside the box. A slick move between Ruel Fox and Scott Sellars paved the way for United's second goal, the ball being quickly delivered into the box where Cole tapped home from close range. By then, the Magpies attacked at will, and it was no surprise when they struck twice more before the break. The first came when Fox was pulled back in the penalty area and Peter Beardsley rammed in the spot-kick. Beardsley, United's chief playmaker, then set up Cole, who drilled the ball into the net. Newcastle were cruising after the interval and allowed Royal Antwerp to hit back with two late goals, one coming from a flying header by Kiekens and the other from a pile-driver by Severeyns. However, they were strikes that only awoke the Magpies goal machine once more. Sellars created a glorious fifth effort by threading his way past three defenders before releasing the ball for Andy Cole to score his hat-trick goal.

MAN OF THE MATCH
Andy Cole – unstoppable in the box.

MATCH RATING	●	●	●		

Cruise control.

STAR COMMENT
Kevin Keegan: 'A really lovely night, with their supporters contributing so much to a magical atmosphere.'

EYEWITNESS
Tim Taylor (*The Journal*): 'It was a question merely of how many Newcastle United would score.'

OPPONENT FILE
Royal Antwerp were an experienced side in Europe, having reached the Cup Winners Cup final only 16 months prior to facing the Magpies. On that occasion, in 1993, they were defeated by Parma at Wembley. They are the oldest club in Belgium but behind Anderlecht, Standard Liege and Club Brugge in the pecking order. Antwerp was given its royal title in 1920 and remains one of the institutions of Belgian football.

STAR VISITOR

Francis Severeyns – A fast and effective striker who joined Antwerp after service with Westmalle, Mechelen and a spell in Italy with Pisa. He had appeared almost 150 times for Antwerp before facing United and was a Belgian international forward who took part in his club's run to the European Cup Winners Cup final in the 1992–93 season. Known as 'Cisse', he showed he had an eye for goal in both games.

DID YOU KNOW
United's aggregate victory of 10–2 over Royal Antwerp remains the highest margin of victory in all the club's European ties.

Tour Stop

Antwerp – Belgium

Royal Antwerp 1994–95

The lively Grote Markt, the attractive centre of the thriving port of Antwerp. It is a city always on the go and bristles with history and museums, too.

The view from the United end at Antwerp's Bosuil Stadion. The Toon Army's giant banner lies behind the goal.

Andy Cole swivels to get a shot at goal despite the attention of two Belgian defenders.

Match magazine on sale in Antwerp.

Bilbao – Spain

Athletic Club Bilbao 1994–95

A pleasant waterfront view of Bilbao, the centre of Basque culture and industry – with a football heart. An intriguing city, it has been much redeveloped in recent years.

Athletic Bilbao's ground situated in the city centre alongside the River Nervion – notice the arched feature on the main stand. The stadium is a symbol of Basque pride.

In an all-blue strip, United attack the Spanish rearguard at St. James' Park with Andy Cole in determined mood.

United's UEFA Cup prog-ramme featuring Rob Lee on the cover.

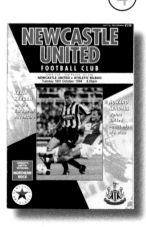

Match 31

1994–95
UEFA Cup, Round 2: Newcastle United v. Athletic Club Bilbao (Spain)
FIRST LEG Tuesday, 18 October 1994, St. James' Park

Athletic Bilbao

UNITED Srníček, Hottiger, Howey, Peacock, Albert, Beresford, Fox, Clark, Beardsley, Sellars, Cole. Subs not used: Watson, Drysdale, Guppy, Jeffery, Hooper. Manager: Kevin Keegan

BILBAO Valencia, Estibariz (Corino), Andrinua, Karanka, Tabuenca (Suances), Larrazabal, Alkiza, Garitano, Mandiguren, Vales, Ziganda. Subs not used: Cortina, Luke, Kike, Burgos. Manager: Javier Irureta

REFEREE H. Krug (Germany)

RESULT Won 3–2 (2–0)

AGGREGATE 3–2

ATTENDANCE 32,140

SCORERS United: Fox (9), Beardsley (34) (pen), Cole (56); Bilbao: Ziganda (72), Suances (80)

MATCH HIGHLIGHTS

For over an hour, Newcastle had this UEFA Cup tie in the bag. Convincingly leading 3–0, the Magpies had displayed their customary free-flowing attacking football to romp to a deserved advantage, and defeat in the tie looked out of the question. Andy Cole and Peter Beardsley had run the show for most of the match; however, Newcastle fatally relaxed and Bilbao pounced to net two late goals – crucial away strikes that saw the advantage rapidly swing to the Basque club. Newcastle had taken an early lead when Cole hooked a ball on for Ruel Fox to race past Larrazabal and slide his effort home from 12 yards. Then, once Cole had been felled in the box, Beardsley put United 2–0 ahead from the spot. Newcastle were in control and after the break it was the same story to start with. An excellent, quick passing move saw the ball ping from Darren Peacock to Beardsley, to Lee Clark and Fox before a well-flighted cross saw Andy Cole place a fine header across the keeper and into the net at the Leazes End. Suddenly, though, the Magpies relaxed their grip on the game and the tie. The Spaniards, always dangerous until that point, pounced and made United pay. Suances flicked the ball on to the impressive Ziganda, who pulled a goal back. Then Suances headed another in for the visitors and the match was turned on its head.

MAN OF THE MATCH

Peter Beardsley – prompted brilliantly from midfield.

| MATCH RATING | • • • • | |

Magnificent for an hour.

STAR COMMENT

Peter Beardsley: 'I guess we were a bit naive. We fell asleep and let them pull two goals back.'

EYEWITNESS

Paul Nunn (*The Journal*): 'Newcastle face a cliffhanger in the Basque country after their Euro romp suddenly turned sour in eight minutes of complacency.'

OPPONENT FILE

A regular in European competition, reaching the UEFA Cup final in 1977 and the second oldest club in Spain, Athletic Club Bilbao owes its origins to British expats – the miners and engineers of north-east England who travelled to the region at the end of the nineteenth century. Fervently Basque, to the extent that at times they insist on playing only players born in the region, Bilbao have rarely overpowered the dominance of Real Madrid and Barcelona in Spain but have always been one of the talented sides below the two giants. They were without two of their star players in Guerrero and Goikoetxea when they travelled to Tyneside.

STAR VISITOR

José Angel Ziganda – An experienced 6-ft. striker who had been a regular scorer for Bilbao at the time. Capped by Spain, he scored 16 goals in La Liga in 1992–93 and 18 in 1993–94. The popular striker joined Bilbao from Osasuna for the 1991–92 season and spent seven years with the Basque club, netting ninety goals in two hundred and ninety-one appearances. He rejoined Osasuna in 1998.

DID YOU KNOW

When United faced Bilbao they were top of the Premiership and buzzing with displays of brilliant football in every match.

Match 32

1994–95
UEFA Cup, Round 2: Athletic Club Bilbao (Spain) v. Newcastle United
SECOND LEG Tuesday, 1 November 1994, Estadi San Mamés (Bilbao)

Athletic Bilbao

UNITED Srníček, Hottiger, Peacock, Howey, Beresford, Fox (Jeffery), Albert, Lee, Sellars (Clark), Watson, Beardsley. Subs not used: Guppy, Drysdale, Hooper.
Manager: Kevin Keegan

BILBAO Valencia, Tabuenca, Andrinua, Karanka, Larrazabal, Larrainzar (Urrutia), Garitano, Alkiza, Mandiguren (Cortina), Suances, Ziganda. Subs not used: Corino, Kike, Luke.
Manager: Javier Irureta

REFEREE A. Amendolia (Italy)

RESULT Lost 0–1 (0–0)

AGGREGATE Drew 3–3, lost on away goals

ATTENDANCE 47,000

SCORERS Bilbao: Ziganda (67)

MAN OF THE MATCH
Peter Beardsley – never gave up.

| MATCH RATING | ● | ● | | | | |

Close encounter.

STAR COMMENT
Scott Sellars: 'We started off very well, and if we had got the goal we deserved it would have been so different.'

EYEWITNESS
Paul Nunn (*The Journal*): 'Newcastle had to perform a fine balancing act, staying solid at the back, always having an eye for goal, and they seemed to be judging it perfectly . . . until Ziganda struck.'

Midfielder
Scott Sellars.

MATCH HIGHLIGHTS
With a three-goal advantage Newcastle would have been comfortable in the fiercely partisan San Mamés stadium in the Basque country, but with that late Spanish rally on Tyneside, it was always going to be difficult. And it was those two Bilbao away goals that proved to be so crucial. United held firm with a gritty and composed performance for most of the match, with the Spaniards enjoying lots of possession but rarely troubling Pavel Srníček. Newcastle managed to keep Bilbao at bay until after the hour mark, before Ziganda broke the deadlock, running on to a pass and firing a shot past Srníček, which took a deflection off Steve Howey. Bilbao were also awarded a late penalty, after they had caught United on the break and John Beresford had felled Suances in the box. However, Garitano struck the post and United had a lifeline. Peter Beardsley, who was inspirational all evening, had a last-minute effort brilliantly saved by Valencia. United did have much of the play on the evening with Lee and Beardsley, in particular, influential. Lee had a flying header go close and another effort from 25 yards whizzed past the woodwork. Indeed, Newcastle were unlucky not to find the net; an away goal would have changed the tie completely. Yet by the end of the match, the San Mamés arena was a sea of red and white and full of noise from the Basque fans, which signalled a victory for the home side.

TOUR STOP – BILBAO
A friendly party atmosphere was created in the streets and bars of Bilbao as some 5,000 Geordies invaded the northern Spanish port. One of Spain's biggest industrial centres, situated on the Bay of Biscay, Bilbao has transformed itself – much like Newcastle – into a popular cultural and tourist-friendly city. Capital of the Basque region, it is an intriguing place with such sights as the Guggenheim Museum and old quarter around the Pozas district and Plaza Nueva. (pop. 355,000.)

STADIA FILE – SAN MAMÉS
Known as La Catedral and first used in 1913, the stadium is the focal point of Basque fervour and pride. It was redeveloped in 1952 and was later enlarged to feature a huge arched main stand – Tyne Bridge style. By 1962, the ground was complete with double-decker stands on all sides and is tightly enclosed by the surrounding streets near to the centre of Bilbao. The World Cup of 1982 saw further modernisation to the ground, with colourful seating and bright white cladding being added to give a pleasing uniformity. The stadium, with a capacity of 46,500, created a terrific atmosphere when Newcastle visited: one of the best experienced on United's European travels so far.

DID YOU KNOW
Athletic Club Bilbao modelled their red-and-white striped shirt on Sunderland, reinforcing the historical links to the north east of England.

Match 33

1996–97
UEFA Cup, Round 1: Newcastle United v. Halmstads BK (Sweden)
FIRST LEG Tuesday, 10 September 1996, St. James' Park

Halmstads

UNITED Srníček, Watson (Barton), Peacock, Howey (Albert), Lee (Gillespie), Clark, Beardsley, Ginola, Asprilla, Ferdinand, Shearer. Subs not used: Elliott, Hislop.
Manager: Kevin Keegan

HALMSTADS Nordberg, Wiberg, Andersson (R) (Ljungberg), Karlsson, Svensson (M), Smith, Arvidsson, Andersson (T), Mattsson, Vougt (Lennartsson), Andersson (R). Subs not used: Stierna, Svensson (H), Selakovic.
Manager: Tom Prahl

REFEREE K. Fisker (Denmark)

RESULT Won 4–0 (2–0)

AGGREGATE 4–0

ATTENDANCE 28,124

SCORERS United: Ferdinand (6), Asprilla (27), Albert (51), Beardsley (54)

MATCH HIGHLIGHTS

Newcastle had an easy opening draw for their new UEFA Cup campaign. Swedish club Halmstads were well beaten by a United side full of attacking flair in a tactical line-up that played only three at the back and brought in Tino Asprilla to join Les Ferdinand and Alan Shearer up front; the Swedes couldn't cope with the trio worth £28.5 million. Newcastle went ahead through an early goal as Ferdinand converted a David Ginola cross, rising ahead of the keeper to power a header into the net after wonderful approach play involving Rob Lee, Beardsley and Shearer. Ferdinand nearly got a second moments later, volleying just wide, while Shearer had a free-kick brilliantly saved. Then Asprilla leapt to crack in a superb volley – again from a Ginola ball into the danger area. Halmstads rarely threatened before half-time, and after the break it was much the same story. Philippe Albert headed another Ginola cross against the woodwork before scoring with the rebound, and, soon after, Peter Beardsley capped a sparkling night when he struck an audacious shot across the keeper for a brilliant fourth goal, following a United short corner. It could have been more as Alan Shearer hit the post and then had two efforts ruled out for marginal offside calls. Newcastle's four-goal haul, though, meant the tie was as good as won.

MAN OF THE MATCH

Tino Asprilla – full of tricks and flair.

MATCH RATING • • • □ □   Splendid show.

STAR COMMENT

Warren Barton: 'We had a terrific forward line that night. There was Alan Shearer, Tino Asprilla and Les, with Peter Beardsley and David Ginola backing up.'

EYEWITNESS

William Johnson (*Daily Telegraph*): 'The part timers from Halmstad had no answer to the tidal wave of Newcastle attacks.'

OPPONENT FILE

The game was the Swedish part timers' first in UEFA Cup action, although Halmstads had already competed in the Cup Winners Cup. However, they were still poles apart in terms of standing when compared to top Premiership clubs like Newcastle United and, for that matter, Sweden's most prominent clubs, AIK Solna and IFK Göteborg. Not many fans in England had heard of any of the Halmstads players, but several went on to have decent careers across Europe in the coming years. The club went on to lift the Swedish title in 1997 and 2000.

STAR VISITOR

Freddie Ljungberg – An up-and-coming player at the time, Ljungberg was already rated as a highly promising midfielder who operated down the right flank and worked tirelessly. A 19-year-old home-grown player and Under-21 international, he was destined to become a regular in the full national side and one of his country's biggest stars in the coming decade. Born in Vittsjö, he joined Arsenal in the 1998–99 season for a fee of £3 million. He has since gone on to win several major prizes with the Gunners.

DID YOU KNOW

United faced three other Arsenal superstars of the future in that 1996–97 UEFA Cup run. Apart from Ljungberg, the Magpies competed with Thierry Henry, Emmanuel Petit and Robert Pires as the season progressed.

Match 34

1996–97

UEFA Cup, Round 1: Halmstads BK (Sweden) v. Newcastle United
SECOND LEG Tuesday, 24 September 1996, Örjans vall Stadion (Halmstad)

Halmstads

UNITED Srníček, Barton, Peacock, Albert, Beresford, Lee, Gillespie, Batty (Clark), Asprilla (Kitson), Ferdinand, Shearer. Subs not used: Elliott, Watson, Hislop.
Manager: Kevin Keegan

HALMSTADS Svensson (H), Jonsson, Arvidsson, Andersson (T), Smith, Svensson (M), Ljungberg (Selakovic), Andersson (R), Andersson (F), Vougt, Lennartsson (Karlsson). Subs not used: Nilsson, Wiberg, Nordberg.
Manager: Tom Prahl

REFEREE S. Piller (Hungary)

RESULT Lost 1–2 (1–0)

AGGREGATE Won 5–2

ATTENDANCE 7,847

SCORERS United: Ferdinand (42); Halmstads: Arvidsson (74), Svensson (M) (79)

MATCH HIGHLIGHTS

Four goals to the good, Newcastle never got going in Scandinavia, seemingly unmotivated for the clash with Halmstads. They didn't serve up an exhibition display for the small Swedish crowd and, in fact, played well below their high standards with the tie already secured after the first leg. The only moment in the whole game that stood out was Les Ferdinand's supreme strike just before half-time to give United the lead. United's striker took the ball from Keith Gillespie on the angle of the box and swivelled brilliantly past his marker before hitting a thundering volleyed shot into the top corner of the net from 16 yards. Halmstads needed a mere six goals now and were never going to get them. Yet the Swedish team battled on, and as United's focus wavered, they rocked the Toon with two goals in a late flurry. Their first strike came by way of a Pavel Srníček error, when he pushed out a shot that had come across his body to Arvidsson, who netted. After that blunder, Srníček brilliantly stopped another shot, but the effort rebounded to Svensson, who guided the ball home. The 2–1 victory against such talented Premiership opposition was a major prize for the tiny Swedish club and an embarrassment for the Geordies.

MAN OF THE MATCH

Les Ferdinand – for his goal alone.

MATCH RATING ● □ □ □ □   Inexcusable display.

STAR COMMENT

Kevin Keegan: 'Maybe being 4–0 up was the problem, but I expected a better performance. We didn't play well, and the better team won on the night.'

EYEWITNESS

Alan Oliver (*Evening Chronicle*): 'For long stretches of the game, it looked as though they were only going through the motions.'

TOUR STOP – HALMSTAD

A port in south-west Sweden on the Kattegat midway between Gothenburg and Denmark's capital Copenhagen, Halmstad is the chief town of the Halland Province. Rich in history and with notable cultural heritage, Halmstad possesses charming pedestrianised streets and squares lined with cafés and restaurants. With a busy harbour guarded by a castle, the town is in many ways a hidden gem. It also boasts a prominent university. (pop. 87,000.)

STADIA FILE – ÖRJANS VALL

A small, compact, homely venue, holding only 19,125, the Örjans vall is situated on the banks of the River Nissan on what was previously the site of a leprosy hospital. Built in 1922 and redeveloped for the 1958 World Cup, it has been upgraded since with the addition of a functional cantilevered stand. Surrounded by a leafy and refined suburb, the stadium is also the home of the Halmia club.

DID YOU KNOW

United's first trip to Sweden was in May 1922 when the Black 'n' Whites played two games: one against GAIS (3–1) and the other against IFK Göteborg (4–0).

The immensely popular Les Ferdinand.

Tour Stop

Halmstad – Sweden

Halmstads BK 1996–97

1. Postcard from Halmstad

Waterside view of the town, a hidden gem on the Swedish coast.

2. Postcard of the Örjans Vall stadium

The homely ground of Halmstads BK, a venue in the 1958 World Cup finals.

3. Match action

Les Ferdinand lets fly to score a terrific goal in Sweden.

4. Matchmagasin

Halmstads' *Matchmagasin* for United's high-profile visit to Scandinavia.

UEFA-CUPEN 96/97
HBK-Newcastle
Tisdag 24 sept. 1996

MATCHMAGASIN

Din Lokaltidning!

Nr 3747

PILKINGTON
SPARA ENERGI ÅT SVERIGE
MED KAPPA ENERGIGLAS

PRIS 20:-

Budapest – Hungary

Ferencváros TC
1996–97

A postcard from Budapest

The celebrated Chain Bridge over the River Danube, looking down from the old town of Buda towards the more modern district of Pest.

A passionate arena and home to Ferencváros, the stadium has distinctive and unusually designed floodlight towers.

David Ginola volleys one of the finest goals witnessed at St. James' Park during the second leg on Tyneside.

Match-day ticket for the UEFA Cup tie at the Ülloi úti Stadion.

Match 35

1996–97

UEFA Cup, Round 2: Ferencváros TC (Hungary) v. Newcastle United
FIRST LEG Tuesday, 15 October 1996, Ülloi úti Stadion (Budapest)

Ferencváros

UNITED Srníček, Watson, Peacock, Albert, Beresford, Gillespie (Ginola), Batty, Lee, Beardsley, Shearer, Ferdinand. Subs not used: Elliott, Clark, Hislop, Asprilla.
Manager: Kevin Keegan

FERENCVÁROS Szeiler, Hrutka, Kuznyecov, Telek, Szucs, Nyilas, Miriuta, Lisztes (Hollo), Nagy (N), Horvath (Zavadky), Nicsenko. Subs not used: Nagy (T), Simon, Arany.
Manager: Zoltan Varga

REFEREE L. Sundell (Sweden)

RESULT Lost 2–3 (2–2)

AGGREGATE 2–3

ATTENDANCE 18,000

SCORERS United: Ferdinand (24), Shearer (34); Ferencváros: Horvath (6), Lisztes (16), (56)

MATCH HIGHLIGHTS

Two away goals from Les Ferdinand and Alan Shearer, after Ferencváros had raced to a 2–0 lead following Newcastle defensive lapses, gave United the edge in this close match. In an intimidating atmosphere, the Magpies started badly: a Pavel Srníček and John Beresford mix-up let in Horvath to score, then another mishap led to Lisztes cracking home a shot following a rebound off the woodwork. After going two goals down, Newcastle clicked into gear and for a half-hour spell dominated the action. They found the net twice, equalising at 2–2 and could have gone in front when a Rob Lee effort struck the post. For the first, a great run and cross by Alan Shearer was headed home by Les Ferdinand, and following David Batty's penetrating run, Shearer turned on the ball to ram it into the net for a scintillating second. But the Hungarians claimed the lead again in the second half after yet another lapse, this time following a Beardsley miscued pass. However, Newcastle travelled back to Tyneside satisfied with two away goals. Indeed, they should have had three when a last-minute Shearer effort was vetoed by the referee, a decision that was proved to be incorrect by television replays. United had been unlucky, because another disallowed goal – this time by Ferdinand – also looked to be good. In the end, two away goals were satisfying, but Newcastle should have arrived back on Tyneside with at least a draw.

MAN OF THE MATCH

Alan Shearer – galvanised the side.

| MATCH RATING | ● | ● | ● | ● | | Thrilling contest. |

STAR COMMENT

Darren Peacock: 'It was a few lapses in concentration that let us down. It was disappointing to lose those bad goals.'

EYEWITNESS

John Edwards (*Daily Mirror*): 'Kevin Keegan's men once again demonstrated their defensive frailties, and it needed Shearer at his best to haul them back into the match.'

TOUR STOP – BUDAPEST

United's second visit to Budapest – now free from communism – was a nostalgic return for the few who had witnessed the scene of United's European triumph 27 years before. In the middle of a vast transformation, the Hungarian capital was rapidly becoming westernised and developing a tourist infrastructure to capitalise on the great sights of the former Habsburg empire. (pop. 1,760,000.)

STADIA FILE – ÜLLOI ÚTI

A modern and comfortable stadium situated on the main route from Budapest's international Ferihegy airport, Ülloi úti has a capacity of 28,000. With distinctive leaning floodlight masts, the stadium is a modern, though largely open, arena. The first game was played there in 1911, and it became a regular international venue after the Second World War. In 1969, Ülloi úti was redeveloped and closed for almost five years. Now completely rebuilt, a section of the stadium behind one goal is cut away to house a statue of the club's founder, which the players pass as they enter the field.

DID YOU KNOW

Newcastle's players needed police protection as they arrived at Ülloi úti, the fiery home fans hurling abuse at Keegan's men as they entered the stadium.

The flamboyant Frenchman, David Ginola.

Match 36

1996–97
UEFA Cup, Round 2: Newcastle United v. Ferencváros TC (Hungary)
SECOND LEG Tuesday, 29 October 1996, St. James' Park

Ferencváros

UNITED Srníček, Peacock, Albert, Elliott, Gillespie (Barton), Batty, Beardsley, Lee, Ginola, Asprilla, Ferdinand. Subs not used: Watson, Kitson, Clark, Hislop.
Manager: Kevin Keegan

FERENCVÁROS Szeiler, Telek, Kuznyecov (Arany), Hrutka, Nyilas, Szucs, Miriuta (Zavadszky), Jagodics, Nagy (N), Horvath (Hollo), Nicsenko. Subs not used: Nagy (T), Simon.
Manager: Zoltan Varga

REFEREE S. Khussainov (Russia)

RESULT Won 4–0 (1–0)
AGGREGATE Won 6–3

ATTENDANCE 35,740

SCORERS United: Asprilla (41), (58), Ginola (64), Ferdinand (90)

MATCH HIGHLIGHTS

The champions of Hungary were a goal up from the first leg of this entertaining, televised tie, but when they landed at Gallowgate for the return leg, they felt the overwhelming might of United's attacking flair, even without the injured Alan Shearer. The first period saw 45 minutes of one-way traffic with Tino Asprilla at his thrilling best and David Ginola having an inspired evening. Peter Beardsley missed a spot-kick, but it was only time before the floodgates opened. The Colombian broke the deadlock, pouncing to sweep home Philippe Albert's knock-down from a corner-kick. Another corner was then converted by the ever-alert Asprilla, guiding a right-foot shot into the net after Darren Peacock's header had caused havoc. United then wrapped the tie up with a stunning goal from Ginola on the edge of the box – arguably, the goal of the season. The Frenchman received the ball, controlled it with his right foot before flicking it to his left and hitting a stunning volley into the top corner past Szeiler. Newcastle were now irresistible and the Hungarians had no answer to a constant attacking flow. Ginola fired against the crossbar, and, near the end, a low cross by Warren Barton was converted by Les Ferdinand from close in to give United a convincing 4–0 victory on the night, and a winning aggregate of 6–3.

MAN OF THE MATCH

David Ginola – at his mesmerising best.

| MATCH RATING | • | • | • | • | • | Simply magnificent. |

STAR COMMENT

Kevin Keegan: 'It really was an outstanding team performance, and I'm delighted so many millions saw us in such an exciting mood.'

EYEWITNESS

Simon Turnbull (*The Independent*): 'David Ginola stamped a goal of world class on a European night that will long be remembered on Tyneside.'

OPPONENT FILE

Hungarian title holders and drop-outs from the Champions League, Ferencváros were no pushovers. The club is the top side in Hungary, and have been winners of the domestic championship and cup on numerous occasions. They possess a loyal support – one, though, that has a fearsome reputation. Known as Fradi in Budapest, they are, in equal measures, the most talked-about, the most loved and the most disliked team in Hungary. Ferencváros possessed a formidable side during the '60s and '70s, reaching three European finals in the Inter Cities Fairs Cup, which they won in 1965, as well as the Cup Winners Cup.

STAR VISITOR

Andras Telek – Skipper of Ferencváros and an accomplished defender. Tall, athletic and a powerful centre-back, Telek had played for his country but had a tough task keeping tabs on Messrs Shearer, Ferdinand and Asprilla. Often operating as a sweeper, he was a tower of strength to the Fradi back-line before joining Slovakian club FC Košice. He twice lifted the title in Hungary and Slovakia. He was also capped 24 times for his country.

DID YOU KNOW

Kevin Keegan reckoned United's display was even better than the 5–0 drubbing handed out to Manchester United only nine days before.

Metz

UNITED Srníček, Barton, Peacock, Albert, Beresford (Elliott), Gillespie, Batty, Lee, Ginola, Asprilla, Beardsley. Subs not used: Kitson, Clark, Watson, Hislop.
Manager: Kevin Keegan

METZ Letizi, Song, Kastendeuch, Serredszum, Pires, Blanchard, Isaias, Traore, Lang, Terrier, Arpinon. Subs not used: Adam, Biancarelli, Strasser, Neumann, Oyawole.
Manager: Joel Muller

REFEREE G. Benko (Austria)

RESULT Drew 1–1 (1–0)

AGGREGATE 1–1

ATTENDANCE 23,000

SCORERS United: Beardsley (30) (pen); Metz: Traore (67)

MAN OF THE MATCH

Philippe Albert – cool and classy under pressure.

| MATCH RATING | ● | ● | | | | Proficient workout. |

STAR COMMENT

Philippe Albert: 'The back four played brilliantly – we did not give them any real chances, and Pav had no saves to make. Their only goal was a mistake.'

EYEWITNESS

Martin Samuel (*The Sun*): 'Loss of discipline was the only threat to Newcastle's supremacy.'

TOUR STOP – METZ

The 2,500 United fans who made the trip to Lorraine in north-east France took note of the great historic importance of the city, prominently recorded in history books since Roman times. Despite being the centre of the French iron and mining industries, Metz retains a charm with splendid squares and quaint narrow streets in its old quarter. It is situated alongside the River Moselle not far from the border with Germany. (pop. 124,000.)

STADIA FILE – STADE SAINT-SYMPHORIEN

With a capacity of 30,000, the Stade Saint-Symphorien is a modern venue built of modest architecture with three cantilevered stands. However, at the time of United's visit, one end was still to be developed. Originally constructed in 1932, the stadium features multi-coloured seating and is immediately adjacent to the river.

DID YOU KNOW

Newcastle United were installed as second favourites for the UEFA Cup behind Milan's Internazionale after the match against Metz. The Magpies were also riding high at the top of the Premiership at the time.

MATCH HIGHLIGHTS

Without the injured pairing of Alan Shearer and Les Ferdinand up front, United produced a professional display and brought a 1–1 draw back to Tyneside on a cold, wintry night in France. Despite the freezing conditions, the Metz crowd created a red-hot atmosphere in the Stade Saint-Symphorien. Newcastle made a good start, and, on the half-hour, Tino Asprilla was felled inside the box by keeper Letizi, as the Colombian tried to take the ball round him. Peter Beardsley stroked home the resulting penalty into the bottom corner of the net to give the Magpies the advantage. David Ginola was back on French territory and had a fine game, while Asprilla, up front on his own, was always a danger. Yet United had to defend for long periods, and the back-line with Philippe Albert and Darren Peacock was resolute. It was a rugged match, too, especially in the midfield battleground where David Batty in particular was prominent. His good performance was in spite of the foul attention meted out by Brazilian Isaias, who at one point punched Batty when he was lying on the turf, resulting in the England man receiving four stitches. The Geordies looked like coming home with a victory, until Metz were gifted a goal when Pavel Srníček misjudged a cross, and Traore gleefully nodded home the equaliser.

Metz

UNITED Srníček, Elliott, Peacock, Albert, Gillespie, Batty, Lee, Ginola (Watson), Beardsley, Asprilla (Clark), Shearer. Subs not used: Kitson, Hislop, Beresford.
Manager: Kevin Keegan

METZ Biancarelli, Song, Kastendeuch, Serredszum, Pires, Blanchard (Iaias), Traore, Lang, Terrier, Arpinon (Oyawole), Strasser. Subs not used: Joubert, Pujade, Jager.
Manager: Joel Muller

REFEREE S. Muhmenthaler (Switzerland)

RESULT Won 2–0 (0–0)

AGGREGATE Won 3–1

ATTENDANCE 35,641

SCORERS United: Asprilla (80), (82)

MATCH HIGHLIGHTS

It was Colombian Tino Asprilla who inspired United to victory, coming alive in UEFA Cup action, with two late goals. His contribution made sure that the Magpies went through to the next round in what was to be Kevin Keegan's last European match as United's boss. However, Metz provided stern resistance and gave Newcastle a number of scares in defence, with Srníček having to be alert as the likes of Robert Pires showed what a great prospect he was. United's keeper, in fact, had to make several fine stops to make sure the French visitors did not take the lead, including a crucial save from Traore, who went clear of United's defence. Metz defended stoutly, too, with David Terrier impressing, so much so that he later joined the Magpies. Newcastle needed something a bit special to break the deadlock, and it was left to the enigmatic Asprilla to turn the game. The at-times brilliant Colombian pounced with a double strike in the space of two minutes. His first came from a Keith Gillespie cross, Asprilla stooping to head home low into the net after Darren Peacock had turned the ball back into the danger area. The second was a gem: from Srníček's clearance, Tino controlled the ball just inside the Metz half, then spun and accelerated past three defenders before flicking the ball into the net. St. James' Park erupted with the popular chant of 'Tino . . . Tino'.

MAN OF THE MATCH

Tino Asprilla – match-winning form.

| MATCH RATING | ● | ● | | | |

Jittery victory.

STAR COMMENT

Kevin Keegan: 'Metz played well and we played very, very much below par. For a while, we were as bad as we could be.'

EYEWITNESS

Ian Murtagh (*The Journal*): 'Too often Newcastle were relying on individual dash rather than collective flair in search of the breakthrough.'

OPPONENT FILE

Before facing United, the French club had only recorded a single victory in European competition and reaching the third round was an achievement in itself for Metz. A side full of youth and talent, the club usually claimed a mid-table position in the *Le Championnat* but at the time excelled and challenged near the head of the table, winning the French league cup as well. The team proudly display the cross of Lorraine on their shirts.

STAR VISITOR

Robert Pires – Born in Reims, Pires began his illustrious career playing for his local club before he joined Metz. He was 23 years old when he faced United and many scouts flocked to watch him from the major clubs of Europe. A fast-raiding winger or midfielder, he could score goals and was destined for the top. Robert joined Marseille soon after and moved on to Arsenal in 2000, becoming a regular for *Les Bleus*, winning the European Championship and World Cup for his country. He has appeared over 50 times for France.

DID YOU KNOW

Tino Asprilla was booked for over-celebrating his second goal: he pulled off his shirt, hooked it to the corner flag and then waved it in the air! He missed the quarter-final as a result. As it happened, he also pulled a hamstring and would have been on the sidelines anyway.

Tour Stop

Metz – France

Stade Saint-Symphorien

FC Metz
1996–97

1. Postcard from Metz

There are some wonderful sights in Metz, including La Porte Serpenoise (top right), La Cathedrale Saint-Etienne (left) and La Porte des Allemands (bottom right).

2. Postcard from Stade Saint-Symphorien

The headquarters of FC Metz, situated next to the Moselle river.

3. Match Action

In a fiery match in France it needed the cool head of Peter Beardsley to send the keeper the wrong way from the penalty spot.

4. Memorabilia

David Ginola is featured on the cover of United's match programme against Metz.

Monaco

AS Monaco
1996–97

1. Postcard from . . . Monaco

Two postcard views showing the dramatic panorama of the principality on the Riviera coast.

2. Postcard from . . . Stade Louis II

A gem of architecture in the heart of Monaco, but frequently criticised for its playing surface and small capacity.

3. Match Action

United's travelling support watch a wonderful strike by Benarbia flash past Shaka Hislop for Monaco's second goal at the Stade Louis II.

4. Memorabilia

The UEFA Cup quarter-final ticket.

1

1

MONACO MONTE-CARLO

2

UEFA CUP
1/4 DE FINALE RETOUR

A.S. MONACO
NEWCASTLE UNITED

1/4 FINALE
18 MARS 97

PESAGES

SCOLAIRES

DIVISION	CATEGORIE	RANG	PLACE
PESAGES		00	0547

938822

SCOLAIRE   104951

Billet à conserver par le spectateur, doit être présenté à toute réquisition

4

3

Match 39

1996–97

UEFA Cup, Quarter-Final: Newcastle United v. AS Monaco (Principality of Monaco/France)
FIRST LEG Tuesday, 4 March 1997, St. James' Park

Monaco

UNITED Hislop, Watson, Peacock, Albert, Elliott, Gillespie, Clark, Barton, Batty, Ginola, Lee. Subs not used: Crawford, Beardsley, Beresford, Srníček, Barratt.
Manager: Kenny Dalglish

MONACO Barthez, Blondeau, Djetou, Dumas, Collins, Benarbia, Anderson, Legwinski, Grimandi, Martin, Henry (Ikpeba). Subs not used: Porarto, Grassi, Irles, Diao.
Manager: Jean Tigana

REFEREE P. Ceccarini (Italy)

RESULT Lost 0–1 (0–0)
AGGREGATE 0–1

ATTENDANCE 36,215

SCORERS Monaco: Anderson (59)

MATCH HIGHLIGHTS

With Kenny Dalglish now in charge of the Magpies for the quarter-final clash, Monaco's victory on Tyneside was completely deserved. The French outfit were a class above an injury-ravaged Magpie side that was forced to play without the considerable presence of Alan Shearer, Les Ferdinand and Tino Asprilla. Rob Lee battled alone up front in an unaccustomed role but had little success as the stylish team from the Côte d'Azur dominated proceedings for long periods. Brazilian Sonny Anderson scored the only goal of the game, almost on the hour mark, set up by Thierry Henry's swift break. Anderson took the pass and crashed the ball into the roof of the net past Shaka Hislop. It was a strike that put the French side in the driving seat for the return leg in the principality. United could have snatched a goal before and after Anderson's strike as Gillespie twice went close, once with a stinging volley. Late on, Fabien Barthez, in goal for Monaco, led a charmed life as Newcastle pressed hard for the equaliser. But a goal never came and the Black 'n' Whites had a mountain to climb in the return leg.

MAN OF THE MATCH

Keith Gillespie – almost gave a lifeline.

| MATCH RATING | • • | | | | Ill-fated night. |

STAR COMMENT

Kenny Dalglish: 'It's obviously difficult for us being a goal behind, but that's not to say it's a foregone conclusion in the second leg.'

EYEWITNESS

Gary Oliver (*Shields Gazette*): 'United's striker shortage left them unable to threaten Jean Tigana's slick Monaco side and Brazilian Sonny Anderson silenced St. James' Park.'

OPPONENT FILE

Managed by the respected Jean Tigana, Monaco had a side full of big names and stars to be. Leaders of the French league at the time, they landed on Tyneside with the title in their grasp. Consistently successful in French football, yet widely unpopular, the club is backed by the wealthy Grimaldi family. With Prince Rainier pouring money into the club during the '60s they became an established force in French football. Their poor support, however, is always under scrutiny, attracting barely 10,000 spectators on a regular basis to their plush home in Monaco. Finalists of the Cup Winners Cup in 1992, they also reached the final of the Champions League a few years after this encounter with United.

STAR VISITOR

Thierry Henry – Only 19 years old when he faced the Magpies, Thierry Henry was already dubbed as the new 'Golden Boy' of French football. His wonderful ball control and piercing runs were even then evident, and he was already being watched by top sides, notably Real Madrid and Juventus. He soon moved to Turin but ended up at Highbury with Arsenal, soon becoming, arguably, the best striker in world football. He lifted the World Cup and Euro Championship with France and has won a host of top honours with the Gunners.

DID YOU KNOW

Monaco's defence was marshalled by experienced centre-back Franck Dumas. He later joined the St. James' Park set-up in June 1999.

Match 40

1996–97

UEFA Cup, Quarter-Final; AS Monaco (Principality of Monaco/France) v. Newcastle United
SECOND LEG Tuesday, 18 March 1997, Stade Louis II (Monaco)

Monaco

UNITED Hislop, Watson, Peacock (Beresford), Albert, Elliott, Barton (Clark), Batty, Lee, Ginola, Beardsley (Gillespie), Asprilla. Subs not used: Crawford, Srníček.
Manager: Kenny Dalglish

MONACO Barthez, Petit, Dumas, Blondeau, Djetou, Collins, Benarbia (Scifo), Legwinski, Grimandi (Martin), Anderson, Henry (Ikpeba). Subs not used: Porarto, Grassi.
Manager: Jean Tigana

REFEREE M. Diaz Vega (Spain)

RESULT Lost 0–3 (0–1)

AGGREGATE Lost 0–4

ATTENDANCE 18,500

SCORERS Monaco: Legwinski (41), Benarbia (50), (67)

MATCH HIGHLIGHTS

United's UEFA Cup run came to a comprehensive end in the millionaire's paradise of Monaco. With Newcastle's side still ravaged by injury, the French league leaders controlled the second leg from the kick-off to the final whistle, and when Sylvian Legwinski opened the scoring before half-time with a powerful shot, after United lost possession of the ball in a dangerous position, Newcastle's European season was all but over. From 30 yards out, Legwinski bent a wonderful right-foot shot round the diving Hislop and into the corner of the net. In the second period, Ali Benarbia struck two more – one a swivelled hook shot from twelve yards, the other an edge of the box free-kick that flew into the net. Thierry Henry and Sonny Anderson were always a handful for United's defence, while in midfield the exceptional talents of Benarbia, John Collins and Legwinski were dominant. The Magpies never got going as an attacking force, with Asprilla and Ginola totally starved of service and thus subdued. Monaco cruised through to the semi-final – yet it could have been different had United been able to field a full strength line-up over the tie and not been deprived of three of Europe's best international strikers in the first game and two in the second.

MAN OF THE MATCH

Steve Watson – kept going against the odds.

| MATCH RATING | ● | | | | | Outclassed. |

Tynesider
Steve Watson.

STAR COMMENT

Rob Lee: 'I believe our best side would have beaten Monaco, even though their side was littered with internationals.'

EYEWITNESS

Christopher Davies (*Daily Telegraph*): 'It could have been worse against opponents who were superior in virtually every respect.'

TOUR STOP – MONACO

Situated on the Mediterranean coast, and enclaved in south-east France, the famous Principality of Monaco is one of the most glamorous destinations in the world. Its clifftop position is dramatic, while Monaco and the resort district of Monte Carlo are home to the rich and famous. A tourist Mecca, its towering skyscrapers, marina area and hilltop palace district are a must see on any Grand Tour of Europe. (pop. 32,000.)

STADIA FILE – STADE LOUIS II

One of the most prominent stadiums in Europe, the Stade Louis II is marvellously situated in the new port complex and thoughtfully designed yet with a relatively small capacity – in comparison to the larger grounds in Europe – of only 20,000. As an arena it packs in so much: car parks, offices, bistros, a sports complex, a swimming pool, shops and, of course, a football venue. This modern masterpiece replaced the original stadium in 1985. It is aesthetically pleasing and was built on four levels at a cost of around £60 million. The road behind the open arched end of the stadium is the unmarked border between Monaco and France.

DID YOU KNOW

Monaco met Internazionale in the semi-final of the competition but lost 3–2 on aggregate. FC Schalke 04 eventually lifted the trophy in the two-legged final.

'Peter Beardsley is a very special person and a very special footballer. You are not supposed to be both'

Kevin Keegan

Peter Beardsley

But for the tragedy of Heysel in 1985, Peter Beardsley would have been an experienced European campaigner by the time he rejoined his home town club in 1993. Winning the league title with Liverpool in 1988 and 1990, the Geordie genius should have taken part in two European Cup runs, as well as a Cup Winners Cup campaign in between. If events had been different, Liverpool could well have increased their remarkable record of reaching European finals and Peter may well have become a European Cup winner. Yet when he appeared for the Black 'n' Whites against Royal Antwerp in September 1994, it was Peter's first match in Continental action due to the lengthy ban on English clubs taking part in European competition in the aftermath of that heart-rending day in Brussels.

Against the Belgians, the Magpies, of course, showed the wider Continental footballing family that Newcastle United had again arrived on the European stage. And Peter Beardsley played his part as the Toon won 10–2 on aggregate. It was a sensational return to European football for the club, and Peter was delighted to get into Continental action for the first time. He said, 'I was especially proud to be captain and lead Newcastle back into Europe.'

Yet Beardsley nearly missed that comeback. He remembered, 'I broke my right cheekbone in the opening game at Leicester City.' He thought he would miss the tie as a result, and although he travelled with the team to Belgium, he later admitted, 'I thought I was going there just to watch.' Peter reckoned he had no chance of playing, but Kevin Keegan had other ideas and was determined to have his skipper on the pitch, even though the Black 'n' Whites had won five games in a row without their experienced star. Beardsley prompted and probed brilliantly that night in Antwerp and also in the return leg at Gallowgate. Opposing manager Urbain Haesaert was full of praise for United's display in both games. He said, 'They are a credit not just to their club but also to the game of football, both in England and abroad. Their two performances against us have been remarkable for the pace, accuracy and quality of their football.'

Despite that remarkable opening, Newcastle were largely novices at that level and against Athletic Club Bilbao in the next round it showed. After Beardsley had inspired the Magpies to a 3–0 lead in the first leg at St. James' Park, United allowed their talented Spanish visitors to claw back two crucial away goals. Beardsley remarked, 'Defeat seemed out of the question. Maybe we thought it was too easy; maybe in our naivety we went chasing another hatful instead of tightening things up. We learned our lesson

Peter Beardsley

the hard way.' United went out on away goals, although Beardsley did his best in the return leg. Putting on a five-star show in Bilbao, he almost sneaked it late on in the match for the Magpies with a superb shot that was brilliantly stopped by goalkeeper Valencia.

The run to the quarter-final of the UEFA Cup in the 1996–97 season saw Peter at the heart of the action. In the opening tussle with Swedish club Halmstads, the Geordie pulled the strings and scored a gem. It was described as an 'audacious shot' straight out of the Beardsley box of tricks. Receiving a short corner from Asprilla, he chipped a delightful strike across the keeper into the far top corner of the net to score a remarkable goal. Newcastle won 4–0 and went on to face Ferencváros in a terrific second-round tie. Pedro, as he is nicknamed at St. James' Park, was the master behind an awesome attacking display in the deciding leg at Gallowgate. Prompting from midfield, and getting quickly into advanced positions to support Les Ferdinand and Tino Asprilla, Peter was magnificent, and United won 4–0 again in one of the club's best-ever Euro displays. All this after he had missed a 22nd-minute spot-kick, striking the outside of the post with his shot.

Another Beardsley penalty was crucial in the next round as United faced French side Metz. This time, however, Pedro was cool and collected and fired the ball true and hard into the bottom corner – sending the keeper the wrong way – in the red-hot atmosphere of the Stade Saint-Symphorien. Newcastle then withstood something of a second-half battering. Peter said, 'We were in control to a large extent and certainly we were happy enough to bring back a 1–1 score line.' The away goal secured in the draw set up United's home victory. Beardsley was confident for the return. He said at the time, 'We can do again what we have done on every occasion we have played a UEFA Cup

PETER BEARDSLEY: FACT FILE

Position: Striker or midfield

Born: Newcastle upon Tyne, January 1961

Joined United from: Vancouver Whitecaps, September 1983, £120,000 and Everton, July 1993, £1.5 million

Left for: Liverpool, July 1987, £1.9 million and Bolton Wanderers, August 1997, £500,000

Other major clubs: Carlisle United, Manchester United, Fulham, Manchester City, Hartlepool United

Full international: England (59 caps, 1986 to 1996)

United career, senior games: 326 app., 119 goals

United Euro record: 10 app., 4 goals

Did you know: Beardsley made guest appearances for both Newcastle's reserve and junior sides when a coach, while in 2002 he turned out for Ponteland against West Allotment Celtic in the Northern Alliance.

game at home recently. We can win to make it five European victories on the trot.' The team's 2–0 success backed up Beardsley's pre-match confidence.

Manager Kevin Keegan said back then, 'It would not surprise me in the slightest if we went all the way to the final – that's how highly I rate the squad.' That, of course, never happened, and remarkably the Magpies' boss was to quickly depart after those comments, replaced by Kenny Dalglish. In the quarter-final, Beardsley was one of a quartet of big names that missed the crucial first leg with Monaco. He missed out with concussion, following an unlucky training ground mishap. The missing star players resulted in the Magpies' downfall both at Gallowgate and on the Côte d'Azur.

While Kevin Keegan's effervescent team far from revolved around one man, Beardsley

Peter Beardsley

certainly had a huge influence. Operating initially between striker Andy Cole and a formidable midfield of Rob Lee, Scott Sellars and Barry Venison, Peter played in a largely free role to perfection. Later, he played alongside Les Ferdinand and Alan Shearer with wingers David Ginola and Keith Gillespie providing the ammunition: it worked a treat. His mere presence in the team was a big bonus. Lee Clark, a fellow Geordie, said at the time, 'Peter Beardsley is a big inspiration to everyone at the club. He leads us by example and by adopting the right attitude.'

With the ability to create goals and score them – usually gems to live long in the memory and put the crowd on the edge of their seats – Beardsley was perhaps the one player in a side of many accomplished individuals that made United tick. Added to the pure football technique and professionalism was an enthusiasm and work rate few could better. His manager Kevin Keegan was to say of his little jewel, 'Peter Beardsley is a very special person and a very special footballer. You are not supposed to be both.' Keegan, writing in Peter's testimonial magazine, added, 'I've played with some of the very best for Liverpool and England. I've also had the pleasure of managing some world-class players, but Peter tops them all for talent and temperament, for all-round excellence and outstanding enthusiasm.'

When Peter returned as a 32 year old to St. James' Park in July 1993 from Everton he was delighted to be joining the Keegan bandwagon. At the time, Peter said, 'The combination of Kevin Keegan and Newcastle United in the Premiership was just irresistible.' Beardsley even took a pay cut to return home. He knew he could be taking part in European football, but didn't really expect that he would very nearly lead his boyhood heroes to the ultimate prize of the Premiership title.

Most people would agree that, in the 1995–96 season, the Magpies should have lifted the league trophy. Leading the pack from the very start, they were brilliantly entertaining throughout the course of the year but just fell short in a late-season slump that allowed Manchester United to overtake them. Defeats in away epics at Liverpool, Blackburn Rovers and Nottingham Forest – three matches United should have collected at least five points from – proved decisive. Beardsley remarked, 'We had only ourselves to blame.'

Peter also didn't think he would go on and play for his country again and collect a special 50th appearance. However, his form with United in that second spell at the club was tremendous and earned the Geordie a recall to the England set-up. Beardsley said, 'Even when there was a lot of speculation about me getting my 50th cap, I just refused to believe that it would happen.' He added, 'I was quite certain I wouldn't play for England again.' But he did, facing Denmark in his return match, and he went on to amass 59 caps for his country.

Born in Longbenton, Peter Beardsley was brought up Black 'n' White daft. In fact, he has been connected with the Magpies in some capacity four times. He was first at St. James' Park as a trialist, then, after starting his career with Carlisle United and in North America with Vancouver Whitecaps, Arthur Cox brought him back to Tyneside to team up with Kevin Keegan during the latter years of the former England skipper's playing career. He then returned to United when Keegan was boss and is currently back at Gallowgate coaching the club's Academy kids.

His first period wearing the black-and-white stripes, back in the '80s, was as eventful as his more recent one a decade later. With Kevin Keegan – the player – captivating the North East and leading United out of the wilderness of the

Peter Beardsley

To many United supporters, Peter Beardsley is
the pick of the celebrated entertainers to have
played for the club.

Star Profile

Peter Beardsley

old Division Two, Beardsley arrived from a spell in North American football to gel perfectly with the former England skipper. The two hit it off from the start and were on the same footballing wavelength. The result was attacking football at its best. United won promotion, and Peter flourished as a player under those early months of Keegan's guidance, eventually reaching international status.

Over a century of goals later, there is little doubt that Peter Beardsley is most supporters' choice as the Toon's most talented player of the modern era. And he stands shoulder-to-shoulder alongside the likes of Jackie Milburn, Hughie Gallacher and Jackie Rutherford in the distant past, too. He is undoubtedly one of United's all-time greats.

It was a great pity that Peter's skills didn't grace the very top level of European football with Liverpool or Newcastle. When the Black 'n' Whites entered the Champions League for season 1997–98, Peter only played a bit-part in the action. With Kenny Dalglish then in charge, Beardsley's days as an automatic choice were over. Now 36 years old, his former colleague and boss at Anfield couldn't guarantee him a place in the side. Peter was on the bench for the all-important qualifier with Croatia Zagreb, but had to be content with a pitch-side vantage point as United took hold of a slender 2–1 advantage at St. James' Park. Thereafter, the United star watched from afar as a Bolton Wanderers player, moving to the Reebok Stadium as the Magpies took on the likes of Barcelona, PSV Eindhoven and Dynamo Kyiv.

Peter moved around during the final years of his career, wanting to play the game he so loved for as long as possible, until his legs, in the end, forced him into retirement. Appearing also for Manchester City, Fulham and Hartlepool United, Peter finally hung up his boots in 1999, some 20 years after his first outing for Carlisle

United. But he wasn't out of the game for long – nor away from St. James' Park, either. After spending a period on the England coaching staff, Beardsley rejoined the club of his blood in 2001 and has become something of a Magpies living legend.

It was the *Sunday Sun*'s Brian McNally who once described Peter Beardsley as 'beguiling, bewildering, breathtaking and brilliant'. He could have added: scintillating, sparkling, stunning and simply superb. Every Newcastle United supporter would agree.

Beardsley in goalscoring acclaim after netting one of his 119 goals for the club.

5

CHAMPIONS LEAGUE BIG TIME

1997–98

The competing teams line up in the vast Olympiyskyi stadium before the Champions League contest between United and Dynamo Kyiv.

The introduction of the Champions League gave European football a whole new meaning. For years, a super-league of Europe's top clubs had been talked about and the evolution of the European Champions Club Cup – the European Cup – into the UEFA Champions League gave football an embryonic version of that super-league, in all but name. Gone was a competition purely for champions. Now the top-ranked clubs in each league qualified for a much wider competition, and the stronger UEFA members – principally Italy, Spain, Germany, France and England – were handed extra places. A UEFA coefficient was also introduced that meant success bred success.

The financial rewards now became huge as worldwide television coverage brought multi-million pound sponsorship. Regular participation in Champions League football now realised a massive increase in both turnover and profit to any successful club, even if a team failed to lift their domestic championship trophy. Those sides in the stronger leagues that finished second or third – and even fourth, as the super-league was extended – now qualified for the Champions League, something that was treated as a huge success in boardrooms around the nations of Europe. And in England, even winning the FA Cup or Football League Cup was seen as being distinctly second best to a place in the Champions League.

Newcastle United were well placed to capitalise on the prestigious blue-chip UEFA competition when it was unveiled. Runners-up to Manchester United in season 1995–96 – when they should have won the title crown – and second again the following season – despite a change in manager as Kevin Keegan sensationally quit – Newcastle found themselves one of the first Champions League non-champions. It was strange to enter the premier competition for so long reserved only for title winners, but Newcastle United didn't make the rules. Magpies boss, and a past winner of the competition, Kenny Dalglish was more than pleased to have 'a shot at this trophy for the first time in Newcastle United's history'.

As runners-up in the Premiership to Manchester United in the 1996–97 season for a second time, the Black 'n' Whites had to battle out a qualifying match to progress into the real competition. However, during the opening weeks of preparation for the 1997–98 campaign United's plans were severely rocked. Dalglish sold David Ginola, then Les Ferdinand, and, to make matters even worse, on the very same weekend that saw the popular Ferdinand head for White Hart Lane to join Tottenham, Alan Shearer was badly injured in an exhibition game with Chelsea at Goodison Park. He was to be out of action for almost six months. United, however, still had the enigmatic Tino Asprilla, but he was soon to join Shearer in the treatment room as well. Before the South American was sidelined, though, he made his mark in history.

Experienced campaigners in Europe, Croatia Zagreb stood between the Magpies and the competition proper. A dramatic tie unfolded that saw United pinch victory with a Temuri Ketsbaia strike at the very end of the 120 minutes of the deciding leg in a tension-filled Maksimir stadium in Zagreb. Influential midfielder Rob Lee remembered, 'It was very emotional because it meant so much to

everyone at the club to get into the Champions League.'

Newcastle were paired with some of the big guns of the Continent in Group C: Dynamo Kyiv, Eastern Europe's most consistent side, PSV Eindhoven, winners in 1988, and the formidable Barcelona, one of the biggest club sides in the world. In response to the draw, Dalglish said, 'We are in the most difficult of the six Champions League groups.'

The opening match staged at St. James' Park for United's historic first Champions League campaign was against Barcelona: and what a match it was. With an Asprilla-inspired Newcastle racing to a 3–0 lead, and eventually winning 3–2, a spectacular showpiece was played out. Alan Shearer, watching on, called United's effort 'an incredible performance', while his boss noted that 'people will respect Newcastle now'.

Newcastle held their own on the long trek to Kiev, but then an injury to Colombian Tino Asprilla made United's already limited options in attack even worse. Against the Dutch champions PSV, United went down in both games and suffered most up front with the loss of Shearer and Asprilla to injury and the sale of Ferdinand. Kenny Dalglish made the comment, 'We have never had a full-strength squad to choose from.' Newcastle needed their top players to compete at that level and injury and suspension robbed Dalglish of a first-choice team in every game. Stuart Pearce pointed out that but for injuries 'Newcastle United could have occupied the top spot and been looking forward to the quarter-final'. The former England defender added, 'I'm sure we would have qualified. I'm pretty sure that we had the firepower in our squad to go through.' Alas, that firepower was too often missing.

United's opening taste of the Champions League ended in something of a disappointment, and many fans pondered on what could have been with an injury-free side on the pitch. However, Kenny Dalglish remarked, 'I'm proud of the seven points we did get, given the problems that beset us from day one.'

Everyone wanted more, though. Players, officials and supporters eagerly looked forward to reaching the glamorous, rich pickings of Champions League action again quickly. It was the competition to be in; nothing could match it.

However, during the season, manager Kenny Dalglish also started to dismantle Kevin Keegan's Entertainers squad. On top of the departure of Ferdinand and Ginola, out went Asprilla, Peter Beardsley and Lee Clark. Their many replacements, including veterans Ian Rush and John Barnes, proved to be less than a match. Only in the longer term would a trio blossom: Gary Speed, Nobby Solano and Shay Given. At the end of the wheeling and dealing process, Newcastle's prospering status, as both a domestic and European giant, was set back five years. Essentially, the club had to start again from scratch in attempting to reach the Champions League. This time, however, they would have to do so with a new boss in charge, one with an enormous European pedigree: Dutchman Ruud Gullit.

Manager and soccer legend Kenny Dalglish, who guided Newcastle into the Champions League for the first time.

The final whistle has gone. John Beresford exchanges shirts and celebrates his two-goal haul in the Champions League clash in Kiev.

MATCHES 41 – 48

Tino Asprilla composes himself before a crucial spot-kick as Croatia Zagreb players debate the decision with the referee.

1997–98

Croatia, Zagreb	v. NK Croatia Zagreb	2–1, 2–2, Agg 4–3	UEFA Champions League, Q
Spain, Barcelona	v. FC Barcelona	3–2, 0–1, Group C	UEFA Champions League, Gp1
Ukraine, Kiev	v. Dynamo Kyiv	2–2, 2–0, Group C	UEFA Champions League, Gp1
Holland, Eindhoven	v. PSV	0–1, 0–2, Group C	UEFA Champions League, Gp1

Euro Facts & Figures

Most Goals
Alan Shearer, 30, 1996 to 2006
Craig Bellamy, 11, 2001 to 2005
Wyn Davies, 10, 1968 to 1970
Shola Ameobi, 10, 2000 to date

Hat-Trick Heroes
Rob Lee v. Royal Antwerp (UEFAC) 1994–95
Andy Cole v. Royal Antwerp (UEFAC) 1994–95
Tino Asprilla v. FC Barcelona (UCL) 1997–98
Alan Shearer v. Bayer 04 Leverkusen (UCL) 2002–03
Alan Shearer v. Hapoel Bnei Sakhnin (UEFAC) 2004–05

To the Dressing Room 1
United dismissals:
Craig Bellamy v. Internazionale 2002–03
Nicky Butt v. Hapoel Bnei Sakhnin 2004–05
Lee Bowyer v. SC Heerenveen 2004–05

Match 41

1997–98
Champions League, Qualifying Round 2: Newcastle United v. NK Croatia Zagreb
FIRST LEG Wednesday, 13 August 1997, St. James' Park

Croatia Zagreb

UNITED Given, Watson, Pistone, Albert (Howey), Pearce, Beresford, Lee, Batty, Ketsbaia, Tomasson (Gillespie), Asprilla. Subs not used: Hughes, Pinas, Crawford, Beardsley, Srníček.
Manager: Kenny Dalglish

ZAGREB Ladic, Saric (Tomas), Simic, Juric, Mladinic, Krznar, Maric (Mujcin), Jurcic, Prosinecki, Viduka, Cvitanovic (I). Subs not used: Ibrahimovic, Stefulj, Brlenic, Cvitanovic (M), Petrovic.
Manager: Marijan Vlak

REFEREE V. Krondl (Czech Republic)

RESULT Won 2–1 (1–0)

AGGREGATE 2–1

ATTENDANCE 34,465

SCORERS United: Beresford (22), (76); Zagreb: Cvitanovic (I) (52)

MATCH HIGHLIGHTS

United's first-ever venture in the Champions League, albeit in the shape of a qualifying match, was a tense and dramatic affair due to the fact that the prize of a place in the competition proper was huge. Without Shearer (injured) and Ferdinand (transferred), United were below strength but did have Tino Asprilla. However, it was full-back John Beresford who emerged as the unlikely hero of United's first-leg qualifying-round victory over Croatia Zagreb. The left-back scored twice in a close contest against a quick-passing Zagreb side who went home satisfied with an away goal. Asprilla began a brilliant one-touch move involving Rob Lee that saw Bez crash home the opener right in front of the posts. The popular Beresford's second – and crucial winner – was a touch fortunate, not to mention controversial. He leapt to volley in a loose ball after the Zagreb keeper had failed to gather under pressure from Asprilla. Hotly disputed by the Zagreb players, all protests for a foul on goalkeeper Ladic were to no avail, and the Czech referee allowed the goal to stand. It was a much-needed strike as the visitors had equalised through Igor Cvitanovic after half-time following a run by Maric, whose delightful through pass was good enough to create a chance for the Croatia striker. With the experienced Prosinecki and emerging Maric prominent, Zagreb showed more than enough to prove that they were going to be difficult to beat in the second leg. If United were going to advance to the glitzy new world of the Champions League, they would have to work hard for it.

MAN OF THE MATCH

John Beresford – in the right place at the right time.

| MATCH RATING | ● ● ● | | | | Charmed and anxious. |

STAR COMMENT

John Beresford: 'Zagreb made us fight all the way and were a bit unlucky to lose.'

EYEWITNESS:

Oliver Holt (*The Times*): 'United's first foray into the European Cup ended amid fierce controversy when a heavily disputed goal gave them a narrow victory.'

OPPONENT FILE

Winning the new Croatian national championship by a massive 21 points and having thrashed old rivals and recent warring enemies Partizan Belgrade to reach the qualifying phase, NK Croatia Zagreb were a talented side, packed with quality players. Formally known as Dinamo, many supporters resented the name change and still insist that the club be known as Dinamo Zagreb. Croatia's top side has a fervent support, both loyal and at times notorious. The team acted as a symbol of national identity during a period of long communist rule, but after facing United, they suffered a player drain, with most of their stars heading to various destinations in the top leagues of Europe. They lifted the Inter Cities Fairs Cup in 1967.

STAR VISITOR

Robert Prosinecki – At times a quite brilliant midfielder who developed as a star with Red Star Belgrade, Prosinecki quickly progressed to the Yugoslav national side as a youngster. Tall, blond and an effective playmaker, Prosinecki was soon the subject of a big move to Real Madrid, later moving on to Barcelona. The star of the Croatian national side as they became a world force, he returned to the Balkans to much acclaim in the summer of 1997 after a spell with Seville.

DID YOU KNOW

Croatia Zagreb's talented forward Silvio Maric impressed United boss Kenny Dalglish so much that he paid £3.58 million in February 1999 for his services. Maric only played thirty-one games for United, though, and scored a mere two goals.

Match 42

1997–98

Champions League, Qualifying Round 2: NK Croatia Zagreb v. Newcastle United
SECOND LEG Wednesday, 27 August 1997, Stadion Maksimir (Zagreb)

Croatia Zagreb

UNITED Given, Barton, Pistone, Albert, Pearce (Howey), Beresford (Gillespie), Batty, Watson, Lee, Tomasson (Ketsbaia), Asprilla. Subs not used: Elliott, Hughes, Crawford, Srníček.
Manager: Kenny Dalglish

ZAGREB Ladic, Maric, Juric, Mladinic, Prosinecki, Viduka (Petrovic), Mujcin, Simic (D), Saric (Simic J) (Tomas), Cvitanovic (I), Jurcic. Subs not used: Ibrahimovic, Stefulj, Brlenic, Cvitanovic (M).
Manager: Marijan Vlak

REFEREE U. Meier (Switzerland)

RESULT Drew 2–2 (1–0) after extra time
AGGREGATE Won 4–3
SENT OFF Zagreb: Juric (43)
ATTENDANCE 34,000

SCORERS United: Asprilla (44) (pen), Ketsbaia (120); Zagreb:

MATCH HIGHLIGHTS

With such a narrow first-leg lead the pressure was on United from the start of this truly breathtaking and compelling evening in Zagreb. Ahead against ten men, the Magpies needed a sensational winning goal in injury time of extra time to avoid a dreaded penalty shoot-out and qualify for the Champions League proper. Despite early pressure, it was the Tynesiders who opened the scoring. Tino Asprilla sent Jon Dahl Tomasson clean through, and as the Dane went round Ladic he was fouled by Juric bang in front of goal. Asprilla confidently stroked home the penalty just before the interval, and as further punishment, Juric was sent off. A 3–1 aggregate lead now looked comfortable. However, ten-men Zagreb fought back to take the match into extra time. With massive backing from the vociferous crowd, Simic reduced the deficit as he headed in unmarked at the far post from a free-kick. Then Newcastle were on their knees as Cvitanovic struck the equaliser in the dying minutes of normal time. David Batty lost the ball and the Croatian crashed home a dramatic leveller to make it 1–2 on the night and 3–3 on aggregate. With a penalty shoot-out looking inevitable, Tino Asprilla set up the dramatic winner for Temuri Ketsbaia with only 38 seconds remaining on the referee's watch. Batty intercepted a poor pass from defence by Zagreb, and the England midfielder made amends for his previous error, releasing the ball quickly to Asprilla. The Colombian swiftly found substitute Ketsbaia on the edge of

the box, and in a flash the ball was in the net. The noisy Maksimir crowd was stunned to silence, while the Black 'n' Whites contingent leapt around in ecstasy. Newcastle were in the Champions League for the first time.

MAN OF THE MATCH

Tino Asprilla – masterly performance.

MATCH RATING	● ● ● ● ●	Electrifying action.

STAR COMMENT

Temuri Ketsbaia: 'I've scored some important goals but never one as important as this.'

EYEWITNESS

Shaun Custis *(The Journal)*: 'Newcastle are set for a £10 million jackpot as they march into Europe's premier competition.'

TOUR STOP – ZAGREB

Capital of the new state of Croatia on the River Sava, Zagreb is rich in history, like most central European capitals. A university centre and manufacturing hub, Zagreb is a green city, too, full of parks and wonderful architecture. Zagreb has an old quarter to rival most, is considered to have some of the most beautifully preserved buildings and streets in the whole of Europe and boasts a party atmosphere around Tkalciceva Street. The most recognisable landmark in Zagreb is the twin spires of St. Mary's cathedral. (pop. 692,000.)

STADIA FILE – STADION MAKSIMIR

Also known as the Hask Gradanski stadium, NK Croatia's home is situated in the Maksimir district, adjacent to the park and zoo, and was built in 1912. It was formerly the home of the pre-war Hask club. Over the years, the stadium has been greatly improved, but it typified many in the old Eastern Bloc: a spacious, oval, concrete bowl with little cover. The Makismir has one main stand, a giant open cantilevered structure opposite this and a running track. It once housed 55,000, but when United visited the city the capacity was only 28,000. Since then, a £40 million refurbishment has taken place, and it is now the Croatian national stadium.

DID YOU KNOW

When substitute Temuri Ketsbaia scored that late dramatic goal in the 120th minute, it was his very first for United since joining the Magpies from AEK Athens.

121

Tour Stop

Zagreb – Croatia

NK Croatia Zagreb 1997–98

St. Mary's cathedral, an architectural gem surrounded by other historic and well-preserved streets which date back to medieval times.

The arena is set in Maksimir Park, one of the largest and most beautiful in Central Europe.

Colombian Tino Asprilla hits a penalty crisply past Ladic during the deciding leg in Croatia.

Geordie favourite Asprilla featured on the cover of United's match programme.

Kiev – Ukraine

Dynamo Kyiv 1997–98

Postcard from Kiev

Situated alongside the important Dnieper river, Kiev is the major urban centre of the former southern Soviet Union. The golden-domed Holy Dormition is pictured.

Postcard from Olimpiysky

The complex has often been packed with over 100,000 spectators, although presently the two-tiered bowl holds up to 83,000 fans.

Match Action

Despite the attention of four Kyiv defenders, John Barnes strikes the ball into the net at St. James' Park.

Memorabilia

UEFA's distinctive Champions League logo was prominent on everything connected to the competition, including match tickets.

Match 43

1997–98
Champions League: Newcastle United v. FC Barcelona (Spain)
GROUP C Wednesday, 17 September 1997, St. James' Park

Barcelona

UNITED Given, Barton, Watson, Albert, Beresford, Gillespie, Batty, Lee, Barnes (Ketsbaia), Asprilla, Tomasson (Peacock). Subs not used: Howey, Rush, Pinas, Hughes, Srníček.
Manager: Kenny Dalglish

BARCELONA Hesp, Reiziger, Celades, Nadal, Sergi, De la Pena, Figo, Enrique, Rivaldo, Anderson (Dugarry), Amuniki (Ciric). Subs not used: Busquets, Abelardo, Amor, Pizzi, Garcia.
Manager: Louis van Gaal

REFEREE P. Collina (Italy)

RESULT Won 3–2 (2–0)
POSITION IN GROUP 2nd/3 pts

ATTENDANCE 35,274

SCORERS United: Asprilla (22) (pen), (31), (49); Barcelona:

MATCH HIGHLIGHTS

Newcastle's debut in the Champions League proper marked one of the most spectacular occasions ever seen at St. James' Park. With a television audience of millions around the world watching, and the stadium bouncing with an excitement rarely matched, United stormed into a 3–0 lead, thanks to a brilliant Tino Asprilla hat-trick, which included two superb Keith Gillespie runs and two copybook Asprilla headers. It was an epic encounter, and for an hour Newcastle were magnificent. Then Barcelona almost, remarkably, saved the game as they took control and netted two late goals, but to begin with, Barca were outplayed as Asprilla took a grip on the contest. After Jon Dahl Tomasson had wasted two early openings, United took the lead when the Dane slotted a ball through for Asprilla to run onto before being felled by keeper Ruud Hesp. Tino stroked home the spot-kick. Eight minutes later, Gillespie roasted Sergi and his accurate cross saw Asprilla leap to bullet a near-post header into the net at the Gallowgate end. Newcastle were on fire and immediately after the interval scored a goal that was a repeat of the first. Gillespie had Sergi toiling as the Irishman's long run and cross tore Barca's defence apart. Asprilla jumped high again and the ball was in the net: 3–0 ahead against one of the world's leading clubs. The Toon Army were in heaven. However, Barcelona hit back as United tired. Dugarry came off the bench and along with Figo and Rivaldo, the Barca stars took hold of the match. Luis Enrique chested in Figo's cut-back 18 minutes from the end, then Rivaldo struck the bar, and David Batty cleared off the

line. United were struggling, and in the dying moments, Figo made it 3–2, hitting the ball through a forest of legs. Time ran out for Barcelona and United hung on. Justifiably, the Black 'n' Whites took much acclaim from the victory.

MAN OF THE MATCH

Tino Asprilla – dazzling style.

| MATCH RATING | • • • • • | Wonderful show. |

STAR COMMENT

Shay Given: 'It was a special night. Gilly played such a big part in Tino's goals, a lot of credit belongs to him.'

EYEWITNESS

Ian Murtagh (*The Journal*): 'This was the night dreamland transformed itself into glorious reality.'

OPPONENT FILE

Qualifying for the Champions League that year by finishing second to Real Madrid, their summer transfers demonstrated the scale of the Barcelona club: selling Ronaldo for £18 million then buying Rivaldo and Sonny Anderson for a combined £28 million. Undoubtedly one of the world's top five clubs, Barca is a Spanish institution, the standard-bearer of the Catalan region. Winners of eight European trophies, reaching thirteen finals altogether, the Barcelona giants are one of the richest and biggest supported clubs in the world, with over 100,000 season-ticket holders. After facing United, Barca lifted the La Liga title in both 1998 and 1999.

STAR VISITOR

Luis Figo – Full of trickery, with a vicious shot and the ability to make and score goals, the Portuguese playmaker Luis Figo had joined Barcelona from Sporting Lisbon in 1995 and was soon to be labelled one of the game's most celebrated forwards. Leader of Portugal's famed 'Golden Generation', Figo lifted the World Player of the Year award in 2001 before his record £37 million and highly controversial switch to Real Madrid. He graced both the European Championships and World Cup and won over 100 caps for his country.

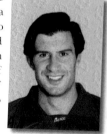

DID YOU KNOW

Referee for the night was Italy's Pierluigi Collina, he of the bulging eyes and balding head fame. He was in charge as the game was broadcast on television to an estimated audience of 200 million worldwide.

Match 44

1997–98
Champions League: Dynamo Kyiv (Ukraine) v. Newcastle United
GROUP C Wednesday, 1 October 1997, Olympiyskyi Stadium (Kiev)

Dynamo Kyiv

UNITED Given, Barton, Peacock, Albert, Beresford, Gillespie, Watson, Batty, Lee (Ketsbaia), Barnes, Asprilla (Tomasson). Subs not used: Hughes, Hamilton, Rush, Howey, Hislop. Manager: Kenny Dalglish

KYIV Shovkovsky, Luzhny (Bezhenar), Golovko, Vashchuk, Dmytrulin, Kossovsky, Shevchenko, Rebrov, Gusin, Khatskevitch (Radchenko), Belkevitch (Mikhailenko). Subs not used: Kernozenko, Samoilov, Shmatovalenko, Volosianko. Manager: Valery Lobanovsky

REFEREE P. Mikkelson (Denmark)

RESULT Drew 2–2 (0–2)

POSITION IN GROUP 2nd/4 pts

ATTENDANCE 98,000

SCORERS United: Beresford (79), (85); Kyiv: Rebrov (4),

MATCH HIGHLIGHTS

On a bitterly cold evening in Eastern Europe, and in front of the biggest-ever crowd to watch United apart from in cup finals, the Magpies were outplayed for almost an hour and found themselves two goals down inside the first thirty minutes. United started disastrously as Serguei Rebrov had the ball in Shay Given's net within the opening five minutes, striking home from close range. And on the half-hour Kyiv's other striking genius, Andriy Shevchenko, ghosted into the area and fired across Given and into the far corner of the United net. Newcastle needed a lifeline, and John Beresford gave the Black 'n' Whites the boost they needed with two unlikely strikes in the last eleven minutes. For the first, the ball broke on the edge of the box and Beresford let fly, his half-hit effort taking a deflection and the ball slipping through the keeper's legs. For the second, he had more luck with another wickedly deflected shot providing the equaliser and earning United a point. It was a hard fought draw, but it came with a price. Newcastle, already without Alan Shearer, now lost Tino Asprilla, carried off with a torn stomach muscle. He was to be missing for the majority of the remaining Champions League fixtures; his loss was a huge blow.

MAN OF THE MATCH

John Beresford – goals from the heavens.

MATCH RATING ● ● ● ☐ ☐   Opportune fight back.

STAR COMMENT

John Beresford: 'Considering we were 2–0 down and looking dead and buried, this has got to be one of our best-ever fight backs.'

EYEWITNESS

Paul Tully (*Black and White* magazine): 'As the Kiev clocks ticked towards midnight, Newcastle United needed a miracle. Two-nil down, United's hopes of any dividend were rapidly slipping away. But then the miracle came along.'

Attack-minded John Beresford.

TOUR STOP – KIEV

On United's first visit to Kiev, the country was just coming to terms with life after communism. The city was still very much a drab Soviet one, but the new capital was to dramatically change in the following years. On the major River Dnieper, a black market then reigned, and the few Newcastle supporters that had travelled found their western goods and cash were much in demand. The centre around Khreshchatik provided the visitors with an insight into life as it was behind the old Iron Curtain. (pop. 2,600,000.)

STADIA FILE – OLYMPIYSKYI

Formerly the Respublikansky Stadion or Krasny (Red) Stadion, the Olympiyskyi is a vast two-tiered concrete bowl constructed on stilts. The pitch is surrounded by the running track compulsory to Eastern-European stadiums. Situated in the heart of Ukraine's capital in a prime location, the Olympiyskyi has many pleasing features, despite its grey concrete mass, including its own metro station portico, Corinthian columns and palatial ticket booths. Prominent floodlights tower above the stadium, which was constructed in 1923. The arena was completely remodelled in 1941 only to be destroyed by the Nazis. Much altered afterwards, it was also upgraded for the 1980 Olympics, when it had a capacity of 101,164. The Olympiyskyi is actually the national stadium: Dynamo only use it for games that are likely to attract large crowds. Their smaller home ground is called Lobanovskyi Dynamo.

DID YOU KNOW

Dynamo's second goal from twenty-one-year-old whiz-kid Shevchenko occurred when United were reduced to ten men: Asprilla was off injured and Tomasson was still warming up on the touchline.

Match 45

1997–98

Champions League: PSV Eindhoven (Holland) v. Newcastle United
GROUP C Wednesday, 22 October 1997, Philips Stadion (Eindhoven)

PSV

UNITED Given, Barton (Albert), Howey, Peacock, Beresford (Ketsbaia), Gillespie, Watson, Batty, Lee, Tomasson, Rush.
Subs not used: Hughes, Brayson, Hamilton, Hislop, Barnes.
Manager: Kenny Dalglish

PSV Waterreus, Vampeta, Stam, Faber, Numan, Petrovic (Moller), Jonk, Cocu, Iwan (Stinga), De Bilde, Nilis (Bruggink).
Subs not used: van Ede, Temrukov, Claudio.
Manager: Dick Advocaat

REFEREE S. Braschi (Italy)

RESULT Lost 0–1 (0–1)

POSITION IN GROUP 2nd/4 pts

ATTENDANCE 29,200

SCORERS PSV: Jonk (38)

MATCH HIGHLIGHTS

Newcastle turned in a solid performance in Holland against PSV, but without star strikers Asprilla and Shearer were goal shy up front. They were disciplined and solid with Darren Peacock and Steve Howey in good form at the heart of United's defence against the talented duo of De Bilde and Nilis. But one lapse was enough to give PSV the points and send United to their first Champions League defeat. In the 38th minute, Dutch international Wim Jonk's volley found the net, going across Shay Given: it was a fine strike from 20 yards, after a neat chest down by De Bilde. United now had to attack but without any real threat up front from Ian Rush or Jon Dahl Tomasson, found chances few and far between. Those that did come fell to Keith Gillespie and Temuri Ketsbaia, but both players lacked the necessary finishing touch in front of goal. The Black 'n' Whites sorely missed Alan Shearer and Tino Asprilla in attack. Newcastle also had a let-off when Peacock handled inside the box, but the referee gave a free-kick outside the area, much to the annoyance of the home support inside the Philips Stadion. Even a draw would have given United a real chance of qualification for the next stage of the Champions League. As it was, United were still in with an opportunity to claim second position behind Kyiv.

MAN OF THE MATCH

Steve Howey – solid at the back.

| MATCH RATING | • | • | | | | Moderate encounter. |

STAR COMMENT

Kenny Dalglish: 'We lost a very competitive game in Holland. It was a good performance.'

EYEWITNESS

Paul Tully (*Black and White* magazine): 'On a bitterly cold night, thanks to the Philips heaters beneath the stand, we were able to watch a stone-cold Newcastle performance in relative warmth.'

TOUR STOP – EINDHOVEN

United's 1,100 supporters enjoyed their visit to the small town of Eindhoven, the centre of the giant Philips electronics empire that dominates almost everything in the area. A prosperous company town near the border with Belgium, Eindhoven largely revolves around two things: Philips and PSV. Typically Dutch, Eindhoven has a pleasant, if undramatic, town centre, the focal point being the De Markt square. (pop. 206,000.)

STADIA FILE – PHILIPS STADION

Centrally located within walking distance of the town centre, the Philips Stadion provides superb facilities for the club, supporters and local businesses. PSV have played on the site since 1913, but it was not until 1977 that the ground was transformed into one of the best small stadiums in Europe. In 1988, it was developed further and was again modified in 1999, after United's visit, with the reconstruction of huge new stands all with a striking white façade. With a capacity of 30,000 when United visited for the first time, the ground houses top-quality corporate and supporter lounges as well as, unusually, a Toys 'R' Us store.

DID YOU KNOW

The Philips Stadion gives supporters the rare opportunity of being kept warm and cosy on a cold evening, such as the one United experienced on their visit. Atttached to the underside of the roofs of the stand are rows of effective heaters that blast hot air onto the spectators beneath.

Match 46

1997–98
Champions League: Newcastle United v. PSV Eindhoven (Holland)
GROUP C Wednesday, 5 November 1997, St. James' Park

PSV

UNITED Given, Barton, Watson, Albert, Pistone, Beresford, Hamilton, Gillespie, Ketsbaia, Barnes, Tomasson. Subs not used: Hughes, Crawford, Peacock, Hislop.
Manager: Kenny Dalglish

PSV Waterreus, Vampeta, Stam, Faber, Numan, Petrovic, Jonk, Cocu, Iwan, Nilis, De Bilde. Subs not used: Bruggink, Moller, Claudio, Stinga, Temrukov, van Ede, Degryse.
Manager: Dick Advocaat

REFEREE G. Benko (Austria)

RESULT Lost 0–2 (0–1)

POSITION IN GROUP 3rd/4 pts

ATTENDANCE 35,214

SCORERS PSV: Nilis (32), De Bilde (91)

MATCH HIGHLIGHTS

Again, the absence of top-class strikers Shearer and Asprilla hit Newcastle hard and the Magpies found that PSV's quality pairing of Nilis and De Bilde up front was the difference between the sides. The Magpies were also forced to play without international midfielders David Batty and Rob Lee, both of whom were suspended. A slick-moving Dutch outfit always caused danger, and United never really got going as an attacking force. Just after the half-hour mark, Luc Nilis converted a slick exchange with his partner De Bilde on the edge of the box to open the scoring, the PSV striker casually rolling the ball past Given. United pressed for an equaliser yet rarely caused goalkeeper Waterreus too much trouble. With Newcastle going forward they were always open to a quick PSV break, and by the final whistle, the Magpies had been hit on the counter-attack. Just before the end, Nilis and De Bilde combined again, the latter gliding past Warren Barton and Shay Given to stroke the ball into an empty net from 12 yards. Newcastle did not pick up a single point against their Dutch rivals, the two most crucial games in the group. Many people felt that had United fielded a full strength side against PSV, results would have been different, and the Magpies would have gone through to the quarter-finals. However, the double defeat now meant qualification was almost impossible.

MAN OF THE MATCH

Steve Watson – gave it a go.

| MATCH RATING | • | • | | | | Sub-standard show. |

STAR COMMENT

Kenny Dalglish: 'I don't think the players could have given us any more than they did.'

EYEWITNESS

Alan Oliver (*Evening Chronicle*): 'The simple fact is, on the night, Newcastle United's patched-up team were not good enough. United were powder-puff up front.'

OPPONENT FILE

Vastly experienced in European football and winners of both the European Cup and UEFA Cup, PSV are backed by the Philips organisation and are one of the most affluent clubs in Holland. Rivalling both Ajax and Feyenoord as the country's top side, they were Dutch champions when they faced United and had developed a master squad under Dick Advocaat. PSV – Philips Sport Vereniging – reached prominence between 1986 and 1992, winning six titles in seven years. They have produced stars galore: from Gullit to Romario and from Ronaldo to van Nistelrooy.

STAR VISITOR

Jaap Stam – Tall at 6 ft 3 in. and strong at the back, Stam was at that time creating much attention and was soon to make a big move to Manchester United. A regular for the Dutch national side, he started his career with lesser clubs Kampen, Zwolle, Cambuur and Willem II before joining PSV. Alex Ferguson spent £10.75 million to take him to Old Trafford where he was an influential figure in the Reds' Treble-winning side of 1999. With over 50 caps for Holland, Stam later moved to Italy with Lazio and AC Milan.

DID YOU KNOW

Two youngsters in the PSV squad were to make a big impression in the years to come: Eidur Gudjohnsen and Boudewijn Zenden both became prominent international players in the Premiership.

Tour Stop

Eindhoven – Holland

PSV
1997–98

Near the border with Belgium, Eindhoven is a town dominated by the giant Philips electronics empire.

A well-equipped, modern venue, the stadium is within walking distance of the town centre.

Temuri Ketsbaia goes close in the first half of the contest in Eindhoven.

Match ticket from the Philips Stadion.

Barcelona – Spain

FC Barcelona 1997–98

Postcard from... Barcelona

The capital of Catalonia and one of Europe's greatest cities. Pictured is Plaça Reial, one of Barcelona's liveliest squares, situated off the famous La Rambla.

BARCELONA   PLAÇA REIAL

Postcard from... Estadi Camp Nou

Undoubtedly one of football's most breathtaking arenas. To the top right of the postcard is Barca's indoor centre and mini-estadi, while away supporters usually had to climb the concrete ramps in the foreground.

Match Action

A dramatic Champions League entry for United at St. James' Park; Tino Asprilla leaps to head into the Barcelona net.

Memorabilia

United's programme for the visit of Barca to Tyneside, perhaps the biggest night in United's history.

Newcastle United
F.C. Barcelona

Match 47

1997–98
Champions League: FC Barcelona (Spain) v. Newcastle United
GROUP C Wednesday, 26 November 1997, Estadi Camp Nou (Barcelona)

Barcelona

UNITED Hislop, Watson, Peacock (Pearce), Albert (Hughes), Pistone, Batty, Hamilton, Beresford, Barnes, Tomasson, Ketsbaia. Subs not used: Elliott (S), Crawford, Pinas, Srníček. Manager: Kenny Dalglish

BARCELONA Hesp, Ferrer, Abelardo, Guardiola (Amor), Couto, Anderson (Pizzi), Giovanni (Nadal), Rivaldo, Ciric, Celades, Reiziger. Subs not used: Busquets, Figo, Xavi, Mario.
Manager: Louis van Gaal

REFEREE M. Batta (France)

RESULT Lost 0–1 (0–1)
POSITION IN GROUP 3rd/4 pts

ATTENDANCE 26,000

STAR COMMENT

Shaka Hislop: 'You don't often get the chance to play in a stadium like that, but the empty stands didn't help the atmosphere.'

EYEWITNESS

Jeff Powell (*Daily Mail*): 'Newcastle's European adventures were swilled down the gutters of a rain-drenched Spanish night.'

TOUR STOP – BARCELONA

The chief port of Spain and the seat of the Catalans, Barcelona is the centre of a nation within a nation. A modern, cosmopolitan and vibrant city, it rivals Madrid in everything, not least football. While there are many historical monuments in the gothic old town, it is also famous for its modernist sights: Gaudí's famous masterpieces the *Sagrada Familia* and *Casa Batlló*. Described as a city that 'sizzles and excites', the tree-shaded La Rambla is busy day and night as is the Port Olimpic marina. (pop. 1,600,000.)

MATCH HIGHLIGHTS

It was supposed to be a sunshine-packed trip to one of the Meccas of football for the travelling 8,000-strong Toon Army. Victory at the Camp Nou was essential to keep Newcastle's Champions League dream alive, but on an evening when the heavens opened and the local public turned its back on the fixture, the match was a huge anti-climax. Newcastle's under-strength side, including 18-year-old debutant Aaron Hughes, who came on at half-time for the unwell Philippe Albert, battled gamely but were second best to the Spanish giants. In torrential rain, Brazilian Giovanni gave Barca victory with a brilliant running chip over Shaka Hislop after he had been sent free by Guardiola's long ball. Newcastle were always chasing the game with Barca perhaps playing within themselves, yet Jon Dahl Tomasson did hit the bar for United with a looping effort that deflected slightly off Couto. But Newcastle's attack was again lightweight and was never able to match the might of Barcelona, even if the Catalan club had by that time given up on a Champions League run and were concentrating all their efforts on chasing domestic trophies.

STADIA FILE – CAMP NOU

One of the most famous arenas in world football, the Camp Nou is also one of the biggest in Europe with a capacity of 98,600 although it has exceeded 120,000 on occasion. Its first stone was laid in 1954 and it opened three years later with subsequent revamps taking place down the years. A huge concrete bowl with three to four steep overhanging tiers at various points around the stadium, its pitch is eight metres below street level. With striking concentric rings of blue-and-red seating, the Camp Nou, however, has little in the way of spectator facilities – or cover from occasional downpours – unless in the impressive main stand. Adjacent is the Mini-Estadi, capable of holding nearly 20,000 spectators, as well as an indoor arena and ice palace. Also on the Barca estate is the club's training centre, office complex and first-class museum and visitor centre.

DID YOU KNOW

Bobby Robson was on the managerial staff of Barca when United faced them. He was at the time responsible for finding new talent. Off scouting, he missed the game at St. James' Park but was in the Camp Nou for the return meeting.

MAN OF THE MATCH

John Beresford – telling attacking forays.

MATCH RATING ● ● ☐ ☐ ☐   Damp squib.

Match 48

1997–98
Champions League: Newcastle United v. Dynamo Kyiv (Ukraine)
GROUP C Wednesday, 10 December 1997, St. James' Park

Dynamo Kyiv

UNITED Hislop, Watson, Peacock, Albert, Pearce, Pistone (Hughes), Batty, Lee, Barnes, Gillespie, Asprilla (Ketsbaia). Subs not used: Elliott (S), Hamilton, Tomasson, Rush, Given. Manager: Kenny Dalglish

KYIV Shovkovsky, Luzhny, Bezhenar, Dmitrulin, Kalitvintsev, Kossovsky, Shevchenko, Rebrov, Gusin, Mikhailenko (Venglinski), Volosianko (Radchenko). Subs not used: Kernozenko, Kardash, Belkevitch. Manager: Valery Lobanovsky

REFEREE H. Krug (Germany)

RESULT Won 2–0 (2–0)

ATTENDANCE 33,694

SCORERS United: Barnes (10), Pearce (21)

FINAL GROUP C TABLE

1	Dynamo Kyiv	11 pts
2	PSV	9 pts
3	Newcastle United	7 pts
4	Barcelona	5 pts

MATCH HIGHLIGHTS

Group C winners Dynamo Kyiv may have not been in top gear with their qualification assured, but Newcastle signed off their Champions League adventure with a deserved victory. And it was the United old guard of Stuart Pearce and John Barnes that ensured the Magpies ended their campaign in style. Barnes scored with a well-placed shot after ten minutes following David Batty's surging run past three players down the right flank. Barnes took the ball inside the box and clipped a perfectly placed 15-yard angled shot into the net. Eleven minutes later, Newcastle went 2–0 ahead when Stuart Pearce hit a characteristic twenty-five-yard free-kick that rocketed into the top left-hand corner of the net. Kyiv stepped up a gear after that and showed why they had been the best side in the group stage. Serguei Rebrov and Andriy Shevchenko became dangerous, causing Shaka Hislop several tense moments, the United keeper saving well on several occasions. However, Newcastle could also have found the net again. John Barnes narrowly missed a Keith Gillespie cross then scraped the post with a header from a corner, and Temuri Ketsbaia whipped in a free-kick that just missed the target. Newcastle wanted to go out in a satisfying manner and they did. To take four points from the group winners tells its own story.

MAN OF THE MATCH

David Batty – dominant performance.

| MATCH RATING | ● | ● | ● | | | A taste for more. |

STAR COMMENT

Kenny Dalglish: 'Playing in the Champions League has been a marvellous experience for everyone connected with the club. We have not disgraced the tournament in any way and if anything have added to the quality.'

EYEWITNESS

Christopher Davies (*Daily Telegraph*): 'Credit to Newcastle for a highly satisfying display, but Dynamo were a pale shadow of the side who romped through group C.'

OPPONENT FILE

The Ukrainian champions and a side that has dominated the country's football since the break from the Soviet Union in 1991, Dynamo recovered from near bankruptcy at one point. Boasting virtually an all-international squad, they were established originally as a police sports club and are now the most successful Eastern European club of the modern era. Twice winners of the Cup Winners Cup in 1975 and 1986 and regulars in UEFA competition, Dynamo are considered a national treasure and are therefore hugely supported, the envy of every other club in the country.

STAR VISITOR

Andriy Shevchencko – Although only 21 years old when he faced United, the young Ukrainian was to develop into one of the world's best strikers in the coming years. He had already impressed many – scoring a memorable hat-trick in the Camp Nou – and during the following season he caught the eye again, netting all three goals as Kyiv put out the holders Real Madrid. He was sold to AC Milan in 1999 for £16 million where he prospered further, becoming, arguably, the finest striker in Europe.

DID YOU KNOW

Newcastle almost made an extra £4.5 million profit from their opening adventure in the Champions League, with a £6 million jump in turnover as a result of increased match revenue.

'He has so many tricks up his sleeve it's unbelievable. I can't think I have seen a striker who can do so many things on the ball.'

Ian Rush

Tino Asprilla

Certain footballers relish the European stage. Give them a run-of-the-mill league affair at Bolton or a League Cup tie against Bradford City and they look decidedly not in the mood. But in the glamour of European football, a clash against the stars of Serie A, La Liga, *Eredivisie* or Le Championnat, they seem to come alive.

Tino Asprilla was one of those players. The different style of football on the Continent appeared to suit the Colombian. In fifty-one domestic matches he managed only nine goals. Yet in UEFA Cup and Champions League football Tino grabbed the same number in only 11 outings. European football was made for Tino. The Colombian himself admitted, 'I find it easier to play against the Continental teams – I am better suited to that.' He said of

the Premiership style of football, 'The pace of the game here is much more frantic than it was in Italy.'

Asprilla was far from a success on Tyneside, especially considering he was an expensive £7.5 million purchase and, at the time, United's record signing. He divided the Toon Army's opinion, but the enigmatic South American gave Newcastle fans some great moments to savour, nonetheless.

It was Kevin Keegan who splashed out that substantial sum of money for the 26-year-old Asprilla in February 1996. The deal was reported at the time as being an 'on/off' affair due to a suspected knee injury, which, in the end, was never a problem for Tino. Keegan took a risk on the unpredictable striker, even though he was known to be at times taxing and someone who seemed to court controversy with an eventful career off the field. But he could also be explosive on the pitch, possessing the ability to win matches on his own with on-the-ball trickery, pace and potent shooting. He also had the gift of being able to baffle defenders who simply never knew what he would do next. In many ways, he fitted the Newcastle United profile perfectly.

Keegan remarked upon his unique style at the time of his signing: 'Tino does things I have never seen a player do before.' He added, 'He is a one-off, a big-stage performer.' His colleagues were soon impressed, too. Les Ferdinand said, 'We've got one hell of a player.' United's centre-forward added, 'He's an exciting player. He will create chances for others and he will score goals himself.'

Asprilla spent almost four years with Parma in Serie A and progressed to two European Cup Winners Cup finals as well as a UEFA Cup final in the space of three years with the Italian outfit. He knew all about the European style of football. He was, seemingly, more at home

Tino Asprilla

with football based on studied build-ups and tactics, rather than the cut and thrust of the Premiership or FA Cup.

He was instrumental in Parma's run to the Cup Winners Cup final against Royal Antwerp at Wembley in 1993, but due to injury sat out the match on the bench and had to frustratingly watch his teammates triumph 3–1. He then took part in the Super Cup: an all-Italian affair that saw Parma topple AC Milan. Another Cup Winners Cup final followed, but Arsenal won the trophy in Copenhagen, while the following season Tino was a winner again as Juventus were beaten in the final of the UEFA Cup in 1995. Asprilla will always be remembered by Parma fans for his stunning hat-trick in the semi-final clash with Bayer Leverkusen. He was an idol at the Ennio Tardini stadium, scoring 25 goals for the Italian club in 84 appearances.

A regular for Colombia, first capped when he was 22 years old and playing in the World Cup finals of 1990, 1994 and 1998, Tino was known in South America as *El Pulpo* (the Octopus) while he was dubbed the 'Black Arrow', the 'Black Gazelle' and *La Pantera Negra* (the Black Panther) in Italy. On Tyneside the Geordies called him, simply, Tino.

Without doubt, Asprilla's finest moment in a black-and-white shirt took place in 1997 against Barcelona on the club's Champions League debut. The *Daily Mail*'s John Richardson wrote, 'Faustino Asprilla's tantalising skills and power-packed hat-trick had just been witnessed by a world-wide audience of more than 200 million.' He was sensational that night. His former manager Kevin Keegan – by this time having moved on – was one of the millions watching on television. He said, 'He was completely unstoppable.' Colleague Shay Given later recalled, 'He was absolutely phenomenal. That's the sort of talent he had.' Asprilla, the man of the moment, said after the game, 'It was a great

TINO ASPRILLA: FACT FILE

Position: Striker

Born: Tulua Valle (Colombia), November 1969

Joined United from: Parma, February 1996, £7.5 million

Left for: Parma, January 1998, £6 million

Other major clubs: Deportivo Cali (Colombia), Atletico Nacional (Colombia), Palmeiras (Brazil), Fluminense (Brazil), Atlante (Mexico), Universidad (Chile), Estudiantes (Argentina)

Full international: Colombia (47 caps, 1990 to 2001)

United career, senior games: 63 app., 18 goals

United Euro record: 11 app., 9 goals

Did you know: Among Tino's many off-the-field antics that grabbed the headlines were several acts of gun toting in Colombia, once firing shots into the air at a hotel disco.

night. I felt so good going into the match. I'm in perfect condition and feel that, at last, the team is playing to my strengths.'

Asprilla was a key figure in United's Champions League opener, with Alan Shearer out of the reckoning and Les Ferdinand now controversially in Tottenham colours. Before the match, Tino said, 'Now I have my chance to shine.' He did that all right. Creating and scoring an early spot-kick, he then twice soared high above the Barca defence to head two brilliant Keith Gillespie crosses past keeper Ruud Hesp. And he very nearly made it a four-goal haul when another header flew narrowly past the wrong side of the post.

His performances against Metz and Ferencváros in UEFA Cup action a year before were almost as good, yet, of course, not as headline grabbing. He scored five goals in that cup run as Newcastle stormed into the quarter-finals. In the first round against Halmstads, as

Tino Asprilla

Kevin Keegan went for all-out attack, adopting a 3-4-3 formation against the Swedish part timers, Asprilla netted a gem of a goal. A deep cross by David Ginola was met full on by Tino's right boot as he jumped to strike a flying volley that gave keeper Bjorn Nordberg no chance.

In the next round, United faced much stronger opposition in Ferencváros. Paul Tully wrote in his club magazine column, 'Tino Asprilla truly began to show what he was capable of.' The rubbery-legged South American was brilliant in the return leg on Tyneside as United turned it on, winning 4–0. Tino scored two of the goals and secured a penalty as well. For one of those strikes, Tino collected the ball from a Darren Peacock knock-down and whipped a shot past Szeiler.

With Shearer and Ferdinand injured much depended on Asprilla in the tie with FC Metz. He was the Black 'n' Whites one-man forward line but was able to rise to the challenge. After the first leg, Tully again wrote, 'Tino came up trumps with a flash of brilliance that had even the hostile French fans applauding.' The Colombian picked up a ball on the left, slipped between two defenders then went outside the advancing keeper Letizi, who caught Tino's ankle to concede the penalty. He was outstanding in the second leg on Tyneside, too: when United needed something special the likeable South American stepped forward.

With the Magpies struggling to break down a solid Metz side and only ten minutes to go in the match, he headed past Biancarelli from close range to break the deadlock and had the crowd roaring their approval of his flamboyant celebration: first doing his customary somersault then draping his shirt around a hoisted corner flag. Within two minutes the chants were again 'Tino . . . Tino' as he ran through the French team's defence before chipping a delightful shot into the net to give United a deserved 2–0

advantage. After scoring that second goal he then tried an extravagant back-heel – in an attempt to please the crowd that loved the entertainment value that he brought to Gallowgate – only to spend the next eight weeks on the sidelines with a torn hamstring as a result.

A frustrating and expensive enigma to many, Asprilla could also, without any doubt, be a match winner. Ian Rush, his teammate at St. James' Park and one of Europe's top forwards himself, once said, 'He has so many tricks up his sleeve, it's unbelievable. I don't think I have seen a striker who can do so many things on the ball.'

From the drug-blighted town of Tulua in the west of Colombia, Tino was always an entertainer. He once said, 'People come to see special things – people come to see a show. Most players can do most things but only a few can do special things. I like to think I can do some of the special things.' He may have looked leggy, loping and lazy in his appearance on the field, but defenders knew he could destroy them with a few seconds of magic.

Unorthodox in style, with deceptive yet explosive pace over a few yards, he could call on an array of extravagant ball skills, frightening ability and sublime balance, and was able to turn defenders in tight situations. His unbelievable talent was first glimpsed during his debut outing for the Magpies against Middlesbrough in February 1996 when he made a short cameo appearance. Brought on as substitute for a brief run-out following his flight to the North East, Tino announced his arrival to the Toon Army by producing a mesmerising back flick and turn that completely bamboozled Boro's Steve Vickers before chipping the ball delightfully for Steve Watson to score.

While Kevin Keegan saw Asprilla's flair and crowd appeal as a special addition to his Entertainers squad, new manager Kenny Dalglish

Tino Asprilla

Tino Asprilla in a race for the ball with Monaco's
Franck Dumas, who later joined the Magpies.

Tino Asprilla

never quite warmed to his erratic style. Dalglish did acknowledge his ability saying, 'Our fans love Tino, and I'm not surprised he really excites them. He excites me too – some of the things he does are just unbelievable. He's just different to anyone I have ever seen.' But Dalglish also said that 'working with Tino was quite an experience'. He added, 'I couldn't always make him understand what I wanted him to do. But half the time he didn't understand what he wanted to do.'

It was no surprise that soon after Tino's fanfare against Barcelona, he fell out of favour. A lack of impact on the Premiership and more off-the-field headlines saw an exit from Gallowgate. Dalglish said, 'He's wonderfully, exceptionally talented.' But United's boss became exasperated with him: 'I lost a little bit of respect for him in his last few days here because of his behaviour.' Dalglish added, 'In the final analysis, if players don't want to play for you then you can't have them here. Tino was disrespectful towards the other players and in the end they lost respect for him.'

The *Evening Chronicle*'s Alan Oliver summed up his time in the North East:

> Enigmatic Colombian Tino Asprilla had driven his managers round the bend. On the field he is breathtakingly instinctive but languid and almost awkward in his movements at times. On occasions it appears the ball is attached to his feet by elastic. At other times he loses possession and puts his side in deep trouble.

Managers, colleagues, fans and the media were totally split over Tino's worth to Newcastle United. Peter Beardsley said, 'He is definitely a very special player. His critics say he gives the ball away too easily, and, yes, there are times when that can be frustrating for the team. But his good points far outweigh the not so good.' Peter added, 'At his best he is absolutely devastating, because he is so unpredictable. He doesn't conform at all.'

He moved back to Parma at the beginning of 1998 and afterwards appeared for a number of clubs in Brazil, Mexico, Colombia, Chile and Argentina. He also had a short spell in the Emirates and even nearly turned out for Darlington in 2002 in a bizarre on/off transfer. Now back in South America, his popularity on Tyneside was shown when he returned to St. James' Park as a match guest in 2005: hero for the day. As he took a bow on the pitch, he was given a huge reception. Everyone will remember Tino with a smile.

Following his magnificent hat-trick against Barcelona, Tino even received the congratulations of Italian referee Perluigi Collina.

6

BELGRADE & SOFIA TO ROME & MUNICH

1998–99, 1999–2000, 2001–02

Alan Shearer turns in celebration after scoring against FC Zurich in Switzerland.

When Ruud Gullit – double European Cup winner with Ajax and AC Milan – took over the reins at St. James' Park in August 1998, the Dutch ace inherited a disjointed squad of players. He needed time to stamp his own impression on United as the Magpies tried to recapture the effervescent footballing days of the Keegan era.

Gullit brought in new faces and discarded many of Kenny Dalglish's acquisitions. Out went the likes of Stephane Guivarc'h, John Barnes, Ian Rush and Stuart Pearce and in came emerging youngster Kieron Dyer – a £6 million purchase from Ipswich Town – big Duncan Ferguson, and defenders Alain Goma and Marcelino.

Amidst Gullit's remodelling of the Magpies, the club made its debut in the European Cup Winners Cup competition in the last year of its existence. Having slipped in league standing, United gained entry into the traditional tournament for domestic cup victors by reaching the 1998 FA Cup final. Although Newcastle lost to the Gunners in the Wembley final, Arsenal had won the Double and would be joining the Champions League draw, paving the way for the Black 'n' Whites to be entered as England's representative in the Cup Winners Cup competition.

The first-round draw was not kind to Gullit and the Geordies, though. United faced a tough contest against Partizan Belgrade.

The Yugoslav side were recognised as being one of the strongest sides in the old Eastern Bloc. However, an added problem for United to contend with was that in 1998 the warring factions in the Balkans had brought NATO to the brink of engaging in the Kosovo War. As a result, an intimidating atmosphere welcomed the Magpies to Belgrade, and both the players and the few supporters who did travel felt decidedly uneasy. Newcastle went out to what was referred to as a 'dodgy' penalty decision and had to focus on domestic issues for the remainder of the season.

Although Gullit's team did show some signs that his recovery plan was working – reaching another FA Cup final and qualifying for the UEFA Cup in the process – Newcastle went through what is for them a regular period of turmoil. Just before starting on the 1999–2000 European campaign, United's Dutch manager caused a huge commotion with his relationship with several of United's leading professionals, notably Rob Lee and Alan Shearer. The unpleasantness led to United slipping to bottom of the Premiership, a spectacular fall-out between Gullit and the club, and the manager's eventual departure back to Holland.

In September 1999, in stepped local hero Bobby Robson, who had been a Newcastle supporter for all of his 66 years, to replace the departed Gullit. Robson possessed a vast knowledge of the game and of European football in particular. From his early days in management with Ipswich Town – when he won the UEFA Cup in 1981 – to successful periods on the Continent with PSV, Sporting Lisbon and at the Camp Nou with Barcelona, not to mention eight years as boss of the England set-up, he gave Newcastle United much-needed experience. With this wealth of footballing acumen behind him, he set about rebuilding a broken super-club that had lost its way under Dalglish and then Gullit.

Having taken charge in the opening weeks of the season, Robson's task was to keep the Magpies in the Premiership then re-establish Newcastle as one of football's modern elite and, in the process, put the Black 'n' Whites back in European contention in the Champions League. The former England supremo was a popular choice, and he soon made an impact, transforming the Tynesiders into a team that was approaching the standard achieved by the much-acclaimed Entertainers a few years previously.

One of his first tasks was to guide United on their return to European action in the 1999–2000 season. Newcastle flew to Bulgaria to face CSKA Sofia, and Robson's knowledge of the Continental football scene was to have great bearing on their opening victories over both Sofia and their next opponents, FC Zurich.

The tie to follow was a European highlight: a double encounter with AS Roma, at the time leaders of Serie A and on their way to the Italian title. Newcastle supporters descended in their droves on Rome, one of the great cities of Europe and the ultimate destination of any Grand Tour. They saw the sights: the Pantheon, Trevi Fountain, the Vatican, Colosseum and the enchanting Spanish Steps. The Toon Army also explored the impressive Stadio Olimpico complex. It typified what playing in Europe is all about: fabulous attractions, big games, striking arenas and an inspiring atmosphere. The Black 'n' Whites were unlucky against Roma, only losing by a solitary goal – a dubious spot-kick converted by Francesco Totti.

Robson ensured that the Geordies were making a steady recovery but they missed out on European action in 2000–01. United also failed to qualify for season 2001–02, which was a big blow. They did, however, take part in the Intertoto Cup qualifying competition. It was much maligned but a UEFA tournament, nonetheless, and a back-door route into the UEFA Cup. Fans should still have been on holiday, sunning themselves around the Mediterranean, while the players prepared hard for the new season but, instead, both focused on the Intertoto Cup matches in July.

Locals in Sofia parade their scarves and banners and give a less than friendly welcome to the Geordies on their trip to Bulgaria in 1999.

Newcastle were too good for CSKA. United's experienced threesome, Gary Speed (left), Nobby Solano (centre) and Alan Shearer (right), get ready for a free-kick.

Robson had now fashioned a new Magpie side centred around senior professionals Alan Shearer at centre-forward, Gary Speed in midfield and Shay Given between the posts. Peruvian Nobby Solano added quality in midfield, too, while Robson purchased forwards Laurent Robert and Craig Bellamy for a combined £16 million. The new team should have been good enough to make the UEFA Cup through the Intertoto, but after an easy romp against Lokeren and another comfortable passage against Munich 1860, United faced an unknown side from Troyes in France. In one of the Intertoto qualifying finals United found themselves 1–4 down to an impressive and quick-moving French side. Yet, in an extraordinary evening, they levelled the game at 4–4 and almost grabbed an injury-time winner. But away goals gave Troyes victory.

Despite their exit on that dramatic night at St. James' Park, manager Bobby Robson's first-stage recovery plan was almost complete. Newcastle were back ready to compete with the best in the Premiership and were soon to resume battle in the Champions League. In the process, Newcastle United would reach the pinnacle of achievement in their first 100 games in European competition.

Sir Bobby Robson revitalised the Magpies and eventually led United into the second group stage of the Champions League.

MATCHES 49 – 62

Joy in Sofia as Temuri Ketsbaia (No. 14) receives congratulations after scoring United's second goal.

1998–99

Yugoslavia, Belgrade	v. FK Partizan	2–1, 0–1, Agg 2–2	European Cup Winners Cup, R1

1999–2000

Bulgaria, Sofia	v. CSKA Sofia	2–0, 2–2, Agg 4–2	UEFA Cup, R1
Switzerland, Zurich	v. FC Zurich	2–1, 3–1, Agg 5–2	UEFA Cup, R2
Italy, Rome	v. AS Roma	0–1, 0–0, Agg 0–1	UEFA Cup, R3

2001–02

Belgium, Lokeren	v. Sporting Lokeren SNW	4–0, 1–0, Agg 5–0	Intertoto Cup, R3
Germany, Munich	v. TSV 1860 Munich	3–2, 3–1, Agg 6–3	Intertoto Cup, SF
France, Troyes	v. Troyes-Aube Champagne	0–0, 4–4, Agg 4–4	Intertoto Cup, Final

Euro Facts & Figures

Countries Opposed
6 times: Holland, France, Spain
5 times: Portugal
4 times: Italy

To the Dressing Room 2
Opponent dismissals:
Lido Vieri (Internazionale), Abas Suan (Hapoel Bnei Sakhnin), Energy Murambadoro (Hapoel Bnei Sakhnin), Goran Juric (NK Croatia Zagreb), Alen Mrtlecki (Sporting Lokeren), Sanel Jahic (NK Zeljeznicar), Miguel Moya (RCD Mallorca), Grigoris Georgatos (Olympiacos CFP), Thanassis Kostoulas (Olympiacos CFP).
Note: The two Olympiacos players were dismissed within 31 minutes of each other in the same match in Piraeus.

Clubs Faced
5 matches: Sporting Clube
4 matches: FC Barcelona, PSV, Feyenoord, Dynamo Kyiv, Internazionale, FK Partizan

Match 49

1998–99

European Cup Winners Cup, Round 1: Newcastle United v. FK Partizan (Yugoslavia)
FIRST LEG Thursday, 17 September 1998, St. James' Park

Partizan Belgrade

UNITED Given, Watson, Dabizas, Charvet, Pearce, Lee, Speed, Glass, Andersson (Solano), Ketsbaia, Shearer. Subs not used: Albert, Gillespie, Guivarc'h, Pistone, Barton, Perez. Manager: Ruud Gullit

PARTIZAN Damjanac, Krstajic, Rasovic, Savic, Trobok, Stojanoski, Ilic (S), Ivic (Pazin), Tomic, Obradovic, Bjekovic (Stojisavljevic). Subs not used: Ilic (R), Duljaj, Gerasimovski, Tesovic, Svetlicic. Manager: Ljubisa Tumbakovic

REFEREE D. Jol (Holland)

RESULT Won 2–1 (1–0)
AGGREGATE 2–1

ATTENDANCE 26,599

SCORERS United: Shearer (12), Dabizas (71); Partizan: Rasovic (69) (pen)

MATCH HIGHLIGHTS

United's first taste of the European Cup Winners Cup paired the Magpies with Partizan Belgrade, in what was perhaps the worst draw the Magpies could have received. Apart from facing a typically solid Yugoslav side, a war was also simmering in the Balkans at the time. With new manager Ruud Gullit at the helm, United had lots of possession but found it difficult to break down a stubborn Partizan defence. The visitors, on the other hand, rarely troubled Shay Given in United's goal. Alan Shearer put the Magpies ahead with a curling shot early into the game, following a move between Rob Lee and Stuart Pearce that handed United's No. 9 the chance just inside the box. Partizan battled into the game, and they received a break when a sloppy Laurent Charvet foul on Bjekovic gave the visitors a penalty, although television replays suggested that the offence was outside the box. Up stepped Rasovic to send Shay Given the wrong way, and the game stood at 1–1 with Partizan having claimed a crucial away goal. New signing Nobby Solano arrived from the bench and twice went close with pin-pointed shots, while Gary Speed missed a clear opening. Newcastle needed a late Nikos Dabizas looping header to give them a narrow advantage in the first leg, the Greek centre-half getting on target after Stephen Glass sent in a hanging cross two minutes after the controversial spot-kick.

MAN OF THE MATCH

Nobby Solano – impressed on his home debut.

MATCH RATING	●	●	●		

Evenly matched.

STAR COMMENT

Nikos Dabizas: 'Everyone was trying to do their best to impress the new manager, but we didn't play particularly well.'

EYEWITNESS

John Richardson (*Daily Mail*): 'Ruud Gullit's unfinished business was left on a knife-edge as Partizan Belgrade stole a precious away goal.'

OPPONENT FILE

One of the superior teams in the Cup Winners Cup, Partizan were top of the Yugoslav table with a young side. Regular champions around that time and one of the Balkans' strongest and most traditional clubs, Partizan were formed as an army side. Constant competitors in the UEFA Cup, they were especially powerful during the communist years when they reached the European Cup final in 1966. The club, though, had recently been rocked by their country's break-up, war and a UN imposed embargo, resulting in financial struggle for the team and a constant exodus of their star players.

STAR VISITOR

Sasa Ilic – Developing into one of the mainstays of the Partizan midfield, Sasa Ilic rose through the ranks at the Belgrade club. He was team captain at an early age and, with his powerful play, was instrumental in Partizan gaining three title victories. Ilic was the player that made Partizan tick, technically accomplished and a regular for Yugoslavia and, afterwards, Serbia. Several top European sides wanted him but for years he remained loyal to Partizan.

DID YOU KNOW

United faced a hot reception in Belgrade for the return leg. Within six months the UK was to all intents and purposes at war with Yugoslavia, and NATO planes were bombing Belgrade as part of Operation Allied Force.

Match 50

1998–99

European Cup Winners Cup, Round 1: FK Partizan (Yugoslavia) v. Newcastle United
SECOND LEG Thursday, 1 October 1998, Stadionu Partizan (Belgrade)

Partizan Belgrade

UNITED Given, Griffin (Albert), Dabizas, Charvet, Pearce, Solano, Speed, Batty, Glass, Ketsbaia, Shearer. Subs not used: Gillespie, Georgiadis, Howey, Barton, Harper, Perez. Manager: Ruud Gullit

PARTIZAN Damjanac, Savic, Stojanoski, Rasovic, Krstajic (Stojisavljevic), Trobok, Ivic, Ilic (S), Tomic, Bjekovic (Tesovic), Kezman (Pazin). Subs not used: Ljubanovic, Duljaj, Gerasimovski, Vukovic. Manager: Ljubisa Tumbakovic

REFEREE M. Diaz Vega (Spain)

RESULT Lost 0–1 (0–0)

AGGREGATE Drew 2–2, lost on away goals

ATTENDANCE 24,000

SCORERS Partizan: Rasovic (53) (pen)

MATCH HIGHLIGHTS

Newcastle's 50th game in Europe took place in a hostile atmosphere in Belgrade, United's trip to Yugoslavia being just prior to the Kosovo crisis. The Magpies had to cope with an at times scary environment in and around the stadium, as well as an onslaught by the home side intent on claiming goals to qualify for the next round. For long periods United defended well, with Nikos Dabizas, Laurent Charvet and Stuart Pearce in particular holding firm against Partizan's bright forwards Bjekovic and Mateja Kezman, who was to face United in future years in both European and Premiership fixtures. But eight minutes after the half-time break, Newcastle fell to another debatable penalty kick when David Batty was judged to have hauled down Ivic. It was a decision hotly disputed by the United camp. Vuk Rasovic's second spot-kick against United was clinical and enough to eliminate the Tyneside Black 'n' Whites. Newcastle had chances to score and also had their own penalty appeal turned down when Shearer was flattened but were only awarded a free-kick outside the box. The best Geordie opportunity fell to Temuri Ketsbaia, who burst through and went for goal on his own, instead of passing to the unmarked Shearer.

England midfielder David Batty.

MAN OF THE MATCH

Alan Shearer – led by example.

MATCH RATING ● ● ☐ ☐ ☐ Intimidating struggle.

STAR COMMENT

Ruud Gullit: 'I think we were very unfortunate – it was a little bit of a dodgy penalty.'

EYEWITNESS

Colin Young (*The Sun*): 'The goal sparked off incredible scenes among the *Grobari*, the home fans known as the Gravediggers.'

TOUR STOP – BELGRADE

Capital of Yugoslavia and then Serbia, Belgrade is beautifully situated on the Danube and Sava rivers. A largely modern city of Eastern-European taste, Belgrade had suffered much damage under German occupation and was about to suffer a modern barrage that again destroyed much of the city. Yet it still retained an old heart around the fortress, which overlooks the Sava, and the Bohemian quarter of Skadarlija. (pop. 1,100,000.)

STADIA FILE – STADIONU PARTIZAN

Also known as the Stadionu JNA (*Jugoslovenska Narodna Armia*/Yugoslav People's Army), Partizan's first match at the ground was in 1949, although the arena was revamped soon afterwards. Home of international matches until 1963, it is situated in parkland and close to the giant and much more modern stadium of their rivals, Crvena Zvezda. A characteristic Eastern-European bowl, Partizan had ambitious plans to redevelop the arena in the years after United's visit. With a capacity of 55,000, it was in much need of refurbishment. Located on one side of the stadium is a museum dedicated to former socialist leader Marshal Tito.

DID YOU KNOW

United faced a side also famed for their black-and-white striped shirts: the Partizan stadium was packed with black-and-white banners and flags – as well as flares and fireworks galore.

Tour Stop

Belgrade – Yugoslavia

(1)

(2)

FK Partizan
1998–99

1. Postcard from Belgrade

A city with a mix of communist-style modernism and treasured architectural gems hidden amongst the concrete. The mighty Danube and Sava rivers provide a pleasing contrast.

2. Postcard from Stadion Partizan

Partizan's ground, also known as the JNA Stadium, was typical of many in the old Eastern Bloc. It has only recently turned into a western-style football venue.

3. Match Action

Gary Speed controls the ball and shoots towards goal, but keeper Damjanac stopped this effort.

4. Memorabilia

A media-pass for United's visit to Belgrade in the club's first and only European Cup Winners Cup tie.

(4)

FUDBALSKI KLUB
PARTIZAN
··
FOOTBALL CLUB
NEWCASTLE UNITED
STADION „PARTIZAN"
1. OKTOBAR 1998.

PRESS **2**

(3)

Sofia – Bulgaria

CSKA Sofia
1999–2000

One of the finest cities in Europe and full of many grand cathedrals and churches, including the Alexander Nevsky capped by gold domes.

Situated in parkland, Sofia's bowl provides little comfort, high-level views or protection from the elements. It is, though, a stadium that creates a terrific atmosphere.

Alan Shearer's equalising goal at Gallowgate against CSKA.

The language barrier that faced the travelling Geordie fans in Sofia is evident on the match programme from the first leg.

Match 51

1999–2000
UEFA Cup, Round 1: CSKA Sofia (Bulgaria) v. Newcastle United
FIRST LEG Thursday, 16 September 1999, Stadion Bulgarska Armia (Sofia)

CSKA Sofia

UNITED Harper, Barton, Goma, Dabizas, Domi, Solano (Hamilton), Speed, Lee, Dyer, Shearer, Ferguson (Ketsbaia). Subs not used: Robinson, Beharall, McClen, Hughes, Karelse.
Manager: Bobby Robson

SOFIA Lukic, Kremenliev (Ivanov G), Mrkic, Trentchev (Litera), Velikov, Petkov, Sharac, Tchoumakov, Mantchev, Hristov (Ivanov D), Berbatov. Subs not used: Iraylo, Ivanov (I), Kovacevic, Paskov, Antonov.
Manager: Dimitar Penev

REFEREE J. Rocca (Spain)

RESULT Won 2–0 (0–0)

AGGREGATE 2–0

ATTENDANCE 20,260

MATCH HIGHLIGHTS

With Newcastle United struggling in the Premiership, they needed a boost from European action. Under the guidance of their experienced and astute new boss, Bobby Robson, they received a lift in the unlikely setting of Sofia, claiming a well-earned away victory. In the first period, the Magpies were disciplined in a daunting atmosphere, although CSKA did go agonisingly close to opening the scoring when they rattled the crossbar with one effort. Newcastle soon quietened the passionate Bulgarian crowd, and two second-half goals brought the Magpies a well-earned away victory. Nobby Solano's delightful free-kick, following a foul on Kieron Dyer, found the net with precision and pace to put United ahead, Shearer stepping over the dead ball, and the Peruvian curling the ball over the wall and past keeper Lukic. Dyer continued to tear holes in the Sofia defence and a run from deep saw the midfielder release the ball to Shearer, who set up Temuri Ketsbaia. The Georgian side stepped two challenges before firing past Lukic to give United a watertight 2–0 advantage. CSKA never got into the game, with the immense Rob Lee and Gary Speed dominating the midfield for United. The only downside for Bobby Robson was an injury to striker Duncan Ferguson.

MAN OF THE MATCH

Kieron Dyer – a free role to cause havoc.

| MATCH RATING | • | • | • | | | Heartening triumph.

STAR COMMENT

Alan Shearer: 'To come back with a clean sheet having scored twice ourselves was very satisfying.'

EYEWITNESS

Paul Tully (Newcastle United match-day programme): 'A reunion of mutual respect between the great Bulgarian international Hristo Stoichkov and Bobby Robson preceded a comfortable victory for United, despite the best efforts of the juvenile CSKA fans to make it otherwise.'

TOUR STOP – SOFIA

One of the oldest cities in Europe, the beautiful Sofia is overlooked by the Vitosha Mountains and is the Continent's second-highest capital after Madrid. Once colonised by the Romans – with the spas left over to prove it – it is a stately city with broad boulevards and large parks. The landmark Alexander Nevsky cathedral with its gold dome is one of the largest in the Balkans. At the time of United's visit, Sofia was in the throes of discarding communism. (pop. 1,100,000.)

STADIA FILE – STADION BULGARSKA ARMIA

Previously known as the Stadion Narodna Armia (People's Army Stadium), the Stadion Bulgarska Armia is, like the majority of football arenas in the Balkans, a concrete bowl. At the time of United's visit it was in poor shape and in need of investment. Compact and tree lined, as well as incorporating an athletics track and bright red seating spelling out the club's name, it was opened in 1957 and featured one stand with a cantilevered roof. The capacity was reduced from 35,000 to 25,000 during the '90s. The ground is situated in the south east of the capital, in parkland next to the much bigger national stadium, Vasilij Levski.

DID YOU KNOW

The victory in Sofia was only United's fourth away victory in European competition at the time, following wins over Újpesti, Dundee United and Royal Antwerp.

Match 52

1999–2000
UEFA Cup, Round 1: Newcastle United v. CSKA Sofia (Bulgaria)
SECOND LEG Thursday, 30 September 1999, St. James' Park

CSKA Sofia

UNITED Harper, Barton, Marcelino, Goma, Domi, Dabizas, Lee (McClen), Speed, Solano, Maric (Robinson), Shearer (Glass). Subs not used: Pistone, Hughes, Charvet, Karelse. Manager: Bobby Robson

SOFIA Lukic, Kremenliev, Mrkic, Velikov, Tomovski, Litera (Deyanov), Antonov, Ivanov (D) (Simeonov), Kiosev, Berbatov, Bukarev (Hristov). Subs not used: Kutchoukov, Ivanov (G), Paskov, Trentev. Manager: Dimitar Penev

REFEREE L. Huyghe (Belgium)

RESULT Drew 2–2 (1–1)
AGGREGATE Won 4–2

ATTENDANCE 36,228

SCORERS United: Shearer (36), Robinson (88); Sofia: Litera (29), Simeonov (90)

MATCH HIGHLIGHTS

It should have been a comfortable stroll for United, already 2–0 up from the first leg, but their over-confidence gave Sofia the opportunity to make an impact on the game and the second leg proved to be far more difficult than it merited. Sofia battled away and rode their luck to carve out a draw on their visit to Tyneside. The 90 minutes of football should have resulted in a United victory with the Magpies creating enough chances to demolish the Bulgarians. Although CSKA had a lot of possession, they created little – only three opportunities in total – while United were always the more potent up front. On the half-hour, the visitors shocked the Gallowgate crowd by taking the lead through Litera's vicious 30-yard pile-driver. But Newcastle stepped up a gear and Alan Shearer quickly equalised, steering home Didier Domi's low cross from close range. The Magpies had sufficient opportunities to comfortably win the fixture, including a Silvio Maric shot that crashed against the post and a marvellous Gary Speed volley that was ruled offside. And when sub Paul Robinson converted a low Stephen Glass cross two minutes from time the game should have been over. However, Simeonov met a cross in injury time to net the equaliser and leave the visitors satisfied with a 2–2 draw. The Magpies, though, had progressed into the second round.

MAN OF THE MATCH

Gary Speed – energetic in midfield.

| MATCH RATING | ● | ● | ● | | |

Indifferent display.

STAR COMMENT

Bobby Robson: 'The objective was to get through and we've done that. We deserved to win it.'

EYEWITNESS

Nicholas Spencer (*Daily Telegraph*): 'Once Alan Shearer restored the two-goal advantage from the first leg, they were never in any danger of slipping up against modest opponents.'

OPPONENT FILE

For many years Sofia were the unrivalled kings of Bulgarian football. The team has been known as CSKA since 1964 when they merged with the Red Banner club. Sofia are well practised in European campaigns and in their time have knocked out the likes of Ajax and Liverpool from the European Cup. With a good UEFA pedigree, they reached European semi-finals in 1967, 1982 and 1989. Like most Eastern Bloc clubs, though, their power base was weakened after the fall of communism in 1991, having been backed and funded by the army up until that point.

STAR VISITOR

Dimitar Berbatov – When he played against the Magpies, Berbatov was an emerging teenage striker. A rising star, he was first capped by Bulgaria as an 18 year old and soon made a big impression on the European scene, so much so that Bayer Leverkusen signed him in January 2001. Since then, Berbatov has become an experienced Bundesliga striker and is approaching 200 games and 100 goals for Bayer. A towering figure up front, he has pace and a deft touch. He also appeared in the 2002 Champions League final.

DID YOU KNOW

In United's previous home fixture – Bobby Robson's first in charge of United at St. James' Park – the Magpies defeated Sheffield Wednesday 8–0 with Shearer netting five goals.

Match 53

1999–2000
UEFA Cup, Round 2: FC Zurich (Switzerland) v. Newcastle United
FIRST LEG Thursday, 21 October 1999, Stadion Letzigrund (Zurich)

Zurich

UNITED Harper, Barton, Hughes, Dabizas, Domi, Solano (McClen), Lee, Speed, Dyer (Serrant), Maric (Robinson), Shearer. Subs not used: Pistone, Kerr, Marcelino, Given. Manager: Bobby Robson

ZURICH Pascolo, Castillo, Stocklasa, Djordjevic, Kebe (Del Signori), Chassot (Douglas), Sant'Anna, Eydelie, Kavelashvili, Bartlett, Frick (Akale). Subs not used: Trombini, Gianni, Malacarne, Andreoli, Mauro. Manager: Raimondo Ponte

REFEREE G. Jacek (Poland)

RESULT Won 2–1 (0–0)
AGGREGATE 2–1

ATTENDANCE 9,600

SCORERS United: Maric (50), Shearer (60); Zurich: Castillo (68)

MATCH HIGHLIGHTS

A lively encounter in Switzerland saw the Black 'n' Whites pave the way for their progress into round three with another away victory. A goalless first half saw a few close things at both ends, but most of the real action occurred after the interval. In the 50th minute, the Magpies took the lead. Alan Shearer flicked on a long ball that Silvio Maric raced onto, the Croatian having some luck with a rebound-cum-mistake from Kebe before producing a deft chip past keeper Pascolo. Ten minutes later, an Aaron Hughes shot looked to be a goal all the way until Pascolo made a brilliant flying stop, pushing the ball onto the crossbar. Shearer, though, picked up the loose ball and lashed it into the net to give United a comfortable 2–0 advantage. Newcastle were cruising but switched off in the final period and allowed the Swiss side to grab a goal back. Castillo went past Carl Serrant and thundered a right-foot shot past Steve Harper. That goal spurred on the home side in the final minutes. Bartlett then struck the bar, and in a final push, FC Zurich almost secured an equaliser. Newcastle held on, though, and achieved a rare victory on their travels.

MAN OF THE MATCH
Nobby Solano – accomplished on the ball.

MATCH RATING	●	●	●		

Commendable win.

STAR COMMENT
Bobby Robson: 'I was not very happy at all in those last 20 minutes. At times we were ripped apart.'

EYEWITNESS
Ian Murtagh (*The Journal*): 'Newcastle never looked assured at the back and truly only clicked into gear during brief spells either side of half-time.'

TOUR STOP – ZURICH
The largest city in Switzerland, Zurich is situated on the banks of the Limmat and Zürichsee, with the Alps providing a dramatic backdrop. Mainly German speaking, the city is an important centre of Swiss industry, commerce and, in particular, banking. It also has a strong tourist industry centred around the fine older districts of the city. The picturesque winding streets of the Altstadt is a lively quarter, while Zurich is noted as an affluent and trendy city: one that knows how to enjoy itself. (pop. 344,000.)

STADIA FILE – STADION LETZIGRUND
Built in 1925, the Stadion Letzigrund was adopted by the city council a decade later. FC Zurich's distinctive arena was upgraded in 1958 to a quirky design, with intriguing angular stands giving a peculiar but pleasing aspect. With a capacity of 23,500, the ground is also used by the Zurich Athletics Club and stages top meetings, including Grand Prix events. The stadium is situated in a built-up, urban area of Zurich.

DID YOU KNOW
Croatian Silvio Maric, after almost nine months on Tyneside, scored his first goal for United on his 20th appearance.

Match 54

1999–2000
UEFA Cup Round 2: Newcastle United v. FC Zurich (Switzerland)
SECOND LEG Thursday, 4 November 1999, St. James' Park

Zurich

UNITED Harper, Barton, Marcelino, Dabizas, Domi, Lee (McClen), Solano, Speed, Maric (Glass), Shearer, Ferguson (Robinson). Subs not used: Charvet, Hughes, Pistone, Karelse.
Manager: Bobby Robson

ZURICH Pascolo, Gianni (Castillo), Eydelie, Kebe (Frick), Sant'Anna, Bartlett (Chassot), Jamarauli, Stocklasa, Quentin, Djordjevic, Kavelashvili. Subs not used: Trombini, Kanga, Andreoli, Douglas.
Manager: Raimondo Ponte

REFEREE D. Messina (Italy)

RESULT Won 3–1 (1–1)
AGGREGATE Won 5–2

ATTENDANCE 34,502

SCORERS United: Maric (33), Ferguson (58), Speed (61). Zurich: Jamarauli (16)

MATCH HIGHLIGHTS

To begin with, Newcastle United made hard work of the return leg with FC Zurich and an early goal from the Swiss side shocked the home crowd. A Jamarauli cross worried Steve Harper and as United's keeper hesitated, in nipped Bartlett to distract the keeper, the ball ending in the net. That shook United into action, and, in the end, Newcastle coasted into round three of the UEFA Cup. Silvio Maric netted the equaliser following up on Alan Shearer's thundering free-kick that hit the crossbar. The visitors were then rocked by two goals in three minutes after half-time. Duncan Ferguson – back after a long lay-off – finished off a move that was set up by Nobby Solano and Gary Speed. The Peruvian was sent clear by Speed, challenged the keeper in a race for the ball and when it ran loose Ferguson stroked it into the open net. Almost immediately from the restart, Newcastle were back threatening the Zurich goal. A corner resulted from the United pressure, and Gary Speed powered home a downward header from the six-yard line to give the Black 'n' Whites a third goal. Newcastle were now in total control, and by the end the Magpies could have scored four or five. It was a comprehensive victory, and the Magpies now looked forward to a meeting with Serie A title contenders Roma.

MAN OF THE MATCH

Duncan Ferguson – an awkward customer.

MATCH RATING	●	●			

Routine victory by the end.

STAR COMMENT

Gary Speed: 'We gave away a bad goal in the first half, but got back in pretty sharpish and in the second half looked quite comfortable winners.'

EYEWITNESS

Damian Spellman (Press Association): 'Sir Bobby Robson was furious when Newcastle returned from Zurich having allowed their hosts a lifeline, and things got worse when the visitors levelled the aggregate score. But two goals inside three minutes assured victory for the Magpies.'

OPPONENT FILE

Fighting to challenge Grasshoppers and FC Basel as Switzerland's top club, FC Zurich have rarely managed to break the stranglehold of their rivals on domestic competitions. Possessing a small but loyal following, the club suffers from a constant supporter drain to the Bundesliga, most notably to Munich. They did have a good spell during the late '50s and '60s and they reached the European Cup semi-final at one point. With another good side, they again reached that stage of the competition in 1977.

STAR VISITOR

Shaun Bartlett – Spotted by Zurich's noted manager and ex-star-player Raimondo Ponte when in South Africa, Bartlett joined the Swiss club in 1998 and was a great success at the Letzigrund. A quick player with a footballing brain, Bartlett plays up front and is capped by South Africa. He was a regular scorer for FC Zurich but was to move to the Premiership in the 2000–01 season when he joined Charlton Athletic for a £2 million fee. Bartlett was born in Cape Town.

DID YOU KNOW

Duncan Ferguson's goal was his first in 341 days of injury heartache, having not scored since his United debut.

Tour Stop

Zurich – Switzerland

FC Zurich
1999–2000

With the Alps as a scenic backdrop, Zurich is a fabulous city. Trendy and affluent, it is situated picturesquely on Zürichsee.

With a design of angled stands which surround the playing surface, FC Zurich's home is distinctive and unusual.

Gary Speed peels away after his near-post header ends up in the Zurich net.

Match ticket from the Letzigrund.

Rome – Italy

AS Roma
1999–2000

The ultimate destination on any Grand Tour. Featured on this postcard are Fontana della Barcaccia and the Spanish Steps (top middle), Piazza Navona (bottom left), the Pantheon (bottom middle) and the Colosseum (bottom right).

An aerial view of the Olimpico complex, now a multi-purpose leisure site located next to the older Foro Mussolini with a grand obelisk, tree-lined walkway and fountain.

Roma's Brazilian defender Aldair blocks Alan Shearer in a race for the ball at the Stadio Olimpico.

Match ticket from the Toon Army's visit to Rome.

Match 55

1999–2000
UEFA Cup, Round 3: AS Roma (Italy) v. Newcastle United
FIRST LEG Thursday, 25 November 1999, Stadio Olimpico (Rome)

Roma

UNITED Harper, Barton, Pistone, Charvet, Dabizas, Hughes, Lee, Speed, Solano, Ketsbaia (Robinson), Shearer. Subs not used: Karelse, Caldwell (S), McClen, Serrant, Glass, Maric. Manager: Bobby Robson

ROMA Antonioli, Rinaldi, Aldair, Zago, Cafu, Assuncao, Candela, Di Francesco, Totti, Montella, Delvecchio. Subs not used: Lupatelli, Zanetti, Bartelt, Alenitchev, Tommasi, Gurenko, Fabio Jnr. Manager: Fabio Capello

REFEREE C. Colombo (France)

RESULT Lost 0–1 (0–0)

AGGREGATE 0–1

ATTENDANCE 45,655

SCORERS Roma: Totti (51) (pen)

MATCH HIGHLIGHTS

With a patched-up team due to injury call-offs, United matched the soon-to-be champions of Serie A all the way and only fell to a contentious penalty kick shortly after the interval. The Magpies gave a gritty first-half performance in the famous Stadio Olimpico, focused on defence – Italian style. The back four of Warren Barton, Laurent Charvet, Nikos Dabizas and Alessandro Pistone – back on his home soil – were determined and held Roma's star forwards, while playmaker Totti was doggedly foiled by Aaron Hughes, who played in a man-marking role. The decisive moment in the match – and, as it happened, the tie – came in the 51st minute and revolved round a controversial refereeing decision by the French official. Delvecchio went to ground after a challenge with Charvet, just inside the box, but television replays suggested United's defender hadn't touched the Roma forward. However, the referee was fooled by the theatrical dive and up stepped Totti to stroke the spot-kick into the net just past Steve Harper, who almost produced a brilliant save. Roma, lifted by their goal, almost made it two when Totti hit the woodwork but then could have been down to ten men when the same player should have been ordered off the field for foul play. In attack, United offered little with Alan Shearer ploughing a lone furrow up front with little support from midfield and receiving something of a battering from the Italian defence. On the night, United went so close to what would have been a marvellous 0–0 draw. Still, all looked forward to an intriguing second leg on Tyneside.

MAN OF THE MATCH

Warren Barton – first-rate in defence.

MATCH RATING	●	●			

Battling performance.

STAR COMMENT

Alan Shearer: 'We man-marked certain players to great effect, gave a very composed and disciplined team performance and deserved to come away with a no-score result.'

EYEWITNESS

Tim Rich (*The Journal*): 'It was time to be desperately proud of Newcastle. A lone-goal defeat keeps the return leg at St. James' Park very much alive.'

The assured Warren Barton

TOUR STOP – ROME

Perhaps the most enchanting city in Europe, with an unrivalled 3,000-year heritage, Rome is situated on the River Tiber and includes the independent state, the Vatican City. With such a rich heritage, United's fans had a lot of sightseeing to pack into their short break. Rome is a city full of grand piazzas, narrow cobbled medieval streets and numerous cafés, bars and restaurants. Built on seven hills, Rome's historical legacy can be seen all over the city from the Pantheon to St Peter's Basilica and from the Trevi fountain to the Colosseum and Forum. (pop. 2,600,000.)

STADIA FILE – STADIO OLIMPICO

Positioned in a tremendous setting, nestling at the foot of Monte Mario and next to the Tiber, the Stadio Olimpico is part of a vast sports complex completed in 1953 as the new home of both Roma and Lazio. Revamped for the 1990 World Cup, with a capacity now of just over 80,000, its symmetrical translucent roof was a major addition to the aesthetically pleasing bowl. Surrounded by cypress trees and now shops, pizzerias, bars and restaurants, it is close to an older sports complex, which comprises the Foro Mussolini, Stadio der Marmi and Cipressi Stadium. The grand entrance to the centre was built by the Fascists and still stands today. A regular venue for Italy's international fixtures, although, due to the athletics track, the crowd is some way from the action.

DID YOU KNOW

Somewhat controversially, Marcelino dropped out of the match considering he was not fit enough to take on the likes of Totti due to a recurrence of a thigh strain. He was replaced by Laurent Charvet, who was already struggling with a blistered foot.

Match 56

1999–2000
UEFA Cup, Round 3: Newcastle United v. AS Roma (Italy)
SECOND LEG Thursday, 9 December 1999, St. James' Park

Roma

UNITED Harper, Charvet, Dumas (Hughes), Dabizas, Pistone, Solano, Lee, Speed, Dyer (Ferguson), Ketsbaia (Glass), Shearer. Subs not used: Given, Barton, Maric, McClen. Manager: Bobby Robson

ROMA Antonioli, Zago, Aldair, Mangone, Cafu, Assuncao, Tommasi, Candela, Delvecchio, Totti, Montella (Di Francesco). Subs not used: Lupatelli, Alenitchev, Tomic, Gurenko, Rinaldi, Choutos. Manager: Fabio Capello

REFEREE H. Strampe (Germany)

RESULT Drew 0–0 (0–0)

AGGREGATE Lost 0–1

ATTENDANCE 35,739

SCORERS none

MATCH HIGHLIGHTS

The leaders of Serie A came to Tyneside intent on holding on to their slender one-goal advantage and put up an ever so typical Italian defensive wall in front of the Magpies. With Brazilians Aldair and Cafu prominent, they repelled all that the Black 'n' Whites could throw at them in a game of very few chances. The best opportunity fell to Temuri Ketsbaia after Rob Lee's marvellous run had taken him past a series of tackles to set up the chance. With only the keeper, Antonioli, to beat, the shaven-headed Georgian struck the ball against the keeper's legs and the chance was spurned. A partially fit Duncan Ferguson entered the action to give Alan Shearer support, and his introduction gave United more impetus, but Roma's rearguard rarely gave a clear opening, although a header from Nikos Dabizas and a Shearer free-kick both went close. As the referee's watch ticked on, Roma became a threat on the counter-attack with Delvecchio and Totti both having efforts that almost sealed the game for the visitors. It had been an absorbing contest: not thrilling or action-packed but a game for the purist, and after 180 minutes of football, only a dubious penalty separated the two sides. United, though, were out of the UEFA Cup.

MAN OF THE MATCH
Robert Lee – accomplished display.

STAR COMMENT
Kieron Dyer: 'We can take great heart. They were top of Serie A, and they're not there for no reason. But we were as good as them over two legs.'

EYEWITNESS
Michael Walker (*The Guardian*): 'Try as Newcastle United did, excitingly and intelligently, they could not break down the Brazil-dominated Roma back-line.'

OPPONENT FILE
Managed by master boss Fabio Capello, Roma were on their way to the *Scudetto* that year, a rare triumph in a country dominated by Juventus and the two Milan giants. For most of the '90s, Roma were also second best to city rivals Lazio, but Capello's remodelled side brought much-needed and much-heralded success. Regulars in European action, they reached the European Cup final in 1984, as well as the last stage of both the Inter Cities Fairs Cup and UEFA Cup. The team is nicknamed the *Giallorossi* (the red and yellows) in Rome.

STAR VISITOR

Francesco Totti – The jewel in Roma's crown, and at the time only 23 years old, Totti was the 'Golden Boy' of Italian football. Tall and elegant, he was a midfielder or striker who could turn a game on his own, and he had already become a regular in the Italian national squad. A genius on the ball, Totti could stroke a match-winning pass or hit a shot that could equally win the game. He joined Roma as a youngster, making his debut when he was 16 years old.

DID YOU KNOW
Franck Dumas suffered a fractured right elbow in the 25th minute and had to be replaced by Aaron Hughes.

Match 57

2001–02

Intertoto Cup, Round 3: Sporting Lokeren SNW (Belgium) v. Newcastle United
FIRST LEG Saturday, 14 July 2001, Daknamstadion (Lokeren)

Lokeren

UNITED Given, Barton, Dabizas, Hughes (Caldwell S), Elliott, Solano, Bassedas (McClen), Speed, Quinn, Bellamy, Ameobi (LuaLua). Subs not used: Harper, Green, Gavilan, Bernard. Manager: Bobby Robson

LOKEREN Zitka, Helgason, Mrzlecki (Zundi), Katana, van Dender, De Beule, Gretarsson, Seyso, Vidarsson, Vonasek (Vodomossi), Kimoto. Subs not used: Davenovic, van Hoey, Muzinga, Moerenhout, De Geest. Manager: Paul Put

REFEREE E. Bernsten (Norway)

RESULT Won 4–0 (3–0)

AGGREGATE 4–0

ATTENDANCE 2,425

SCORERS United: Quinn (14), Ameobi (24), (40), LuaLua (86)

MATCH HIGHLIGHTS

United returned to European action when they entered UEFA's recently introduced pre-season Intertoto Cup tournament, which offered the reward of qualification for the UEFA Cup. While most supporters, and no doubt some players, would have rather still been on a Mediterranean beach, the prize was highly important. United strolled through their opening game in the mini-tournament. The team looked fresh and set off at a high tempo with the Belgians simply unable to cope with the huge gulf in class – even without facing the likes of Alan Shearer and Kieron Dyer. Nineteen-year-old Shola Ameobi made his mark on the game with two fine goals after the unlikely Wayne Quinn had opened the scoring. Christian Bassedas had set up new signing Craig Bellamy and his pull-back from the goal line had found Quinn, who put United 1–0 up. Bellamy was again instrumental in the second goal, Ameobi's first. The former Coventry striker drilled through a ball for the tall United youngster to round Zitka and stroke the ball into the net. Ameobi was soon back on target, putting United 3–0 ahead before half-time. A marvellous six-man move was rounded off with a cool finish. After the interval, Newcastle stepped down a gear and went into cruise control, using the game as more of a pre-season workout. But they still found enough to register a fourth goal, and what a corker it was. Lomana LuaLua's finale was spectacular, a sensational scissor-kick four minutes from time. It could have easily been

more than 4–0, but Lokeren keeper Zitka produced a string of good stops to ensure his side were not humiliated.

MAN OF THE MATCH

Craig Bellamy – brilliant start for United.

| MATCH RATING | ● | ● | ● | | | A class apart.

STAR COMMENT

Bobby Robson: 'We were missing six players but we explained to those who played how important this game was.'

EYEWITNESS

Jason Mellor (*The Journal*): 'A comprehensive victory against opponents no stronger than a Belgian Brentford.'

TOUR STOP – LOKEREN

A small town between the giant cities of Antwerp and Brussels near to Ghent, Lokeren is located on the important River Durme in the Waasland district of East Flanders. A fertile region, it is a principal local town and features several historic buildings including a fine Town Hall and several Flemish Renaissance houses. (pop. 37,000.)

STADIA FILE – DAKNAMSTADION

With a capacity of 18,000 at the time, the Daknam stadium is a neat, compact arena originally constructed in 1956 and upgraded twice since – in 1974 and more recently between 2000 and 2004. When Newcastle visited, the crowd of only 2,425 created little atmosphere. It was the lowest attendance for a United European match and one of the smallest on record for any senior fixture.

DID YOU KNOW

Craig Bellamy made his debut for United against the Belgians following his £6.5 million transfer from Coventry City. The 22 year old sported silver boots for the occasion.

Match 58

2001–02

Intertoto Cup, Round 3: Newcastle United v. Sporting Lokeren SNW (Belgium)
SECOND LEG Saturday, 21 July 2001, St. James' Park

Lokeren

UNITED Given, Barton, Dabizas, Hughes, Elliott, Solano, Bassedas (McClen), Speed, Quinn (Bernard), Bellamy (LuaLua), Ameobi. Subs not used: Griffin, Harper, Caldwell (S), Gavilan.
Manager: Bobby Robson

LOKEREN Dabanovic, Helgason (Mrzlecki), Soley, Katana, van Dender, Zoundi (Bangoura), Gretarsson, Vidarsson, El Bodmossi, Kimoto (Muzinga), De Beule. Subs not used: Zitka, De Geest.
Manager: Paul Put

REFEREE E. Steinborn (Germany)

RESULT Won 1–0 (0–0)

AGGREGATE Won 5–0

SENT OFF Mrzlecki (81)

ATTENDANCE 29,021

SCORERS United: Bellamy (60)

MATCH HIGHLIGHTS

Expectations were high in anticipation of another walkover against Lokeren in the second leg at St. James' Park, but the Belgian visitors were determined this time not to cave in to United's forward threat. Lokeren showed a firm defence and were robust at times in their method of keeping the Magpies at bay, so much so that they had defender Mrzlecki ordered off for over-zealous tackling in the second half. United had to work for their victory but were, of course, in no danger at all, having secured a four-goal advantage from their trip to Belgium. Craig Bellamy again showed he was going to be a potent acquisition for the Black 'n' Whites and on his home debut netted the only goal of the game, picking off Nobby Solano's downward header to drive past keeper Dabanovic. Lokeren's substitute Mrzlecki, who had been the main culprit of some crude tackles, was deservedly sent off in the 81st minute for one too many rough challenges and Newcastle strolled into the next round of the competition, favourites to qualify for the UEFA Cup from their Intertoto pool.

MAN OF THE MATCH

Aaron Hughes – cool and assured.

MATCH RATING ● □ □ □ □   Low-key encounter.

STAR COMMENT

Bobby Robson: 'Lokeren came here for the second leg to defend and get a respectable score line.'

EYEWITNESS

Simon Rushworth (*The Journal*): 'This largely unspectacular fixture soon settled into a pattern of midfield movements, uncommitted challenges and stout defence.'

OPPONENT FILE – SPORTING LOKEREN

United's opponents had been reformed as late as 1999 following a merger between local sides KSC and St. Niklaas Waasland, after an earlier association between the Standard and Racing clubs. Having a best-ever season in 1980–81 when they finished as runners-up in Belgium, they reached the quarter-final of the UEFA Cup the following year. Way behind Anderlecht and Club Brugge in the pecking order of Belgian football, Lokeren had already played four games in the Intertoto Cup before facing the Magpies.

STAR VISITOR

Okitankoyi Kimoto – One of several players on the Lokeren staff from Africa, Kimoto hailed from Zaire while other teammates were born in the Ivory Coast, Congo, Guinea and Cameroon. Nicknamed 'Papy', he was fast and well built, a striker who had scored in Lokeren's previous Intertoto Cup victories over Toftir and Zaglebie Lubin.

DID YOU KNOW

Lokeren had played five games before meeting Newcastle – four of them competitive – while the Magpies had barely had time to unpack their suitcases after their summer break.

Tour Stop

Lokeren – Belgium

1

Sporting Lokeren SNW 2001–02

A small arena in a rural setting in central Belgium, Lokeren's Daknamstadion.

Lomano LuaLua came off the bench in the second leg against Lokeren and dazzled the Belgians.

United's first taste of the Intertoto Cup. Match-day programme featuring Shola Ameobi together with a ticket from the trip to Belgium.

NEWCASTLE UNITED

OFFICIAL MATCHDAY PROGRAMME
2001/02 SEASON • INTERTOTO CUP SPECIAL • £1.00

SPORTING LOKEREN
SATURDAY 21st JULY 2001
ST. JAMES' PARK • KICK-OFF 7.00PM
3RD ROUND   2ND LEG

INTERTOTO CUP

ntl: adidas

3

SP. Lokeren SNW Sportstadion
14/07/2001 20:00 Intertoto
STAANPLAATS / PLACE DEBOUT

4017

SP. Lokeren SNW
Newcastle

Tribune 3   Blok-Bloc   STAANPLAATS
Ingang-Entree   **VAK6**   922
V6   PLACE DEBOUT

Jupiler   THUIS
Basisprijs
GARAGE VAN WINKEL M. n.v.   BEF 600.00
Mercedes Benz Lokeren   EUR 14.87

2

Munich – Germany

TSV 1860 Munich 2001–02

1 Postcard from... Munich

Marienplatz at the heart of the Bavarian capital. Frauenkirche cathedral with its distinctive onion domes is to the left and Neues Rathaus (town hall) is to the right.

2 Postcard from... Olympiastadion

One of Europe's most spectacular sporting venues with vast transparent canopies and situated in landscaped parkland, it is visible from almost anywhere in Munich thanks to its 950-ft landmark tower.

3 Match Action

Peruvian Nobby Solano netted three times against TSV, here striking one of two penalty-kicks into the net.

4 Memorabilia

TSV's magazine for the tie in Munich.

Match 59

2001–02

Intertoto Cup, Semi-Final: TSV 1860 Munich (Germany) v. Newcastle United
FIRST LEG Wednesday, 25 July 2001, Olympiastadion (Munich)

TSV 1860

UNITED Given, Barton, Dabizas, Elliott, Solano, Bassedas (Caldwell S), Hughes, Speed, Quinn (Bernard), Bellamy, Ameobi (LuaLua). Subs not used: Griffin, McClen, Gavilan, Harper.
Manager: Bobby Robson

TSV 1860 Jentzsch, Riseth, Zelic, Tapalovic, Wiesinger, Mykland, Hassler, Dheedene (Ipoua), Weissenberger, Schroth (Max), Agostino. Subs not used: Ehlers, Pfuderer, Passlack, Bierofka, Hoffman.
Manager: Werner Lorant

REFEREE S. Bre (France)

RESULT Won 3–2 (1–0)
AGGREGATE 3–2

ATTENDANCE 15,000

SCORERS United: Solano (11), (54) (pen), Hughes (83); TSV 1860: Agostino (57), Tapalovic (67)

MATCH HIGHLIGHTS

The small crowd in the sprawling and vast Olympic complex made for an eerie atmosphere, but the few present enjoyed a tremendous game of football with some excellent goals. The match got off to a great start with a brilliant opening effort in the 11th minute from United's Peruvian midfielder Nobby Solano. In a dazzling 50-yard run from his own half, the little South American danced into the heart of the German defence and clinically finished with a delicate chip over keeper Jentzsch. Newcastle were in command for much of the first hour of the match, and it was no surprise when the Geordies went 2–0 up after Craig Bellamy had been felled in the box. Solano stepped up to drill the spot-kick into the net. TSV 1860 had some good moments, though, and they pulled a goal back three minutes later, Agostino blasting the ball past Shay Given in spectacular style. Newcastle then found themselves on the rack for a period, and the Germans equalised on 67 minutes when Tapalovic capitalised on a goalmouth scramble to make it 2–2. The game could have gone either way in the closing twenty minutes, with chances created at both ends, but it was

Ulsterman Aaron

the Black 'n' Whites that grabbed the winner seven minutes from time. A Solano cross was met by Aaron Hughes, who headed cleanly and firmly past Jentzsch.

MAN OF THE MATCH
Nobby Solano – terrific display.

| MATCH RATING | ● | ● | ● | ● | |

End-to-end action.

STAR COMMENT
Bobby Robson: 'Nobby Solano scored what has to be the best goal of his life, chipping the keeper after a long run.'

EYEWITNESS
Gary Oliver (*Shields Gazette*): 'Nolberto Solano's exquisite individual goal deserved a better stage than the Intertoto Cup and the paltry 15,000 attendance.'

TOUR STOP – MUNICH
A vivacious, bohemian city, Munich is set against the backdrop of the Alps and is distinguished by splendid buildings of much historical interest. The city is also characterised by its art and cultural activity, and is famous for its numerous beer halls, clubs and cafés. With the largest university in Germany, Munich's young population is extremely active and enthusiastic about its football. Marienplatz and Konigsplatz lie at the heart of the Bavarian capital, which is also a major commercial centre and one-time headquarters of the Nazi movement. (pop. 1,300,000.)

STADIA FILE – OLYMPIASTADION
During the '90s, TSV 1860 moved from their home in the Giesing district to the Olympiastadion, but the move was an unpopular one, with the club having to share the vast sports complex with their more affluent neighbours, Bayern. One of Europe's classic arenas, built for the 1972 Olympics, it is best known for its unique tent-like glass roof that sweeps around the stadium. Situated in the Olympiapark and overlooked by the giant Olympic tower, the whole complex is a tourist stop in its own right. With a capacity of 69,000, it was completely refurbished during the '90s. TSV 1860 and Bayern moved to an equally spectacular new stadium named the Allianz Arena in 2005.

DID YOU KNOW
Newcastle had previously visited Munich for an exhibition match against a combined city XI during the summer of 1955 (lost 1–2) then faced TSV 1860 in a friendly at St. James' Park in October 1958 (won 3–0).

Match 60

2001–02

Intertoto Cup, Semi-Final: Newcastle United v. TSV 1860 Munich (Germany)
SECOND LEG Wednesday, 1 August 2001, St. James' Park

TSV 1860

UNITED Given, Barton, Dabizas, Elliott, Solano, Lee (Caldwell S), Hughes, Speed (Acuna), Quinn, Bellamy (LuaLua), Ameobi. Subs not used: Harper, Griffin, Bernard, Bassedas. Manager: Bobby Robson

TSV 1860 Jentzsch, Pfuderer, Riseth, Greilich, Borimirov, Tapalovic (Agostino), Hassler, Mykland, Tyce, Max, Schroth. Subs not used: Hofmann, Wiesinger, Weissenberger, Dheedene, Ehlers, Ipoua. Manager: Werner Lorant

REFEREE I. Baskakov (Russia)

RESULT Won 3–1 (1–1)
AGGREGATE Won 6–3

ATTENDANCE 36,635

SCORERS United: Speed (5), LuaLua (80), Solano (90) (pen); TSV 1860: Schroth (41)

MATCH HIGHLIGHTS

This semi-final decider was in United's hands, with TSV 1860 having to score at least twice to have any chance of overtaking the Black 'n' Whites. In the end, the Germans never looked like doing that, although they did show the decent-sized crowd that they could play attractive football, with veteran playmaker Thomas Hassler the architect of everything good about their play. However, as with many foreign opponents who had come to Tyneside, their neat, possession-orientated approach play was rarely matched by any decisive work in the danger area, and it was left to the Magpies to be the more dangerous attacking side. United's early opening goal, after five minutes, gave Newcastle the cushion they wanted, Gary Speed powering in an unstoppable header past Jentzsch from a Nobby Solano free-kick. United relaxed after that and allowed TSV 1860 to grab an equaliser just before half-time when Borimirov found space and coolly drilled a low ball across the box for Schroth to net. The visitors had a glimmer of hope but that was extinguished when Robson sent on the sprightly Lomana LuaLua for Craig Bellamy. The Congo striker livened the match up, and Newcastle got back into the groove, striking two late goals. For the first, LuaLua harried Riseth, robbed the ball and then rounded the keeper to strike low and hard from the narrowest of angles for a fine goal. Then, right on full-time, Wayne Quinn's dangerous cross was handled in the area and Solano stroked the resulting penalty into the netting.

MAN OF THE MATCH

Gary Speed – wholehearted effort.

MATCH RATING ● ● ● Comfortable by the whistle.

STAR COMMENT

Bobby Robson: 'The players have come back to play four competitive games in three weeks. We scored 11 goals, and we couldn't have done much better than that.'

EYEWITNESS

Paul Tully (*Scene@StJames* magazine): 'Lomana LuaLua's first St. James' Park goal, taken round the goalkeeper and fired in from a narrow angle, offered great promise of things to come from the Congoese box of tricks.'

OPPONENT FILE

At their peak during the mid-'60s, TSV (*Turn & Sport Verein*) 1860 reached the final of the Cup Winners Cup but lost to West Ham United at Wembley in 1965 and went on to lift the German championship a year later. Since then, though, they have suffered a yo-yo existence between the Bundesliga and the regional Bavarian league, only re-establishing themselves in the top flight in 1993. Still a multi-sports club, they are very much in the shadow of Bayern; however, they possess a loyal and very local fan base, unlike their rich neighbours.

STAR VISITOR

Thomas Hassler – A veteran of German football, at 35 years of age Hassler showed he could still dictate a game from midfield with his control, vision and never-ending work ethic. Magnificent at set-pieces: free-kicks and corners were his speciality. Born in Berlin, he won over 100 caps for his country and was one of the architects of Germany's victory over Bobby Robson's England in the 1990 World Cup semi-final. Hassler joined TSV 1860 from Borrusia Dortmund. He also played for Juventus and Roma during his career.

DID YOU KNOW

French international Laurent Robert was unveiled as United's new £9.5 million signing from Paris St-Germain before the game with TSV 1860.

estac *Match 61*

2001–02
Intertoto Cup, Final: Troyes-Aube Champagne (France) v. Newcastle United
FIRST LEG Tuesday, 7 August 2001, Stade de L'Aube (Troyes)

Troyes-Aube

UNITED Given, Barton, Dabizas, Hughes, Elliott, Solano, Lee, Speed, Quinn, Ameobi, Bellamy (LuaLua). Subs not used: Harper, Griffin, Caldwell (S), Bernard, Acuna, Bassedas. Manager: Bobby Robson

TROYES Heurtebis, Thomas, Bradja, Berthe, Amzine, Celestine, Leroy (Rothen), Zavagno, Ghazi, Boutal (Saifi), Gousse (Djukic). Subs not used: Herve, Hamed, Niang. Manager: Alain Perrin

REFEREE T. Ovrebo (Norway)

RESULT Drew 0–0 (0–0)

AGGREGATE 0–0

ATTENDANCE 10,414

SCORERS None

MATCH HIGHLIGHTS

The first leg of the Intertoto Cup final proved to be a difficult one for a Newcastle side that was outplayed by a slick-moving French outfit. With a place in the UEFA Cup at stake, the price of failure was large, and the Black 'n' Whites were fortunate to come back to Tyneside with their defence intact. On a balmy, wet summer evening, Troyes made all the running and pinned United into their own territory for most of the first half. They could have been two goals up inside the first ten minutes as Shay Given had a couple of lucky escapes in goal. And it didn't end there as Gousse, Ghazi, Boutal and Leroy all went agonisingly close to opening the scoring. Newcastle came out after the interval with a more resolute attitude, and the one-way traffic was stemmed. Yet it was Troyes that went closest to breaking the deadlock and gaining a crucial advantage when Saifi had a marvellous opportunity to score, but he blazed the chance wide of the post.

MAN OF THE MATCH

Shay Given – showed his worth.

MATCH RATING ● ●   Jaded display.

STAR COMMENT

Bobby Robson: 'We were fortunate to come away from France on level terms.'

EYEWITNESS

Simon Rushworth (*The Journal*): 'United deserved little against a technically superior and physically fitter outfit playing Continental football.'

TOUR STOP – TROYES

A historic town and industrial community to the east of Paris, Troyes became prosperous in the Middle Ages. On the River Seine, it has a picturesque and quaint old city centre with well-preserved sixteenth-century houses situated along narrow streets. In the heart of Troyes stands one of France's most magnificent Gothic cathedrals, St-Pierre-et-St-Paul. The town is the former capital of the Champagne region. (pop. 61,000.)

STADIA FILE – STADE DE L'AUBE

Originally opened in 1956 and renovated in 2000 and 2003, the Stade de L'Aube is now a modern stadium and usually creates a terrific atmosphere, with its stands close to the pitch. With a capacity of only 18,000, it still manages to generate a cauldron-like environment for big games. It is bright and breezy with multi-coloured seating and four separate two-tiered stands.

DID YOU KNOW

England's other Intertoto Cup entrant was Aston Villa, who also reached one of the three finals, defeating FC Basel 5–2 on aggregate. PSG and Brescia contested the other final.

stac *Match 62*

2001–02
Intertoto Cup, Final: Newcastle United v. Troyes-Aube Champagne (France)
SECOND LEG Tuesday, 21 August 2001, St. James' Park

Troyes-Aube

UNITED Given, Barton (O'Brien), Dabizas, Hughes, Elliott, Solano (LuaLua), Lee, Speed, Quinn (Bernard), Ameobi, Bellamy. Subs not used: Harper, Acuna, Bassedas. Manager: Bobby Robson

TROYES Heurtebis, Thomas, Bradja, Meniri, Hamed, Saifi (Tourenne), Leroy, Rothen, Zavagno, Boutal (Djukic), Gousse (Ghazi). Subs not used: Sekli, Jbari, Thomas, Zambernardi. Manager: Alain Perrin.

REFEREE T. Fiorenzo (Italy)

RESULT Drew 4–4 (1–2)

AGGREGATE 4–4, lost on away goals

ATTENDANCE 36,577

SCORERS United: Solano (2), Ameobi (65), Speed (70) (pen), Elliott (90); Troyes: Leroy (25), Gousse (28), Boutal (47), (62)

MATCH HIGHLIGHTS

The deciding leg of the Intertoto Cup final with French unknowns Troyes provided the large attendance with a thoroughly entertaining match, despite a disappointing outcome for the home supporters. It was a remarkable contest with United going in front early on, before being hit by a Troyes onslaught that left the Magpies trailing 1–4 with less than half an hour to go. However, Newcastle mounted a thrilling fight-back in the final stages of the match. The Geordies started brilliantly with a spectacular Nobby Solano goal after only two minutes. He latched onto the ball on the edge of the box and crashed a 20-yarder into the net, but United did not capitalise on that early breakthrough, and Troyes showed that they were a composed and highly efficient side. Indeed, they could have been European Champions for the way they pushed the ball around and tore United open in the next hour. The visitors were on level terms after 25 minutes when Leroy's long-range drive took a deflection and swerved past Shay Given from 30 yards. Immediately afterwards, Gousse slipped through the defence to put his team ahead. The same player was then involved again when one of his efforts struck the woodwork, only for the rebound to drop kindly for Boutal, who forced the ball home and put Troyes 3–1 ahead with one foot in the UEFA Cup. It seemed all over for United when Boutal was again on target just after the hour, heading unmarked past Given at the far post. But then came United's fight-back. Against the odds, Shola Ameobi started a revival, hitting the top corner of the net from a Solano cross. Then Ameobi won a penalty, Speed crashing the ball home in emphatic fashion to make it 3–4. With the St. James' Park crowd roaring United on, Robbie Elliott headed a stoppage-time equaliser, but it wasn't enough. In the remaining few minutes, United couldn't grab what would have been a remarkable winner, and Troyes went through on away goals.

MAN OF THE MATCH

Nobby Solano – transfer speculation, but proved his worth.

MATCH RATING	● ● ● ● ●	Astonishing 90 minutes.

STAR COMMENT

Craig Bellamy: 'It's hard to get over a game like that. When you score four goals at home, you expect to win.'

EYEWITNESS

Paul Gilder (*The Journal*): 'Robson will surely have the defending manuals out when his side return to training tomorrow.'

OPPONENT FILE

Troyes-Aube were only founded in 1986 and made a steady rise from the French Fourth Division to top-level football, in a progression that was reminiscent of Wimbledon's in England. They finished in seventh position in 2000–01 and entered the Intertoto Cup, their first taste of European football. Totally unknown outside their own country, they were a highly talented side that surprised many people during the early years of the decade.

STAR VISITOR

Sladjan Djukic – A veteran Yugoslav midfielder, Djukic gave Troyes' young side the experience needed for top-level football. At 34 years of age, he was a long-serving player for Troyes and a great favourite of the crowd as the club rose from obscurity. Joining the club from Lorient, Djukic was always capable of scoring goals, hitting double-figures in each of his last three seasons with the club.

DID YOU KNOW

It was the first time United had conceded more than three goals at St. James' Park in a European fixture.

Tour Stop

Troyes – France

Troyes-Aube Champagne 2001–02

1. Postcard from . . . Troyes

Part of Troyes' tastefully restored town centre. On the River Seine, the magnificent St-Pierre-et-St-Paul cathedral is pictured.

2. Postcard from . . . Stade de L'Aube

The colourful Stade de l'Aube: small, bright and cheerful with a record attendance of just under 18,000 for the visit of PSG in 2000.

3. Match Action

Nobby Solano's early stunning opening strike against the French at St. James' Park.

4. Memorabilia

Match ticket for United's visit to Troyes.

'I don't think there's been a more-consistent South American in this
country since Ossie Ardiles and Ricky Villa'
Sir Bobby Robson

Star Profile

Nolberto Solano

In the modern age of global line-ups, Newcastle United have fielded players from all over Europe, including France, Holland, Denmark, Italy, Greece and Georgia. The team has featured players from further afield, too. South America, in particular, has been a source of talent with a number of Chileans and Argentinians arriving at St. James' Park over the years. Stars from Brazil and Colombia have also settled on Tyneside, and one special midfielder came all the way from Peru – the first from that captivating country to appear in Britain – Nolberto Solano.

Known as Nobby to all, Solano can be recognised as one of the very best imports from South America in modern times. Many players from that continent have arrived, briefly dazzled, faded and then headed off to new shores or footballing oblivion. Few have taken root and really impressed. World Cup winners Ossie Ardiles and to a lesser extent Ricky Villa did so at Tottenham Hotspur. More recently, Arsenal's Brazilians Edu and Gilberto have showed much skill and ability but without ever reaching the level of their north London rivals' earlier imports, while Gus Poyet, and now Gabriel Heinze, have performed well, too. On Tyneside, United's many South Americans – including, more recently, Clarence Acuna, Christian Bassedas and Daniel Cordone, and in earlier years, Mirandinha – failed to come to terms with the English brand of football. Even the popular Tino Asprilla never really established himself as a Premiership force.

However, Nobby Solano did acclimatise to English football, becoming one of Kenny Dalglish's rare successful imports. Joining the Black 'n' Whites as a virtual unknown on these shores, Dalglish picked a good 'un in Solano, even if much of his footballing pedigree had only been witnessed on video tape. By the time Sir Bobby Robson had taken charge of the Magpies, he hailed Solano as a special player. United's boss said, 'I don't think there's been a more consistent South American in this country since Ossie Ardiles and Ricky Villa.' In an interview in *The Journal* he added:

> Nobby has been magnificent for Newcastle United. He is an incredibly consistent performer even though he's of such slight build. He copes with the rigours of the English game increasingly well and that's thanks to his technical ability.

One of the most reliable footballers that United has acquired from abroad, Solano initially spent almost six years on the St. James' Park staff, becoming an extremely popular player. His success at the club is all the more remarkable by virtue of his having to come to terms with

Nolberto Solano

NOBBY SOLANO: FACT FILE

Position: Midfield

Born: Callao (Peru), December 1974

Joined United from: Boca Juniors (Argentina), August 1998, £2.76 million and Aston Villa, January 2005, £1.5 million

Left for: Aston Villa, January 2004, £1.75 million

Other major clubs: Sporting Cristal (Peru), Deportivo Municipal (Peru)

Full international: Peru (76 caps, 1994 to date)

United career, senior games: 248 app., 40 goals (to 7 Jan 06)

United Euro record: 31 app., 7 goals (to 7 Jan 06)

Did you know: Having played alongside the great Diego Maradona at Boca Juniors in Buenos Aries, the pair struck up a friendship, and Solano was invited to appear in the Argentinian's tribute match.

rapid changes in the manager's office during his early years: first Dalglish was replaced by Ruud Gullit, then the Dutchman was succeeded by Bobby Robson. His record of over 230 appearances and almost 40 goals in his first spell on Tyneside ranks with the records of the very best midfielders to have played for the club in recent years – only Robert Lee and Gary Speed have scored more goals from the engine-room of midfield for United in modern-day football.

A star in South America, winning championships in Peru, and a regular for his country, Solano joined United in August 1998 as a 23-year-old rising star. He quickly settled on Tyneside and was determined to master English as soon as possible. In the process, he had to come to grips with the Geordie dialect, too, although that took a bit longer to master. Within a few short months, Solano had settled into life in the North East, and by the time of his fifth year, the Peruvian was more than happy to still be in the area and playing in the Premier League for Newcastle. He said, 'I'm proud to still be here. I love it so much that I cannot see myself playing anywhere else in Europe.'

Both a maker and scorer of goals, the little Peruvian was consistently high in the stats rankings for assists. He made goals for his teammates, time and time again, from accurate crosses, deft through balls, exquisite free-kicks and corners. He was frequently on the score sheet himself, able to bend dead balls round a defensive wall or steal into the box for a shot on goal. After a season adapting to the pace and competitive edge of Premier League football, he learnt to track back and support his full-back. In short, Nobby came to terms with the Premiership style. He said, 'It is special, but it is very different to anywhere else in the world. You have to fight for every ball and work up and down the pitch, with every player being able to attack and defend.' The South American added, 'I realised it was not enough for me to be talented and to play good football. You need more than that.'

In European matches, the style of football suited Solano, too. He could spray passes around and link up with the forwards, supporting strikers Shearer and Bellamy. In Newcastle's UEFA Cup campaign of 1999–2000 he was prominent, while he was also influential as United qualified for Champions League football in the 2001–02 season. At that time, United had, arguably, the best wide pairing in the division: Solano on the right flank, balanced by the left foot of Robert on the opposite wing.

Champions League football suited Nobby. He once made the comment, 'It is a different type of football – a higher standard: the World Cup of club football.' Against many of his fellow South Americans in the opposition teams –

Nolberto Solano

Solano in Champions League
action against Barcelona.

men like Barcelona's Saviola, Rochemback and Motta, Juve's Montero, Salas and Zalayeta, and Inter's Zanetti, Crespo and Recoba – Solano excelled. Intelligent and creative, technically sound with the ball despite being a little short of pace, Solano was able to take opponents on and beat them using thought and craft rather than athleticism.

In the San Siro against Internazionale during the 2002–03 run, he played a major part in United reaching what was perhaps the pinnacle of their recent European adventures. Cracking the ball against the woodwork in the fifth minute made his intentions clear. He was not out of place in such surroundings and alongside such star names.

Solano also scored goals in United's European exploits, and the few who witnessed his marvellous solo effort against TSV 1860 in the magnificent Olympiastadion will never forget it. In the opening minutes, he got United

off to a wonderful start – later described as a 'moment of magic' – with a 'dazzling 50-yard run and finish'. *The Journal* recorded the goal: 'Following a neat one-two with fellow South American Christian Bassedas, the former Boca [Solano] man embarked on a mazy run forward.' As space opened up for the United midfielder, Solano 'calmly chipped keeper Simon Jentzsch to score surely his best in a black and white shirt'. A goal of that quality deserved to grace a higher stage than the derisory Intertoto Cup game played in front of a paltry crowd in the huge stadium in Bavaria.

It was a pity that a simmering club versus country dispute surrounding his international call-ups soured relationships somewhat. Solano had to make regular trips to South America – a 13- to 14-hour flight to Lima – to represent Peru, and the jet lag that he suffered, moving between the different time zones, also disrupted United's team plans. Solano confirmed, 'It can

Nolberto Solano

take me six or seven days to change round.' It was a far from ideal situation, considering the congested match schedule in England. More than once, manager and player had words. Nobody at United wanted Nobby to jet off to the other side of the world in the middle of an important fixture programme but, surely, few could criticize him for it. As Peru's captain, he wanted to appear for his country. And, after all, United knew perfectly well when they purchased him he would continue to play international football, especially in World Cup qualifiers and the prestigious *Copa America*.

In the end, his commitment to the Peruvian national side had an impact on his departure from St. James' Park in January 2004. To many judges, inside and outside Gallowgate, the sale of 29-year-old Solano to Aston Villa for what was considered to be a cut-price £1.75 million was a slip-up. The transfer appeared to be a somewhat risky one, with Sir Bobby Robson attempting to fill the gap left by Nobby by playing the inexperienced youngster Darren Ambrose, fielding Lee Bowyer out of his true position, or shuffling Jermaine Jenas or Kieron Dyer to wide roles they did not take to.

Bobby Robson's Newcastle United side was never quite as balanced without Nobby's talented right foot. The Magpies struggled to fill the right-midfield slot with a player naturally suited to the role and missed the consistent performances that Solano had delivered. At that time, Solano had developed into one of the top-rated players in the Premiership and one with vast experience at club, European and international level. Villa manager David O'Leary was delighted to have caught him for such a bargain price.

The Toon Army were not pleased at all. When news of Solano's impending departure, in his sixth season at Gallowgate, hit the street, there was much dismay among the ranks. Still highly popular with the fans, Nobby apparently did not want to go and sadly his transfer to Villa Park was surrounded by sniping by the manager and player in the media. There were, as Neil Farrington of the *Sunday Sun* reported, claims from St. James' Park that Solano had engineered his own move, something that Nobby denied. However, the player did confirm that relationships had deteriorated, noting that 'my problem with the manager was not made obvious in words but in his general attitude towards me'. Solano added, 'It was clear he just didn't rate me anymore, not like he had in the past.' It was a difficult decision for Robson, who confirmed that agreeing to let the little Peruvian depart was 'as tough a decision as I've ever had to make'. Robson also noted that Solano had been 'a blue-chip player for this club'. On the arrival of Graeme Souness as boss of Newcastle United, there was even talk of the Black 'n' Whites attempting to re-sign the player. This was, perhaps, acknowledgement that the Magpies had been too hasty in letting him head south for Birmingham.

At Villa Park, Nobby continued where he left off at Gallowgate. Playing on the right-hand side of midfield, he patrolled up and down the flank and continued to hit balls into the danger area but now for fellow South American striker Juan Pablo Angel to capitalise on, instead of his ex-United teammates.

Soon, though, Solano was to head back to St. James' Park. On the eve of the 2005–06 season, manager Graeme Souness brought him back to Gallowgate from a reluctant 19-month exile. The Peruvian said, 'I was very, very happy to come back,' and added, 'Coming back to Newcastle is even better than signing the first time.'

Nobby Solano stands out as a special player and a huge Tyneside favourite. He can be recognised alongside the great '50s FA Cup-winning star George Robledo as the Magpies' finest-ever South American import.

7

DRAMA IN ROTTERDAM & MILAN

2002–03

Newcastle and Inter enter the San Siro for their epic Champions League clash in 2003.

The Magpies' second taste of the Champions League big time in the 2002–03 season resulted in an incident-packed campaign that was something of a roller-coaster ride – in true Newcastle United tradition. Concluding the 2001–02 season in fourth spot, after a year in which the Black 'n' Whites even flirted with a real bid for the Premiership title, was extremely satisfying and showed that Sir Bobby Robson – by now knighted for his services to football – had re-established the club as a credible force.

Sir Bobby's Newcastle United line-up had developed in the two years since he had taken over management of his boyhood idols. In midfield and attack the Geordies were a potent force with the talismanic Geordie icon Alan Shearer leading the way. Alongside the former England skipper up front was Craig Bellamy, who had established a good partnership with Shearer, the young Welshman's pace perfectly complementing the power of his captain. On the flanks, Laurent Robert and Nobby Solano were influential, while Kieron Dyer and Gary Speed provided the engine-room of the side in midfield. In addition, Robson brought in talented youngsters in the shape of Jermaine Jenas and Hugo Viana. Only in defence were the Magpies a touch suspect, but the imminent arrival of Leeds and England centre-half

Jonathan Woodgate would bolster the back four.

Following a comfortable passage through the qualifying stage against Bosnians Zeljeznicar, United were paired in Group E with some accomplished performers at that level: Feyenoord, Dynamo Kyiv and Juventus. It looked a demanding group, United having to face three sides of exceptional pedigree, including Turin giants Juve, one of the world's most successful sides and twice winners of the trophy.

The difficulty of progressing from their group was, therefore, apparent and Newcastle could not have had a more disappointing start to their Champions League campaign, losing their first three contests. The games were tough, but as Bobby Robson said at the time, 'In all three UEFA Champions League games so far, we've not been outplayed, outfought, outskilled or outshone, but we have no goals and not a single point, which is cruel and disheartening.' United's boss added, 'We have a mountain to climb.' Yet with an inspiring 1–0 home victory over Juventus they got off the mark, and United started to climb that mountain.

The Magpies' amazing and what was to be record-breaking fight-back continued with three more points against Kyiv and then a truly dramatic victory in Holland, at the De Kuip arena in Rotterdam, home of Feyenoord. Newcastle needed another win in their final group match and Juventus to help them out in the Ukraine, if they were to qualify for the next phase of the competition. Newcastle got both: a sensational Craig Bellamy injury-time winner and a Juve victory against Kyiv sending the Magpies through to the next stage of the competition to much acclaim. Alan Shearer said of that thrilling encounter, 'It was such a see-saw game, such a roller-coaster ride, and if we had a slice of luck to win it then, overall, I think we've earned that luck.' United's skipper added, 'I cannot remember any better games for sheer excitement and passion. It really was an incredible game.'

It didn't come any easier for United in the next phase of the Champions League. Newcastle were this time drawn in Group A with last year's finalists Bayer Leverkusen and two more giants of the European scene: Internazionale and Barcelona. Once more, United began badly with a 1–4 home defeat to Inter in a match that saw Newcastle down to ten men within the first five minutes when Bellamy was ordered off. Worse was to follow when his strike partner Alan Shearer also received a suspension. In the next match, a depleted side lost again, this time to Barcelona in the Camp Nou, but the Magpies spirit was outstanding and another fight-back took place. A double triumph over the German side Leverkusen gave the Geordies a chance to qualify and set up a terrific encounter with Inter in the San Siro.

That evening in Milan saw Newcastle reach the pinnacle of their European development. Against one of the Continent's most prominent teams, and in one of Europe's finest and most daunting stadiums, the Black 'n' Whites took the game to the Italians and were unlucky not to secure all three points rather than the 2–2 draw they came away with. Newcastle had reached the top table of Europe and showed that they could compete at the highest level. And United's 10,000 travelling support did their bit too, giving terrific backing to the team as the Toon Army's tour of Europe reached a climax. Flags, banners and black-and-white shirts were to be seen everywhere in Milan and produced an inspiring atmosphere in the Piazza Duomo all the way to the awesome Giuseppe Meazza arena.

In the end, the Magpies needed those extra two points that they perhaps should have brought home from Milan. A victory in the San Siro would have given them a real opportunity of progressing even further in the Champions League and would have made the final clash with Barcelona at Gallowgate a mouth-watering contest. As it was, there was little at stake when the Catalans arrived on Tyneside, yet over 50,000 turned up as the people of Newcastle

Skipper Alan Shearer, pictured bandaged and
bloodied, was in the wars against Dynamo Kyiv.

demonstrated their continued bond with European football. Newcastle bowed out of the Champions League with a defeat at the hands of Barcelona, but with a little more fortune they could have made it to the quarter-finals.

After Newcastle's second foray into the world's greatest club competition, Bobby Robson said, 'This season has been a great European education and experience for us.' He went on to note that it had been a 'real test of mental strength, character and ability, and we have acquitted ourselves extremely well'.

Robson's task was now to ensure that the Black 'n' Whites would challenge Arsenal, Manchester United, Liverpool and a fast-emerging Chelsea, for the right to play Champions League football year after year. If he could achieve that, Newcastle United would earn massive additional revenue, much prestige and progress towards the goal of becoming one of Europe's biggest clubs. However, that target was not an easy one to hit due to a number of unfortunate circumstances: continual injury woe, ill-fortune and Newcastle's abiding tendency to self-destruct. As a result, the riches of the Champions League remained something to aspire to, rather than a regular certainty.

The rain in Spain . . . United's Aaron Hughes, Steven Caldwell and Michael Chopra experience the Barcelona downpour.

MATCHES 63 – 76

Craig Bellamy's dramatic last-minute winner against Feyenoord in the De Kuip arena.

2002–03

Bosnia, Sarajevo	v. NK Zeljeznicar	1–0, 4–0, Agg 5–0	UEFA Champions League, Q
Ukraine, Kiev	v. Dynamo Kyiv	0–2, 2–1, Group E	UEFA Champions League, Gp1
Holland, Rotterdam	v. Feyenoord	0–1, 3–2, Group E	UEFA Champions League, Gp1
Italy, Turin	v. Juventus	0–2, 1–0, Group E	UEFA Champions League, Gp1
Italy, Milan	v. Internazionale	1–4, 2–2, Group A	UEFA Champions League, Gp2
Spain, Barcelona	v. FC Barcelona	1–3, 0–2, Group A	UEFA Champions League, Gp2
Germany, Leverkusen	v. Bayer 04 Leverkusen	3–1, 3–1, Group A	UEFA Champions League, Gp2

Euro Facts & Figures

Youngest & Oldest

Youngest player to appear for United: Aaron Hughes, 18 years 18 days v. FC Barcelona (UCL) 1997–98 (a)

Oldest player to appear for United: Stuart Pearce, 36 years 160 days v. NK Partizan (ECWC) 1998–99 (a)

Youngest player to score for United: Alan Foggon, 19 years 17 days v. Vitória Setúbal (ICFC) 1968–69 (h)

Highest Attendances

98,000 v. Dynamo Kyiv (UCL) Olympiyskyi Stadium, 1997–98

75,580 v. Glasgow Rangers (ICFC) Ibrox Park, 1968–69

Lowest Attendances

2,425 at Sporting Lokeren (ITC) 2001–02

6,200 at FK ZTS Dubnica (ITC) 2005–06

7,847 at Halmstads BK (UEFAC) 1996–97

8,000 at Panionios (UEFAC) 2004–05

Match 63

2002–03

Champions League, Qualifying Round 3: NK Zeljeznicar (Bosnia-Herzegovina) v. Newcastle United
FIRST LEG Wednesday, 14 August 2002, Kosevo Olimpijski Stadion (Sarajevo)

Zeljeznicar

UNITED Given, Hughes, Dabizas, Bramble, Bernard (Quinn), Solano, Dyer, Jenas, Viana (Elliott), Shearer, LuaLua (Ameobi). Subs not used: Harper, O'Brien, Bassedas. Manager: Bobby Robson

ZELJE Hasagic, Jahic (Alagic), Karic, Alihodzic, Mulaosmanovic (Mudrinic), Mulalic, Gredic, Cosic, Mesic, Seferovic, Guvo. Subs not used: Kruzik, Zeric, Radonja. Manager: Amar Osim

REFEREE L. Michel (Slovakia)

RESULT Won 1–0 (0–0)

AGGREGATE 1–0

ATTENDANCE 36,000

SCORERS United: Dyer (55)

MATCH HIGHLIGHTS

Newcastle United faced a volatile home crowd in the Balkans, and a less than perfect pitch, as they attempted to gain the upper hand in the vital opening Champions League qualifying match. There was plenty of vocal support in Sarajevo and the Magpies' young line-up – with an average age of 23 – coped well in the electric atmosphere. United's youngsters – especially midfielders Kieron Dyer and Jermaine Jenas – displayed supreme confidence as the Black 'n' Whites claimed the advantage. The opening half remained goalless, although Lomana LuaLua could have put United in front, missing a golden opportunity. Jahic did likewise for Zelje, while Shay Given made a wonderful acrobatic stop from Guvo. Newcastle's crucial away goal came ten minutes after the interval, in what was a brilliant team effort. LuaLua set off on a piercing run that tore a hole in the home defence. Dyer took the ball on and a perfect one-two passing movement with skipper Alan Shearer saw the young midfielder take the return in his stride before clipping the ball past Hasagic. It was a goal of quality that just about put the Magpies into the money-spinning Champions League group stages. After that, Newcastle gained total control, holding the midfield battleground and firm

Emerging midfielder Jermaine Jenas.

in defence. Nevertheless, the partisan crowd roared their Zelje favourites on in one of the noisiest venues United have experienced on their European travels.

MAN OF THE MATCH

Kieron Dyer – superb in support up front.

MATCH RATING	●	●	●		

Professional display.

STAR COMMENT

Kieron Dyer: 'We know only half the job is done, but we have got a crucial away goal.'

EYEWITNESS

Luke Edwards (*The Journal*): 'The noise on the arrival of the two teams was deafening and the level rarely abated.'

TOUR STOP – SARAJEVO

Only around 400 United fans made the trip to the war-torn Balkan city, which was still displaying signs of the conflict, the buildings scarred by bullet and mortar fire. On the River Miljacka, Sarajevo is surrounded by hills and marked by church towers, minarets and tower blocks. On United's visit, the traditional café life was just starting to return to some semblance of normality, especially along the pedestrianised Ferhadija and in the old quarter. The infamous location of the assassination of Archduke Franz Ferdinand in 1914, the city later became the focal point of the ethnic war that tore apart the old Yugoslavia. (pop. 401,000.)

STADIA FILE – KOSEVO OLIMPIJSKI STADION

Also known as the Kosovo Stadium, the Kosevo Olimpijski Stadion historically belongs to arch rivals FK Sarajevo. It was used for the fixture with United due to the damage Zelje's Grbavica arena had sustained during the war not having been repaired sufficiently to meet UEFA's standards. A picturesque open, low-angled arena, the Olimpijski had a capacity of 45,000 and was the venue for the 1984 Winter Olympics. Complete with running track and green seats, the stadium is close to a vast graveyard, a harrowing reminder of the recent war.

DID YOU KNOW

In an intimidating atmosphere in the Kosovo Stadium, Kieron Dyer was hit by a plastic bottle as he celebrated his second-half strike.

Match 64

2002–03

Champions League, Qualifying Round 3: Newcastle United v. NK Zeljeznicar (Bosnia-Herzegovina)
SECOND LEG Wednesday, 28 August 2002, St. James' Park

Zeljeznicar

UNITED Given, Hughes, Bramble, Dabizas (O'Brien), Bernard, Solano (Kerr), Dyer, Speed, Viana, LuaLua (Ameobi), Shearer. Subs not used: Harper, Elliott, Jenas, Griffin.
Manager: Bobby Robson

ZELJE Hasagic, Mulalic, Jahic, Alihodzic, Mulaosmanovic, Radonja, Karic (Tica), Biscevic, Seferovic, Cosic (Mudrinic), Guvo (Alagic). Subs not used: Kruzik, Kajtaz, Mesic, Silic.
Manager: Amar Osim

REFEREE F. De Bleeckere (Belgium)

RESULT Won 4–0 (2–0)

AGGREGATE Won 5–0

SENT OFF Jahic (69)

ATTENDANCE 34,067

SCORERS United: Dyer (23), LuaLua (36), Viana (73), Shearer (80)

MATCH HIGHLIGHTS

Newcastle United cruised through the second leg of the qualifying match to secure the riches that a place in the Champions League proper promised. Once the Magpies had penetrated a determined Zelje defence inside the opening half-hour, United completed the game at a canter. The important breakthrough came when Nobby Solano lofted a ball into the box with a perfectly weighted pass for Dyer to run onto, and the England midfielder beat the keeper with a neat lob into the net. With a two-goal aggregate advantage, Zelje had little hope. Thirteen minutes later, they were dead and buried when Lomana LuaLua squeezed past a defender on the edge of the box and curled a lovely shot with pace and accuracy into the bottom corner of the net. The Black 'n' Whites were in complete control and after the break could have run up a cricket score. Alan Shearer twice struck the woodwork, while Hugo Viana, Solano and Gary Speed all went agonisingly close, too. Following a red card for Jahic, the visitors found it even more difficult, and it was no surprise when Newcastle doubled their lead. For the third goal, Dyer carved out an opening and fed Viana on the left who cracked a rising shot into the net. Dyer was also involved in United's final goal, his long ball finding his skipper who galloped clear and drilled a classic Alan Shearer shot under the keeper and into the net.

MAN OF THE MATCH

Kieron Dyer – instrumental all evening.

| MATCH RATING | ● | ● | ● | | | | Superior show. |

STAR COMMENT

Bobby Robson: 'We got four goals and could have had seven by the end of the match.'

EYEWITNESS

Simon Rushworth (*The Journal*): 'United were happy to build with measured balls from the back, while their opponents were drilled to break with purposeful penetration.'

OPPONENT FILE

Zelje are one of two passionately supported teams in the football-mad city of Sarajevo and to be simply involved in the UEFA Champions League after a bitter and bloody war was enough for the club. Like many sides from the former Yugoslavia, Zelje have a good history in Europe and reached the semi-finals of the UEFA Cup in 1985. They were also Yugoslav champions in 1972. On the resumption of normal football service after the war in 1995, Zelje quickly became the country's leading club, dominating the championship in a newly formed and fully integrated Muslim–Croatian league.

STAR VISITOR

Jure Guvo – A lively striker, the 24-year-old Croatian forward joined Zeljeznicar in the 2001–02 season and soon proved his worth in attack. He scored two goals in his side's earlier Champions League qualifier tie against Akranes. Tall and fast, Guvo was prominent in the title triumph that won Zelje entry to the Champions League qualifying stages.

DID YOU KNOW

A £15 million fortune awaited the Magpies in the Champions League proper and games against the likes of Internazionale, Barcelona and Juventus.

Tour Stop

Sarajevo – Bosnia

NK Zeljeznicar 2002–03

SARAJEVO

BOSNIE HERZEGOVINE

The focus of the recent Balkan war, the city is now being slowly rebuilt after much damage.

Sarajevo's national stadium was the venue of United's Champions League qualifier, because Zelje's Grbavica arena was undergoing refurbishment.

Kieron Dyer sprints clear of the Zelje defence to net United's crucial away goal in Sarajevo.

Match ticket from the contest in Bosnia.

Kiev – Ukraine

Dynamo Kyiv
2002–03

**1. Postcard from . . .
Kiev**

Khreschatyk, the busy main
thoroughfare and business
centre of Kiev. It was United's
second visit to the Ukrainian
capital.

**2. Postcard from . . .
Olympiyskyi**

An internal view of Dynamo's
multi-purpose Olympiyskyi
stadium, which boasts
some fine-art detail,
including bronze statues and
decorative plaques.

3. Match Action

Alan Shearer drives a
penalty-kick past the Kyiv
keeper at St. James' Park.

4. Memorabilia

Match programme from the
Magpies' return visit to Kiev.

Match 65

2002–03
Champions League, Group E: Dynamo Kyiv (Ukraine) v. Newcastle United
Matchday 1, Wednesday, 18 September 2002, Olympiyskyi (Kiev)

Dynamo Kyiv

UNITED Given, Griffin, O'Brien, Dabizas, Bernard (Robert), Hughes (Solano), Dyer, Speed, Viana, Bellamy, Shearer (Ameobi). Subs not used: Harper, Jenas, Bramble, LuaLua. Manager: Bobby Robson

KYIV Reva, Ghioane, Peev, Sablic, Nesmachnyi, Husin, Khatskevich (Gavrancic), Leko, Leandro (Melaschenko), Cernat, Shatskikh. Subs not used: Khudzhamov, El Kaddouri, Rincon, Bodnar, Skoba. Manager: Oleksiy Mykhaylychenko

REFEREE E. Gonzalez (Spain)

RESULT Lost 0–2 (0–1)

POSITION IN GROUP 4th/0 pts

ATTENDANCE 42,500

SCORERS Kyiv: Shatskikh (17), Khatskevich (63)

MATCH HIGHLIGHTS

United's long journey to the Ukraine ended in frustration and defeat as United opened their Champions League campaign. The Magpies started the game well and looked able to cope with the home side's attacking raids, but they were rocked by a one-in-a-million strike by Maksim Shatskikh in the 17th minute. The Kyiv striker collected the ball on the edge of the box and from 25 yards banged a scintillating long-range shot that flew into Shay Given's net. After that, much of the play saw the Ukrainians keeping United's defence occupied, and it was no surprise when they added another goal midway through the second period. Melaschenko's shot was parried by Given, but the ball looped up for Khatskevich to dive forward and head home. Kyiv created other chances, too, and had a strong penalty appeal turned down, much to the dislike of the home crowd. At the other end of the field, United found it hard work breaking down a dominant Kyiv central pairing, with Alan Shearer battling largely on his own up front. The Magpies hardly created a chance in the whole 90 minutes and were a well-beaten side by the final whistle.

United's Welsh international Gary Speed.

MAN OF THE MATCH

Gary Speed – overworked in midfield.

| MATCH RATING | ● | ● | | | |

Cheerless journey.

STAR COMMENT

Bobby Robson: 'Dynamo were tremendous at the back, and there was simply no way past them.'

EYEWITNESS

Paul Tully (Newcastle United match-day programme): 'The first goal altered the entire course of the game, and as Kyiv grew in confidence, we found ourselves pushed back more and more.'

TOUR STOP – KIEV

United's second visit to the Ukrainian capital saw around 200 fans make the long and expensive trip. A lot had changed in the city since the Geordie faithful were there five years before, with a strong Western influence emerging all over the vast capital. Fashion shops, entertainment clubs, bars and the ubiquitous McDonalds had taken hold. Even tourism had arrived. Now free from the Soviet Union, Friendship Arch and Independence Square had become symbols of the city. (pop. 2,600,000.)

STADIA FILE – OLYMPIYSKYI

On United's first visit to the vast stadium in 1997, the ground was almost full with a near 100,000 attendance. This time, it was only halfway to capacity yet still created a cauldron of noise. With a capacity of 82,893 on the Magpies' second visit, and once called the Khrushchev Stadium, Kyiv's arena is one of the finest in Eastern Europe. Also known as the National Sports Complex, it has an athletics track like most venues in the old Eastern Bloc and distinctive floodlighting pylons. The Olympiyskyi was renovated in 1999.

DID YOU KNOW

Alan Shearer played on despite being bloodied and bandaged due to a nasty head wound that needed four stitches.

Match 66

2002–03

Champions League, Group E: Newcastle United v. Feyenoord (Holland)
Matchday 2, Tuesday, 24 September 2002, St. James' Park

Feyenoord

UNITED Given, Griffin, O'Brien, Dabizas, Hughes, Solano, Dyer, Speed, Robert, Bellamy (LuaLua), Shearer. Subs not used: Harper, Jenas, Bramble, Ameobi, Bernard, Viana.
Manager: Bobby Robson

FEYENOORD Zoetebier, Emerton, van Wonderen, Paauwe, Rzasa, Song, Bosvelt, Ono, Pardo (Lurling), van Hooijdonk, Buffel. Subs not used: Gyan, Kalou, Bombarda, de Haan, van Persie, Lodewijks.
Manager: Dick van Marwijk

REFEREE C. Colombo (France)

RESULT Lost 0–1 (0–1)
POSITION IN GROUP 4th/0 pts

ATTENDANCE 40,540

SCORERS Feyenoord: Pardo (4)

MATCH HIGHLIGHTS

Thirty-four years and sixty-five games later, Newcastle United re-enacted the club's first game against European opponents Feyenoord, but the outcome was very different. While the Dutch defence collapsed back in 1968, they put up a strong wall of resistance and pinched a victory following an early blunder that had gifted them an opening goal. Inside the first five minutes, Feyenoord took the lead when van Hooijdonk tried to pick out Buffel, Andy Griffin and Andy O'Brien both miscued their clearances and the ball fell for Pardo, who lashed home a dipping 20-yard volley from the edge of the penalty area. The Magpies spent the remaining 86 minutes trying to grab an equaliser, but Feyenoord's excellent defence stood firm. Newcastle matched the Dutch and for long periods held the advantage but lacked the spark in the box to create a clear opening. Newcastle did go close to scoring at times: a Shearer header beat keeper Zoetebier but Ono cleared off the line, while Craig Bellamy crashed a great volley against the top of the bar. That single-goal defeat left United rooted to the bottom of Group E with no points and no goals. The Champions League had proved to be a stern examination indeed and one that would test United to the limit.

MAN OF THE MATCH

Nobby Solano – immaculate distribution.

| MATCH RATING | ● | ● | | | | Luckless night. |

STAR COMMENT

Bobby Robson: 'They cashed in on our mistake, but they never gave us any present. We weren't outplayed by any manner or means.'

EYEWITNESS

Luke Edwards (*The Journal*): 'United swept forward, wave after wave of attacks battering their opponents, but they never managed to find their target.'

OPPONENT FILE

UEFA Cup holders and now challenging in the Champions League, Feyenoord had a fine side built around the experienced threat of van Hooijdonk up front and the guile of Bosvelt in midfield. One of the Continent's top sides since European competition took hold in the '60s, Feyenoord may not have the world-wide image of rivals Ajax, but in the Netherlands they are the club with the most passionate support.

STAR VISITOR

Pierre van Hooijdonk – A classical centre-forward with a devastating shot, especially from set pieces, Dutchman van Hooijdonk joined Feyenoord after a stint with Benfica. Much travelled, he also appeared for Celtic and Nottingham Forest in Britain and made headlines on his departure from the UK. Nicknamed 'Pi-Air' for his aerial menace, van Hooijdonk has been a regular in the Dutch squad but with limited opportunities due to the striking riches available to the Netherlands.

DID YOU KNOW

Feyenoord's Brett Emerton, Paul Bosvelt and Robin van Persie soon landed in the Premiership, United very nearly signing the Australian Emerton before he joined Blackburn Rovers.

Match 67

2002–03
Champions League, Group E: Juventus (Italy) v. Newcastle United
Matchday 3, Tuesday, 1 October 2002, Stadio Delle Alpi (Turin)

Juventus

UNITED Given, Griffin (Ameobi), O'Brien, Dabizas, Hughes, Solano (Viana), Speed, Jenas (LuaLua), Robert, Dyer, Shearer. Subs not used: Bernard, Harper, Elliott, Bramble. Manager: Bobby Robson

JUVENTUS Buffon, Thuram, Juliano, Montero, Moretti, Baiocco (Fresi), Tudor (Brindelli), Davids, Nedved, Di Vaio (Trezeguet), Del Piero. Subs not used: Ferrara, Salas, Camoranesi, Chimenti. Manager: Marcello Lippi

REFEREE R. Temmink (Holland)

RESULT Lost 0–2 (0–0)

POSITION IN GROUP 4th/o pts

ATTENDANCE 41,424

SCORERS Juventus: Del Piero (66), (81)

MATCH HIGHLIGHTS

It was a black-and-white derby as United faced one of the most famous clubs in the world in Turin. And it was Alessandro Del Piero, one of the world's greatest players of modern times, who proved to be the difference on the night as the Italian star fired in two goals of real quality. Newcastle, though, held their own for long periods in an entertaining match and, before Del Piero struck, could have gone in front themselves. After Juve had pressed United early on – Del Piero striking the crossbar with a brilliant 25-yard shot – the Magpies showed they could be a danger, too. Both Alan Shearer and Laurent Robert could have given the Tynesiders the lead in one glorious attack that cut Juventus apart, but the chance was missed. In the second half, the Stadio Delle Alpi erupted when Del Piero whipped in a free-kick, after Nikos Dabizas had been penalised for a foul on the Italian international striker. However, the Black 'n' Whites from England were not out of it and minutes later had what looked like an excellent leveller ruled out for offside. Shearer headed home from Gary Speed's far-post cross, but the linesman's flag was up against Dyer, even though it could be argued that he was not interfering with play. Juventus then sealed the match, and the Champions League points, when Del Piero raced on to meet an Edgar Davids cross, the ball deflecting into Given's net. It was a cruel blow to a Newcastle side that performed well and deserved something from the match.

Disappointingly, United still had no points and no goals to show for their efforts.

MAN OF THE MATCH

Alan Shearer – manfully contested everything.

| MATCH RATING | ● | ● | ● | | | |

Encouraging display.

STAR COMMENT

Bobby Robson: 'We were never outplayed or outclassed. Our players have every right to take pride in their performance against the current Italian champions.'

EYEWITNESS

Simon Rushworth (*The Journal*): 'Two second-half goals emphatically ended United's brave resistance.'

TOUR STOP – TURIN

Around 4,000 of the Toon Army engulfed the vast Piazza San Carlo of Turin (Torino to the locals). Capital of the Piedmont region in north-western Italy and throne of the old House of Savoy, Turin is a city of grace and charm with superb baroque architecture. A commercial giant, it is the centre of the Fiat motor empire, while it is also a city of much culture and home to the Turin Shroud, noted as 'the most famous – and most dubious – holy relic of them all'. On the River Po, the snow-capped Alps are an hour's drive away. (pop. 865,000.)

STADIA FILE – STADIO DELLE ALPI

Built for the 1990 World Cup and shared by Juve and Torino, the Stadio Delle Alpi is an awesome sight, sunk ten metres below ground level with a striking design and a spectacular silver-cladded roof split into two halves. It is an architectural gem but a stadium much loathed by local supporters for its lack of atmosphere, distance from the pitch and out of city location. With three tiers of seating, the arena has the Alps as its marvellous backdrop. With a capacity of 69,041, the ground was for many years owned by the local authority and lacked facilities, so much so that, at that time, Juve had ambitious plans to completely revamp the arena.

Greek defender Nicos Dabizas.

DID YOU KNOW

Juve striker Di Vaio was carried off the field following a clash of heads, an ambulance ending up on the pitch to ferry the striker to hospital. The match was held up for over

Juventus

UNITED Harper, Griffin, O'Brien, Bramble, Hughes, Solano, Jenas, Speed, Robert (Viana), LuaLua (Ameobi), Shearer. Subs not used: Given, Bernard, Elliott, Acuna, Kerr. Manager: Bobby Robson

JUVENTUS Buffon, Thuram, Juliano, Ferrara, Brindelli, Camoranesi (Zambrotta), Davids (Conte), Tacchinardi, Nedved, Del Piero, Di Vaio (Zalayeta). Subs not used: Chimenti, Fresi, Moretti, Baiocco. Manager: Marcello Lippi

REFEREE R. Pedersen (Norway)

RESULT Won 1–0 (0–0)
POSITION IN GROUP 4th/3 pts

ATTENDANCE 48,370

SCORERS United: Griffin (61)

MATCH HIGHLIGHTS

One of the biggest nights of United's European history resulted in a much-needed victory over one of football's strongest clubs. Just about everyone wrote the Magpies off, but Bobby Robson's side began a remarkable recovery with three points against the Italian champions and leaders of Group E. United were patient, assured and professional, while around the penalty box they showed the ability to open up the Juve defence. United created plenty of half chances and the odd real opportunity; Laurent Robert, in particular, was provided with a fabulous opening after good work from Nobby Solano and Gary Speed, but the Frenchman put his shot just wide. An Alan Shearer header was powered just over the crossbar, and Buffon made a magnificent save from the No. 9's thunderbolt. After the interval, the Black 'n' Whites got the breakthrough they thoroughly deserved. On the hour, a Robert free-kick was cleared out to full-back Andy Griffin at the corner of the box. The young United defender surged past oncoming defenders then struck a fierce shot from an acute angle that flew into the net off Buffon's fist. The Gallowgate arena erupted to acclaim United's first goal of the Champions League campaign. And what an important goal it was – enough to secure victory. Newcastle could have made it two after that, Solano going close and bringing about another tremendous stop from Buffon. But Juventus were always a danger, especially in the closing stages of the match when they strode forward in search of an equaliser. Indeed, they came within a whisker of making it 1–1 when Zalayeta fired against the crossbar.

MAN OF THE MATCH

Andy Griffin – a stunning goal.

| MATCH RATING | ● | ● | ● | | | Celebrated victory. |

STAR COMMENT

Bobby Robson: 'Tactically we were outstanding, and everybody did well. We had big resolve and big tenacity.'

EYEWITNESS

Luke Edwards (*The Journal*): 'Sir Bobby Robson's side delivered the performance of the season, outplaying, outfighting and at times outclassing the Italian champions.'

OPPONENT FILE

The most successful European side United have faced, even outstripping Barcelona in terms of stature, Juventus have lifted six European trophies and reached fourteen finals altogether (to the start of the 2005–06 season). There are few more famous clubs around, notwithstanding Real Madrid, AC Milan, Manchester United and Barca. Eventually finishing the Champions League campaign as runners-up, the famous Turin outfit are also Italy's most successful team, where they are known as the 'Zebras' and the *Bianconeri* (the white and blacks). Backed by the Agnelli family of Fiat fame, Juve were Italian champions when United faced them in 2002 and lifted the Scudetto again in 2003.

STAR VISITOR

Alessandro Del Piero – Once the shining light of Italian football, the gifted Del Piero recaptured much of his form during the period he faced United, following a lengthy spell of average performances after a bad knee injury. A regular goalscorer for club and country, he joined Juve from Padova in 1993 as a teenager and quickly became an automatic choice for the Azzurri. Del Piero scored a record ten goals in the 1997–98 Champions League tournament. Without doubt a world-class striker, he has appeared over 70 times for Italy.

DID YOU KNOW

United played in a silver-grey coloured kit allowing Juventus to wear the famous black-and-white stripes – the Toon Army for once having to support the side without the traditional stripes on home soil.

Tour Stop

Juventus 2002–03

1

2

3

4

1. Postcard from . . . Turin

A panorama of Turin with the Mole Antonelliana prominent, the city's tallest landmark which gives spectacular views to the Alps.

2. Postcard from . . . Stadio Delle Alpi

Juve's modern and stylish Stadio Delle Alpi. The arena was constructed for the 1990 World Cup but is loathed by many locals for its sterile atmosphere.

3. Match Action

Full-back Andy Griffin breaks the deadlock against Juventus on Tyneside, and Newcastle's revival takes off.

4. Memorabilia

United's Champions League programme with Juve featuring two of Europe's greats: Alan Shearer and Edgar Davids.

Rotterdam – Holland

Feyenoord
2002–03

1. Postcard from ... Rotterdam

The Magpies' second visit to Rotterdam in European action gave supporters the opportunity to visit some unusual Dutch architecture: the cubic houses pictured around the pleasant old harbour district.

2. Postcard from ... De Kuip Stadion

A UEFA five-star venue and one of the finest on the Continent, Feyenoord's De Kuip had been recently modernised and upgraded at the time of Newcastle's visit.

3. Match Action

Hugo Viana's left foot strikes the ball past two Feyenoord defenders to put United 2–0 ahead in Rotterdam.

4. Memorabilia

Match ticket from the epic contest at the De Kuip Stadion.

Datum : 13-11-2002
Aanvang : 20:45
Ingang : Poort 07-12
Sector : ORANJE
Prijs : EUR 50.00

RIJ : 15
Stoel : 16

Feyenoord –
Newcastle United
Champions League

Seizoen 2002 / 2003

Match 69

2002–03

Champions League, Group E: Newcastle United v. Dynamo Kyiv (Ukraine)
Matchday 5, Tuesday, 29 October 2002, St. James' Park

Dynamo Kyiv

UNITED Harper, Griffin, O'Brien (Bernard), Bramble (Dabizas), Hughes, Solano (Dyer), Jenas, Speed, Robert, Shearer, Ameobi. Subs not used: Given, Viana, LuaLua, Acuna.
Manager: Bobby Robson

DYNAMO KYIV Reva, Peev, Gavrancic, Ghioane, Husin, Nesmachnyi, Leko (Rincon), Dmytrulin, El Kaddouri (Cernat), Belkevich, Shatskikh. Subs not used: Leandro, Bodnar, Sablic, Shovkovskyi, Melaschenko.
Manager: Oleksiy Mykhaylychenko

REFEREE J. Marin (Spain) (sub; J. Losantos)

RESULT Won 2–1 (0–0)
POSITION IN GROUP 3rd/6 pts

ATTENDANCE 40,185

SCORERS United: Speed (58), Shearer (68) (pen); Kyiv: Shatskikh (46)

MATCH HIGHLIGHTS

The return match with Dynamo Kyiv saw another step in the Newcastle recovery plan, securing three more points with a well-earned victory. But the Magpies had to achieve it the hard way, coming back from a goal down having lost both centre-backs to injury. When Andy O'Brien and Titus Bramble were both taken off, many of the fans feared it was going to be one of those nights, especially when Shatskikh opened the scoring just after the interval. Peev's through pass was met by the Dynamo striker and Shatskikh drilled his shot past Steve Harper. But Newcastle were both gritty and determined and battled back into the match. Ten minutes later, Gary Speed levelled the game with a fine diving header from Solano's corner-kick – the Toon's fourth corner in quick succession. Newcastle continued to pile on the pressure and their attacking strengths told in the 68th minute. A ball was hoisted into the danger area for Shearer to run on to, Husin blatantly held back United's skipper, and the Spanish official had little hesitation in awarding a penalty. Up stepped United's talisman to drive the ball into the bottom left corner, sending the keeper the wrong way in the process. It was a crucial spot-kick, securing three points that now put the Magpies in with a real chance of qualification for the next group stage – and this after being dead and buried four weeks previously. The match wasn't quite over, though, as Kyiv almost grabbed another goal,

but Andy Griffin cleared off his own goal line to save the day. It was a clearance that was as vital to United's progress as Shearer's penalty kick.

MAN OF THE MATCH

Gary Speed – action-man performance.

MATCH RATING ● ● | | | | Rousing result.

STAR COMMENT

Jermaine Jenas: 'They were a difficult side to play against – really organised and hard-working.'

EYEWITNESS

Simon Rushworth (*The Journal*): 'United's Champions League hopes were, as they have been all season, hanging by a thread.'

OPPONENT FILE

The pride of the Ukrainian nation, Dynamo Kyiv made their second visit to St. James' Park in competitive football as favourites to accompany Juventus out of Group E. But the Kyiv that visited United the second time round were not the same potent side as the Dynamo team of a few years before and had for the first time in a decade failed to lift their domestic championship. However, they were still extremely well organised and strong at the back, experienced at playing European football, and the most successful of all the old Eastern Bloc clubs in UEFA competition.

STAR VISITOR

Maksim Shatskikh – Kyiv's replacement for Andriy Shevchenko and purchased in 1999 from Baltika in Russia, the tall, strapping Shatskikh, from Uzbekistan, was a quality striker and had a sensational first season in Dynamo's colours. He topped the Ukraine goal-scoring charts in 2000 and 2001 and was quickly recognised around Europe as a forceful leader of the attack. A regular for his country, he could strike a ball with power and accuracy.

DID YOU KNOW

Referee Juan Antonio Marin pulled a hamstring late in the first half and Javier José Omar Losantos, Marin's fellow countryman and fourth official, took over, subsequently awarding United a crucial spot-kick.

Match 70

2002–03
Champions League, Group E: Feyenoord (Holland) v. Newcastle United
Matchday 6, Wednesday, 13 November 2002, De Kuip Stadion (Rotterdam)

Feyenoord

UNITED Given, Griffin, O'Brien, Dabizas, Hughes, Jenas, Speed, Dyer, Viana (Bernard), Shearer, Bellamy. Subs not used: Solano, Acuna, LuaLua, Ameobi, Caldwell (S), Harper. Manager: Bobby Robson

FEYENOORD Lodewijks, Gyan, van Wonderen, Paauwe, Rzasa, Song (Bombarda), Bosvelt, Emerton, Lurling, Kalou, Buffel. Subs not used: Collen, de Haan, van Persie, Pardo, Loovens, L'Ami. Manager: Bert van Marwijk

REFEREE F. Wack (Germany)

RESULT Won 3–2 (1–0)

FINAL GROUP E TABLE

1	Juventus	13 pts
2	Newcastle Utd	9 pts
3	Dynamo Kyiv	7 pts
4	Feyenoord	5 pts

ATTENDANCE 44,500

SCORERS United: Bellamy (45), (90), Viana (49); Feyenoord: Bombarda (65), Lurling (70)

MATCH HIGHLIGHTS

On a night when both teams needed a victory in order to have a chance of securing a place in the second stage of the Champions League, it turned out to be quite an evening. The Magpies appeared to be cruising at 2–0 ahead and were hoping for a favour by Juventus in Kiev, before the Dutch hit back to level the game. However, a late and dramatic winner from Craig Bellamy sent the Tynesiders through. Newcastle had opened the scoring just before the interval when an Alan Shearer header set up Bellamy, who closed in on goal from the angle of the box to steer a superb shot across the keeper and into the net. Four minutes after the half-time break it was 2–0. Another excellent move saw Hugo Viana picked out by Kieron Dyer on the edge of the box. The Portuguese midfielder chested the ball down and struck a brilliant left-foot drive past Lodewijks to put United two ahead, but the match was far from over. Feyenoord got back into the game and awoke their raucous crowd. A chance fell to Bombarda, and he drove a stinging shot past Shay Given, then five minutes later the De Kuip faithful erupted when the Dutch grabbed an unlikely equaliser, Lurling firing home an 18-yard volley. Feyenoord were now in the driving seat, after being second best for most of the match. But Newcastle's line-up had spirit and battled back, always posing a danger up front.

Bellamy's pace, contributing to an effective partnership with Shearer, caused the Feyenoord defence all sorts of problems. In injury time, Dyer broke through on goal but his shot was pushed out by Lodewijks. Bellamy, though, pounced on the loose ball as quick as a flash to steer it home from an acute angle into the net. It was a heart-stopping finale. Then, all eyes were on Kiev: Juventus had won, and United were through. It was an amazing feat considering their woeful start to their Champions League campaign.

MAN OF THE MATCH

Craig Bellamy – pace that threatened.

MATCH RATING	•	•	•	•	•	Out of this world.

STAR COMMENT

Craig Bellamy: 'I knew it was going to be the biggest game of them all and that the fans were going to make it special – and they did.'

EYEWITNESS

Niall Hickman (*Daily Express*): 'Robson had called for a football miracle, and that is what he got.'

TOUR STOP – ROTTERDAM

The Geordies' second visit to the Dutch port of Rotterdam proved a fulfilling journey, although many of the travelling masses stayed in Amsterdam and made the short trip south for the match only. Those who didn't travel to the De Kuip just for the game could wander through the Oudehaven, Rotterdam's old harbour area that has been rebuilt in somewhat daring and avant-garde styles. The Kijk-Kubus (Cube Houses) is one of several unusual architectural gems that can be found in the city. (pop. 600,000.)

STADIA FILE – DE KUIP

The Stadion Feijenoord, to give it its more formal Dutch title, had undergone huge changes since United's visit 34 years previously. The De Kuip is now recognised as a UEFA 5-star arena, with a capacity of 51,180. Completely modernised in 1994 and now a state-of-the-art venue, the stadium, nicknamed 'The Tub', has first-class facilities of every kind, including an adjacent training complex and a museum. It has been reconstructed with an impressive uniform design of steel bracing and silver cladding.

DID YOU KNOW

No team in Champions League history had ever qualified after losing its first three group matches. Newcastle were the first side to achieve such a comeback, and the 3,000 travelling Toon Army were jubilant.

Match 71

2002-03

Champions League Phase 2, Group A: Newcastle United v. Internazionale Milano (Italy)
Matchday 7, Wednesday, 27 November 2002, St. James' Park

Internazionale

UNITED Given, Griffin, O'Brien, Dabizas, Hughes (Caldwell S), Solano, Dyer, Speed, Viana (Robert), Bellamy, Shearer. Subs not used: Harper, Acuna, Jenas, LuaLua, Ameobi. Manager: Bobby Robson

INTER Toldo, Zanetti, Materazzi (Cordoba), Cannavaro, Pasquale, Okan (Dalmat), Emre, Almeyda, Morfeo, Crespo (Recoba), Vieri. Subs not used: Fontana, Di Biagio, Gamarra, Coco.
Manager: Hector Cupar

REFEREE S. Bre (France)

RESULT Lost 1–4 (1–3)
POSITION IN GROUP 4th/0 pts
SENT OFF Bellamy (5)
ATTENDANCE 50,108

SCORERS United: Solano (71) Inter: Morfeo (2), Almeyda (34), Crespo (45), Recoba (80)

MATCH HIGHLIGHTS

United's first venture into the latter stages of the Champions League, which included all the big guns of European football, started in sensational fashion. Inter's arrival on Tyneside 32 years before, in the Inter Cities Fairs Cup, caused quite a stir, and the same was true as this Champions League encounter got under way. Within 66 seconds the visitors were in front when the unmarked Morfeo caught United cold after a penetrating run and cross from Zanetti. Worse was to follow. On the five minute mark, Craig Bellamy kicked out at centre-half Materazzi and he was red-carded. A goal behind and down to ten men against one of Europe's top sides, it couldn't get any worse. But it did. In a fiery contest, Alan Shearer almost followed Bellamy down the tunnel when he was caught in the box and retaliated. Inter then forced in two more goals before the break. For the first, Crespo powered a shot that hit Andy Griffin but Almeyda brilliantly struck the rebounded ball from 25 yards to score. Just before the half-time whistle Okan went past Aaron Hughes on the touchline and slid a pass to the near post where Crespo converted the chance. There was no way back for the Magpies, although to their credit they fought on and did grab a goal when Nobby Solano coolly finished after a Laurent Robert diagonal ball had picked him out. Soon after, the Peruvian could have got another when he missed a great chance, while Robert also twice went close. But Inter's attack always spelled danger to

the under-strength Magpies, and it was no surprise when substitute Recoba scored a gem of a fourth goal. Picking up the ball wide on the right, the South American cut inside and delivered a marvellous shot across Shay Given that curled into the net.

MAN OF THE MATCH

Alan Shearer – battled away despite the odds.

| MATCH RATING | ● | ● | ● | | | Calamitous start. |

STAR COMMENT

Craig Bellamy: 'I've made a right mess of tonight. I have let the fans down, I have let my teammates down and I have let the manager down.'

EYEWITNESS

Paul Gilder (*The Journal*): 'To their credit, the Magpies refused to lie down and showing the kind of spirit which has seen them defy the odds in Rotterdam, set about trying to repeat those heroics.'

OPPONENT FILE

Recently revamped and resurgent under the guidance of Hector Cupar, Inter were striving to reclaim a leading position in European football and emulate the success of Italian rivals AC Milan and Juventus. Despite a lack of success in the Champions League, they lifted three UEFA Cup titles in the '90s, reached another final and remained a major force. The team is known as *La Beneamata* (The Beloved) in Italy.

STAR VISITOR

Christian Vieri – A forceful and much travelled leader, in the mould of Alan Shearer, the Inter centre-forward joined the Milan club from Lazio for a record £32.1 million deal in July 1999. Tall and exceptional in the air, he has forged telling partnerships for Inter with both Ronaldo and Hernan Crespo. A regular in the Italian side, Vieri was born in Bologna and hails from a family of footballers. He started his career in Australia where he was raised as a child.

DID YOU KNOW

Alan Shearer, like Bellamy, was in trouble with UEFA. He reacted to an elbow by Cannavaro, and although the referee missed the incident, United's skipper was caught by video evidence and handed a two-game ban. Bellamy received a three-match suspension.

Match 72

2002–03
Champions League Phase 2, Group A: FC Barcelona (Spain) v. Newcastle United
Matchday 8, Wednesday, 11 December 2002, Estadi Camp Nou (Barcelona)

Barcelona

UNITED Given, Griffin, O'Brien, Hughes, Bernard, Solano, Dyer, Speed, Robert, Ameobi, LuaLua (Chopra). Subs not used: Harper, Caldwell (S), Dabizas, Acuna, Jenas, Cort. Manager: Bobby Robson

BARCELONA Bonano, Puyol, De Boer, Reiziger (Christanval), Cocu (Mendieta), Riquelme, Xavi, Motta, Overmars, Dani (Saviola), Kluivert. Subs not used: Enke, Gerard, Rochemback, Giovanni. Manager: Louis van Gaal

REFEREE F. de Bleeckhere (Belgium)

RESULT Lost 1–3 (1–2)
POSITION IN GROUP 4th/o pts

ATTENDANCE 45,100

SCORERS United: Ameobi (24); Barcelona: Dani (7), Kluivert (35), Motta (58)

MATCH HIGHLIGHTS

Without the suspended Alan Shearer and Craig Bellamy, United went into the cauldron of the Camp Nou with a relatively inexperienced attack of Shola Ameobi and Lomana LuaLua. Yet the two stand-ins performed admirably as United matched their famous opponents for long periods, and, for a spell, it looked like United could get something from the match. Although Barca opened the scoring, when Dani converted a Xavi cross with a fine left-foot volley, United battled back and deserved their equaliser. A run from Nobby Solano and good build-up play from Kieron Dyer ended with Ameobi hitting a crisp low shot past Bonano. At that time, the Magpies were on top, but a killer goal from Patrick Kluivert on 35 minutes gave the Catalan side the advantage. Overmars caused mayhem on the left and his fellow Dutchman swept home a low shot past Shay Given. In the second half, Barca increased their lead as Motta's header from a corner found the net, off Dyer's half-hearted and somewhat casual attempt at a clearance on the line. Although the points were heading Barca's way, Newcastle went close and should have scored again – Ameobi having two fine headers that were cleared off the line. Two games and no points. The Champions League second phase had begun the same way for the Magpies as the first had.

MAN OF THE MATCH

Shola Ameobi – a real handful.

| MATCH RATING | ● | ● | ● | | | Undeserved score line. |

STAR COMMENT

Bobby Robson: 'Barcelona and Inter are now in pole position, but we will do our best to recover.'

EYEWITNESS

Simon Rushworth (*The Journal*): 'Against a Barcelona side seeking a record tenth successive Champions League victory, United created enough clear chances to have won an engaging Group A fixture.'

TOUR STOP – BARCELONA

For United's second visit to one of the great centres of European football, there was, once again, a mass exodus from Tyneside. Newcastle supporters filled the Plaça Reial and tree-lined La Rambla, while some also explored the imposing cathedral and old Barri Gotic, as well as the impressive Olympic complex at Parc de Montjuic. Barcelona is a truly exciting destination for all tastes. (pop. 1,600,000.)

Shola Ameobi, creative in attack.

STADIA FILE – CAMP NOU

Barcelona's giant stadium was at least half full for United's second visit and this time created something of an atmosphere, unlike the Magpies' previous outing five years before. Situated in Les Corts district, west of the city centre, the Camp Nou is a cauldron of Catalan fervour and the original architects made provision in the design for an expansion that would take the capacity to a huge 150,000. Unusually, the Camp Nou has a chapel adjacent to the dressing-rooms.

DID YOU KNOW

For the second time on visiting Barcelona's noted arena, the Magpies were swamped by a rainstorm. Indeed, the match had to be called off due to the deluge of water and was played the following day. United's 5,000 travelling support had to either return home or rearrange flights and stay in Barcelona for another 24 hours.

Tour Stop

Barcelona – Spain

1

2

NOU CAMP - BARCELONA

TA:10/12/2002 **FCBARCELONA**

CHAMPIONS 20:45 HORES UEFA CHAMPIONS LEAGUE
LEAGUE

uefa.com

FC BARCELONA – NEWCASTLE UNITED FC

LOCALITAT TRIBUNA 3 GRADERIA

ACCES: 14   BOCA: 412
PORTA: 27   FILA: 0003
               SEIENT: 0016
PREU: 62,00 EUROS

IVA INCLÒS

ENTRADA

4

3

FC Barcelona 2002–03

The famous La Sagrada Familia, a must see on any trip to the Catalan capital.

A fine aerial postcard of Barca's vast Camp Nou complex, opened in 1957. On both United's Champions League visits, the heavens opened – and the rain was very much in Spain.

Newcastle had little luck in the return match at Gallowgate; Alan Shearer is pictured firing towards goal.

Match ticket for the game in Barcelona; the contest was switched to the following evening because of torrential rain.

Leverkusen – Germany

Bayer 04 Leverkusen 2002–03

At the centre of the industrial Ruhr region, Leverkusen is a company town dominated by the Bayer chemical plant.

Financed by Bayer, the arena contains a luxury hotel complex at one end of the stadium (left). It is one of the finest small grounds in Europe.

Shola Ameobi proved to be a useful striker in European action. Here he is pictured netting in the BayArena.

United's allocation of away tickets for the smaller stadiums was usually meagre.

Match 73

2002-03

Champions League Phase 2, Group A: Bayer 04 Leverkusen (Germany) v. Newcastle United
Matchday 9, Tuesday, 18 February 2003, BayArena (Leverkusen)

Bayer Leverkusen

UNITED Given, Hughes, O'Brien, Bramble, Bernard, Jenas, Dyer, Speed, Robert, Ameobi (Cort), LuaLua (Chopra). Subs not used: Harper, Acuna, Griffin, Kerr, Caldwell (S). Manager: Bobby Robson

BAYER Butt, Preuss (Schneider), Kleine, Cris (Bracher), Ojigwe, Balitsch (Kaluzny), Neuville, Simak, Basturk, Brdaric, Franca. Subs not used: Vranjes, Babic, Zivkovic, Starke. Manager: Thomas Horster

REFEREE T. Hauge (Norway)

RESULT Won 3–1 (3–1)
POSITION IN GROUP 3rd/3 pts

ATTENDANCE 22,500

SCORERS United: Ameobi (5), (15), LuaLua (32); Bayer: Franca (26)

MATCH HIGHLIGHTS

The unpredictable talents of Shola Ameobi and Lomana LuaLua again showed up well, and United secured their first points of the second phase in the BayArena. The first of a double-header with the German outfit, United had to win to stand any chance of qualification, and they destroyed the Bundesliga outfit with three clinical goals in the first half. Ameobi struck twice in the opening 15 minutes of the match. For the first, LuaLua worked his way down the flank before searching out Ameobi with a fine cross. Shola picked his spot and nodded United into the lead. Then Ameobi was back for a second, quite brilliant, goal. He robbed defender Cris, glided past Kleine and struck the perfect shot into the right-hand corner of the German goal. Bayer did pull a goal back in an entertaining opening half, Franca scoring after he collected a pass from Basturk, but the Magpies retained control and scored a wonderful third. Their two-goal advantage was restored when Olivier Bernard gathered the ball on the touchline and fed Laurent Robert. His quick cross found LuaLua in acres of space, the young forward jumping to volley a beauty into the net. There was time before the interval for Ameobi to be denied a hat-trick by a marginal offside decision. The second period was never going to be as frenetic, and United held firm. Bayer enjoyed some possession without creating much by way of a threat in the penalty box and the Magpies

saw out the rest of the match, picking up a much-needed victory and with it three points.

MAN OF THE MATCH

Shola Ameobi – perplexed the Germans.

MATCH RATING ● ● ● ● ☐   Impressive show.

STAR COMMENT

Bobby Robson: 'We knew that if we could take the lead early on, we would be able to control the match from then on.'

EYEWITNESS

Luke Edwards (*The Journal*): 'The best has yet to come from Robson's young side, but, in many respects, this was a coming-of-age performance.'

TOUR STOP – LEVERKUSEN

Situated in the heart of the industrial Rhineland and Ruhr region, Leverkusen is a town dominated by Germany's largest chemical plant owned by Bayer, the maker of aspirin and other well-known products. Sandwiched between the major centres of Düsseldorf and Cologne – where most of United's fans stayed – and situated alongside the noble Rhine, Leverkusen is a largely modern, uninspiring town but one that staunchly supports its football club. (pop. 162,000.)

STADIA FILE – BAYARENA

Also known as the Ulrich-Haberland Stadion, the 22,500 arena is purpose built and ultra modern, complete with a hotel complex and panoramic restaurant. Bayer moved from the modest Sportpark in 1958 and thereafter developed the site, within walking distance of the town centre. Financed by Bayer, the BayArena was modernised into a streamlined, bright and compact ground. The small stadium is something of a masterpiece with uniform white cantilevered stands around the pitch. It also has an innovative conference and event centre with a variety of VIP clubs.

DID YOU KNOW

United boss Bobby Robson celebrated his 70th birthday in Leverkusen. It was also Jermaine Jenas's birthday. United's 2,000 fans in the BayArena waved celebration banners for the pair.

Match 74

2002–03

Champions League Phase 2, Group A: Newcastle United v. Bayer 04 Leverkusen (Germany)
Matchday 10, Wednesday, 26 February 2003, St. James' Park

Bayer Leverkusen

UNITED Given, Griffin, Bramble, Caldwell (S), Bernard, Kerr (Viana), Dyer (Solano), Speed, Robert, Ameobi, Shearer (LuaLua). Subs not used: Harper, O'Brien, Cort, Hughes. Manager: Bobby Robson

BAYER Butt, Preuss, Kleine, Cris (Zivkovic), Placente, Ramelow (Babic), Kaluzny, Neuville (Brdaric), Basturk, Simak, Franca. Subs not used: Starke, Ojigwe, Bracher, Dogan.
Manager: Thomas Horster

REFEREE C. Larsen (Denmark)

RESULT Won 3–1 (3–0)
POSITION IN GROUP 3rd/6 pts

ATTENDANCE 40,508

SCORERS United: Shearer (5), (10), (35) (pen); Bayer: Babic

MATCH HIGHLIGHTS

Alan Shearer was back to lead United's attack and guided United to a victory as they kept alive their hopes of qualifying for the Champions League quarter-finals. The Magpies were determined to collect three points and burst forward at every opportunity against their German visitors. The match was all but over by half-time as Shearer bagged three goals to destroy any hopes Bayer had of a shock result. Inside the opening five minutes, the skipper rose to meet a Gary Speed cross and bulleted a header in at the far post. Six minutes later, Shearer intercepted a bad defensive clearance and released Shola Ameobi, whose low cross ended up at the feet of Shearer: United were 2–0 up. It was almost one-way traffic, but the Germans did win a dubious penalty, only for Shay Given to stop Neuville's spot-kick. Before the break, Shearer sealed the points with his third goal. Dyer burst into the box and as he shaped to fire towards goal, Kleine tugged him back with an arm around his chest. The Danish referee had no hesitation in pointing to the spot. Up stepped Shearer to drive the penalty high into the top corner. United's No. 9 could have made it four in the second period, missing a sitter from only eight yards, while other chances could have seen Newcastle substantially increase their lead, too. Leverkusen got a consolation goal in the 73rd minute when Babic latched onto a good pass from the impressive Basturk to fire past Given.

MAN OF THE MATCH

Alan Shearer – back with a bang.

MATCH RATING	●	●	●			Easy romp.

STAR COMMENT

Bobby Robson: 'I didn't imagine we would have the game won so early on.'

EYEWITNESS

Paul Gilder (*The Journal*): 'A master class in goalscoring from a player still rightly regarded as one of Europe's great strikers.'

OPPONENT FILE

When they faced United, Leverkusen were going through a harrowing season, following a monumental campaign in which they had just missed out on the German Double and Champions League trophy, reaching the final at Hampden but falling to Real Madrid. Having sold several key players, including Michael Ballack, Bayer had just sacked their manager Klaus Toppmoller. The club was backed by the Bayer Company and although formed in 1904, they had only become a force in Germany in the '80s. Since then, they have rapidly grown in stature, winning the UEFA Cup in 1988. The team is now a respected European competitor.

STAR VISITOR

Yildiray Basturk – A young Turkish midfielder, Basturk rose to prominence in the 2001–02 season, helping Bayer to come within a whisker of winning an amazing Treble and his country to third spot in the World Cup. Busy and skilful, he soon became the influential player in Bayer's engine-room after moving from Bochum. Born in Germany of Turkish descent, Basturk was especially prominent as Bayer knocked out Arsenal, Manchester United and Liverpool from the Champions League.

DID YOU KNOW

Alan Shearer's hat-trick was his first in Europe and was only United's fourth treble by any player – following Rob Lee (v. Antwerp), Andy Cole (v. Antwerp) and Tino Asprilla (v. Barcelona).

Match 75

2002–03

Champions League Phase 2, Group A: Internazionale Milano (Italy) v. Newcastle United
Matchday 11, Tuesday, 11 March 2003, Stadio di San Siro (Milan)

Internazionale

UNITED Given, Griffin, O'Brien (Hughes), Bramble, Bernard, Solano (LuaLua), Jenas, Speed, Robert (Viana), Shearer, Bellamy. Subs not used: Harper, Ameobi, Kerr, Caldwell (S). Manager: Bobby Robson

INTER Toldo, Zanetti, Cordoba, Cannavaro, Coco, Conceição, Di Biagio, Okan, Guly (Martins), Emre (Pasquale), Vieri. Subs not used: Fontana, Gamarra, Vivas, Franchini, Napolitano. Manager: Hector Cupar

REFEREE L. Batista (Portugal)

RESULT Drew 2–2 (1–0)

POSITION IN GROUP 3rd/7 pts

ATTENDANCE 53,459

SCORERS United: Shearer (42), (49); Inter: Vieri (47), Cordoba (61)

MATCH HIGHLIGHTS

United needed a victory in a mighty showdown in the San Siro, and they very nearly grabbed one. Indeed, Newcastle could have taken all three points in a pulsating match played in an awe-inspiring atmosphere. The Black 'n' Whites' start to the match showed that they meant business, taking the game to Inter from the off. Nobby Solano cracked a terrific volley against the bar in a game that flowed from end to end. Just before the interval, the deadlock was broken when Craig Bellamy, back with purpose after suspension, flew past Cannavaro and Cordoba on the right flank and picked out Shearer at the far post with a low cross. United's No. 9 got to the ball ahead of Zanetti to guide the ball home, sending United's huge travelling support wild in the process. Immediately after the break, Inter equalised as Vieri leapt to send a great header past Shay Given after a cross by Conceição. Yet within two minutes United were back in front, and it was that man Shearer again. Laurent Robert whipped in a vicious low ball in front of the keeper on the six-yard line. Toldo pushed the ball out only for Shearer to pounce on the rebound and put the Magpies ahead again. However, for a second time, the Milan club levelled the contest with a header, this time from Cordoba, who climbed above United's static defence to make it 2–2. At times, the encounter turned ugly and fiery but, thankfully, never got out of control, and by the end, both sides were content with a point each. The draw meant that qualification for the quarter-finals rested on the very last match of the group stage.

MAN OF THE MATCH

Alan Shearer – top-class show.

| MATCH RATING | ● ● ● ● ● | Outstanding epic. |

STAR COMMENT

Bobby Robson: 'We were the better side in the San Siro, if not by a lot, and I believe we did deserve victory.'

EYEWITNESS

Simon Rushworth (*The Journal*): 'If Newcastle now fail to make further progress in world football's elite club competition, then it will not be for the want of trying.'

TOUR STOP

Thousands more Tynesiders made the trip to the smart and chic city of Milan the second time around. The city is bustling and prosperous, while nothing is more important than football (*calcio*) in the metropolis. Perhaps the football capital of Europe, Milan is a city with a population that lives for their two main clubs, Inter and AC Milan. The Toon Army took 10,000 members to Italy and filled Milan's city centre with boisterous Geordie noise and good-natured humour. (pop. 1,250,000.)

STADIA FILE – SAN SIRO

Milan's celebrated stadium had undergone vast redevelopment by the time United played there for the second time. Totally refurbished for the 1990 World Cup, a third tier was added to the structure, which also saw the introduction of vast spiral towers and a huge overhanging trussed roof. Now a concrete, steel and glass temple to football, the San Siro is perhaps the best in Europe. Situated in a fashionable and plush district, with a capacity of 83,679 and the pitch close to the spectators, the Milan arena boasts an intimacy and colourful atmosphere few stadiums can match.

DID YOU KNOW

The Toon Army's support in the San Siro was extraordinary, the pinnacle of Tyneside's Grand Tour. That night even saw the creation of a witty operatic aria that started 'Have you ever seen a Mackem in Milan . . .' and ended 'We're in Milan-you-know, Sunderland's going down-io'.

Skipper Alan Shearer.

Match 76

2002–03

Champions League Phase 2, Group A: Newcastle United v. FC Barcelona (Spain)
Matchday 12, Wednesday, 19 March 2003, St. James' Park

Barcelona

UNITED Given, Griffin, O'Brien, Bramble, Bernard, Solano (Viana), Dyer, Jenas, Robert (Ameobi), Shearer, Bellamy. Subs not used: Harper, Hughes, LuaLua, Kerr, Caldwell (S). Manager: Bobby Robson

BARCELONA Victor, Gabri, Andersson, De Boer, Reiziger, Rochemback, Xavi (Gerard), Motta, Mendieta (Iniesta), Riquelme, Kluivert (Sergio). Subs not used: Bonano, Overmars, Christanval, Oleguer. Manager: Radomir Antic

REFEREE J. Wegereef (Holland)

RESULT Lost 0–2 (0–0)

FINAL GROUP A TABLE

1	Barcelona	16 pts
2	Inter	11 pts
3	Newcastle United	7 pts
4	Bayer Leverkusen	0 pts

ATTENDANCE 51,883

SCORERS Barcelona: Kluivert (59), Motta (74)

MATCH HIGHLIGHTS

The final match of Group A was the proverbial game of two halves. With victory a must – and even then perhaps not enough if Bayer were to fail to beat Inter – United created plenty of chances in the opening half as they dominated proceedings. But they failed to find the net, and, in the second period, Barca stepped up a gear. The visitors clinically took their opportunities and confirmed their status as the best side in the group. Newcastle's chances fell for Craig Bellamy, and while he caused the Barcelona defence all kinds of problems, the Welsh striker wasted a number of good opportunities in front of goal. United should have been two or even three goals in front by the interval – striking the post twice – but were frustrated by the time the Dutch referee blew for the recess. After the break, two defensive errors were capitalised on by the Spanish visitors. The first came almost on the hour mark, Titus Bramble making a costly blunder in the box by hesitating with his clearance. In a flash, Patrick Kluivert pounced to stroke the ball past Shay Given. Then, from a Riquelme free-kick, Motta was left unmarked and from six yards found the net off Given and the crossbar. United had made two dilatory defensive mistakes that were clinically punished at Champions League level. It was all academic anyway; Inter toppled Bayer Leverkusen so even with a victory, the Magpies would not have qualified for the quarter-finals. United's 14-game Champions League run had come to an end. They were out of the competition but had earned much praise for their performances in the first and second stages and enriched their reputation in Europe.

MAN OF THE MATCH

Kieron Dyer – penetrating pace.

MATCH RATING	•	•				Tame finale.

STAR COMMENT

Alan Shearer: 'What we have achieved this season is something of which everyone connected with Newcastle United can be very proud.'

EYEWITNESS

Simon Rushworth (*The Journal*): 'Bellamy, both hero and villain in this wonderful competition, was the vibrant catalyst as a black and white wave washed over the visiting defence.'

OPPONENT FILE

As the new century opened, the Catalan giants Barcelona were determined to halt a slide in the club's fortunes and revive their position as one of Europe's top performers. In recent years, they had been in the shadow of Real Madrid and Valencia, but with a procession of superstars, they were starting to recapture their form and style, recording a 14-game unbeaten Champions League run that included their win over the Magpies.

STAR VISITOR

Patrick Kluivert – One of Europe's great centre-forwards, Kluivert boasted a record goals haul for Holland: 40 goals in 79 games. Tall, elegant and highly skilled, the striker made a name for himself as a teenager in the Ajax side that lifted the European Cup in 1995 and reached another final the following season. He quickly became a star of Netherlands football and earned a big move to AC Milan in 1997, moving on to the Camp Nou for a £9 million fee a year later.

DID YOU KNOW

Dutchman Patrick Kluivert scored in both group matches against United and also in a friendly at the start of the season. He became a United player in the summer of 2004 while so did, a year later, two other opponents from Group A, Inter's Emre and, albeit briefly, Francesco Coco.

Tour Stop

Milan – Italy

Internazionale
2002–03

1. Postcard from . . . Milan

Not many of the Toon Army made the trip to Milan on United's visit in 1970, but in 2003, 10,000 invaded the streets around the impressive Duomo (centre).

2. Postcard from . . . Stadio di San Siro

The awesome Stadio Giuseppe Meazza – commonly known as the San Siro throughout football – perhaps the best arena on the Continent.

3. Memorabilia

Match ticket from the rousing clash in Milan.

4. Match Action

Centre-forward Alan Shearer stretches to convert United's second goal in the San Siro.

An end-to-end battle in the San Siro.

Above and right: Shearer in characteristic goal celebration runs towards the Geordie masses after netting his double against Inter.

Above: United's top marksman gets to the ball before Zanetti to turn in Craig Bellamy's cross for United's opening strike.

Right: The atmosphere from the near 54,000 crowd inside the San Siro was terrific. The occasion showed exactly what Champions League football is all about.

Star Profile

'He is one of the top goalkeepers in Europe, successful at club and international level – and still getting better'

Mick Martin

Shay Given

Just as Alan Shearer has been Newcastle United's guiding spirit and talisman in attack for most of the last decade, goalkeeper Shay Given has been an inspiration to the back-line. A dependable and at times quite brilliant wall of resistance, he is a goalkeeper who can be counted with the very best. Sir Bobby Robson once said, 'I wouldn't swap him for anybody in the Premiership.' And Graeme Souness echoed these sentiments during his period in charge.

It is claimed that football clubs can increase their chances of being successful – however relatively so – if they possess a top-class keeper, and in Shay Given the Magpies have a last line of defence surpassed by few in the Premier League over the last few years. Just as his skipper Alan Shearer took the praise by striking the goals, Given often claims the headlines by making breathtaking saves.

An Irishman like Willie McFaul, the Black

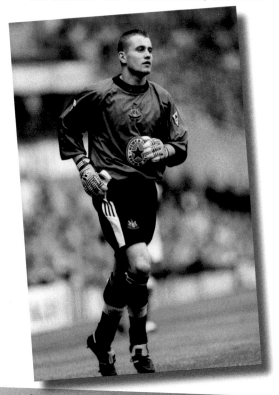

'n' Whites' last goalkeeper of real note who lifted the Inter Cities Fairs Cup with United, Shay Given headed to Britain from his native Donegal in 1992. After a trial at Old Trafford with Manchester United, he travelled across the border to join Irish legend Liam Brady, who was at that time the boss of Celtic. As an apprentice at Parkhead, he worked with coach and fellow Irishman Mick Martin, an ex-United midfield star. Talking about Given in those early days, Mick said, 'He was too young to tell if he would make it then. But now he is one of the top goalkeepers in Europe, successful at club and international level – and still getting better.'

A change in management saw Given walk out on the Hoops in 1994, when he was 18 years old, to join Kenny Dalglish at Blackburn, but with England international keeper Tim Flowers barring his way at Ewood Park, the youngster went out on loan in search of first-team experience. Shay appeared for Swindon Town then had an extended spell with Newcastle's local rivals Sunderland during the second half of the 1995–96 season. It brought him to the attention of many clubs. Given's agility and goalkeeping prowess became apparent, and in recording a string of clean sheets, the young keeper was marked down as a star of the future.

By that time, Kenny Dalglish had moved on from Ewood Park, eventually landing on Tyneside as the successor to Kevin Keegan, and the new United boss rated the emerging Given highly. He paid £1.5 million to bring the young goalkeeper to Newcastle in the summer of 1997 in a deal settled by a tribunal after Rovers asked for substantially more cash.

Over eight years of the Magpies' roller-coaster ride later, Shay Given is approaching four hundred outings for the club and is United's record appearance holder in European football with over fifty games to his name. Given

Shay Given

has produced a series of accomplished displays in Continental action, especially in United's Champions League adventures.

He has said that UEFA's premier tournament is a must for professionals these days: 'As a youngster, I always wanted to play at the highest possible level. It's where you want to be. It's the top club competition in the world, and as players, it's where we aspire to play.'

The Irishman's first game in European competition was in the crucial Champions League qualifier with Croatia Zagreb in August 1997, which proved a tense and thrilling encounter. Given looked assured in both games and made several important stops. He saved well against Viduka and Cvitanovic at St. James' Park, while in Zagreb he was much busier, making a string of crucial blocks, especially a memorable late save from a Robert Prosinecki drive. Newcastle held on to their advantage against a fired-up ten-man Zagreb side, and afterwards Given said, 'They shouldn't have been able to get back into it with ten against eleven but they did. They were a very good side. When they got back at 1–1, early in the second half, it gave their crowd a lift; the fans really got behind them, and their players were up for it from then on.' Given added, 'We had it won when they scored their second goal in injury time. That was the worst moment.' Zagreb had clawed themselves back to level the game on aggregate and take the tie into extra time. That second goal by the highly talented Igor Cvitanovic was a beauty. Shay recalled, 'I never got anywhere near it to be honest. It was right across me and inside the far post.'

Boss Kenny Dalglish had to work hard and fast to gee up United's players before the restart. Given remembered, 'All the lads were down because we thought we had it won, but Kenny Dalglish got us going. Everything he said lifted us all again for extra time.' Newcastle

SHAY GIVEN: FACT FILE

Position: Goalkeeper

Born: Lifford, April 1976

Joined United from: Blackburn Rovers, July 1997, £1.5 million

Other major clubs: Celtic, Sunderland, Swindon Town

Full international: Republic of Ireland (70 caps, 1996 to date) (to cs 2005)

United career, senior games: 359 app., 0 goals (to 7 Jan 06)

United Euro record: 54 app., 0 goals (to 7 Jan 06)

Did you know: Shay Given has won more international caps while playing for Newcastle than any other player on the club's books. He passed Alf McMichael's previous record in April 2003 and has collected the vast majority of his games for the Republic as an United player.

eventually went through to the Champions League proper, thanks to Temuri Ketsbaia's sensational last-minute winner, which was right out of a make-believe comic strip. Afterwards, Given described his opening tie in Europe as 'quite an introduction'.

United's first crack at the Champions League also remains embedded in Given's memory, most notably the Magpies' terrific opener with the Catalan giants. He said, 'They were obviously favourites to beat us, but before Barcelona knew it Tino was knocking in the goals and we were 3–0 up. Barcelona came back at us, and even though they scored two goals late on, I remember making a few good saves – important saves, too – as they came at us.' In the last period of the match, the superstars of Barca started to turn it on, and Given had to be at his best as an onslaught came his way.

Shay Given

He kept out a Rivaldo free-kick, then hurled himself to his right to parry away a rocket from the Brazilian. Nadal's volley was tipped over the bar, he kept out another Rivaldo effort with his legs and then was relieved to see yet another Rivaldo free-kick crash against the woodwork to safety. Given added, 'It was a bit nerve-racking. However, we held out. It was very special out there.' Shay concluded, 'It's probably the best match that I've ever been involved in at St. James' Park.'

Given has been the hero on several other occasions, too. During the Black 'n' Whites next Champions League campaign, in 2002–03, he was also prominent. In the qualifier against Bosnians Zelje, there was enormous pressure to succeed. He recalled, 'We knew we were more than capable of doing the business. We won the first leg in Bosnia, and once we scored the early goal at St. James' Park, we were comfortable and deserved winners.'

The 2002–03 European programme was probably United's best-ever season in terms of the prestige that it brought the club. Shay said, 'People stood up and took notice of Newcastle United, and it turned out to be a very exciting season for all concerned at the club.' In reaction to the tough group that Newcastle were drawn in, Given said, 'We weren't overawed – we never are. Rather, we were excited and looking forward to the challenge.'

Newcastle, however, started badly: 'We were disappointed, but the spirit [of the team] was good throughout. We knew having lost the first three games we were capable of winning the return fixtures, and that's exactly what we did. Whilst it was still possible to qualify, we gave it everything we could.'

Qualifying for the second stage on a dramatic night in Rotterdam was special, and that match stands out for Given as much as the historic opener against Barcelona does.

He said, 'Dramatic hardly sums it up. It was an amazing game, and when Bellars scored right at the death, our emotions were all over the place. It wasn't until the final whistle sounded that we all knew what it meant to us.'

Newcastle started the same way in the second stage as they had in the first, with defeats against Inter and Barcelona. Shay recalled, 'We were determined as ever, but this time it didn't quite fall for us. I thought we matched Barca for large periods of the game but conceded a couple of bad goals at bad times. Shola [Amoebi] took his goal well, and they certainly knew they had been in a contest.'

A crucial match in Milan followed, and United's Irishman remembers that evening in the San Siro as another marvellous occasion. He said, 'Perhaps the best atmosphere of all, with all the Geordies there that night. They were magnificent, quite unbelievable really, all banked up in huge numbers behind the goal – what a noise they made.

'I think we should have beaten Inter. We took the game to them and were very unlucky. Al [Shearer] took his goals very well, and 2–1 would have been a fairer reflection of the game.'

Having to fight hard for the No. 1 jersey with Steve Harper, another very capable goalkeeper, the Irishman made the position his own with steady and reliable performances. Given said, 'Goalkeeping is about consistency, and I believe I've got that consistency. And I think experience helps: the more games you play, the more you understand the game.'

Given's rise to the top has been achieved – unlike that of some contemporaries playing for other clubs – with a far from convincing back four in front of him. Newcastle's continual struggle in the last decade to blend together an effective rearguard has never helped him. A series of fragile defensive formations have

Shay Given

Irish international Shay Given has developed into one of the world's best goalkeepers.

always made it difficult for the keeper and kept him busy, and although Given has made some costly mistakes – as, of course, all keepers do – they have been few and far between.

Now approaching 80 caps for the Republic of Ireland, Shay appeared in the 2002 World Cup finals in Japan and Korea, in which he was outstanding. He is now an experienced international goalkeeper and arguably better in his position than any of the keepers that the neighbouring United Kingdom's teams can currently boast. Certainly no one could say that Scotland, Wales, Northern Ireland or even England – with their wider choice – have latterly fielded someone better. Are David

James, Robert Green, Maik Taylor, Paul Jones or Rab Douglas more accomplished keepers? Few will say 'yes'. Paul Robinson, who has recently made the England No. 1 shirt his own, has the potential to be very good but also has a long way to go before he accomplishes what Given has on the international stage.

Shay is experienced in big games on the Continent at both club and international level and should go past Packie Bonnar's record of 80 appearances in goal for Ireland. Given is also not far from Steve Staunton's overall record of 102 caps, and if he reaches that milestone, it would give him legendary status in his home country, not to mention elevate him into a select

Shay Given

group of players who have reached a century of international appearances worldwide.

The popular Irishman is also very much on course to be recognised as United's finest goalkeeper. Only two other Magpie custodians have appeared more often for the Toon in senior matches: Willie McFaul (387 appearances) and Jimmy Lawrence (507 appearances). If he keeps clear of injury and remains at St. James' Park, he could also top Lawrence's all-time appearance record. At only 29 years of age and with maybe eight seasons still to play as a keeper, that longstanding total is well within Shay's reach.

Along the way, Shay Given might also play a major part in bringing silverware back to St. James' Park. He was gutted when United tumbled out of the UEFA Cup at the hands of first Marseille and then Sporting Lisbon in the 2003–04 and 2004–05 seasons. Given said, 'I truly believed that we could win the UEFA Cup. To me the UEFA Cup was Newcastle's big chance of making the breakthrough and finally winning a trophy.' The defeat in Lisbon was disheartening for everyone. Shay said, 'It was the biggest kick in the teeth in my eight years at the club.'

With his exceptional talent the likeable Irishman needs to be a winner. As Given once said, 'I wouldn't like to retire after playing so many games for Newcastle and have people ask "what did you win?" and have to say "nothing".' Shay is at the very top of his profession and

Goalkeepers need to ignore the sometimes intimidating crowd in big European ties. Shay Given takes little notice of the flares and fireworks.

8

TROPHY BID IN PROVENCE

2003–04

A marvellous picture that captures the atmosphere of European football: Shola Ameobi has just scored beneath the lights of FC Basel's St. Jakob Park.

For any club to win the modern version of the UEFA Cup it is a long haul. In the 2003–04 season, Newcastle very nearly reached the final, failing at the last hurdle when the Black 'n' Whites were rocked by injuries to key players. They played 14 games in Europe that season, from a Champions League qualifier in August to the semi-final of the UEFA Cup during May. It was an eventful campaign.

Newcastle began the season with their eyes on bigger fish than the UEFA Cup when they qualified for another crack at the Champions League by finishing in third place in the Premiership table, fighting off rivals Chelsea and Liverpool by two points for a chance of entry into the big time – United's third in six years. The Magpies faced a difficult preliminary test against Partizan Belgrade, but it was a qualifying tie Newcastle should have won. United's second defeat at the hands of the Serbs in a decade – by way of a penalty shoot-out at St. James' Park after a marvellous away victory in hostile Yugoslavia – took many weeks to recover from. The club was stunned by the exit. Not only had they lost a multi-million pound jackpot, the depressing defeat affected domestic form for the first half of the season. Manager Sir Bobby Robson said after the game, 'Everybody is distraught. That's how it's affected us.' Chairman Freddy Shepherd said the defeat was a 'severe setback for Newcastle United'. He added, 'After the success we enjoyed in the Champions League last season, a second run this term would have been a major plus for us in terms of both prestige and finance.'

Towards the end of the previous campaign, Robson had strengthened his side with the £8 million signing of Jonathan Woodgate from Leeds United. The young England defender was purchased to marshal the defence and mentor either Andy O'Brien or Titus Bramble towards becoming an effective partner. Lee Bowyer, Woodgate's former teammate at Elland Road and an experienced competitor in midfield, also arrived at St James' Park.

The dramatic exit at the hands of the fanatically supported Balkan club had to be put to one side and be forgotten. Easier said than done, perhaps, but United did have the consolation of entry into the UEFA Cup. They were installed as one of the favourites for the trophy alongside Barcelona, Feyenoord, Valencia and Liverpool. The teams that would drop out of the Champions League in February, following the group stage, were also likely to be potential winners.

After initial hopes of further contests with the might of European football in the Champions League – against the likes of Real Madrid, Bayern Munich or AC Milan – the Geordies' UEFA Cup campaign started with an unglamorous tie with NAC Breda of the Netherlands. The contrast between the two competitions was striking. Not surprisingly, the Black 'n' Whites sailed through round one. Following a decent encounter with FC Basel that featured six goals, another lacklustre tie came next, against Norwegians Vålerenga, although it gave the travelling Toon Army a chance to visit Oslo, the capital of the fjords, at the height of a Scandinavian winter.

The competition did not really come alive until the minnows had been despatched and the Champions League third-placed teams entered the competition. Illustrious names such as Internazionale and PSV joined the action. The UEFA Cup was now a tournament with an edge

to it. The draw paired United with Spanish side Real Mallorca, winners of the Copa del Rey in the previous season, although struggling at that time in La Liga. Newcastle passed that test with plenty to spare, winning 7–1 on aggregate.

PSV, Bobby Robson's ex-club and old foes from Champions League combat, faced the Magpies in the quarter-final. The tie was much closer, United edging through by a single goal after two competitive games, one at the Philips Stadion and the other at St. James' Park. Alongside United in the draw in Nyon for the last four were Valencia, Villareal and Olympique Marseille – four noted clubs, all with a European pedigree. Newcastle were paired with *L'Om* – as they are commonly known – the French giants from Provence.

Bobby Robson's side needed to keep clear of injury in the run up to the much anticipated semi-final in April and May, but fortune was not kind to the Magpies. They lost Craig Bellamy, who pulled a muscle at Villa Park, and Kieron Dyer, out with hamstring problems. Then Jermaine Jenas was sidelined, too, and, crucially, central-defender Jonathan Woodgate hobbled to the treatment room in a match against Chelsea with what looked to be only a thigh strain. In fact, it proved to be an injury that would keep the talented stopper out of the 2004 European Championships in Portugal and out of action for much of the next 12 months, following a summer headline-making move from Tyneside to the Bernabéu and Real Madrid. United needed his calm and controlling influence at the back, while losing the cutting pace of Bellamy and Dyer up front also proved to be crucial.

At St. James' Park, United were held to a scoreless draw. However, despite having nothing to show for their efforts, they had importantly kept a clean sheet and not conceded an away goal. The semi-final was still very much in the balance. As a result, nearly 60,000 spectators packed themselves into Marseille's Velodrome arena. With a depleted line-up, the Geordies were up against both a vociferous crowd and

The UEFA Cup semi-final trip to the south of France to face Marseille was an enjoyable experience despite the result. **Top**: United supporters relax in the Vieux Port. **Below**: A section of Marseille support in the Velodrome that created such a magical atmosphere.

home side spearheaded by the dangerous Didier Drogba. Two goals from the highly rated centre-forward gave L'Om victory.

It was Marseille that made arrangements for the final in Gothenburg's Gamla Ullevi stadium and not United. Alan Shearer noted, 'To get so close to the final and not reach it leaves a dreadfully hollow feeling.' Many people on Tyneside felt that with a full-strength side

Robson's team would have been too powerful for Marseille and it would have been United crossing the North Sea to face past European Cup-winners Valencia in Sweden instead. But it was not to be. Newcastle, though, were to have another go at the UEFA Cup the following season and would attempt to go a stage further. They would be playing towards a final in Lisbon but with a new manager at the helm.

Sir Bobby Robson surveys the 57,500 crowd inside the Velodrome for United's UEFA Cup semi-final.

MATCHES 77 – 90

Alan Shearer rises first to the ball to score against PSV in the UEFA Cup quarter-final at St. James' Park.

2003–04

Serbia, Belgrade	v. FK Partizan	1–0, 0–1, Agg 1–1	UEFA Champions League, Q
Holland, Breda	v. NAC Breda	5–0, 1–0, Agg 6–0	UEFA Cup, R1
Switzerland, Basel	v. FC Basel	3–2, 1–0, Agg 4–2	UEFA Cup, R2
Norway, Oslo	v. Vålerenga IF	1–1, 3–1, Agg 4–2	UEFA Cup, R3
Spain, Palma	v. RCD Mallorca	4–1, 3–0, Agg 7–1	UEFA Cup, R4
Holland, Eindhoven	v. PSV	1–1, 2–1, Agg 3–2	UEFA Cup, QF
France, Marseille	v. Olympique de Marseille	0–0, 0–2, Agg 0–2	UEFA Cup, SF

Euro Facts & Figures

St. James' Park Attendances
Highest:
59,309 v. RSC Anderlecht (EFC) 1969–70
59,303 v. Glasgow Rangers (ICFC) 1968–69
59,234 v. Újpesti Dózsa (ICFC) 1968–69
Lowest:
19,046 v. Bohemian FC (UEFAC) 1977–78
25,135 v. FK ZTS Dubnica (ITC) 2005–06
26,156 v. SC Heerenveen (UEFAC) 2004–05
26,599 v. NK Partizan (ECWC) 1998–99

Average Attendance
Best average attendance in a season at St. James' Park:
55,392 (ICFC) 1968–69 (6 matches)
Overall average attendance at St. James' Park:
39,702 (51 matches) (to cs 2005)

Club Debuts in Europe
David Young (1969–70), Ian Mitchell (1970–71), Aaron Hughes (1997–98), Olivier Bernard (2001–02), Craig Bellamy (2001–02), Hugo Viana (2002–03), Titus Bramble (2002–03), Steven Taylor (2003–04), Martin Brittain (2003–04), Peter Ramage (2004–05), Lewis Guy (2004–05), Emre (2005–06), Scott Parker (2005–06).

Match 77

2003–04

Champions League, Qualifying Round 3: FK Partizan (Serbia and Montenegro) v. Newcastle United
FIRST LEG Wednesday, 13 August 2003, Stadionu Partizan (Belgrade)

Partizan Belgrade

UNITED Given, Griffin, Woodgate, O'Brien, Bernard, Solano (Jenas), Speed, Dyer, Robert (Ameobi), Shearer, Bellamy.
Subs not used: Harper, Elliott, Hughes, Bramble, Chopra.
Manager: Bobby Robson

PARTIZAN Kralj, Djordjevic, West, Bajic, Cirkovic, Duljaj (Drulovic), Ilic, Nadj, Malbasa, Delibasic (Stojanoski), Iliev.
Subs not used: Radakovic, Savic, Rzasa, Zavisic, Cakar.
Manager: Lothar Matthaus

REFEREE V. Hrinak (Slovakia)

RESULT Won 1–0 (1–0)

AGGREGATE 1–0

ATTENDANCE 32,500

SCORERS United: Solano (39)

MATCH HIGHLIGHTS

Landing one of toughest qualifying draws available, Newcastle United pulled off an impressive victory in the Serbian capital. And like their previous visit to Belgrade, they had to contend with a fiery atmosphere and stifling heat. The Geordies of Tyneside – sporting an all silver-grey kit – frustrated Partizan with a purposeful and professional performance. They were sound in defence, and even though most of the action was at the Magpies' end of the field, they were always able to cause a threat going forward. In the 39th minute, they converted one of their limited opportunities. After soaking up all the early home pressure, Laurent Robert fired over a good cross-field pass for Alan Shearer and Partizan centre-half West to battle for the ball in the box. West's challenge could have easily resulted in a penalty being conceded, but, instead, the ball dropped nicely for Nobby Solano at the far post, and he guided it back across keeper Kralj and into the net. At times, the contest was rough and physical, while Shay Given had a few lucky escapes in goal as Partizan piled on the pressure. United's goalkeeper played his part, saving well on several occasions, and in the final minute he made a remarkable stop. Stonjanoski looked a certain scorer, but the Irishman blocked well, and Ilic missed the rebound. Victory by a single goal, away from home, had very much given the Magpies the advantage in what was a demanding qualifier.

MAN OF THE MATCH

Shay Given – famous performance.

| MATCH RATING | ● | ● | ● | | |

Marvellous contest.

STAR COMMENT

Shay Given: 'We got a superb result, but the tie's not over yet, not by a long way.'

EYEWITNESS

Paul Gilder (*The Journal*): 'The result was built on a stout defensive display, with Jonathan Woodgate and Shay Given performing heroics.'

TOUR STOP – BELGRADE

In 2003, Belgrade was a rather better place to visit than when United had first been there, five years earlier. However, there was still a hostile feel to the city, with many Serbs harbouring resentment over the break-up of Yugoslavia, and the buildings still showed scars of the conflict. But a new spirit of freedom existed, and extensive refurbishment to rebuild the Central-European capital, situated alongside the Danube, was under way. (pop. 1,100,000.)

STADIA FILE – STADIONU PARTIZAN

Known as the JNA Stadium in the days of communism, huge lettering on the vast uncovered seating of the typical Eastern-European bowl now spelt out 'Partizan' in red and blue colours. Overlooked by several tower blocks, the arena generates a terrific atmosphere despite its open aspect.

DID YOU KNOW

Newcastle's fans in Belgrade were barred from sightseeing by heavily armed police and were made to stay inside their hotel. The British Embassy came to the rescue and invited the travelling Geordies to the Ambassador's residence for a party. The Toon Army, of course, behaved impeccably.

Match 78

2003–04
Champions League, Qualifying Round 3: Newcastle United v. FK Partizan (Serbia and Montenegro)
SECOND LEG Wednesday, 27 August 2003, St. James' Park

Partizan Belgrade

UNITED Given, Hughes, O'Brien, Woodgate, Bernard, Solano (LuaLua), Dyer, Speed (Jenas), Viana (Robert), Ameobi, Shearer. Subs not used: Harper, Griffin, Bramble, Chopra. Manager: Bobby Robson

PARTIZAN Kralj, Djordjevic, West, Cirkovic, Duljaj, Malbasa, Nadj, Ilic, Stonjanoski, Delibasic (Cakar), Iliev. Subs not used: Radokovic, Rzasa, Bajic, Drulovic, Brnovic, Savic. Manager: Lothar Matthaus

REFEREE J. Wegereef (Holland)

RESULT Lost 0–1 (0–1) after extra time
AGGREGATE Drew 1–1, Lost 3–4 on penalties

ATTENDANCE 37,293

SCORERS Partizan: Iliev (49)
Penalty shoot-out, lost 3–4 – United: Shearer, Dyer, Woodgate, Hughes (all missed), Ameobi, LuaLua, Jenas (scored); Partizan: Malbasa, Stojanoski, Iliev (all missed), Cakar, Nadj, Ilec, Cirkovic (scored)

MATCH HIGHLIGHTS

For the second time in five years, Partizan gave United a challenging contest and sent the Magpies out of Europe. On this occasion, the prize of the Champions League was huge, and Newcastle took several months to recover from the disappointment of their loss. The Serbians largely stifled United's attacking play, defending well and giving the Magpies little space or time on the ball for the whole 90 minutes, and for much of extra time, too. They also converted one of their few chances to level the tie just after the interval. A counter-attack saw Nadj chip a pass into the path of Sasa Ilic, who drew Given before slipping the ball to Illiev, who was 12 yards out. The conversion was easy and Partizan had drawn level at 1–1. Newcastle did come close on occasions, in a match that saw few clear-cut opportunities created. Despite the lack of chances, it was still an absorbing and nerve-tingling contest with such an important prize at stake. The visitors forced extra time and no one from Tyneside relished the thought of a penalty shoot-out, the Magpies having an extremely poor record from the spot in the past. However, the game did go to the wire and, eventually to penalties. Newcastle started the shoot-out badly, failing with their first three kicks – even the dependable Alan Shearer fired his spot-kick over the bar. But it was all level at 2–2 after five kicks each. As the tension mounted, Jenas converted United's sixth penalty and United

were a single save, or Partizan miss, away from qualification to the Champions League. Ilic, though, scored and the Russian-roulette of the penalty shoot-out turned Partizan's way. Aaron Hughes missed the seventh kick, lifting his shot over the bar and Cirkovic didn't. Partizan were through and United were shell-shocked. After that great result in Belgrade, Newcastle should never have let the tie out of their grasp. Instead of the glittering Champions League, the Magpies headed for the UEFA Cup.

MAN OF THE MATCH

Kieron Dyer – wasted endeavour.

| MATCH RATING | ● | ● | | | | Disastrous outcome. |

STAR COMMENT

Alan Shearer: 'It was a massive blow to the club, and there was little consolation to be had. We didn't play well. We let it slip.'

EYEWITNESS

Paul Tully (Newcastle United match-day programme): 'Partizan came to St. James' with a carefully worked out game plan and executed it perfectly.'

OPPONENT FILE

FK Partizan – commonly referred to as Partizan Belgrade – were managed at the time by one of football's legends, the German midfielder of 150 international caps, Lothar Matthaus. He had forged a strong, well-organised team in the mould of the fine Yugoslav club sides of the '60s and '70s. They were champions of Serbia and were always going to be a threat to United's progress.

STAR VISITOR

Taribo West – A tough centre-back from Lagos in Nigeria, Taribo West was once described as a 'wandering minstrel of the European scene'. Once linked with a move to St. James' Park, West joined the Partizan club in January 2003 and was the cornerstone of their defence. The much-capped player had spells with Auxerre, for Italian giants Inter and AC Milan, and also for Derby County and Kaiserslautern. He took part in the World Cups of 1998 and 2002.

DID YOU KNOW

United lost around £10 million by not progressing into the Champions League, not to mention missing out on the prestige and glamour that would have gone with competing in UEFA's top competition.

Tour Stop

Belgrade – Serbia

FK Partizan 2003–04

Evening view of the huge urban sprawl of Serbia's capital.

Known for a long time as Stadion JNA, the stadium's former title translates to the Yugoslav People's Army Stadium with origins back to the height of the communist Eastern Bloc.

United players acknowledge their travelling fans in Belgrade after snatching a 1–0 victory: Champions League qualification almost achieved – or so everyone thought.

United's match magazine for the return leg featuring Nobby Solano being congratulated after his goal in Belgrade.

Breda – Holland

NEC Breda
2003–04

Near the Dutch border with Belgium, Breda is steeped in history and boasts a wonderful fortress (pictured) as well as typical European squares filled with cafés and bars.

This postcard souvenir was published when Breda's well-appointed arena was sponsored by Fujifilm. By the time of United's visit, it had changed its name to the MyCom Stadion.

Laurent Robert drives the ball precisely to secure a 1–0 victory in Holland.

Breda's match programme from the visit of the Premiership millionaires.

de groeten uit Breda

FUJIFILM STADION

OCTOBER 15TH 2003 • KICK OFF 20.15 HRS

Breda

UNITED Given, Hughes, O'Brien, Bramble, Bernard (Viana), Dyer (Ambrose), Jenas, Speed, Robert, Shearer, Bellamy (Ameobi). Subs not used: Caig, Griffin, Caldwell (S), LuaLua. Manager: Bobby Robson

BREDA Babos, Feher, Schenning, Penders, Gudelj, Diba (Boussaboun), Peto, Slot (Koning), Engelaar, Seedorf, Elmander. Subs not used: Coutinho, Collen, Stam, Vos, Barakat.
Manager: Ton Lokhoff

REFEREE N. Ivanov (Russia)

RESULT Won 5–0 (2–0)

AGGREGATE 5–0

ATTENDANCE 36,007

SCORERS United: Bellamy (30), (36), Bramble (58), Shearer (76), Ambrose (88)

MATCH HIGHLIGHTS

Newcastle United needed to pick themselves up from the disappointment of their Champions League exit as they faced the lesser names of European football in the UEFA Cup. Opponents NAC Breda were certainly of lesser quality, demonstrating the gulf between the UEFA Cup and Champions League, especially in the early stages of the competition. Breda, with a following of over three thousand noisy fans, were no match for the Premiership club, and United strolled to a five-goal victory. For the opening half-hour, the Dutch side held their own, but as soon as United scored their first goal, the floodgates opened. Craig Bellamy caused the initial damage, netting twice in six minutes. For the first, O'Brien's long ball was flicked on by Alan Shearer, and Bellamy raced into space to coolly lob the keeper. Then, Kieron Dyer skipped past two challenges to feed Laurent Robert, and the winger's pass across the face of goal gave Bellamy the chance to side-foot home. After the interval, Titus Bramble headed the ball past Babos from a Robert corner for United's third. Shearer had missed a sitter earlier in the match, but the United captain made amends when Robert tapped a free-kick on the edge of the box into his path, and the skipper thundered a right-footed shot into the left-hand corner of the net. Substitute Darren Ambrose scored the fifth on his home debut, almost on the final whistle, heading down and

into the net following another Robert cross. Newcastle were all but over the first hurdle in the UEFA Cup.

MAN OF THE MATCH

Laurent Robert – undefendable left foot.

| MATCH RATING | ● ● ● ● | | Glittering attack. |

STAR COMMENT

Andy O'Brien: 'I think we shocked Breda. We played well throughout, and once Craig Bellamy got his two goals, they fell apart a bit.'

EYEWITNESS

Luke Edwards (*The Journal*): 'It may not be the Champions League but nobody was complaining at the final whistle.'

OPPONENT FILE

Latterly rescued by the local council, after Dutch tax authorities threatened insolvency, NAC (*Noad Advendo Combinatie*) Breda had finished in fourth place in the Dutch table and had qualified for Europe for the first time in 30 years. They were in good form, having just defeated Ajax, and they possessed a good team spirit but no real superstars. Their visit to St. James' Park was recognised as one of their greatest nights. The club has only once lifted the Dutch title, in 1921, while they also secured the Dutch cup in 1974.

STAR VISITOR

Stefano Seedorf – Many pundits reckoned Seedorf was a star of the future. The young player was the nephew of AC Milan and Holland star Clarence Seedorf, who was a winner of the European Cup with three different clubs. At the time, Stefano was still an Ajax player, on a long-term loan deal with Breda to give the youngster experience. A very talented midfielder, he was born in Zaandam in the Netherlands.

DID YOU KNOW

Titus Bramble and Darren Ambrose, both ex-Ipswich players, scored their first goals for United against Breda. Ambrose also became one of United's youngest European goalscorers at 19 years and 208 days old.

Breda

UNITED Harper, Griffin, O'Brien, Bramble (Caldwell S), Bernard, Solano (Ambrose), Jenas, Viana, Robert, Dyer (LuaLua), Ameobi. Subs not used: Given, Shearer, Speed, Hughes.
Manager: Bobby Robson

BREDA Babos (Coutinho), Coflen, Penders, Koning (Barakat), Gudelj, Seedorf, Slot, Engelaar, Stam, Boussaboun (Vos), Elmander. Subs not used: Risamasu, Haemhouts.
Manager: Ton Lokhoff

REFEREE E. Bernsten (Norway)

RESULT Won 1–0 (0–0)

AGGREGATE Won 6–0

ATTENDANCE 15,564

SCORERS United: Robert (86)

MATCH HIGHLIGHTS

With a 5–0 advantage, United travelled to Holland for the second leg in the comfort zone and even had the luxury of resting Alan Shearer, Gary Speed and Shay Given. United's 80th fixture in European action was no classic and became an academic exercise, almost like a training run-out for the Magpies. Breda had little hope and what little there was took a jolt when their goalkeeper Gabor Babos clashed with Titus Bramble early in the contest and had to be replaced by Coutinho. However, the home side did press the Black 'n' Whites and struck the woodwork with one effort. The Magpies played within themselves at all times and as the Dutch tired in the last 20 minutes, stepped up a gear. Newcastle landed the killer blow four minutes from time to secure the victory and win the tie 6–0 on aggregate. Jermaine Jenas advanced through midfield and sent Laurent Robert, cutting in from the wing, clean through with an immaculate pass. The Frenchman measured the angle and stroked the ball past the advancing keeper. Before the final whistle, United could have doubled the score when Shola Ameobi created another opening, this time for Lomana LuaLua. The Congo international should have scored but from only four yards out managed to fire his effort against the post.

MAN OF THE MATCH

Laurent Robert – another polished display.

MATCH RATING	●	●				

Regulation victory.

STAR COMMENT

Bobby Robson: 'It was a professional job. We didn't make mistakes and didn't give anything away.'

EYEWITNESS

Simon Rushworth (*The Journal*): 'A night which showcased two-legged cup football at its worst.'

TOUR STOP – BREDA

Situated south of Rotterdam near the border with Belgium, Breda is a historically important town and the focus of several notable moments in European history. It is home to the Dutch Royal Military Academy, has a fine castle and boasts the landmark *Groote Kerk*. Breda is described as a quiet student town but one with a warm atmosphere and plenty of nightlife. (pop. 164,000.)

STADIA FILE – MYCOM STADION

Newly constructed, NAC moved to the MyCom Stadion in 1996. Originally known as the FujiFilm Stadium, the arena was later rebranded 'MyCom' by new sponsors. An almost perfectly rectangular arena, it has unusual small floodlight towers and a prominent entrance area. Having a capacity of 16,400, the ground is usually well populated, Breda attracting an average attendance of around 15,000.

DID YOU KNOW

United's triumph in Breda was Bobby Robson's 100th victory in charge of the Magpies.

Match 81

2003–04
UEFA Cup, Round 2: FC Basel (Switzerland) v. Newcastle United
FIRST LEG Thursday, 6 November 2003, St. Jakob Park (Basel)

Basel

UNITED Given, Hughes, O'Brien, Bramble, Bernard, Solano (Ambrose), Jenas, Speed, Robert (Viana), Shearer, Ameobi. Subs not used: Harper, Caldwell (S), Dabizas, LuaLua, Chopra.
Manager: Bobby Robson

BASEL Zuberbuhler, Degan (P), Yakin (M), Zwyssig, Atouba, Huggel, Cantaluppi, Yakin (H) (Rossi), Chipperfield, Streller, Gimenez (Barberis). Subs not used: Rapo, Quennoz, Ze Maria, Degen (D), Smiljanic.
Manager: Christian Gross

REFEREE T. Ovrebo (Norway)

RESULT Won 3–2 (2–2)
AGGREGATE 3–2

ATTENDANCE 30,000

SCORERS United: Robert (14), Bramble (37), Ameobi (75); Basel: Cantaluppi (11), Chipperfield (15)

MATCH HIGHLIGHTS

FC Basel were a much tougher proposition in the second-round tie than Breda had been in the first. However, United put themselves firmly in the driving seat by scoring three away goals in an entertaining contest in Switzerland. Basel started well, but United were always a danger in attack and came back strongly after conceding two early goals. A 25-yard drive from Cantaluppi gave the home side the lead, but Laurent Robert quickly levelled matters. Jermaine Jenas fed Shola Ameobi, who in turn gave Robert the ball after he had cut in from the flank. He had plenty of time to pick his spot, shooting low into the corner. In a frenetic opening, Basel regained the lead only a minute later. A throw-in was weakly headed away to the edge of the box and Chipperfield fired in a low shot that clipped Jenas as it went past Shay Given. Twenty-two minutes later, it was all square again at 2–2. A Robert corner caused panic, and Titus Bramble belted the ball through a forest of legs into the net. Basel almost took the lead once more in a frenzied, end-to-end first half, the post coming to United's rescue after one Basel attack. Bobby Robson installed some discipline during the interval break, and for the second period, the game was controlled by the Black 'n' Whites. They grabbed a winner 15 minutes from time. Nobby Solano delivered an inviting pass to Shola Ameobi on the edge of the box. The tall Nigerian-cum-Geordie weaved his way past the defence before striking a left foot shot beneath the keeper and into the net.

MAN OF THE MATCH
Laurent Robert – always a threat.

MATCH RATING	● ● ● ●

Exciting clash.

STAR COMMENT
Bobby Robson: 'Our movement was good, and we were always going to cause them problems and make inroads into their defence.'

EYEWITNESS
Paul Gilder (*The Journal*): 'The Magpies put themselves in the driving seat in a tie of fluctuating fortunes.'

TOUR STOP – BASEL
An old university city that straddles the Rhine, Basel is situated on the river bend where Switzerland meets France and Germany. A cosmopolitan, picturesque city with an old medieval heart, it is a maze of fine old streets with an imposing cathedral overlooking the mighty Rhine. With vibrant entertainment and a varied cultural scene, it proved an agreeable port of call. (pop. 165,000.)

STADIA FILE – ST. JAKOB PARK
Although built originally in 1954, St. Jakob Park is now a modern and eye-catching arena. The stadium has undergone much redevelopment and is one of the finest small stadiums in Europe. With a capacity of 33,010, it boasts a bright and breezy exterior of translucent cladding, is impressively lit in the evening and has a colourful interior of blue and red. A uniform two-tiered structure surrounds the pitch, while a corporate complex includes shopping facilities. St. Jakob Park also has its own railway, motorway and tram links.

DID YOU KNOW
Jermaine Jenas almost missed the match when he sustained a freak back injury in the dressing-room just before the warm-up. Frantic treatment made sure he played the full 90 minutes.

Match 82

2003–04
UEFA Cup, Round 2: Newcastle United v. FC Basel (Switzerland)
SECOND LEG Thursday, 27 November 2003, St. James' Park

Basel

UNITED Given, Hughes, O'Brien, Bramble, Bernard, Dyer (Solano), Jenas, Speed, Robert (Ambrose), Shearer, Ameobi. Subs not used: LuaLua, Woodgate, Caldwell (S), Viana, Harper.
Manager: Bobby Robson

BASEL Zuberbuhler, Degan (P), Quennoz, Zwyssig (Smiljanic), Atouba, Barberis (Degen D), Cantaluppi, Chipperfield, Yakin (H), Streller, Rossi (Tum). Subs not used: Ze Maria, Duruz, Rapo.
Manager: Christian Gross

REFEREE K. Fisker (Denmark)

RESULT Won 1–0 (1–0)

AGGREGATE Won 4–2

ATTENDANCE 40,395

SCORERS United: Smiljanic (13) (own goal)

MATCH HIGHLIGHTS

Although United did not score a hatful of goals, they recorded a comfortable victory against their Swiss visitors and moved into round three, joining the Champions League drop-outs in the draw. The Magpies effectively won the tie as early as the 13th minute when they went into a commanding 4–2 advantage on aggregate. Laurent Robert's vicious corner-kick whipped past several defenders before striking the unfortunate Smiljanic's boot. The ball ricocheted over the line despite Chipperfield attempting to make a desperate clearance. The linesman flagged for a goal, and Newcastle were on their way. Yet Basel looked a good side at times, passing the ball quickly and neatly and were unlucky not to be level on terms as a result of their free-flowing football. Yakin came close for the visitors when a free-kick clipped a post, while Newcastle could have increased their tally with Robert and Alan Shearer chances. In a sometimes bruising encounter – Shearer sustained a cut to the head – both sides concentrated on neat midfield build-up play, but little goalmouth action was provided as a result.

MAN OF THE MATCH

Gary Speed – outstanding attitude.

MATCH RATING ● ● □ □ □   Anxious at times.

STAR COMMENT

Gary Speed: 'We didn't play well and won 1–0, which says something for us.'

EYEWITNESS

Paul Gilder (*The Journal*): 'The Magpies finally brushed off the bitter disappointment of their Champions League failure by completing an aggregate win over FC Basel.'

OPPONENT FILE

The Swiss championship leaders managed by ex-Tottenham boss Christian Gross, FC Basel were a veteran of UEFA competition and had a decent run in the Champions League the previous season. They are an affluent club that had only recently re-emerged after a spell out of the limelight in the shadow of Grasshoppers. Title holders in 2002 and 2003, Basel were recognised as the best-supported club in Switzerland, having a loyal following in their region.

STAR VISITOR

Hakan Yakin – Younger of the two Yakin brothers – his elder brother Murat did not appear at Gallowgate – Hakan was established in Europe as a top midfield player with a wonderful left foot. He and his brother were the stars of Basel, both having shone in Champions League and UEFA Cup football, notably against Juventus, Manchester United, Liverpool and Celtic. With the ability to carve open defences and a feared dead-ball expert, Yakin could also play as an extra striker. A Swiss international, he was previously with Grasshoppers and Paris St-Germain.

DID YOU KNOW

Still in the hat for the UEFA Cup trophy were several European giants, including Barcelona, Benfica, Celtic, Marseille, PSV, Valencia, Inter, Roma and Liverpool.

Tour Stop

Basel – Switzerland

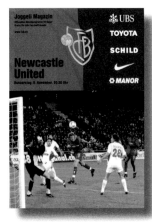

FC Basel
2003–04

1. Postcard from... Basel

The old town of Basel alongside the Rhine provides plenty of scope for exploring the medieval sights and lively nightlife.

2. Postcard from... St. Jakob Park

One of the best pocket-sized arenas on the Continent. In the foreground is St. Jakob Park's main stand incorporating shops and offices as well as FC Basel's HQ.

3. Match Action

United scored three times in Basel. Robert's excellent first-half strike is pictured.

4. Memorabilia

Match magazine from the Black 'n' Whites' visit to Switzerland.

Oslo – Norway

Vålerenga IF
2003–04

1

Karl Johansgate, the main city-centre artery of Norway's capital with the Royal Palace in the distance (top left). This postcard replicates almost exactly the wintry conditions of United's visit.

2

Vålerenga switched the UEFA Cup tie to the national Ullevaal Stadion, which had recently been transformed into a showpiece arena fitted out with colourful seating.

Craig Bellamy gave United the lead in Oslo, volleying the ball past keeper Bolthof.

The Norwegians' match programme from the tie.

3

4

Match 83

2003-04

UEFA Cup, Round 3: Vålerenga IF (Norway) v. Newcastle United
FIRST LEG Thursday, 26 February 2004, Ullevaal Stadion (Oslo)

Vålerenga

UNITED Given, Hughes, O'Brien, Bramble, Bernard, Ambrose (Dyer), Jenas, Speed, Viana (Robert), Bellamy, Ameobi (Bridges). Subs not used: Harper, Elliott, Shearer, Taylor.
Manager: Bobby Robson

VÅLERENGA Bolthof, Hagen, Rekdal, Hovi (Edvardsen) (Krogstad), Brocken, Gashi, Hanssen, Normann (Ovrebo), Berre, Santos, Holm. Subs not used: Hjulstad, Bohinen, Lund.
Manager: Kjetil Rekdal

REFEREE G. Gilewski (Poland)

RESULT Drew 1–1 (1–0)

AGGREGATE 1–1

ATTENDANCE 17,039

SCORERS United: Bellamy (39); Vålerenga: Normann (54)

MATCH HIGHLIGHTS

Manager Bobby Robson controversially left out Alan Shearer, Kieron Dyer and Laurent Robert from his usual starting XI against Norwegians Vålerenga. On a bitterly cold evening in Oslo, where the snow was a foot thick in places, Newcastle's 1–1 draw was a decent enough result; however, judges in the media and many supporters were very disappointed at the uninspiring display against a side Newcastle should have comprehensively beaten. After United had gone in front, just before the interval, the Black 'n' Whites should have finished the tie as a contest but instead allowed a spirited home fight-back. United's strike came from a Hugo Viana corner, the midfielder collecting a rebound from his initial kick to send the ball into the box. Viana's second cross found Bellamy in space and his clinical volley found the net off the upright. With the backing of a lively home crowd, Vålerenga had a go at their Premiership visitors after the break, and they scored a deserved equalising goal in the 54th minute. Normann rose above Aaron Hughes to get to a cross, and his header found the net past Shay Given. It could have been worse, too, as United's goalkeeper had to be alert to make two fine saves late on.

MAN OF THE MATCH

Craig Bellamy – lively all evening.

STAR COMMENT

Alan Shearer: 'I was disappointed to be left out and angry to be left out, but that's the manager's decision. They were unlucky not to win the game.'

EYEWITNESS

Simon Rushworth (*The Journal*): 'Sir Bobby Robson's often hesitant team painted a frustratingly poor picture of Premiership football.'

TOUR STOP – OSLO

Capital of Norway at the head of the Oslo Fjord, Oslo is a charming tour stop, especially around the revamped harbour area at Aker Brygge. With a dramatic setting and guarded by the Akershus *Slott* (Castle), Oslo is also an emerging tourist destination, with a lively and attractive city centre. The city is surrounded by mountains, which were covered in snow at the time of United's visit and provided an impressive backdrop to the match. (pop. 522,000.)

STADIA FILE – ULLEVAAL STADION

Although most of Vålerenga's home fixtures are played at the much smaller, crumbling Bislett arena near the city centre, their UEFA Cup match was switched to the national Ullevaal Stadion. With a capacity of 27,000, the ground had recently been upgraded and extended into a showpiece venue filled with colourful blue and red seating and an adjoining shopping complex.

DID YOU KNOW

Due to heavy snow there were doubts about the fixture and suggestions were made that the tie could be played at Oslo's indoor arena, the Valhall. There was also talk that the match would be switched to Middlesbrough's Riverside Stadium or even to Holland. UEFA insisted the game should take place in Oslo, and, in the end, the Ullevaal was cleared of snow and was totally playable.

Powerful centre-half, Titus Bramble.

Match 84

2003–04
UEFA Cup, Round 3: Newcastle United v. Vålerenga IF (Norway)
SECOND LEG Wednesday, 3 March 2004, St. James' Park

Vålerenga

UNITED Given, O'Brien, Woodgate, Bramble, Hughes, Bridges (Brittain), Jenas, Speed, Robert, Shearer, Bellamy (Ameobi). Subs not used: Harper, Orr, Taylor, Elliott, Viana. Manager: Bobby Robson

VÅLERENGA Bolthof, Brocken, Hagen (E), Rekdal (Normann), Hovi, Hanssen (Waehler), Berre, Gashi, Jalland, Holm, Santos. Subs not used: Bohinen, Ovrebo, Lund, Hjulstad. Manager: Kjetil Rekdal

REFEREE E. Braamhaar (Holland)

RESULT Won 3–1 (1–1)

AGGREGATE Won 4–2

ATTENDANCE 38,531

SCORERS United: Shearer (19), Ameobi (46), (88); Vålerenga: Hagen (24)

MATCH HIGHLIGHTS

In what was a very long road to a possible final in Gothenburg, United went through to the fourth round with a satisfying victory over the Norwegians, thanks to a couple of second-half goals from Shola Ameobi. However, prior to the Magpies taking control, Vålerenga battled for everything and gave United an uncomfortable opening spell. The Norwegian side tested Shay Given before Alan Shearer broke the deadlock, with some assistance from the hapless visiting goalkeeper. Oyvind Bolthof, Vålerenga's last line of defence, looked nervous all night, and in the 19th minute he carried the ball out of his box and gave away a dangerous free-kick. Shearer ran onto a Jermaine Jenas pass to fire the ball through the keeper and into the net. However, the plucky Norwegians hit back, claiming an equaliser from a corner when Hagen volleyed past Given. At the interval, all was level on aggregate, and United needed to step up their performance. The team-talk must have done the trick as within a minute Shola Ameobi – on for the injured Craig Bellamy – had put United in front. He turned Hagen outside the box, then cut back between two more defenders before hitting the net with a shot that went off the keeper, who perhaps should have stopped it. It was a good effort from Ameobi, nevertheless, and from that moment onwards, the Magpies largely took charge of the match without ever putting the game beyond their opponents. They also knew that a slip-up would give Vålerenga the tie on away goals. Newcastle made it 3–1 and

eased those fears near the end of the game when a ball down touchline by Alan Shearer found Jermaine Jenas, who rolled it into the path of Ameobi to score his second of the night.

MAN OF THE MATCH

Shola Ameobi – made the difference.

MATCH RATING ● ● ● ◻ ◻   Undistinguished victory.

STAR COMMENT

Bobby Robson: 'We cannot give a performance like that in the next round against a real quality side.'

EYEWITNESS

Simon Rushworth (*The Journal*): 'Another dubious showing. Another fortunate home victory and another unconvincing display.'

OPPONENT FILE

Vålerenga had qualified for the UEFA Cup by winning the Norwegian cup and had progressed to play United without actually winning a game, recording five draws along the way. They were a club that had gone through massive financial problems and a yo-yo existence, being promoted and relegated several times over the years. The tie against the Magpies was, therefore, a huge draw for Vålerenga. Way behind Rosenborg in Norway's pecking order, the club had raised the profile of football in the capital, which was never a footballing hotbed.

STAR VISITOR

Kjetil Rekdal – Player-coach of Vålerenga and considered to be one of Norwegian football's all-time greats, the veteran Rekdal was a former midfield general who had now switched to the back-line. For most of his career, though, he was a fine box-to-box player, capped 83 times for his country, captain of Norway and a servant of Borussia Monchengladbach, Lierse, Rennes and Hertha Berlin.

DID YOU KNOW

Youngster Martin Brittain came on as substitute for Michael Bridges and made his debut for the Magpies in the tie.

Real Mallorca

UNITED Given, Hughes, O'Brien, Bramble, Bernard, Dyer (Ambrose), Jenas, Speed, Robert, Shearer, Bellamy. Subs not used: Caig, Elliott, Woodgate, Viana, Bridges, Ameobi.
Manager: Bobby Robson

MALLORCA Franco, Cortes, Nino, Lussenhoff, Moya, Campano, Nagore, Colsa (Marcos), Nene, Eto'o, Correa (Finidi). Subs not used: Miki, Nadal, Ramis, Olaizola, Marcos, Perera.
Manager: Luis Aragonés

REFEREE A. Hamer (Luxemburg)

RESULT Won 4–1 (0–0)
AGGREGATE 4–1
SENT OFF Moya (82)

ATTENDANCE 38,012

SCORERS United: Bellamy (66), Shearer (70), Robert (73), Bramble (83); Mallorca: Correa (56)

MATCH HIGHLIGHTS

It was the fifth occasion that the Magpies had entertained Spanish opposition on Tyneside, and it took the Geordies over an hour to break the visitors down. It was an essential breakthrough, though, as Mallorca had taken the lead in the 56th minute when Correa headed home following an Eto'o effort that struck the bar. When they eventually found a way through the Spanish defensive wall, United went on to put the tie beyond Mallorca. Newcastle managed a late rally and scored three goals in a seven-minute spell. Mallorca's lead had only lasted ten minutes before Alan Shearer flicked on a Titus Bramble long ball and Craig Bellamy was in on goal, drilling his shot to the keeper's left. Then a Laurent Robert corner was thudded home by Shearer, who rose to meet the ball with his head at the near post. Three minutes later, Newcastle made the score 3–1 with a Robert special: a free-kick down the middle from 30 yards that the keeper misjudged by diving to his left. Newcastle were in control now, and on 83 minutes, Bramble met a Robert free-kick to volley past the keeper Franco. To compound the visitors' problems, Moya was sent off for felling Shearer, while the physical Spaniards had six other players booked as well. After an hour of run-of-the-mill football from United, they finished the game in style and almost booked a place in the quarter-final.

MAN OF THE MATCH

Craig Bellamy – a constant menace.

| MATCH RATING | • | • | • | • | | Satisfying result. |

STAR COMMENT

Jonathan Woodgate: 'I thought our first-half performance wasn't up to scratch, but we were brilliant in the second half.'

EYEWITNESS

Paul Tully (Newcastle United match-day programme): 'Suddenly, someone clicked the "On" button, and a very different Newcastle United came to life.'

OPPONENT FILE

RCD (Real Club Deportivo) Mallorca were struggling in 17th place in La Liga when they faced United. However, in Europe they enjoyed better fortune and hoped to emulate their formidable achievement in the 1998–99 season when they reached the European Cup Winners Cup final led by Hector Cupar. They qualified for the UEFA Cup by lifting the Copa del Rey, the club's first major honour since its formation in 1916.

STAR VISITOR

Samuel Eto'o – Fast, powerful and extremely skilful, the 23-year-old Eto'o was rated as one of the hottest properties in Spain and was soon to make a big move to Barcelona. The Cameroon international had already played in two World Cups and won over fifty caps for his country despite his tender age. Eto'o arrived in Palma on loan from Real Madrid as a teenager and established himself as Mallorca's star player and a regular goalscorer, netting the goals that lifted the Spanish cup for his club in 2003.

DID YOU KNOW

Craig Bellamy scored his fifth goal in six games against Real Mallorca, following five months on the sidelines with a serious knee injury.

Match 86

2003–04
UEFA Cup, Round 4: RCD Mallorca (Spain) v. Newcastle United
SECOND LEG Thursday, 25 March 2004, Estadi Son Moix (Palma)

Real Mallorca

UNITED Given, O'Brien (Taylor), Woodgate, Bramble, Bernard, Ambrose, Jenas, Speed (Bellamy), Robert (Viana), Shearer, Ameobi. Subs not used: Harper, Elliott, Orr, Chopra. Manager: Bobby Robson

MALLORCA Miki, Ramis (Eto'o), Lussenhof, Poli, Finidi, Marcos (Campano), Nagore, Gonzalez (Nino), Perera, Bruggink, Nene. Subs not used: Moya, Correa, Vincente. Manager: Luis Aragones

REFEREE K. Pluatz (Austria)

RESULT Won 3–0 (0–0)

AGGREGATE Won 7–1

ATTENDANCE 11,500

SCORERS United: Shearer (46), (89), Bellamy (78)

MATCH HIGHLIGHTS

The dynamic strike partnership of Alan Shearer and Craig Bellamy crushed Real Mallorca at a wet Son Moix arena as Newcastle comfortably reached the last eight of the tournament. Real's manager decided to rest several of his best players, including Samuel Eto'o, in order to concentrate on a relegation struggle at home. As at St. James' Park, the first half was largely forgettable, but, again, the second period sprung into life with the Magpies scoring three goals. It took Alan Shearer only 37 seconds after the restart to put United ahead, capitalising on a Miki error, the goalkeeper kicking out his clearance straight to the Newcastle skipper. Shearer, 25 yards from goal, curled a well-placed shot around the diving keeper and into the net. Craig Bellamy was brought off the bench, and Mallorca now had Newcastle's first-choice strike-force to contend with. It took a while for United to find the net again, but the goal was worth waiting for. On 78 minutes, Bellamy picked the ball up deep on the halfway line and launched a counter-attack. The Welsh striker galloped to the Real Mallorca box before drawing the keeper and chipping cleverly past Miki. Before the close, Alan Shearer managed another goal. Getting on the end of a hard and low cross by Olivier Bernard, the former England centre-forward converted with a simple tap-in. It was United's 150th goal in European competition. A 7–1 aggregate victory against a Primera Liga team of any standard was a first-class effort.

MAN OF THE MATCH

Titus Bramble – a powerhouse at the back.

MATCH RATING ● ● ●   First-class display.

STAR COMMENT

Bobby Robson: 'We played the first half like a practice match but in the second half showed more grit.'

EYEWITNESS

Rob Stewart (*Daily Telegraph*): 'Sir Bobby Robson was quickly able to look forward to returning to one of his former clubs, PSV Eindhoven, but he will be aware they will certainly provide far sterner opposition.'

TOUR STOP – PALMA

The main commercial centre of the Balearic Islands, Palma has long been a favourite haunt of British travellers. Impressive and spectacular, Palma's vast gothic cathedral dominates the town and overlooks the marina and Bahai de Palma. The community is guarded by the historic Castell de Bellver and is described as a 'chic little capital'. A fun city in the sun, Palma is packed with tapas bars, restaurants and pubs in the old quarter as well as by the bay. (pop. 378,000.)

STADIA FILE – ESTADI SON MOIX

Real Mallorca moved to the newly built Son Moix bowl on the outskirts of the city in 1999, leaving their historic home to other sporting clubs. Developed in a joint agreement with the local council, the Son Moix stadium was originally built for the University Games and has a capacity of 23,142. It features two large cantilevered stands along the touchlines and smaller covered ends behind each goal. The athletics facilities mean that the pitch is some way from the seating area.

DID YOU KNOW

Steven Taylor, the 18-year-old England youth-team starlet, made his first-team debut for United, coming on as a substitute for Andy O'Brien.

Media pass for the Estadi Son Moix.

Tour Stop

Palma – Mallorca

1

RCD Mallorca 2003–04

This postcard shows a Balearic scene that many people will have visited: Palma's waterfront and the Gothic Sa Seu cathedral, a stop-off on many a Geordie holiday.

2

Real Mallorca's municipal all-purpose stadium, opened in 1999 with a capacity of just over 23,000.

Craig Bellamy guides the ball past Franco; Newcastle recorded four goals against Real Mallorca on Tyneside.

Match ticket from the visit to Mallorca.

4

3

Eindhoven – Holland

PSV
2003–04

It was back to Holland and a return visit to Eindhoven. The street cafés in De Markt overflowed with the Toon Army once more.

Since this postcard was published, the Philips Stadion has seen the construction of a major stand replacing the low-level structure that is pictured in the foreground.

Jonathan Woodgate clashes with Mateja Kezman (right) and Jermaine Jenas sends a header into the PSV net just before half-time during the first leg in Holland (below).

PSV's match programme for United's visit.

PSV FLITS

PSV - NEWCASTLE UNITED
Donderdag 8 april 2004, 20.45 uur

Match 87

2003–04

UEFA Cup, Quarter-Final: PSV Eindhoven (Holland) v. Newcastle United
FIRST LEG Thursday, 8 April 2004, Philips Stadion (Eindhoven)

PSV

UNITED Given, Hughes, Woodgate, Bramble, Bernard, Ambrose, Jenas, Speed, Robert, Shearer (Ameobi), Bellamy. Subs not used: Harper, Elliott, O'Brien, Bridges, Viana, Brittain.
Manager: Bobby Robson

PSV Waterreus, Bogelund, Colin, Bouma, Lee, Park, van der Schaaf (Vogel), van Bommel, de Jong (Rommedahl), Kezman, Vennegoor of Hesselink. Subs not used: van Dijk, Vonlanthen, Addo, Wuytens, Bomfim.
Manager: Guus Hiddink

REFEREE G. Veissiere (France)

RESULT Drew 1–1 (1–1)
AGGREGATE 1–1

ATTENDANCE 32,500

SCORERS United: Jenas (45); PSV: Kezman (15)

MATCH HIGHLIGHTS

In an evenly contested match in Holland, United scored a precious away goal that did much to send them into the semi-final. PSV were a step-up from all of United's previous UEFA Cup opponents, and at last the competition proved to be a highly competitive one. An intriguing contest took place with opportunities created at both ends. PSV went close thanks to their danger man Mateja Kezman, while Alan Shearer tested keeper Waterreus. But it was the Dutch side that opened the scoring with a fine Kezman effort. Robbing Aaron Hughes, the PSV striker moved forward to strike a lovely curling shot round Shay Given from 20 yards. Newcastle, though, were now experienced European campaigners, and they kept their heads, put up a strong wall of defence and forced their way back into the match. Their equaliser came at the perfect moment, right on the stroke of half-time. Laurent Robert's free-kick was met by Jermaine Jenas, who climbed above everyone to head home from six yards. The second period belonged largely to PSV, but although they enjoyed lots of possession, they created few opportunities: United's centre backs, Titus Bramble and Jonathan Woodgate, were holding firm. Only once did PSV get a look in, when Bouma's effort struck the woodwork. At the other end, Shearer cracked a 25-yarder that the PSV keeper turned over the crossbar.

MAN OF THE MATCH

Olivier Bernard – solid in defence, dangerous in attack.

| MATCH RATING | ● | ● | ● | | | |

Hard-fought draw.

STAR COMMENT

Jermaine Jenas: 'After their early goal, we settled down and started to get at them. We played well defensively to keep them out.'

EYEWITNESS

Luke Edwards (*The Journal*): 'Newcastle United held their line superbly to gain the upper hand in their first full-scale battle in the competition.'

TOUR STOP – EINDHOVEN

Newcastle's second journey to Eindhoven in the south of the Netherlands saw most United supporters stop off in Amsterdam en route. However, Eindhoven is itself a lively city, especially around De Markt, Wilhelminaplein and Stratumseind, notable as the street with the most bars in the whole of Holland. A green city with parks and biking routes, it has grown from a small provincial town into an important commercial centre. (pop. 206,000.)

STADIA FILE – PHILIPS STADION

Despite possessing only a modest capacity of 30,024, the Philips Stadion remains one of the finest small arenas on the Continent. Developed from a basic pitch in an open park, PSV's home is a popular venue and one that has seen plenty of big-match action in both the UEFA Cup and Champions League.

DID YOU KNOW

PSV's unusually named striker Jan Vennegoor of Hesselink took his title from a land deal and the merger of two farms in the Enschede region of Holland.

Match 88

2003–04
UEFA Cup, Quarter-Final: Newcastle United v. PSV Eindhoven (Holland)
SECOND LEG Wednesday, 14 April 2004, St. James' Park

PSV

UNITED Given, Hughes, Woodgate, Bramble (O'Brien), Bernard, Ambrose (Ameobi), Jenas, Speed, Robert (Viana), Shearer, Bellamy. Subs not used: Harper, Elliott, Dyer, Bridges.
Manager: Bobby Robson

PSV Waterreus, Bogelund, Colin, Bouma, Lee, van Bommel, Vogel (Vonlathen), de Jong, Rommedahl (Vennegoor of Hesselink), Kezman, Park. Subs not used: van Dijk, Leandro, van der Schaaf, Addo, Wuytens.
Manager: Guus Hiddink

REFEREE M. Gonzalez (Spain)

RESULT Won 2–1 (1–0)
AGGREGATE Won 3–2

ATTENDANCE 50,083

SCORERS United: Shearer (8), Speed (65); PSV: Kezman (50) (pen)

MATCH HIGHLIGHTS

The quarter-final tie was finely balanced after the first leg, and the two teams were evenly matched in the deciding encounter. It was a close tussle, and it took United's most experienced pros, Alan Shearer and Gary Speed, to steer the Magpies through to a semi-final meeting with Olympique Marseille. Both United's strikes were from close in and both were headers from set pieces. For the first goal, Laurent Robert's wicked in-swinging corner was met by Shearer at the near post after only eight minutes of play. It was the start the Toon Army wanted, but PSV were not going to be beaten lightly. They kept possession well and forced a penalty after a double error in United's back-line. Both Darren Ambrose and Olivier Bernard could have dealt better with a PSV cross, and Park Ji-Sung was upended in the penalty area. Kezman stepped up to drill the spot-kick past Shay Given. The game remained level until Speed delivered the winning strike in the 65th minute. Another vicious Robert corner was this time met by the Wales skipper, beating the flapping PSV keeper Waterreus to the ball. The final period of the match proved to be nail-biting, with PSV striving to score the winner, but Jonathan Woodgate and Titus Bramble held the line, and, after 35 years, Newcastle United had once more reached the semi-final of a European competition.

MAN OF THE MATCH

Jonathan Woodgate – commanding at the back.

MATCH RATING • • • •   Excellent scrap.

STAR COMMENT

Shay Given: 'It was "Game On" when they scored, but the lads stayed focused and came back at PSV. Even at 2–1 it was tense.'

EYEWITNESS

Alan Oliver (*Evening Chronicle*): 'Those last 20 minutes scared the life out of every Newcastle United fan. There wasn't anyone who did not know that if PSV scored again then United were out of the competition.'

OPPONENT FILE

PSV had entered the UEFA Cup via the Champions League. They had qualified for Europe's premier competition seven years in a row and were, without doubt, a quality outfit. Regulars at the top level in Europe, the club was at that time behind Ajax in the race for the Dutch championship. PSV were managed by experienced boss Guus Hiddink, who had already led them to four titles and the European Cup. Hiddink guided the team to the Champions League semi-final the following season, too.

STAR VISITOR

Mateja Kezman – Having faced United as a youngster when playing for Partizan Belgrade, the Serbian moved to Holland for £7 million after that encounter in 1998 to replace Ruud van Nistelrooy in PSV's attack. Noted as one of the most prolific goalscorers on the Continent, being quick and elusive, Kezman is a regular for the Serbian national side and attracted the attention of several top clubs while in the Netherlands. After the game between Newcastle and PSV, Kezman was even linked with a move to Tyneside but eventually joined Chelsea for £5 million in the summer of 2004, although goals were hard to come by in the Premiership.

DID YOU KNOW

Sir Bobby Robson lifted two Dutch titles with PSV and had at his disposal such players as Ronaldo and Romario, as well as Ruud van Nistelrooy in a later spell.

Match 89

2003–04

UEFA Cup, Semi-Final: Newcastle United v. Olympique de Marseille (France)
FIRST LEG Thursday, 22 April 2004, St. James' Park

Marseille

UNITED Given, Hughes, Woodgate, O'Brien, Bernard, Ambrose, Speed, Viana, Robert, Shearer, Ameobi (Bridges). Subs not used: Harper, Elliott, Bramble, Brittain, Orr, Chopra.
Manager: Bobby Robson

MARSEILLE Barthez, Beye, Hemdani, Meite, Ferreira, N'Diaye, Flamini, Dos Santos, Batlles (Celestini), Meriem, Drogba. Subs not used: Gavanon, Christanval, Vachousek, Ecker, Cicut, Ba.
Manager: José Anigo

REFEREE V. Ivanov (Russia)

RESULT Drew 0–0 (0–0)
AGGREGATE 0–0

ATTENDANCE 52,004

MATCH HIGHLIGHTS

The Magpies needed to be at their best – and at full strength – to take care of French giants Marseille. They also needed to take a lead to the partisan Mediterranean port for the deciding leg; however, without stars Kieron Dyer, Craig Bellamy, Lee Bowyer and Jermaine Jenas, they had an uphill task. In a fabulously noisy atmosphere at a packed St. James' Park, the Magpies gave it a go but found most openings falling to Shola Ameobi and not the clinical Alan Shearer. In the space of five minutes, Ameobi had two great opportunities to put United in front, running onto passes from Shearer and Laurent Robert only to see a header go off target and Barthez block the second effort with his knee. Gary Speed also missed a golden chance – an open goal – after a Shearer shot had been blocked. But it was one of those nights for the Black 'n' Whites: nothing would go past an inspired Fabien Barthez in the Marseille goal. At the other end of the field, the French danger man Didier Drogba showed much ability and volleyed the ball onto the inside of the post in the 64th minute, following a Meite cross, but the ball rebounded to safety. Newcastle headed to Provence with Marseille holding the advantage. United needed a clean bill of health and the return of influential figures. Instead, they unluckily faced another injury setback when defensive kingpin Jonathan Woodgate pulled out of the deciding match.

MAN OF THE MATCH

Jonathan Woodgate – a master at centre-half.

| MATCH RATING | ● | ● | ● | | | Unfortunate outcome. |

STAR COMMENT

Alan Shearer: 'Nil-nil might not have been a great result, but it's certainly not a bad one. They know as well as we do that if we get an away goal they have got to get two to win.'

EYEWITNESS

Rob Robertson (*The Herald*): 'If anyone was going to score on the night it was Drogba. Indeed, the Marseille striker could be the difference between whether Robson's European dream comes true or not.'

OPPONENT FILE

Marseille dropped out of the Champions League group stage and had just eliminated Internazionale. While they were only sixth in the French league, L'Om found their form in European action. France's biggest club with a huge and fanatical support, they had reached the pinnacle of their success during the '90s, lifting a succession of domestic honours as well as reaching two European Cup finals, winning the competition in 1993. However, a highly controversial financial scandal disgraced the club and only latterly had Marseille recovered their status in Europe. They are backed by the adidas corporation.

STAR VISITOR

Didier Drogba – A striker who rose to prominence in France in double-quick time, Drogba is from the Ivory Coast. He was outstanding for Marseille in the 2003–04 season, scoring regularly and at the highest level in the Champions League. An international player, Drogba joined Marseille from Guingamp and was soon under scrutiny from Europe's top clubs. His penetrating runs, physical presence and lethal finishing eventually resulted in a move to Chelsea after a massive £24 million deal.

DID YOU KNOW

Apart from the big summer move of Drogba to Chelsea, Marseille's young midfielder Mathieu Flamini was pinched by London rivals Arsenal. He went on to play an important role in the Gunners' season.

Match 90

2003–04
UEFA Cup, Semi-Final: Olympique de Marseille (France) v. Newcastle United
SECOND LEG Thursday, 6 May 2004, Stade Velodrome (Marseille)

Marseille

UNITED Given, Hughes, O'Brien, Bramble, Bernard, Ambrose, Viana (Bowyer), Speed, Robert, Shearer, Ameobi. Subs not used: Harper, Taylor, Elliott, Caldwell (S), Bridges, Chopra.
Manager: Bobby Robson

MARSEILLE Barthez, Beye, Hemdani, Meite, Ferreira, Flamini, N'Diaye, Dos Santos, Marlet (Batlles), Drogba (Vachousek), Meriem. Subs not used: Gavanon, Ecker, Christanval, Celistini, Merlin.
Manager: José Anigo

REFEREE L. Michel (Slovakia)

RESULT Lost 0–2 (0–1)

AGGREGATE Lost 0–2

ATTENDANCE 57,500

MATCH HIGHLIGHTS

In a hostile Velodrome arena, over 50,000 roared L'Om to victory against a United side rocked by more injury woe. England centre-half Jonathan Woodgate missed the match adding to the list of casualties that Bobby Robson already had to contend with. With Woodgate only able to watch from the sidelines, Didier Drogba proved to be the difference between the two sides, the Marseille centre-forward scoring two goals of quality – one in each half – to make sure the French side reached the final in Sweden rather than Newcastle. United's patched-up line-up missed Kieron Dyer and Craig Bellamy's pace in attack, and with Laurent Robert rarely involved, the Magpies only created one real opportunity. With 13 minutes to go and a goal behind, it was a crucial stage of the match. The ball fell for substitute Lee Bowyer on the six-yard line following an Ameobi header. His effort, though, went agonisingly past the wrong side of the post. If United had scored a goal at that point – and an away one at that – the outcome might have been very different. As it was, Drogba went up the other end of the field and converted a Batlles free-kick, firing home his second of the contest from an unmarked position. Marseille had landed the killer blow. His earlier 18th-minute goal had given the French side the advantage and got their big crowd fully behind them. Hugo Viana lost possession, Drogba's power and pace forced him past Aaron Hughes, and he calmly stroked the ball past Given into the

net. Marseille went on to face Valencia in the Gothenburg final and lost 0–2.

MAN OF THE MATCH
Titus Bramble – battled against the odds.

| MATCH RATING | ● | ● | ● | | | Bitter defeat. |

STAR COMMENT
Bobby Robson: 'It has been a long competition, and it is the first match that we have lost in 12 games in Europe, so I think we should be proud about that.'

EYEWITNESS
Simon Rushworth (*The Journal*): 'The Stade Velodrome rocked to Drogba's beat.'

TOUR STOP – MARSEILLE
Described as a 'bubbling, maritime melting-pot of a city', Marseille is the major port in France and has a diverse ethnic community. A hotbed of football, it is the oldest city in France. Set on the Mediterranean, it has the hills of Provence as its backdrop. The centre of the city revolves around the Vieux Port, a hive of activity of every sort, while there are also many grandiose buildings to see, including Vieille Charité and the Notre-Dame-de-la-Garde, which offers fabulous views. (pop. 796,000.)

STADIA FILE – STADE VELODROME
Built to coincide with the 1938 World Cup in France with a cycling track that gave the arena its name, Marseille's famous Stade Velodrome has undergone much alteration, most notably for the 1998 World Cup. An intimidating arena when full, the Velodrome holds 60,000 and is the biggest club ground in France. Almost totally open to the elements with one main stand, the arena, nevertheless, creates a tremendous and colourful atmosphere.

DID YOU KNOW
Lee Bowyer's appearance was his first European game for 12 matches, after serving a lengthy suspension handed out during his Leeds United days. An administrative mishap led to the player having to serve double the sentence, making it one of the longest Euro bans on record.

Tour Stop

Marseille – France

①

②

④

③

Olympique de Marseille 2003–04

1. Postcard from Marseille

The Stade Velodrome is pictured in the foreground of this bird's-eye view of Marseille, France's second city. The lively Vieux Port area is situated to the top right of the postcard.

2. Postcard from Stade Velodrome

Marseille's Velodrome, housing a fanatical home-team support, proved an intimidating venue for United's UEFA Cup semi-final clash.

3. Match Action

The atmosphere in Marseille was terrific; the stadium was full of noise, colour, flares and fireworks.

4. Memorabilia

Match ticket from the semi-final contest.

'He can be frustrating at times, but we know the brilliance is in there just a case of getting it out of him'
Alan Shearer

Laurent Robert

Every side needs a touch of magic and flair, even the most resolute of teams. After all, football is entertainment and supporters pay to be entertained. Especially so at St. James' Park, a club with a tradition of big names and celebrity players who have delighted the Gallowgate crowd down the years.

From the same enigmatic mould as the likes of Tino Asprilla and Jinky Smith before him, Laurent Robert is a player who could be both quite brilliant and infuriatingly mediocre in the space of a few moments. But he was a match-winner: a player who could turn the course of a game with a piece of virtuoso skill that only a select few could produce. When he joined United Robert said, 'I'm going to bring that little bit extra to Newcastle that has been lacking to make them into the great team they were before.' It was hoped that he would be the final piece in a rebuilding strategy that would see the Magpies back in contention at both the top of the Premiership and in Europe. It worked . . . for a while.

Born on the Indian Ocean island of Réunion – a French colony since the seventeenth century and some 8,000 miles from Europe – Robert joined United as a 26 year old in August 2001. Having become a noted performer in Le Championnat, he cost United a hefty £9.5 million fee from Paris Saint-Germain, which is still one of the club's highest transfer fees on record. Like David Ginola, United's previous star signing from France, Robert very quickly became a firm favourite of the Toon Army. Both could get the crowd roaring and both had the ability to whip the ball in from the flanks. Ginola perhaps had more flair and razzmatazz but he never scored enough goals. Robert, on the other hand, may not have been so stylish but he not only made goals, he scored them too, often with stunning shots that swerved and dipped from 20 to 35 yards out.

Goalkeepers could never judge what would happen when Robert got within shooting distance. Sometimes they would be relieved to see the ball fired high over the bar. Sometimes, though, Robert caught it just right, and the ball turned one way, then the other, before flying past the unfortunate goalkeeper and into the net.

In Laurent's first season he claimed ten goals, then another five in 2002–03, and twelve the following year. He provided the side with goals from midfield and created twice as many from his vicious crosses and dead-ball kicks. In Bobby Robson's new-look attack alongside Alan Shearer and Craig Bellamy, Robert was an important addition. Captain Alan Shearer said at the time, 'Laurent gives us great width on the left. There are not many players in the Premiership like Laurent, and, certainly, we don't have another player like him here at Newcastle. He whips a great ball in.'

In Continental action, having appeared for PSG in the early days of the Champions League,

Laurent Robert

Robert knew what to expect. He became a big favourite at the Parc des Princes, enjoying a wonderful 2000–01 season and performing well in Europe for the Parisian side that year. Alongside some talented players, including Nicolas Anelka and Jay-Jay Okocha, Robert took on the likes of Bayern Munich and Scandinavian sides Rosenborg and Helsingborg. PSG qualified for the second phase with comfort but faced stiffer opponents in a tough group with Deportivo La Coruna, Galatasaray and AC Milan. The French club struggled, but Robert did find the net against AC Milan.

His 15 goals that season brought him to the attention of many managers around Europe and persuaded Bobby Robson to write that sizeable cheque. Robert went on to be a prominent member of Robson's Champions League qualifying side in the 2001–02 season, while his experience was important during United's European run the following year. He started to impress in the double-header with Juventus, in the Stadio Delle Alpi and in the return leg at Gallowgate, while he continued to be a threat against Dynamo Kyiv. Robert missed the deciding Group E match in Rotterdam with Feyenoord due to injury, but was back for the second phase. He was effective in both games against Germany's Bayer Leverkusen and in the San Siro when United took on Inter.

Yet his inconsistency caused conflict between the player and his boss, and Robson once admitted that 'sometimes we have screaming matches'. Sir Bobby worked hard to make Robert a top player. He said, 'As a manager, Laurent is my greatest challenge since Romario, but we will make him a better player.' Some time later, he also ironically added, 'When I finally get him right, I will be 120 years of age!'

The following year, as United headed for the latter stages of the UEFA Cup, no one in or out of the dressing-room knew which Laurent Robert

LAURENT ROBERT: FACT FILE

Position: Outside-left/Midfield

Born: Saint-Benoît (Réunion), May 1975

Joined United from: Paris Saint-Germain, August 2001, £9.5 million

Left for: Portsmouth, June 2005, loan

Other major clubs: Brest (France), Montpellier (France), Benfica (Portugal)

Full international: France (9 caps, 1999 to date)

United career, senior games: 181 app., 32 goals

United Euro record: 35 app., 5 goals

Did you know: Laurent Robert made his debut for France against Northern Ireland alongside such eminent names as Fabien Barthez, Bixente Lizarazu, Patrick Vieira, Laurent Blanc, Marcel Desailly and Robert Pires. In goal for the Irish that night was ex-United keeper Tommy Wright.

would be on show from match to match. He was terrific against Breda and Basel. However, against Marseille in the semi-final, United were badly affected by injuries and needed a big performance from the Frenchman. But, as is the way with many players of his breed, he lacked drive and did not look in the mood for a match-winning display, either at St. James' Park or in the Velodrome.

When Graeme Souness came in as the Magpies' new boss, he also felt the same frustrations as his predecessor at Gallowgate. The Scot worked hard to make Robert recognise that while United had to entertain, they also needed to be winners. Souness stressed to Laurent that in the modern game wingers – or wide midfielders – had to do much more than wait around for the ball to come to them. They had to contribute in all areas of the field. On

Laurent Robert

Laurent Robert could be a match winner but also an expensive luxury.

more than one occasion, the man from Réunion was frustrated at being left on the sidelines. Robert said in an interview, 'The manager has no confidence in me.' He added, 'He says I am lazy in training.' Despite this, he also noted, 'I want to stay with United, I really do, but if I am not going to play, then I will move on.'

However, the two appeared to create a working relationship in the end but, as it turned out, only for a short period. Robert initially acknowledged that his boss was right and Souness admitted that United's attack needed Laurent's magic. The manager said, 'In terms of his abilities at dead-ball situations, Laurent is up there with all the top players around.' Alan Shearer remarked, 'We all know the ability Laurent has. He can be frustrating at times, but

we know the brilliance is in there – it's just a case of getting it out of him.'

That touch of magic and brilliance was in evidence in the UEFA Cup match against Dutch side Heerenveen as United made a bid for the trophy. With Shearer, Patrick Kluivert and Shola Ameobi selected up front, United's front line looked decidedly awkward, while the midfield lacked creative ability, especially from the flanks. Robert came off the bench for Ameobi and immediately made an impact. Shearer and Kluivert now had some service and United prospered.

Against Olympiacos in Piraeus, the Frenchman scored a wonderful trademark free-kick that put the Magpies in charge, but after that, Robert went back into his shell. The

Laurent Robert

relationship between the manager and player broke down again as Robert was often substituted following ineffectual displays. Once more, the crunch came in the big-match arena: this time the quarter-final against Sporting Clube. His performance at St. James' Park prompted Graeme Souness to say, 'I was looking for more from him, a lot more.' So were the fans.

In the return leg in Lisbon, Robert was conspicuous by his absence – literally so. The Black 'n' Whites needed the experienced Robert to be full of fire against Sporting Clube. Instead, he was not even on the bench. Another bust-up with his manager on the eve of one of the club's biggest-ever weeks saw Souness 'disappointed and amazed' at the Frenchman's media outburst criticizing his managerial reign and United's lack of progress. Some of the comments made by Robert may have had some merit, but the timing was appalling: it was as if he planned to disrupt the build-up to the Magpies' crucial games against Sporting and then Manchester United in the FA Cup semi-final.

Always popular with United's faithful, Robert once said, 'To hear the fans sing my name is very good for me. I appreciate the support.' However, many supporters, like Robson and Souness, were at times utterly frustrated with the Frenchman. They moaned both when he was on the pitch, if he appeared lethargic, and when he was on the bench, willing him to come on and turn the game. He was the ultimate enigma. Robert had the talent to be ranked with the best of his country – with Robert Pires and Thierry Henry, for example – but often appeared to lack the ambition, the motivation and the work ethic for the English game. He also seemed to lack the big-match temperament to be considered as the equal of those two Arsenal and Les Bleus stars.

The Toon Army expected, at the very least, consistent displays from Robert, if not regular match-winning performances. However, all too often, what they got instead was mediocre, moody efforts from the Frenchman. The fans longed for the moments of magic that the left boot of Robert could produce. Moments like his spectacular double strike against Tottenham Hotspur: a dipping volley at the Leazes End and a wonder screamer at Gallowgate. Then there were earlier gems against Arsenal: a lovely run and shot at Highbury followed by a fired-up effort of equal quality at St. James' Park. There were also stunning long-range goals at Derby and at Anfield, not to forget the volleyed corker that he flew past the Villa keeper and an often remembered free-kick that sailed past Manchester United's Fabien Barthez. Latterly, exquisite dead-ball opportunities hit the net against Sochaux and Olympiacos as well as in Premier League action against Manchester City and Liverpool.

Unfortunately, it was not to be. By the end of the 2004–05 season, Robert was heading to a new club and a new start. Having scored over 30 goals in 181 games for the Magpies, his record looked a decent one, but it could and should have been much better. As Souness began to remodel his United squad during a busy summer, Robert was one of several stars to move on. The 30-year-old French international joined Portsmouth during June with a view to a permanent deal. Alan Oliver wrote in the *Evening Chronicle*, 'The enigmatic French winger is undoubtedly one of the most talented players United have had in recent seasons.' He added, 'Robert continued to alternate between being brilliant and looking as though he did not care, leaving steam coming out of Souness' ears.'

9

THE LONG ROAD TO LISBON

2004–05

United and Olympiacos players enter the Karaiskakis
Stadium to a vociferous welcome.

Sir Bobby Robson was still in charge as the 2004–05 season began, and the experienced boss needed to pick his side up following a disappointing end to the last programme: losing the UEFA Cup semi-final to Marseille then failing by a whisker in another chase with Liverpool for a Champions League spot. Newcastle should have qualified in fourth place with room to spare, but a late-season slump and poor away record, compounded by those injuries that hindered their effort against Marseille, saw the Anfield club overtake the Magpies and secure the lucrative prize. For the second year running, the Black 'n' Whites missed out on the financial windfall of Champions League football.

Once again, Robson's team was competing in the UEFA Cup but this time in a newly introduced format featuring an initial group stage followed by a traditional knockout phase. Again, if any side was going to lift the trophy, they faced a tough schedule: 15 matches including the final at the remodelled and impressive Estádio José Alvalade in Lisbon.

United's veteran boss, however, was to take no part in Newcastle's latest UEFA Cup bid. The Magpies' pre-season and early league results were unacceptable to the board, and the manager was also tainted by the controversy of dressing-room unrest and a bust-up with star midfielder Kieron Dyer. Robson was axed at the end of September after five years in charge, just before the Magpies were to face Hapoel Bnei Sakhnin, an unknown quantity from Israel, in the first round of their UEFA Cup campaign. Three-times European Cup winner Graeme Souness was brought in to take the reins and guide the team through what was going to be a long schedule that would see the club reach the milestone of a century of European fixtures. Souness had an impressive pedigree in Continental football as a player and manager, most notably with Liverpool and Glasgow Rangers.

The former Blackburn Rovers boss would have Robson's summer signings Patrick Kluivert and Nicky Butt at his disposal, both of whom were, like their new manager, past winners of UEFA's premier competition. Tottenham's international full-back Stephen Carr and young England hopeful James Milner were also added to the squad.

Newcastle found the early games of the UEFA Cup to be somewhat unattractive yet they made comfortable progress. They won their first five matches against less than quality opponents at a canter, scoring fourteen goals and conceding only a single effort. However, they did face trips to new and appealing destinations: Athens and Tel Aviv included. As with the season before, many critics said that the competition only really started in February. By this time, most of the lesser clubs are eliminated and the third-placed Champions League sides join the fray. There were, therefore, some big names contesting the UEFA Cup by then. Newcastle United and neighbours Middlesbrough were the British representatives, while the likes of Benfica, Valencia, Ajax and old foes Dynamo Kyiv were all still in the competition.

On paper, the squad Graeme Souness possessed looked good, packed with a mix of youthful talent and experienced heads. The manager acknowledged he had some 'world-class players' and added, 'I am inheriting a group of footballers who are only going to get better.' Souness said, 'The club is in great nick,

everything is in place.' His target for the season was qualification for the Champions League, and, on the way, the team might even lift the UEFA Cup. However, hidden in the dressing-room was a hornets' nest of trouble for the new boss to cope with, and blending the mix of seasoned professionals and temperamental young superstars proved increasingly difficult. In addition, injury too often disrupted United's progress – yet again. The injured list that season included Patrick Kluivert, who when fit and eager looked a class apart, Kieron Dyer and Titus Bramble, who as the season unfolded increasingly looked like he might be the answer to Newcastle's defensive problems.

As Souness settled into life at St. James' Park he soon found he had many issues to resolve. Player power spilled over, and the Scot had to show the team who was boss. Craig Bellamy was sent into exile following a headline-making exchange with the manager, while Olivier Bernard joined Southampton and Laurent Robert became frustrated at his lack of playing opportunities. New faces of international quality arrived: Celestine Babayaro, Amdy Faye and the £8 million signing of French centre-half Jean-Alain Boumsong, although he took no part in the UEFA Cup run having already played in the competition for Rangers.

United's back-line was strengthened by the introduction of Carr and Babayaro, and the emergence of Titus Bramble, while youngster Steven Taylor also contributed. Dyer was rehabilitated in midfield and Robert came to accept the manager's philosophy on football – initially at any rate. Nicky Butt, Amdy Faye, Jermaine Jenas and a rejuvenated Lee Bowyer gave the side a formidable midfield choice. Up front they were still led by the old warhorse Alan Shearer – in what was labelled as his last season, although he played on for a further year. He operated alongside either Patrick Kluivert or Shola Ameobi. After an initial difficult period under Souness, United's new-look line-up eventually clicked and set out on a double cup bid: at home in the FA Cup and on the

Continent in the UEFA Cup.

Newcastle continued to cruise through the early rounds of the UEFA Cup impressively, and were unbeaten in ten games. Apart from nine victories, they also drew once against Sporting Lisbon in a largely meaningless final group-stage contest. The Magpies topped their league table and went into the knockout phase in confident mood, having previously defeated the Athens-based Panionios, the once-mighty Dinamo Tbilisi and FC Sochaux.

As the tournament really got started, Newcastle took care of Dutch side Heerenveen with ease before facing Olympiacos. The Toon Army were able to enjoy another trip to the ancient and cosmopolitan city of Athens, or to be more accurate, the neighbouring port of Piraeus. It was a tough draw: the Greek side had performed well in the Champions League and were unlucky to be one of the refugees in the UEFA Cup. However, Newcastle were again commanding with both Shearer and Kluivert in goalscoring form, striking 11 goals between them up to that point and eventually scoring 16 all told. In a stirring first leg at the Karaiskakis Stadium, in which the Greeks had

Graeme Souness almost guided United to another semi-final but was to depart soon after.

United's bench in Piraeus with the travelling Toon Army behind. Left to right: manager Graeme Souness, assistants Terry McDermott, Alan Murray and physio Derek Wright.

two men sent off, United won 3–1. They then eased into the last eight of the competition 7–1 on aggregate, following a 4–0 romp at St. James' Park in a match that marked the club's much-heralded 100th European fixture. Graeme Souness was highly satisfied and said, 'We look like a confident side now.' The Black 'n' Whites also looked like winners and were hailed as one of the hot favourites to lift the trophy. Chairman Freddy Shepherd was proud of the club's European milestone. He said, 'To reach a century of European matches is a truly magnificent achievement – one which only six other English clubs before us have been able to claim.' Significantly, Shepherd also added, 'And when it is taken into account that 72 of those 100 games have taken place since 1994, it indicates the rise of Newcastle United as an international football power.'

The Magpies marched on into their next century of European matches with real hope of lifting the UEFA Cup in the enticing city of Lisbon. However, as is Newcastle's way, little went according to plan.

With an ever-so-typical Continental crowd in the background, Alan Shearer leads United out in Athens alongside the Panionios skipper.

MATCHES 91 – 100 & ON

Newcastle's line-up in Tel Aviv. Back row, left to right: Hughes, O'Brien, Bowyer, Bernard, Robert, Kluivert; front: Jenas, Shearer, Given, Carr, Bellamy.

2004–05

Israel, Tel Aviv	v. Hapoel Bnei Sakhnin	2–0, 5–1, Agg 7–1	UEFA Cup R1
Greece, Athens	v. Panionios	1–0, Group D	UEFA Cup, Gp
Georgia, Tbilisi	v. Dinamo Tbilisi	2–0, Group D	UEFA Cup, Gp
France, Sochaux	v. FC Sochaux-Montbéliard	4–0, Group D	UEFA Cup, Gp
Portugal, Lisbon	v. Sporting Clube	1–1, Group D	UEFA Cup, Gp
Holland, Heerenveen	v. SC Heerenveen	2–1, 2–1, Agg 4–2	UEFA Cup, R3
Greece, Piraeus	v. Olympiacos CFP	3–1, 4–0, Agg 7–1	UEFA Cup, R4
Portugal, Lisbon	v. Sporting Clube	1–0, 1–4, Agg 2–4	UEFA Cup, QF

Euro Facts & Figures

On the Bench

United players to have appeared on the bench as substitute but who have made no senior appearance:
Dave Clarke (1968–69), Jason Drysdale (1994–95), Paul Barrett (1996–97), Brian Pinas (1997–98), Stuart Elliott (1997–98), Lionel Perez (1998–99), Stuart Green (2001–02), Tony Caig (2003–04 & 2004–05), Bradley Orr (2003–04), Paul Huntington (2005–06)

Competition Analysis (to cs 2006)

UEFA Champions League
P18 W7 D2 L9   17%

UEFA Champions League qualifiers
P6 W4 D1 L1   6%

UEFA Cup
P46 W28 D8 L10   43%

Inter Cities/European Fairs Cup
P24 W13 D6 L5   23%

European Cup Winners Cup
P2 W1 D0 L1   2%

UEFA Intertoto Cup
P10 W6 D2 L2   9%

Match Record (to cs 2006)

Overall:
P106 W59 D19 L28 F188 A111
Success-rate 56%

Home:
P53 W39 D6 L8 F112 A42
Success-rate 74%

Away:
P53 W20 D13 L20 F76 A69
Success-rate 38%

Match 91

2004–05
UEFA Cup, Round 1: Newcastle United v. Hapoel Bnei Sakhnin (Israel)
FIRST LEG Thursday, 16 September 2004, St. James' Park

Bnei Sakhnin

UNITED Given, Carr, O'Brien, Elliott, Hughes (Bernard), Dyer (Butt), Bowyer, Jenas, Robert, Ameobi (Milner), Kluivert. Subs not used: Harper, Shearer, Bellamy, Ambrose.
Manager: Graeme Souness

HAPOEL Murambadoro, Kassom (Edri), Danan, Etchi, Ghnaim (Salameh), Rabah, Eliyahu, Suan, Hamud (Rodrigues), Masudi, Agoye. Subs not used: Hillik, Shalaata, Khalaili, Salah.
Manager: Eyal Lachman

REFEREE A. Costa (Portugal)

RESULT Won 2–0 (2–0)

AGGREGATE 2–0

SENT OFF Butt (61), Suan (61)

ATTENDANCE 30,221

SCORERS United: Kluivert (3), (40)

MATCH HIGHLIGHTS

Many judges reckoned Newcastle would win the game at a canter, the difference in status between the clubs being so huge, but the energetic Israelis proved to be annoying opponents, breaking up Newcastle's flow with a mix of fouls and enthusiasm. With new boss Graeme Souness in charge for the first time and without the rested Alan Shearer and Craig Bellamy, United did just enough against a rugged defence. With Dutch star Patrick Kluivert up front, the Magpies still had sufficient firepower to ensure a comfortable victory. Kluivert twice opened up the Sakhnin defence to register United's two goals at either end of the first half. For the first, a Laurent Robert cross caused problems and the big striker pounced on a loose ball to net the opener. The Dutchman was then twice denied by the Sakhnin goalkeeper Energy Murambadoro, while Jermaine Jenas had a goal-bound effort saved, too. Robert had the ball in the net but it was ruled out by the referee, and Dyer missed a great opportunity to put United two goals in front. However, just before the interval Kluivert again met a Robert corner, and his header went in off the post and crossbar. In the second half, Newcastle could and should have registered more goals as the game deteriorated into an ill-tempered affair with the visitors picking up six yellow cards as the result of over-zealous tackling. The match boiled over just as Nicky Butt came on from the substitutes bench, the former England man immediately becoming embroiled in a confrontation with the Sakhnin skipper Suan and both were sent off by referee Costa. Newcastle, however, had done enough to give themselves the advantage for the return leg in Tel Aviv.

MAN OF THE MATCH

Patrick Kluivert – alone in class and guile.

MATCH RATING	●	●			

Bland tussle.

STAR COMMENT

Robbie Elliott: 'It was a physical sort of game. Sakhnin came with a game plan to get about us and disrupt the play.'

EYEWITNESS

Tim Rich (*The Independent*): 'For Sakhnin to be here at all was remarkable. The town's entire population would have comfortably fitted into St. James' Park twice over.'

OPPONENT FILE

Unheard of outside their own country, Sakhnin were the first Arab side to ever appear in UEFA competition. The club had enjoyed a meteoric rise since being formed by the merger of Hapoel and Maccabi in 1993, and despite a constant financial struggle, they forged a strong identity in Sakhnin, a small community in the north of Israel. Their entry into the competition was likened to 'Whitley Bay getting into the UEFA Cup'.

STAR VISITOR

Ernst Etchi – An experienced central defender with over 30 caps for Cameroon, Etchi possessed plenty of big-game experience, including appearances in the World Cup finals and African Nations Cup. At 29 years old, he was tall and powerful, his club's key player and was instrumental in Sakhnin lifting Israel's domestic cup in 2004. Previously, Etchi played his football in France and Belgium, while he has also appeared in Champions League football.

DID YOU KNOW

Nicky Butt was ordered off only 133 seconds after coming on as a substitute in place of hamstring victim Kieron Dyer for grabbing the Israeli captain Abas Suan by the throat.

Match 92

2004–05

UEFA Cup, Round 1: Hapoel Bnei Sakhnin (Israel) v. Newcastle United
SECOND LEG Thursday, 30 September 2004, Ramat Gan Stadium (Tel Aviv)

Bnei Sakhnin

UNITED Given (Harper), Carr, O'Brien, Hughes, Bernard, Bellamy, Bowyer, Jenas, Robert (Ambrose), Shearer, Kluivert (Milner). Subs not used: Elliott, Taylor, Ramage, Brittain. Manager: Graeme Souness

HAPOEL Murambadoro, Rabah (Rodrigues), Etchi, Danan, Ghnaim, Kassom, Eliyaha, Masudi, Khalaili, Arshid (Edri), Agoye (Salah). Subs not used: Hillik, Nidal, Salameh, Hamud.
Manager: Eyal Lachman

REFEREE J. Santiago (Spain)

RESULT Won 5–1 (3–1)

AGGREGATE Won 7–1

SENT OFF Murambadoro (88)

ATTENDANCE 14,000

SCORERS United: Kluivert (9), Shearer (37), Kluivert (41), Shearer (51), (90); Hapoel: Masudi (13)

MATCH HIGHLIGHTS

On a hot and dry evening in Tel Aviv, Newcastle's power and class, especially from Alan Shearer and Patrick Kluivert, tore the Israeli side apart. United's front pair, two of the finest European strikers of the last decade, were far too good for the Sakhnin defence, and, in the end, it was ruthlessly exposed. Kluivert netted twice in the first half, and Shearer grabbed a hat-trick as Newcastle largely dominated the match. Chances were quickly carved out, and Newcastle took the lead in the ninth minute when Jenas cleverly set up Kluivert with a marvellous back-heel. The Dutchman swept home his shot with ease. As in the first leg on Tyneside, Sakhnin showed plenty of passion and were rugged with it, and they equalised against the run of play within four minutes of Newcastle scoring. After slack United defending, Masudi turned in a cross by Kassom. At that point, United stepped up a gear. A Lee Bowyer shot was spilled by Murambadoro and Shearer was on the spot to make the score 2–1 – 4–1 on aggregate – and Kluivert struck again before the interval. A Laurent Robert run and pass was clinically finished off by the former Barcelona striker. After the break, Newcastle were so much on top that it looked more like a training-ground match and more goals were scored. Jenas was bundled over in the box and Shearer struck home the penalty, sending the keeper the wrong way. Then the eccentric Murambadoro handled the

ball outside his box to stop Craig Bellamy. The Sakhnin keeper was ordered off by referee Santiago and Khalaila took over between the posts. The stand-in was soon picking the ball out of his goal, though, as a Shearer shot flew past him and into the net.

MAN OF THE MATCH
Patrick Kluivert – the touch of a master.

| MATCH RATING | ● | ● | ● | | | Ill-matched encounter. |

STAR COMMENT
Graeme Souness: 'They were just reckless in their challenges, and I would have liked the referee to have been a bit stronger.'

EYEWITNESS
Luke Edwards (*The Journal*): 'Sakhnin hustled, bustled and kicked; Newcastle passed, moved and scored.'

TOUR STOP – TEL AVIV
It was Newcastle's first-ever visit to Israel and to Tel Aviv, a fascinating city full of energy, life and a vibrant edge. A mix of ancient and modern, it is where East meets West. The old streets of Jaffa give the flavour of the Middle East of old, while the Tayelet beachfront is very much Mediterranean in style. The first all-Jewish city in the region and the country's largest, Tel Aviv has to cope with a constant terrorist threat, and tight security was evident at every corner. (pop. 360,000.)

STADIA FILE – RAMAT GAN
With Sakhnin's tiny and somewhat dilapidated stadium on the edge of the Galilee Hills being far from the minimum UEFA standard, the game was switched 60 miles to the Israeli national arena in Tel Aviv. Holding over 40,000, the venue is an open bowl with brightly coloured seating that slopes gently down to an athletics track and pitch. Also featuring one vast two-tiered stand, the arena is the home to Maccabi Tel-Aviv.

DID YOU KNOW
Newcastle played in a new European away kit of bright yellow tops with black trim and black shorts.

Goalkeeper Steve Harper.

Tour Stop

Tel Aviv – Israel

Hapoel Bnei Sakhnin 2004–05

The marina on Tel Aviv's waterfront showing several of the city's high-rise hotels. The UEFA Cup tie with Sakhnin gave Newcastle the opportunity to visit Israel for the first time.

An evening view of Tel Aviv's national arena, Ramat Gan, a sprawling open bowl with a vast double-decked stand along one touchline.

Patrick Kluivert leaps to head a goal into the Gallowgate net during the first leg on Tyneside.

Match ticket from Israel, in Hebrew.

Athens – Greece

Panionios
2004–05

One of the wonders of the world: the Acropolis, majestically overlooking Athens. The Greek capital may be the spiritual home to the Olympics, but football is now king.

The modest home of Panionios. No one knew it at the time, but the Toon Army would be soon back in Athens – just a mile from the Nea Smyrni to face Olympiacos in Piraeus.

Captain Alan Shearer crashes home the spot-kick in Athens after Shola Ameobi had been fouled.

Match ticket for the game in Greece showing the newly introduced UEFA Cup branding.

Nea Smyrni Stadium

Match 93

2004–05

UEFA Cup, Round 2, Group D: Panionios (Greece) v. Newcastle United
Matchday 1, Thursday, 21 October 2004, Nea Smyrni Stadium (Athens)

Panionios

UNITED Given, Carr, O'Brien, Elliott, Bernard, Milner (Ameobi), Jenas, Bowyer, Robert, Shearer, Bellamy. Subs not used: Harper, Taylor, Brittain, Hughes, Bramble, Ambrose. Manager: Graeme Souness

PANIONIOS Colceag, Spiropoulos, Giannopoulos, Vlcek, Makos, Domoraud, Dodd, Zimonjic (Goundoulakis), Tziolis, Parodi (Lagonikakis), Breska. Subs not used: Exouzidis, Mitrou, Meszaros, Mantzios, Sotiriou. Manager: Karol Pecze

REFEREE R. Rosetti (Italy)

RESULT Won 1–0 (0–0)

POSITION IN GROUP 2nd/3 pts

ATTENDANCE 8,000

SCORERS United: Shearer (86) (pen)

MATCH HIGHLIGHTS

Newcastle started the new UEFA Cup group format with a frustrating performance against Greek side Panionios in Athens. In a drab contest on a poor pitch, United clinched the game late on with a spot-kick from skipper Alan Shearer. In the end, it was a hard-earned result and showed that Newcastle could go away from home, play badly and pinch a result. In the first half, Panionios were content to pack men behind the ball in a bid to frustrate United, and with the Magpies unable to create much going forward, the match deteriorated into a dour spectacle. Jermaine Jenas could have scored, but the young midfielder skied a fabulous opportunity from 12 yards out over the bar. Newcastle had to be patient and after the break did start to control the match, keeping possession of the ball and spraying it around the field, but chances were hard to come by against a packed defence. However, a change from the bench made a difference. Graeme Souness sent on Shola Ameobi in the 66th minute, and he soon caused problems in the box for the Greeks. After Shearer saw a header turned over the bar and a Laurent Robert free-kick went close, Ameobi had a penalty appeal turned down. Minutes later, the same player was again felled in the box as he attempted to slip past two defenders. Makos had raised his knee, and, this time, the Italian referee Rosetti awarded the spot-kick. Up stepped centre-forward Alan Shearer to fire the ball hard and high into the net to secure three points for United in Group D.

MAN OF THE MATCH

Robbie Elliott – comfortable and assured.

| MATCH RATING | ● | | | | | Tedious skirmish. |

STAR COMMENT

Alan Shearer: 'We were never going to lose the game. Panionios didn't get people forward and tried to play on the break, and their tactics did make life difficult for us.'

EYEWITNESS

Simon Rushworth (*The Journal*): 'United's doleful Athenian adventure will be quickly forgotten.'

TOUR STOP – ATHENS

A cosmopolitan, ancient capital, Athens had just undergone a pleasing multi-million refurbishment for the 2004 Olympics when United visited the dramatic city. With sights galore, including the citadel of the Acropolis, the new Olympic complex and the old town of Plaka with its narrow winding streets, Athens was a tourist gem for the travelling Toon Army. It is also a vibrant, modern city and the population is football obsessed. Athens has a coastal stretch at Piraeus, too, where United would soon play one of their most dramatic ties. (pop. 746,000.)

STADIA FILE – NEA SMYRNI

With a capacity of only 11,700 – reduced due to the structural failure of one of the stands – the Nea Smyrni arena is situated in a plush suburb of Athens on the way to the coast and Piraeus. With bright red and blue colours, the stadium has been upgraded in recent years with the addition of upper tiers, while the the floodlit Acropolis provides a magnificent backdrop to the arena in the evening. It was originally constructed in 1940.

DID YOU KNOW

United's victory was the club's 50th in Europe since their debut back in 1968: P93 W50 D18 L25.

Experienced defender Robbie Elliott.

Dinamo Tbilisi

UNITED Given, Hughes, O'Brien, Elliott (Bramble), Bernard, Bellamy, Jenas, Bowyer (Ambrose), Robert, Kluivert, Shearer (Milner). Subs not used: Harper, Ameobi, Taylor, Brittain. Manager: Graeme Souness

DINAMO Mamaladze, Kashia (Silagadze), Salukvadze, Shashiashvili, Melkadze (Gancharov), Kakaladze, Kandelaki, Kankava, Aladashvili (Akhalaia), Nemsadze, Kvirkvelia. Subs not used: Zoidze, Dvali, Makharadze, Gigauri. Manager: Gia Gegucahdze

REFEREE E. Bernsten (Norway)

RESULT Won 2–0 (1–0)

POSITION IN GROUP 1st/6 pts

ATTENDANCE 27,218

SCORERS United: Shearer (37), Bellamy (55)

MATCH HIGHLIGHTS

United's victory over Dinamo Tbilisi almost secured them a place in the knockout stage of the UEFA Cup, with three of the five sides in each group going through. Once Alan Shearer had blazed Newcastle into the lead in the 37th minute, only one side was going to collect all three points. On top for most of the match, Newcastle should have been comfortably ahead before Shearer's strike. A mix of poor finishing and good goalkeeping kept Tbilisi in the hunt, but that was to soon change. Shay Given's long punt was headed on by Laurent Robert. Patrick Kluivert picked up the loose ball in midfield and played a first-time precision lay-off into the path of Shearer. The Newcastle No. 9 struck a 14-yard shot that flashed past keeper Mamaladze and into the net at the near post. Once more, Kluivert was a class apart at this level. He went close on a number of occasions and was unlucky not to score the goal that his performance deserved. Newcastle made it 2–0 in the second half when Craig Bellamy latched onto a poor headed clearance from a Robert corner, the Welshman volleying the loose ball into the back of the net. Dinamo showed neat touches on the ball in midfield, but a lack of penetration meant they rarely threatened United's goal, and it was left to the Magpies to create the chances. The Geordies should have scored more, but a poor final delivery stopped the visitors heading back home to Georgia with an embarrassing score line to their name, as chance after chance was wasted.

MAN OF THE MATCH

Patrick Kluivert – too good for this level.

| MATCH RATING | ● | ● | | | | Run-of-the-mill engagement. |

STAR COMMENT

Graeme Souness: 'We dominated the game throughout but were disappointed we didn't score more.'

EYEWITNESS

Paul Tully (Newcastle United match-day programme): 'Tbilisi were honest and brave but strictly limited, and United's attacking football should and would have produced more goals had the final ball into the box been more precise.'

OPPONENT FILE

Since first playing in Europe back in 1973, Dinamo Tbilisi have been regular UEFA participants and won the Cup Winners Cup in 1981 by defeating Carl-Zeiss Jena. The leading club in Georgia, without question, Dinamo were also a force to be reckoned with in the communist era, twice being crowned as champions of the Soviet Union. Since the establishment of Georgia's own football league in 1990, they have lifted a remarkable ten titles in a row.

STAR VISITOR

Giorgi Nemsadze – Skipper of Dinamo at 32 years old, Giorgi Nemsadze was an experienced international midfielder for Georgia, having been capped on 72 occasions. Nemsadze started his career with Tbilsi and returned home in 2004 after a respectable tour of Europe with clubs in Germany, Turkey, Switzerland and Italy; he also played for Dundee in Scotland. He lifted the Swiss title with Grasshoppers and saw regular action on the European scene. Nemsadze was a hugely influential player on his day.

DID YOU KNOW

Alan Shearer's goal was Newcastle United's 100th home strike in Europe since Jim Scott's opener against Feyenoord in 1968.

Sochaux

UNITED Given, Hughes, Bramble, Elliott, Bernard, Butt, Bowyer (Dyer), Ambrose (Taylor), Milner (Robert), Ameobi, Bellamy. Subs not used: Harper, Kluivert, Jenas, Brittain. Manager: Graeme Souness

SOCHAUX Richert, Daf, Diawara, Paisley, Mathieu, Isabey (Diarra), Lonfat (Boudarene), Pitau, Oruma, Ilan, Menez (Santos). Subs not used: Gnanhouan, Tall, De Carvalho, Lavie. Manager: Guy Lacombe

REFEREE C. Davila (Spain)

RESULT Won 4–0 (1–0)

POSITION IN GROUP 1st/9 pts

ATTENDANCE 15,713

SCORERS United: Bowyer (28), Ameobi (46), Bellamy (74), Robert (89)

MATCH HIGHLIGHTS

Newcastle United's first victory on French soil at the sixth attempt was an impressive performance, and the score line could have easily been much wider had United taken their chances as the game came to a close. On a bitterly cold evening on the French border, United kept their 100 per cent record in the UEFA Cup intact and cruised into the latter stages of the competition by giving Sochaux a footballing lesson in the second half. However, before United took command, Sochaux tested Shay Given on several occasions and the Magpies keeper had to show his shot-stopping ability, saving well from Menez, Ilan and Isabey. As the home side tested United, Lee Bowyer gave the Black 'n' Whites the lead – against the run of play – by drilling home a shot across the keeper from Shola Ameobi's deflected pass. Newcastle then missed a sitter when Craig Bellamy and James Milner combined from a brilliant Given clearance-cum-pass. After the break, however, Newcastle got off to a flying start and never looked back. Within 40 seconds, Ameobi picked up a loose ball after the keeper had been wrong footed by a deflection from an Olivier Bernard cross, and the tall United striker side footed the ball home. Sochaux did have a chance to get back into the game when they were awarded a penalty, but Mathieu drove his shot weakly past the post. It was a costly miss for the home team as United stepped up to fire another two goals into Richert's net. A Dyer run cut Sochaux apart, and the ball was neatly slid through for Aaron Hughes to

square it back for Craig Bellamy, who coolly finished off a well-worked move. After incessant attacking by United, Laurent Robert, brought on as sub as the game came to a close, hit a wonderfully struck free-kick that curled into the corner of the net. There was still time for both Ameobi and Robert to waste glaring opportunities, yet United were more than content with a convincing 4–0 victory over a side that were challenging in Le Championnat and had just beaten Marseille.

England Under-21 defender Steven Taylor.

MAN OF THE MATCH

Shay Given – showed he is the best.

MATCH RATING	•	•	•		

Surprising romp.

STAR COMMENT

Graeme Souness: 'It was a good performance, but we could have been more clinical in front of goal.'

EYEWITNESS

Simon Rushworth (*The Journal*): 'Four memorable goals, a deserved clean sheet and a 100 per cent record in the UEFA Cup are statistics to satisfy the most demanding of football perfectionists.'

TOUR STOP – SOCHAUX-MONTBÉLIARD

The sprawling base of the Peugeot car empire that comprehensively backs the club, Sochaux and the neighbouring historic town of Montbéliard are situated on the border with Germany and Switzerland. The area is largely an industrial centre; however, the heart of Montbéliard offers all the charm of an old Germanic town and is in the shadow of a fifteenth-century castle. On the Rhine–Rhone canal, it is an important staging post and within the sight of the dramatic Alps. (pop. 35,000.)

STADIA FILE – STADE AUGUSTE BONAL

A much-modernised stadium paid for by Peugeot euros, the Stade Auguste Bonal has a capacity of only 20,000 but provides a good atmosphere in a covered arena. A rectangular stadium with continuous stands of smooth lines in grey cladding, the arena is like most in the country: small, modern and functional with a touch of French imagination and flair.

DID YOU KNOW

Shay Given made his 300th United appearance against Sochaux and recorded his 44th European match for the Magpies – more than any other player. He was to become the first Newcastle player to reach 50 games in Europe.

2004–05

UEFA Cup, Round 2, Group D: Newcastle United v. Sporting Clube de Portugal
Matchday 5, Thursday, 16 December 2004, St. James' Park

Sporting Clube

UNITED Given, Taylor (O'Brien), Bramble, Hughes, Elliott, Milner, Ambrose, Jenas, Bernard, Bellamy (Guy), Ameobi. Subs not used: Harper, Ramage, Brittain.
Manager: Graeme Souness

SPORTING Ricardo, Enakarhire, Beto (Tello), Polga, Rogerio, Tinga, Rochemback, Custodio, Paito, Liedson, Pinilla (Douala). Subs not used: Danny, Garcia, Barbosa, Ferreira, Tiago, Sa Pinto.
Manager: José Peseiro

REFEREE P. Allaerts (Belgium)

RESULT Drew 1–1 (1–1)

FINAL GROUP D TABLE

1	Newcastle United	10 pts
2	FC Sochaux	9 pts
3	Sporting Clube	7 pts
4	Panionios	3 pts
5	Dinamo Tbilisi	0 pts

ATTENDANCE 28,017

SCORERS United: Bellamy (5); Sporting: Custodio (39)

MATCH HIGHLIGHTS

Both clubs had all but qualified for the next stage of the UEFA Cup, but Newcastle needed to top Group D – by avoiding defeat at the hands of Sporting – to earn a more advantageous draw in the next stage. If they did so they would avoid the Champions League teams dropping out of that competition and into the UEFA Cup. Graeme Souness fielded a largely inexperienced side – partly because of injury and partly by choice – yet the depleted United team, to their credit, easily held their Portuguese visitors. Sporting kept the ball for long periods but rarely troubled Shay Given and with chances few and far between at both ends of the field, the match ended in a predictable and uninspiring draw. Newcastle took an early lead when Craig Bellamy looped a header over Ricardo after he had run onto a Shola Ameobi flick. However, six minutes before the break, Sporting drew level. Aaron Hughes committed a foul, and Rochemback's delightful cross from the resulting free-kick found Custodio, who leaped above United's defence to head past Given. Without Alan Shearer and Patrick Kluivert, only Bellamy offered anything in attack, and Ricardo had a largely quiet evening. Nevertheless, the job was done convincingly enough

and Newcastle ended the group stage at the top of the Group D table. The Magpies were now rated as one of the favourites for the competition, winning five and drawing one of their six matches to that point to remain unbeaten.

MAN OF THE MATCH

Craig Bellamy – lively and dangerous.

| MATCH RATING | ● | | | | | Monotonous action. |

STAR COMMENT

Graeme Souness: 'We had a relatively inexperienced side, and we worked hard against a team that is good on the ball. We didn't create very much, but we didn't have to.'

EYEWITNESS

George Caulkin (*The Times*): 'This listless draw did not stray towards the inspirational, and nor did it signal a reversal of recent fortunes, but it secured their passage to the knockout phase.'

OPPONENT FILE

Having faced United in a pre-season tournament at St. James' Park, the two clubs knew each other well and were to meet face to face, yet again, later in the competition. Sporting were impressive in the Portuguese *SuperLiga*, challenging for top spot alongside Porto and Benfica. Recently, the famous Lions' performances have been less than satisfactory to their supporters, although they reached the UEFA Cup semi-final in 1991. They were fancied to have a real go at reaching the final, which was to be held at their very own Estádio José Alvalade.

STAR VISITOR

Ricardo Pereira – Goalkeeper for the Portuguese national side, Ricardo starred in the European championships for his country and ruined England's hopes of glory by saving penalties – and converting one – in an epic quarter-final. He joined Sporting Clube from Boavista where he had lifted the national title. Ricardo was an agile and acrobatic keeper but one prone to costly errors, too. He has won over 30 caps for Portugal.

DID YOU KNOW

Hugo Viana was an important part of Sporting's side that year, but the Newcastle player on loan to the Portuguese club for the season was barred from playing against the Magpies as part of the transfer deal.

Tour Stop

Sochaux – France

FC Sochaux-Montbéliard 2004–05

MONTBELIARD

Montbéliard and Sochaux virtually merge into one town. Sochaux is dominated by the Peugeot auto plant, while Montbéliard (pictured) has a pleasant old centre around the castle.

A new and modern complex built with Peugeot euros.

Lee Bowyer fires the ball low and hard to find the net against Sochaux in France.

Match-day ticket for the tie with the Le Championnat club.

Heerenveen – Holland

SC Heerenveen
2004–05

1. Postcard from Heerenveen

Situated away from the bustle of Amsterdam, the town of Heerenveen boasts two major arenas: the ice-skating centre (top left) and the Abe Lenstra Stadion (bottom).

2. Postcard from Abe Lenstra Stadion

In the midst of major enlargement when Newcastle took to the field, Heerenveen's ground was doubling in size, with the stands pictured being substantially enlarged.

3. Match action

Alan Shearer strikes the ball perfectly and United are all level in Holland.

4. Memorabilia

Match ticket for the tie in Friesland.

Match 97

2004–05

UEFA Cup, Round 3 (Round of 32): SC Heerenveen (Holland) v. Newcastle United
FIRST LEG Thursday, 17 February 2005, Abe Lenstra Stadion (Heerenveen)

Heerenveen

UNITED Given, Carr, O'Brien, Bramble, Babayaro (Hughes), Bowyer, Faye, Jenas, Kluivert, Shearer (Ambrose), Ameobi (Robert). Subs not used: Caig, N'Zogbia, Milner, Taylor. Manager: Graeme Souness

HEERENVEEN Vandenbussche, Bakkati, Hansson, Breuer, Rzasa, Vayrynen, Prager (Rose), Hestad, Yildirim, Huntelaar (Samaras), Bruggink (Sikora). Subs not used: Haarala, Waterman, Wolfgang, Drost. Manager: Gertjan Verbeek

REFEREE Z. Szabo (Hungary)

RESULT Won 2–1 (0–1)

AGGREGATE 2–1

SENT OFF Bowyer (85)

ATTENDANCE 19,500

SCORERS United: Shearer (69), Bowyer (82) Heerenveen: Huntelaar (24)

MATCH HIGHLIGHTS

The cut and thrust of knockout competition returned as United headed for Holland on a cold and wintry evening to play Heerenveeen at the Abe Lenstra arena. United should have taken an early lead when Bowyer headed a good opportunity over the bar. Heerenveen were lively in front of their noisy home support, and with Yildirim finding space, they caused United a few tense moments during the first period of the match. Indeed, they took the lead and exposed United's defensive frailty in the process. Titus Bramble made a hash of a clearance, Heerenveen's Prager stole the ball and then set up Huntelaar for a rising shot that zipped past Shay Given. With Souness fielding Alan Shearer, Shola Ameobi and Patrick Kluivert in attack, Newcastle's formation never worked. It was only when Ameobi was withdrawn and Laurent Robert entered the action that the Magpies looked like an effective unit. With Kluivert happier further up field alongside Shearer and Robert out wide, the Black 'n' Whites were a different side. Newcastle soon grabbed an equaliser, Shearer scoring in typical fashion. In the 69th minute, Robert and Kluivert combined brilliantly with a neat interchange, and the ball fell for Shearer, who converted the chance right-footed past Vandenbussche from 15 yards. As Heerenveen began to tire in the last quarter of the match, United took control, and the winner came in the 82nd minute. Stephen

Carr made a surging run down the flank, and his telling low ball into the box was met by Kluivert, whose flick set up an opening for Lee Bowyer to neatly and cheekily back heel home. Three minutes later, Bowyer was again the centre of attention, this time in trouble with referee Szabo. He was sent off for a second bookable offence, forcing United to play out the remaining few minutes with ten men. However, Newcastle hung on to record their fourth away victory in a row.

MAN OF THE MATCH

Alan Shearer – master marksman.

| MATCH RATING | ● | ● | | | |

Tolerable away success.

STAR COMMENT

Graeme Souness: 'Even though we were the better team, we gave away a poor goal to go behind, and that gave them an enormous lift.'

EYEWITNESS

Paul Gilder (*The Journal*): 'Just as the Magpies seemed to be in danger of sliding to a new low, Alan Shearer and Lee Bowyer raced to the rescue to ease the heat on United's under-fire board.'

TOUR STOP – HEERENVEEN

Situated in a thinly populated area of Holland between Amsterdam in the south and Groningen in the north, Heerenveen is a town keen on sport. It is home to Europe's fastest speed-skating ice rink – a popular pastime in Holland – while the football club enjoys a considerable local following, too. It has a modern city centre and is described as a 'small, cosy city'. It has canals running through the area, and several majestic restored houses from the medieval era remain as landmarks. (pop. 42,000.)

STADIA FILE – ABE LENSTRA STADION

Named after a famous past player who accomplished much for Heerenveen and for Holland, the Abe Lenstra arena was in the midst of upgrading and enlargement from the previous capacity of 17,653 when United played there. A modern, attractive stadium on the outskirts of the town, the venue generates a rousing flag-waving pre-match atmosphere in typical Dutch style.

DID YOU KNOW

The Hungarian referee's assistant Peter Hegyi lived in Whitley Bay and worked at Newcastle University. He was given special permission by UEFA to run the line.

Match 98

2004–05
UEFA Cup, Round 3 (Round of 32): Newcastle United v. SC Heerenveen (Holland)
SECOND LEG Thursday, 24 February 2005, St. James' Park

Heerenveen

UNITED Given, Carr, Bramble, O'Brien (Taylor), Hughes, Dyer (Jenas), Faye, Butt, Robert, Ameobi, Shearer (Milner). Subs not used: Caig, N'Zogbia, Ambrose, Ramage.
Manager: Graeme Souness

HEERENVEEN Vandenbussche, Bakkati, Hansson, Breuer (Seip), Rzasa, Vayrynen, Radomski, Hestad, Yildirim, Huntelaar (Samaras), Bruggink (Sikora). Subs not used: Waterman, Rose, Haarala, Prager.
Manager: Gertjan Verbeek

REFEREE D. Delevic (Yugoslavia)

RESULT Won 2–1 (2–0)
AGGREGATE Won 4–2

ATTENDANCE 26,156

SCORERS United: Breuer (10) (own-goal), Shearer (24); Heerenveen: Bruggink (79) (pen)

MATCH HIGHLIGHTS

After a period of criticism, and a week of turmoil within the ranks, the victory over Heerenveen perhaps marked the point at which Graeme Souness turned the corner and his United line-up started to get it right. The Magpies' success over the Dutch side was the start of a 12-game unbeaten run that propelled the Magpies into the latter stages of both the UEFA Cup and the FA Cup. In atrocious weather, with rain, sleet and snow pouring down, the Black 'n' Whites cruised into the next round. Laurent Robert played an influential role all night, and an early goal killed off any chance that Heerenveen had of creating a shock. After ten minutes, an own-goal from Breuer gave United the lead, following a characteristically vicious Robert cross, the French winger having been set up by Alan Shearer. The ball struck the Dutch defender a yard from the line, and the ball ricocheted into the net past Vandenbussche. A second followed soon after, Alan Shearer wrapping up the tie in the 24th minute with a copybook free-kick won by Dyer. The ball was touched to one side, and the Magpies' captain walloped it past the wall and goalkeeper into the net. Newcastle should have scored more, but Shola Ameobi missed three good chances, while Kieron Dyer, Nicky Butt and Laurent Robert all went close. Newcastle were in total control, and it wasn't until late in the game that Heerenveen got a look in, gaining a consolation penalty when Ameobi handled in the box, although he appeared to have been pushed. Bruggink stroked the kick past Shay Given.

MAN OF THE MATCH
Laurent Robert – in the mood.

MATCH RATING	●	●			

Should have been more.

STAR COMMENT
Alan Shearer: 'It was a job well done. The contest was possibly over when the first goal went in, but it was definitely over when the second one hit the net.'

EYEWITNESS
George Caulkin (*The Times*): 'If any individual has been responsible for the pendulum swinging so dramatically in the manager's favour, it is Robert.'

OPPONENT FILE
An emerging Dutch provincial club and the pride of Friesland, Heerenveen had grown dramatically in stature in the last decade, having only reached the big time in 1993 when they were promoted to Holland's Premier Division. Although lacking the pedigree of other Dutch clubs in Europe, Hereneveen have a solid fan base. They finished fourth in the Eredivisie the previous season to qualify for the UEFA Cup and were surprise runners-up in the league in 2000.

STAR VISITOR

Arnold Bruggink – A veteran striker and experienced campaigner in European football, Bruggink had already faced United for both PSV and Real Mallorca in previous meetings. The Dutch forward had scored goals wherever he played and joined Heerenveen in the summer of 2004 from Mallorca. Winner of two Dutch championships, he scored over fifty goals in six seasons for PSV.

DID YOU KNOW
Heerenveen once fielded such quality strikers as Jon Dahl Tomasson – later to join United from the Dutch club – and Ruud van Nistelrooy.

Match 99

2004–05
UEFA Cup, Round 4 (Round of 16): Olympiacos CFP (Greece) v. Newcastle United
FIRST LEG Thursday, 10 March 2005, Karaiskakis Stadium (Piraeus)

Olympiacos

UNITED Given, Carr, O'Brien, Bramble, Hughes, Dyer (Jenas), Faye (N'Zogbia), Butt, Robert (Milner), Shearer, Kluivert. Subs not used: Harper, Ameobi, Taylor, Bowyer. Manager: Graeme Souness

OLYMPIACOS Nikopolidis, Kostoulas, Anatolakis, Schurrer, Mavrogenidis, Maric, Stoltidis, Djordjevic (Kafes), Georgatos, Rivaldo (Pantos), Okkas (Giovanni). Subs not used: Giannou, Castillo, Vallas, Philipakos. Manager: Dusan Bajevic

REFEREE A. Ibanez (Spain)

RESULT Won 3–1 (2–1)

AGGREGATE 3–1

SENT OFF Georgatos (12), Kostoulas (43)

ATTENDANCE 30,595

SCORERS United: Shearer (13) (pen), Robert (33), Kluivert (68); Olympiacos: Djordjevic (15) (pen)

MATCH HIGHLIGHTS

On the day that Newcastle visited Olympiacos, the Greek side were celebrating their 80th birthday, and it proved to be an eventful party at the daunting Karaiskakis arena. Referee Arturo Ibanez was the centre of attention as he awarded two penalties inside the first sixteen minutes and sent off two Olympiacos players. The already charged and somewhat hostile crowd became even more intimidating. Newcastle, though, were cool and collected in the bad-tempered atmosphere and thoroughly professional in gaining a first-leg advantage that eventually won them the tie. Djordjevic and Georgatos of Olympiacos impressed early on, but United took the lead with a spot-kick after Kieron Dyer had been pushed when making a break into the box. His initial shot was blocked, but as he followed up the rebound for a certain goal, Georgatos flattened the United midfielder and was sent off as a further punishment. Shearer lashed home the penalty high into the net. However, the referee evened matters up when Andy O'Brien tugged Stoltidis as he ran to meet a free-kick and the other skipper, Djordjevic, whacked the ball past Given in similar fashion. Shearer then had a header cleared off the line, but United took the lead once more when they were awarded a free-kick for a foul on Laurent Robert on the edge of the box. The Frenchman took the kick himself and brilliantly curled a shot around the wall and into the net from 20 yards. A second red card for a home-side player caused mayhem in the crowd. Kostoulas caught Nicky Butt with a late challenge, and the Olympiacos player received a second yellow card and

his marching orders. Down to nine men, the Greeks had no chance, and in the second period United capitalised on their advantage and controlled the game, passing the ball around. The Magpies also had to make sure they were not the victim of a tit-for-tat sending-off, but the Spanish referee wasn't intimidated by the hostile crowd, and Newcastle's players were disciplined, being careful not to get caught up in any confrontations. United scored a third goal when substitute James Milner danced his way to the byeline before pulling the ball back for Kluivert to strike the ball first time into the net.

MAN OF THE MATCH

Alan Shearer – cool-headed and professional.

| MATCH RATING | ● | ● | ● | | | Absorbing encounter.

STAR COMMENT

Alan Shearer: 'We handled the situation extremely well, didn't do anything silly, and finished the match with 11 men on the pitch and a very handy two-goal advantage.'

EYEWITNESS

Peter Lansley (*The Times*): 'The Greek league leaders had two players sent off in a surreal first half as Newcastle United showed admirable composure to maintain a 100 per cent away record in Europe.'

TOUR STOP – PIREAUS

Adjoining Athens on the Saronic Gulf and a major port, Piraeus is the third largest city in Greece. Lively and modern with an ancient centre, the city is surrounded by the hills of Profitis Ilias and Athens itself. On a natural harbour, it is the main link to the Greek Islands, while its waterfront is packed with marinas and tavernas of all descriptions. (pop. 176,000.)

STADIA FILE – KARAISKAKIS STADIUM

The home of Olympiacos was first built back in 1895, remodelled in 1936 and now is one of the finest small arenas in Europe. With a 33,500 capacity, Olympiacos had to move home for several years while a dispute simmered over the redevelopment, but they moved back in 2004 to a fanfare welcome. Named after a general of the Greek revolution, it is an ultra-modern complex, designed with giant steel-tower supports around the streamlined bowl. The arena is situated on the coastal strip next to the equally spectacular Peace and Friendship indoor stadium.

DID YOU KNOW

United's £8 million centre-half Jean-Alain Boumsong was unable to play in any of the UEFA Cup matches as he was cup-tied, having already appeared in European competition that year for Rangers.

2004–05

UEFA Cup, Round 4 (Round of 16): Newcastle United v. Olympiacos CFP (Greece)
SECOND LEG Wednesday, 16 March 2005, St. James' Park

Olympiacos

UNITED Given, Carr (Ramage), Hughes, O'Brien, Taylor, Jenas, Bowyer, Butt, Robert (N'Zogbia), Dyer (Milner), Shearer. Subs not used: Harper, Faye, Ambrose.
Manager: Graeme Souness

OLYMPIACOS Nikopolidis, Mavrogenidis, Anatolakis, Vallas, Pantos, Maric, Kafes, Stoltidis (Taralidis), Djordjevic (Okkas), Castillo, Giovanni (Philapakos). Subs not used: Giannou, Schurrer, Kouloucheris, Joaquim.
Manager: Dusan Bajevic

REFEREE K. Plautz (Austria)

RESULT Won 4–0 (1–0)

AGGREGATE Won 7–1

ATTENDANCE 32,163

SCORERS United: Dyer (17), Shearer (44), Bowyer (53), Shearer (68)

MATCH HIGHLIGHTS

Newcastle United's landmark centenary game in Europe resulted in an easy romp, with much credit going to Graeme Souness and the team for the way in which they despatched their respected Champions League opponents. That they won without several key players who had been rested for the second leg made their performance all the more impressive. It was a notable victory, United's attacking prowess proving to be far too hot for the Greeks to handle. The Magpies dominated the match, so much so that keeper Shay Given had only one shot to save and that almost on the final whistle. Kieron Dyer's astute movement racing forward opened up the Greeks, and Newcastle soon took the lead. After a Nicky Butt shot had rattled the bar, Dyer burst through to reach a Laurent Robert header and with his back to the net cheekily back-heeled a classy goal. Shearer then went close on a trio of occasions before at last finding the net just before the break. Dyer again surged into the danger area and pulled the ball back for his captain, who controlled and executed the chance with his left foot. Soon after the interval, Newcastle made it 3–0 when Bowyer drilled a shot home after his header was blocked. Shearer then grabbed his second, running onto a Jermaine Jenas pass before easing round Nikopolidis and ramming a shot into the roof of the net. By the end of the tie, United were in cruise-control and fielded an experimental back-line of Peter Ramage (making his debut as a sub), Andy O'Brien, Steven Taylor and Aaron Hughes.

MAN OF THE MATCH

Alan Shearer – never gave up the cause.

| MATCH RATING | ● | ● | ● | | | Amazing victory. |

STAR COMMENT

Graeme Souness: 'We made a good start, and kept them on the back foot throughout. We made a good team look very ordinary.'

EYEWITNESS

Paul Gilder (*The Journal*): 'The industrious Magpies strode to victory to ensure the club's centenary celebrations did not fall flat.'

OPPONENT FILE

The Greek championship leaders and a respected side that had collected ten points in their Champions League group – defeating Liverpool, Monaco and Deportivo – Olympiacos were, on paper, the best side United had faced that year by some considerable distance. Known as the Manchester United of Greece, Olympiacos are the most popular and most decorated side in the country. They were Greek champions from 1997 to 2004 and are regular participants in the Champions League as well as the UEFA Cup. Known as Thrylos in Greece, which can be translated as . . . 'the Legends'.

STAR VISITOR

Giovanni – One of two Brazilian stars in the Olympiacos line-up – along with Rivaldo, who missed the match at Gallowgate – Giovanni was no stranger to the Magpies, having netted the winner for Barcelona in the Camp Nou back in 1998. Aged 33 and with 19 caps for his country, the tall and skilful striker or midfielder was a popular player in Piraeus and netted 21 goals the season before as his side lifted the title once again. From Belem in Brazil, he appeared for Santos before heading for Europe with Barcelona.

DID YOU KNOW

Ex-Newcastle United and Greece midfielder George Georgiadis, then 32, was on the Olympiacos playing staff but missed the return to St. James' Park with a long-term injury.

100 MATCH RECORD

Only six other English clubs have reached the century milestone in European football: Liverpool, Manchester United, Arsenal, Leeds United, Chelsea and Tottenham. United's record was: P100 W56 D19 L25.

Piraeus – Greece

Olympiacos CFP 2004–05

It was back to the cosmopolitan city of Athens and its adjoining port of Piraeus for the clash with Olympiacos. The Greek Parliament building on Syntagma Square is pictured.

Newly constructed in 2004 and a marvellous landmark on the Piraeus coast.

Referee Arturo Ibanez shows the red card to Olympiacos defender Kostoulas. Brazilian Rivaldo (right) looks on.

United marked their 100th game in Europe with a special edition programme for the return match with the Greeks.

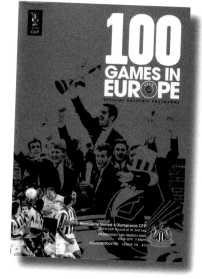

. . . and on to Lisbon

Having reached the significant milestone of one hundred European fixtures, the Magpies had a wonderful chance of reaching the final – indeed of lifting the UEFA Cup trophy. Newcastle United now set their sights firmly on Lisbon. The final was on 18 May, but the Black 'n' Whites ended up in the charming Portuguese capital some five weeks early. In the quarter-final they were drawn against Sporting Clube at the same venue as the final was to be staged, the José Alvalade arena.

After the headline-making highs and lows of Alan Shearer's announcement that he was going to continue playing and the bizarre altercation on the pitch between Lee Bowyer and Kieron Dyer in a game against Aston Villa, four days in the middle of April – described by manager Graeme Souness as 'the biggest week in the club's recent history' – shaped United's often turbulent season. Their quarter-final meeting in Lisbon and a FA Cup semi-final clash with Manchester United would prove to be decisive in determining the success of the team's efforts that year.

Newcastle took a 1–0 victory to Lisbon following a tight first leg that saw a bulleted Shearer header give United their slender advantage. In the majestic rebuilt Estádio José Alvalade, United's tactics looked perfect for an hour of the match. Newcastle had a semi-final place well in their sights once Kieron Dyer – playing up front alongside Alan Shearer and causing mayhem – hit the net with a lightning run and shot that put the Black 'n' Whites 2–0 ahead on aggregate. Sporting now needed to score at least three times and that – for the first hour – looked highly improbable. Indeed, with Dyer's menacing pace, it was Newcastle who were the more likely side to find the net. The Magpies should have coasted through.

But football can change so quickly. Just as in the Magpies' last bid for UEFA Cup glory, the team's fortunes ran out as the competition moved into the later decisive stages. Injuries to Jermaine Jenas, Titus Bramble and, critically, Dyer – as the clock ticked towards that fateful hour mark – meant Souness had to make three enforced changes. It turned the game. United's boss said afterwards, 'If we had managed to keep our starting XI on the pitch it would be a much different story.' Laurent Robert's pre-match outburst and subsequent absence also compounded the manager's difficulties by limiting his selection choice. Newcastle self-destructed and conceded three goals in the last twenty minutes to go down 1–4. It should never have happened. But it did. Newcastle tumbled out of the tournament in depressing fashion. And worse was to follow three days later when United lost, by the same score line again, to Manchester United at the Millennium Stadium. Souness made the comment that the defeat in Portugal 'inflicted an enormous psychological blow'. The long road to Lisbon had ended in disappointment instead of triumph.

Left: Local newspaper marking the quarter-final in Lisbon.
Right: The towering monument of Cristo Rei overlooking the Tagus and Ponte 25 de Abril.

A quarter-final exit in Lisbon

Match 101

UEFA Cup Quarter-Final:
Newcastle United v. Sporting Clube de Portugal (Portugal)

FIRST LEG Thursday, 7 April 2005, St. James' Park

UNITED Given (Harper), Carr, Taylor, O'Brien, Hughes, Faye, Jenas, Dyer (Bowyer), Robert (Milner), Ameobi, Shearer. Subs not used: Butt, Elliott, Ambrose, N'Zogbia.
Manager: Graeme Souness

SPORTING Ricardo, Rogerio, Beto, Polga, Jorge, Martins (Mota), Rochemback, Moutinho, Barbosa (Tello), Sa Pinto, Liedson. Subs not used: Tiago, Niculae, Garcia, Sergio, Paito.
Manager: José Peseiro

REFEREE Y. Baskakov (Russia)

RESULT Won 1–0 (1–0)
AGGREGATE 1–0

ATTENDANCE 36,753

SCORERS United: Shearer (36)

MAN OF THE MATCH Steven Taylor – Positive and commanding.

STAR COMMENT Graeme Souness: 'We can play a lot better, but for all the ball Sporting had, they didn't cause us problems.'

EYEWITNESS Luke Edwards (*The Journal*): 'A clean sheet with a makeshift defence will enable United to use the counter-attacking football which suits them.'

Match 102

UEFA Cup Quarter-Final:
Sporting Clube de Portugal (Portugal) v. Newcastle United

SECOND LEG Thursday, 14 April 2005, Estádio José Alvalade (Lisbon)

SPORTING Ricardo, Rogerio, Beto, Polga, Jorge, Martins (Barbosa), Moutinho, Sa Pinto (Custodio), Rochemback, Niculae (Pinilla), Douala. Subs not used: Mota, Garcia, Tello, Nelson.
Manager: José Peseiro

UNITED Given, Carr, Bramble (O'Brien), Taylor, Babayaro, Faye, Jenas (Milner), Bowyer, N'Zogbia, Dyer (Kluivert), Shearer. Subs not used: Butt, Ambrose, Ameobi, Harper.
Manager: Graeme Souness

REFEREE P. Frojdfeldt (Sweden)

RESULT Lost 1–4 (1–1)
AGGREGATE Lost 2–4

ATTENDANCE 33,309

SCORERS United: Dyer (19); Sporting: Niculae (39), Sa Pinto (70), Beto (76), Rochemback (90)

MAN OF THE MATCH Kieron Dyer – Had Sporting in tatters.

STAR COMMENT Kieron Dyer: 'We shot ourselves in the foot and only have ourselves to blame. The spirit was good and for 60 minutes we were comfortable. Then we blew a gasket.'

EYEWITNESS George Caulkin (*The Times*): 'A desperate run of injuries and a ceaseless courting of painful headlines may have caught up with them.'

FINAL BLOW

Sporting Clube went on to topple Dutch side AZ Alkmaar in the semi-final, winning with a last-minute goal, then faced CSKA Moscow in the final at their home stadium, the José Alvalade. However, they went down 3–1 on the night to the huge disappointment of the mainly Portuguese crowd.

The newly constructed Estadio José Alvalade.

'He is an idol and will go on to become a legend'
Sir Bobby Robson

Alan Shearer

Alan Shearer collects awards and records almost for fun: from Player of the Year and Footballer of the Year trophies to being crowned the Premiership's all-time goal-king and official Player of the Decade, Shearer has won a hatful. He also toppled the great Jackie Milburn's record of 200 goals for Newcastle United. No wonder his former boss Sir Bobby Robson once claimed, 'He is an idol and will go on to become a legend.' United's No. 9 is also the club's record scorer in Europe by far. For years, big Welshman Wyn Davies held that accolade with 10 goals in 24 matches, scored during United's first encounter with European football. Alan Shearer has demolished that total and now heads the honours list with 30 goals in 49 games, including the 2005–06 Intertoto campaign.

Of course, playing football on the Continent was nothing new for Alan Shearer.

On international duty with England he has faced top defenders from Spain, Italy, Holland and France, as well as from wider afield when playing against such teams as Argentina and Brazil. The likes of Laurent Blanc, Frank de Boer, Fabio Cannavaro and Roberto Ayala have all had to face up to the threat of the Geordie centre-forward. His exceptional goal record of 30 in 63 appearances for his country proves he was a danger to both European and worldwide defences at international level. It was that experience that gave Newcastle United an edge in many of their meetings with Continental club sides, as the Magpies became regular competitors in UEFA action.

Alan first tasted European football in one of the earliest versions of the Champions League format with Blackburn Rovers during the 1995–96 season. He also took part in Rovers' debut in Europe the year before that, but neither campaign went too well. Blackburn lost to Swedish part timers Trelleborg in the opening round of the UEFA Cup, which was a big disappointment for everyone at Ewood Park. However, winning the Premiership title gave Rovers and Shearer the chance to participate in Europe's most prestigious competition. Unfortunately, they lost their first three games in Group B and did not progress any further.

Following his world record £15 million move from Lancashire back home to Tyneside in the summer of 1996, Shearer pulled on the black and white shirt in European action for the first time in a UEFA Cup run during the 1996–97 season. That campaign included an intense contest with Hungarian champions Ferencváros, and a goal in Budapest remains one of Shearer's very best, rated in Alan's own top ten. The man himself said it was 'a very important goal as well as a very good one'. In the Ülloi úti stadium, United were locked in an end-to-end clash that saw the Magpies go two goals down. However,

Alan Shearer

the Geordies battled back to equalise with two important away goals. After Les Ferdinand had converted a great run and cross by Shearer, Alan grabbed a marvellous second. Taking a pass from David Batty, Shearer remembered his effort well. He said, 'When the ball came to me I pivoted and got the volley exactly right, up into the top corner of the net.'

After taking care of the Hungarians and reaching the quarter-finals in that run, he was unlucky to miss the Toon's own debut in the Champions League and that ever-so-spectacular opening performance against Barcelona in 1997. United's expensive purchase badly damaged his lower leg and ankle in a pre-season exhibition match against Chelsea at Goodison Park and was to be on the sidelines for half the season. As a consequence, he watched all of the Black 'n' Whites' European campaign from the stands. And how the Magpies missed him, especially when Tino Asprilla was also sidelined soon after the feast of football on show against Barca.

Shearer, however, made up for his frustration at his early European experiences with Newcastle by leading them from the front in their Cup Winners Cup, UEFA Cup and Champions League challenges in the seasons that followed. During the 2002–03 Champions League campaign, United had arguably their best-ever season in Europe, reaching the second stage of the competition and matching some of the very best clubs in Europe. Newcastle could have easily reached the quarter-final of the European Champions Cup that year, and Alan Shearer was very much in the headlines.

After an agonising start to that year's competition, Shearer led by example as the Magpies secured victory over Juventus at St. James' Park. Points were also needed against Dynamo Kyiv, and Shearer made sure the Black 'n' Whites seized all three with a nerve-racking

ALAN SHEARER: FACT FILE

Position: Centre-forward

Born: Newcastle upon Tyne, August 1970

Joined United from: Blackburn Rovers, July 1996, £15 million

Other major clubs: Southampton

Full international: England (63 caps, 1992 to 2000)

United career, senior games: 389 app., 200 goals (to 7 Jan 2006)

United Euro record: 49 app., 30 goals (to 7 Jan 2006)

Did you know: Alan Shearer is one of only three footballing personalities to be honoured with the Freedom of the City of Newcastle upon Tyne, the others being Jackie Milburn and Sir Bobby Robson.

penalty in the 68th minute. He was magnificent in the De Kuip stadium when Newcastle reached the second stage in dramatic fashion. The Shearer and Craig Bellamy partnership caused Feyenoord's defence problems all evening.

Unfortunately, United's centre-forward was then suspended for two games following a fiery encounter with Inter at St. James' Park. Hardly ever one to lose his cool, despite receiving some rough treatment down the years, Shearer was caught up in the heat of a fierce contest with the Italians. Soon after Craig Bellamy had been sensationally sent off in the opening minutes of the game for kicking out at Marco Materazzi, Shearer tangled with Fabio Cannavaro in the Inter box as Solano prepared to flight a free-kick into the middle. The international defender pulled and tugged at the No. 9, and United's skipper, as *The Journal* reported, caught 'the defender with a swinging elbow'. Referee Stephane Bre missed the incident, but UEFA's

Star Profile

Alan Shearer

video camera did not, and Alan was handed a two-match ban. It was a double blow on top of Bellamy's three-match suspension.

Shearer was back with a bang against Bayer Leverkusen, scoring a hat-trick at Gallowgate. The skipper was awesome that night. United's publications editor Paul Tully wrote, 'The Leverkusen back four were breaking out in a cold sweat every time Alan got near the ball in their penalty area.' *The Journal* described his display as 'a scintillating performance' and reported that he 'registered a thrilling hat-trick inside the opening 36 minutes'. His first came from a Gary Speed cross towards which Shearer stooped forward to head the ball past Butt. Then, from Ameobi's low centre the ball found its way to United's skipper who was barely three yards from the goal-line. He had the most simple of chances to nod home his second. Alan's hat-trick goal came from the spot after Kieron Dyer had been pulled back, Shearer striking a ferocious penalty that gave the overworked Hans-Jorg Butt little chance.

Against Internazionale in the return match, Newcastle needed something special, and they almost claimed a marvellous victory thanks to two more goals from Shearer. Those strikes proved to be two of the most satisfying he has scored in his outstanding career, and with over 400 to choose from, that is saying something. Alan said, 'The two in Milan stand out, because of the occasion, the opposition, the stage and the fantastic support we had on the night.' That sort of support, as Alan recalled, gave everyone a lift: 'It was absolutely phenomenal, magnificent. Sometimes you're lost for words – on that occasion I was.'

His double strike was vintage Shearer: he was always clinical in the danger area. The first came after a Bellamy run and cross. The former England captain pounced on his partner's low ball across the face of goal and fired it into the back of the net from the edge of the six-yard box. Then it was Robert's turn to send in a vicious cross that Toldo, the Inter goalkeeper, couldn't cope with. As the ball ran loose, Shearer poked it into the net. He had scored two opportunist goals from close in, rather than the spectacular efforts that he was capable of. However, they were still two goals that will be recalled by United fans forever. That stirring match ended in a 2–2 draw, but it was not quite enough for United to progress into the knockout stage.

Shearer continued his European goals trail in the UEFA Cup runs of 2003–04 and 2004–05 that saw Newcastle head for the latter stages of the competition. United had a real go at winning the trophy, and, in the process, Shearer grabbed a hatful of goals. Had it not been for injuries to influential players at the wrong time, he could well have proudly led the Magpies to one, if not two, finals. Many fans considered that a full line-up would have gone all the way in those back-to-back bids for another taste of long-overdue European glory.

First, though, the Geordies had to get over the huge blow of missing out on a Champions League place by falling in a crucial qualifier against Partizan Belgrade. Shearer recalled, 'We were confident. We knew we were capable of winning, but it didn't happen. It was very tough and a massive blow for the club, the staff, players and supporters. After winning the first leg in Belgrade, we blew it in the return. We should have won, but at the end of the night, we weren't good enough to progress.'

Shearer was almost lost for words as to why United failed so miserably in the penalty shoot-out. He said, 'There's no reason to explain it. They are a lottery to a certain extent, but until anyone finds a better way of deciding a drawn match, penalties are the best way I know. All in all it was a huge disappointment.'

So it was UEFA Cup action for United, and

Alan Shearer

United's talisman Alan Shearer, the club's record goalscorer in Europe and of all time.

the run to face Marseille in the semi-final of 2004 saw Alan bag six goals. A year later, United's skipper collected even more, this time scoring 11. However, the UEFA Cup was not up to the same standard as the Champions League, and some of the opposition were decidedly inferior. Alan said, 'They weren't necessarily top drawer, but you can only beat what's there on the pitch in front of you. Clearly, the Champions League is the top competition, with a better standard

of player and team, but let's not degrade the UEFA Cup. There are some top sides battling it out for the trophy each season.'

Newcastle were totally focused on lifting that impressive UEFA Cup trophy. 'It would mean a tremendous amount to everyone connected to the club. I've seen all the old film of Bobby Moncur lifting the old Fairs Cup back in 1969 – a year before I was born – and it looked to me to be an absolutely marvellous occasion.'

Alan Shearer

Both UEFA Cup runs were long hauls. Alan said, 'It was gruelling but more so the travel than the matches. Playing Sunday, Thursday, Sunday all the time, with flights and hotels as constant companions, is tough.' In the first of those European trophy bids, United faced two good sides. Shearer noted, 'Basel were a decent team. Remember, they had done well in the Champions League the previous year with the same group of players. Over the two legs we deservedly won through, and our victory across there was one of our best results of the campaign.

'PSV are always going to be a force – look at how well they have done in the Champions League afterwards. We got a good score draw in Holland, and the success at St. James' Park was one of those nervy European nights as we held on for a tight aggregate win.'

That victory over the Dutch took United into the semi-final and up against Marseille. Shearer recalled, 'They were a very good team and Drogba was an exceptionally good striker – that's why he demanded a transfer fee of £20 million plus the following summer. But we were capable of beating Marseille. A full squad may well have done the business.

'We needed to take a lead to France. Although we kept a clean sheet at St. James' Park, it was not to be enough. We were forced to field a weakened team, and it showed over the two legs. When you're at that stage of the competition, indeed any big game, you need to have your big guns fit and firing on all cylinders. Unfortunately, we didn't.'

The following season, the run into the final rounds of the tournament was equally draining, and this time Newcastle were even stronger favourites to reach the final. By the time United had disposed of Olympiacos and faced Sporting Lisbon in the quarter-final Shearer said, 'I think ourselves and Sporting will be looking at the rest of the sides in the competition and thinking we have an excellent chance of winning it.'

But, once again, United had no luck when it really mattered. 'We went to Lisbon and, after doing well for an hour, got badly hit by injuries and conceded three late goals. We were going along nicely, we had an away goal, and at 1–1 with 20 minutes to go we were in the driving seat. But it finished 4–1, and that defeat was really hard to take.' Alan confirmed that it 'was the biggest disappointment of my career'.

Shearer added, 'Kieron [Dyer] going off was crucial to the outcome – he had been causing them a lot of problems. Titus [Bramble] was also a big miss, and, suddenly, the injury crisis was hitting really hard.'

United tumbled out of the UEFA Cup. They could only dream of what might have been and look forward to their next opportunity to travel the roads of the Continent. Shearer emphasised how essential European football is now for major clubs. He said, 'It is very important. The top teams and the top players all play regularly in UEFA competitions, and it's something you need to do to stay in touch with the rest of the leading clubs. If you don't, you can easily fall off the pace.

'The Champions League is undoubtedly the top competition. As a player you want to play against the best there is – both players and teams – and that's what the Champions League gives you.' Shearer added, sentiments echoed by everyone at St James' Park, 'Newcastle United needs to be in European football – it's as simple

Postscript: 2005–06 Intertoto Cup

At the beginning of season 2005–06, United played four games in the Intertoto Cup in a bid to qualify for the UEFA Cup. Match details are as follows:

Round 3

Match 103 FK ZTS Dubnica (Slovakia) v. Newcastle United

FIRST LEG Sunday, 17 July 2005, Mestsky Stadion

UNITED Harper, Taylor, Boumsong, Elliott, Babayaro, Milner, Butt, Faye, N'Zogbia, Shearer, Chopra (Brittain). Subs not used: Given, Ramage, Huntington.

Manager: Graeme Souness

DUBNICA Pernis, Pleva, Novak, Svestka, Zimen, Izvolt (Grendel), Drzik (Filo), Kopacka, Kiska (Brusko), Tesak, Adam. Subs not used: Postrk, Svikruha, Skultety, Augustini.

Manager: Lubos Nosicky

REFEREE Y. Alon (Israel)

RESULT Won 3–1 (2–1)

AGGREGATE 3–1

ATTENDANCE 6,200

SCORERS United: Chopra (4), N'Zogbia (6), Milner (70); Dubnica: Tesak (42).

Round 3

Match 104 Newcastle United v. FK ZTS Dubnica (Slovakia)

SECOND LEG Saturday, 23 July 2005, St. James' Park

UNITED Given, Carr, Taylor, Boumsong, Babayaro, Bowyer, Faye, Jenas (Chopra) (Brittain), N'Zogbia, Milner, Shearer. Subs not used: Harper, Elliott, Butt, Ramage.

Manager: Graeme Souness

DUBNICA Pernis, Pleva, Novak, Svestka, Zimen, Izvolt, Drzik, Kopacka (Skultety), Kiska (Augustini), Tesak, Adam (Svikruha). Subs not used: Grendel, Brusko, Zapotoka, Postrk.

Manager: Lubos Nosicky

REFEREE K. Kircher (Germany)

RESULT Won 2–0 (0–0)

AGGREGATE Won 5–1

ATTENDANCE 25,135

SCORERS United: Shearer (70), (90).

Semi-final

Match 105 RC Deportivo La Coruña (Spain) v. Newcastle United

FIRST LEG Wednesday, 27 July 2005, Estadio Municipal De Riazor

UNITED Given, Carr, Boumsong, Taylor, Babayaro, Milner (Chopra), Bowyer, Butt, Faye, N'Zogbia, Shearer. Subs not used: Harper, Elliott, Ramage, Huntington, Brittain.

Manager: Graeme Souness

DEPORTIVO Molina, Pablo, Andrade, Romero, Capdevila, Munitis, Duscher (Victor), Sergio, Luque (Scaloni), Castro, Tristan (Valeron). Subs not used: Manua, Juanma, De Guzman, Hector.

Manager: Joaquin Caparros

REFEREE S. Gumienny (Belgium)

RESULT Lost 1–2 (0–1)

AGGREGATE 1–2

ATTENDANCE 16,000

SCORERS United: Bowyer (47); Deportivo: Castro (10), Andrade (57).

Semi-final

Match 106 Newcastle United v. RC Deportivo La Coruña (Spain)

SECOND LEG: Wednesday, 3 August 2005, St. James' Park

UNITED Given, Carr, Boumsong, Taylor, Elliott, Faye (Ameobi), Parker, Emre (Brittain), Bowyer, Milner (N'Zogbia), Shearer. Subs not used: Chopra, Ramage, Harper.

Manager: Graeme Souness.

DEPORTIVO Molina, Pablo, Andrade, Romero, Capdevila, Scaloni, Sergio (Valeron), Duscher, Munitis, Castro (Juanma), Tristan (Luque). Subs not used: Victor, Acuna, De Guzman, Mallo.

Manager: Joaquin Caparros

REFEREE H. Fleischer (Germany)

RESULT Lost 1–2 (1–1)

AGGREGATE Lost 2–4

ATTENDANCE 34,215

SCORERS United: Milner (38); Deportivo: Andrade (44), Munitis (46).